W9-BNV-702

HOUGHTON MIFFLIN

Reading

A Legacy of Literacy

Give It All You've Got

HOUGHTON MIFFLIN   BOSTON · MORRIS PLAINS, NJ

California · Colorado · Georgia · Illinois · New Jersey · Texas

Design, Art Management and Page Production: Kirchoff/Wohlberg, Inc.

ILLUSTRATION CREDITS
26-30. 32-47 Joe Cepeda. **48-57, 59-69** Wayne Alfano.

PHOTOGRAPHY CREDITS
4 J. Henry Fair/Retna Ltd. **5** AP/Wide World Photos. **6** Robert
Holmes/Corbis. **7** PhotoDisc. **8** AP/Wide World Photos. **9** Corbis/
Bettmann. **10** PhotoDisc. **11** Gail Mooney/Corbis. **12-3** Bill Ross/Corbis.
14 AP/Wide World Photos. **15** © Chris Lee. **16** AP/Wide World Photos.
18 P. Souza/Liaison International. **20** PhotoDisc. **21** AP/Wide World
Photos. **22** Friedman/Liaison International. **23** Friedman/Liaison
International. **24** J. Henry Fair/Retna Ltd. **25** PhotoDisc.Buck Leonard
70 National Baseball Hall Of Fame Library, Cooperstown NY. **71** National
Baseball Hall Of Fame Library, Cooperstown NY. **72** (t) Todd Gipstein/
Corbis. **72** (b) Corbis/Bettmann. **73** National Baseball Hall Of Fame
Library, Cooperstown NY. **74** AP/Wide World Photos. **75** National
Baseball Hall Of Fame Library, Cooperstown NY. **76-7** Pittsburgh
Courier/Archive Photos. **78** AP/Wide World Photos. **79** Corbis/Bettmann.
80 Sporting News/Archive Photos. **81** (t) Todd Gipstein/Corbis. **81** (b)
AFP/Corbis. **82-3** National Baseball Hall Of Fame Library, Cooperstown
NY. **84** Sporting News/Archive Photos. **85** National Baseball Hall Of Fame
Library, Cooperstown NY. **86** National Baseball Hall Of Fame Library,
Cooperstown NY. **88** Corbis/Bettmann. **89** Corbis/Bettmann. **90** National
Baseball Hall Of Fame Library, Cooperstown NY. **91** National Baseball Hall
Of Fame Library, Cooperstown NY.

Printed in U.S.A.

ISBN: 0-618-04407-8

12 13 14 - VH - 06 05 04

Give It All You've Got

Contents

Meet Yo-Yo Ma
by Meish Goldish

Strategy Focus

How did Yo-Yo Ma become one of the finest musicians of our time? As you read, be sure to **evaluate** the facts and the opinions about this famous cello player.

Yo-Yo Ma is playing the cello. It sings for him warmly and deeply, as if it had a human voice. Yo-Yo Ma's face shows how completely the music has captured him.

The listeners' faces show their feelings too. Some people even have tears in their eyes.

Audiences everywhere are thrilled to hear Yo-Yo Ma play. He is among the finest cello players in the world.

Paris, France

Like many great musicians, Yo-Yo Ma started playing as a young boy. He came from a musical family who lived in Paris, France. His father was a music teacher and composer. His mother was a singer. Both had left China to live in France years before Yo-Yo was born.

Yo-Yo's older sister was learning to play the violin. Yo-Yo was only four years old. He tried the violin too. But he decided that he wanted a different stringed instrument — a bigger one. He wanted a cello. Yo-Yo needed help just to hold the cello. "I had to sit up on three telephone books, and there was always trouble finding the right size chair," he later remembered.

Isaac Stern

Yo-Yo's father was his first teacher. Mr. Ma gave his son difficult music to play. It was written by the great composer Johann Sebastian Bach (YO-haan Seb-AST-shun Bah-k). Mr. Ma told Yo-Yo to learn just a little bit at a time. Every day, Yo-Yo learned a little more than the day before.

By the time he was five, Yo-Yo could play some of the Bach works by heart. He was performing at the University of Paris. In the audience was a famous violinist, Isaac Stern. Stern told people that Yo-Yo Ma's talent was "extraordinary."

Yo-Yo liked playing the cello. More importantly, he was starting to love great classical music.

Johann Sebastian Bach

Growing up in New York City

When Yo-Yo was seven, the family left
France to live in New York City.

In New York, Yo-Yo's new music teacher
saw that the young cellist was remarkably
gifted. Yo-Yo performed on television when he
was eight. He gave a concert at Carnegie Hall
when he was nine. That same year, he entered
the Juilliard School of Music. It is one of the
finest music schools in the world.

Yo-Yo was very small and shy. He had been taught to obey his parents quietly and without question. Now, in the United States, his music teacher wanted him to show his feelings more. At school, he was supposed to speak up. American children were expected to ask lots of questions about everything.

Yo-Yo Ma felt torn. How could he fit in with other American kids and still be a good son?

Yo-Yo continued to study music. His cello playing began to change. It felt freer, more full of feeling.

Carnegie Hall

A Big Decision

Yo-Yo Ma had been performing in public since early childhood. Then, at the age of seventeen, he faced a choice. Should he try to earn a living as a performer? Or should he get a college education? Yo-Yo Ma chose college.

At Harvard University, Yo-Yo Ma studied more than music. He explored literature and history and other subjects. He learned to form his own ideas about the things he was studying in class.

Harvard University in Cambridge, MA

Yo-Yo Ma has said that choosing an education was the "best decision" he ever made. It gave him more choices in life. He knew he could have a career outside of music if he wished to someday. He said, "It's not that I'm stuck playing the cello because it's the only thing I can do."

Yo-Yo Ma performs at Carnegie Hall.

 Becoming a Great Cellist

At Harvard, Yo-Yo Ma continued to perform and to learn about music. Cellists must know how to use their fingers and the bow in just the right way. Yo-Yo Ma had developed plenty of skills for the cello since his childhood. He had learned from great teachers. He regularly practiced for long hours. But as Yo-Yo Ma grew older, he was learning more than skills.

In 1998, Yo-Yo Ma played in a celebration in Washington, D.C. It was to honor the music of J. S. Bach.

Yo-Yo Ma was learning to draw on something deep inside himself to share with listeners. It was more than talent or skill. It was the special quality that made truly great musicians. He was learning how to make the cello come alive with feelings. He was learning to show the fear, dreaminess, joy, hope, and sorrow that live in the music.

"When your brain and heart are engaged, you can't go wrong," Yo-Yo Ma later said. And by the time Yo-Yo left Harvard, he seldom did go wrong.

Overcoming Trouble

Yo-Yo Ma married Jill Hornor in 1978. His career was growing quickly now. He was being invited to give concerts all over the world. He traveled nearly every week of the year. When he wasn't performing, he was making recordings. He didn't get home as often as he had wanted. So, it got harder and harder for him and Jill to see each other.

But Yo-Yo's new, busy life came to a sudden stop. When he was 25, Yo-Yo faced a serious health problem. He had something wrong with his back, called a curved spine. It was now giving him great pain. His doctors told him he needed to have an operation to fix it. It had to be done while his body was still young. If he waited too long, the operation might not work.

There was another, scarier risk. The doctors told Yo-Yo that the operation might harm his nerves. If that happened, Yo-Yo might never be able to play the cello again.

Still, Yo-Yo kept a positive attitude. He told Jill, "If I come out of this alive but not able to have control of my fingers, I will have had a very fulfilling life in music."

Yo-Yo went ahead with the operation. Fortunately, the operation was a complete success. And although Yo-Yo Ma's upper body was in a cast for six months, he still practiced the cello. He was determined that his life in music would go on.

Once Yo-Yo had fully recovered, he got busier than ever. Yo-Yo Ma couldn't say no when someone asked for just one more concert in a city. It was hard for him to turn down exciting chances to play for people. But Yo-Yo also knew he was needed at home, now more than ever. In 1984 he and Jill had a son. Two years later, the family grew again when their daughter was born.

Yo-Yo Ma decided to cut back on his performing dates. He was determined to pay as much attention to his family as he did to playing cello. He never regretted his decision.

Yo-Yo Ma performs with the Mark Morris Dance Company in Boston, MA.

Sharing the Music

Most audiences for classical music are older adults, especially in the United States. But Yo-Yo Ma wanted young people to learn to enjoy the works of great composers. He remembered the joy of growing up in a home filled with music. That's how he wanted his children to grow up.

Yo-Yo began appearing with his cello on children's television programs such as *Sesame Street* and *Mister Rogers' Neighborhood*. Maybe children who had never heard a cello before would feel its beauty.

Yo-Yo Ma shares a smile with popular singer Bobby McFerrin.

Today, Yo-Yo Ma is a musical superstar.
With adoring fans and nonstop attention,
superstars can start to think they are too
important. But audiences sense Yo-Yo Ma's
basic warmth. His cheerfulness, patience, and
good humor come across when he's on stage.
"I am playing the music not to show off or
prove anything," he has said. "I want to share
something of what the music means."

More than forty years ago, a little boy
named Yo-Yo Ma began to learn the music of
Johann Sebastian Bach. Through the years,
Yo-Yo Ma has continued to play those same
works. The music "constantly enriches," he
has said. It always gives him something new
to think about. To Yo-Yo Ma, the music is
what matters most.

Responding

Think About the Selection

1. Why do you think Yo-Yo Ma's cello playing changes after he moves to New York?

2. What does Yo-Yo Ma mean when he says, "When your brain and heart are engaged, you can't go wrong"?

3. Give one example each of a fact and an opinion in the story.

Fact and Opinion

Copy this chart on a piece of paper. Write whether each sentence is a fact or an opinion.

Clue	Fact or Opinion?
Yo-Yo Ma is among the finest cello players in the world.	?
Yo-Yo Ma's father was his first teacher.	?

Victor Sews

by Lee S. Justice

illustrated by Joe Cepeda

Strategy Focus

Is sewing class too hard for Victor? As you read, stop and **summarize** each part of the story.

It was the first day of sewing class. Ms. Lee was telling us about the pants we'd be making. "Keisha and Thomas are wearing the pants they made last term," said Ms. Lee.

Keisha and Thomas stood at the front of the room to model their pants. They looked like they wanted to be somewhere else. But the pants weren't bad.

"They're like pajama pants," Ms. Lee went on. "But they're for everyday wear. I think it's important for kids to make something they can actually wear and be proud of."

I liked the idea of sewing. But that was before I tried it.

First of all, we had to iron our paper patterns. The patterns were like the plans for making the pants.

"Victor," Ms. Lee said to me, "may I suggest that you spread out the pattern more smoothly?"

I looked around. Everybody else's patterns were smooth. My patterns were wrinkled. There were even a few rips.

"Oops," I said.

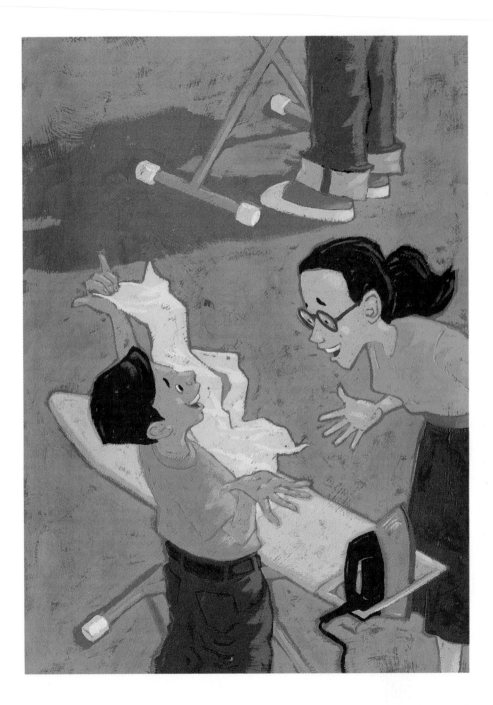

Next we were supposed to pin the patterns to the cloth we had picked out. Mine was black with little yellow squares and triangles on it. "That's a nice design," Nina said to me.

Nina is a girl I've liked for a long time. So her compliment made me feel good. I kept pinning, trying to come up with something nice to say back.

The next thing I knew, Ms. Lee was beside me. "Victor," she said, "remember what I said about pinning to the other side of the fabric? The side that will be the outside of the pants."

I saw that I had laid down the cloth the wrong way. Everybody else's cloth *was* pinned on the outside. How come nobody but me had a problem?

I pulled out the pins, flipped the cloth over, and started pinning again. I worked fast.

"Victor," said Ms. Lee a short while later. "Do you really need *that* many pins?" I looked down. Sure enough, about a million pins were sticking out of my pattern paper. What could I have been thinking?

Carmen pointed at my work. "Victor's making porcupine pants," she said.

I made a goofy face, pretending to be surprised by all those pins. Everybody laughed.

"How's that sewing class going?" Mom asked me a few weeks later.

"OK," I said.

"It's good that boys take sewing these days," Mom said. "When I went to school, boys took wood shop, and girls took sewing. I'm glad those days are over. Things are more fair now. Who knows? Maybe you'll have the talent of my uncle Oscar."

"Who's he?" I asked my mother.

"My grandmother's brother. He was a tailor. He even made suits for the Yankees."

"He sewed the Yankees' uniforms?" I asked.

"No, their *suits* — the clothes they wore off the field" said Mom. "Some of the ballplayers would come to Uncle Oscar's shop to get their suits tailored. He did good work. I took you to his shop once when you were very small. I guess you don't remember."

That night I had a weird dream. I dreamed I was playing for the Yankees. But I couldn't move right because my uniform didn't fit. Every time I swung the bat, I heard the sound of cloth ripping.

When I woke up, the sheets and blankets were tightly wrapped around me.

Then I remembered it was Tuesday. Oh, no! Sewing class again.

I got to sewing class just before the bell. Everyone was already working away.

We practiced on the sewing machines using a small piece of cloth.

I sat down at my machine and slipped the cloth under the needle.

Ms. Lee suddenly appeared at my back. "Slow and steady, Victor," she said. I pushed down the foot pedal. "Slo-o-o-w, Victor, gently, GENTLY, **GENTLY!!**" It was too late. My cloth was a tangled wad. Ms. Lee had to cut it out of the machine with scissors.

Next, I used one of the tracing wheels. The tracing wheel looks like a pizza cutter. You roll it in chalk then you roll it on the cloth around the pattern. It traces out a line.

Once again, Ms Lee spotted me. "Victor," she said. "You're supposed to trace onto the other side of the fabric."

Another time, cutting with scissors gave me trouble. I had cut too much. The pants looked like they'd fit a four-year-old. "I'll go on a diet," I said.

When the class laughed, Ms. Lee told me to stop clowning around.

I saw why it took a whole term to sew a pair of pants. There were so many steps! You had to iron, then pin, then trace, then iron again. It went on and on. When we started, I barely knew what a needle was. Now I knew, but it was not a pretty picture.

Finally, I got the hang of using the machine. The needle poked in and out of the cloth nicely. So what if the seam wasn't exactly straight?

"I need more cloth," I told Ms. Lee. "I messed up a little on the back part." Somehow, my sewing had changed the cloth into a tattered rag.

"There should be more in the box," said Ms. Lee, pointing me to the fabric rolls. "Remember to do all the steps in the right order, Victor."

I grabbed the fabric, spread it out, cut, and began pinning the pattern. I worked so fast that I felt like a real pro. "I bet this is how Uncle Oscar did it," I thought. I pictured the Yankees at my shoulder, admiring my skill.

I didn't notice it at the time, but this cloth did not exactly match the cloth for the front of my pants. This one was yellow with big black squares and triangles.

Why didn't I notice the difference?

"**I**s your sewing class still good?" Mom asked me that night.

"It's OK," I answered. "The best part about it is that it's almost over."

The last step was hemming the pant legs. I was supposed to do that by hand. But I thought the machine would do it faster. That was mistake number two zillion. It did go fast — too fast. Before I knew it, I had hemmed one leg shut.

I tried picking the thread out of the cloth. After ten minutes, I had picked out three stitches. If I kept up at that pace, I'd be done in about two years.

"I'll just cut and hem again," I decided quickly.

On the last day of sewing class, we were each supposed to parade around the room in our new pants. I put on my pants and looked in the bathroom mirror.

That's when I noticed that the front and the back had different designs. One leg ended just below the knee. The other ended at the ankle. I thought about running away.

"Well, if I look like a clown, I may as well act like one," I told myself.

I entered the room strutting. There were roars and shrieks of laughter. I took a few bows.

When the laughter quieted down, I heard Nina's voice. "Look at how Victor matched up the designs on the front and back. They're *almost* the same. That's so artistic."

"Actually, those pants are cool," said Carmen.

I looked closely at their faces. Were they kidding?

Ms. Lee smiled at me. "You're a style maker, Victor," she said

A few days later, Carmen showed up in pants she had sewn at home. The front and the back didn't match. One leg was a little longer than the other.

Whatever Carmen does, a lot of other kids do. Soon the school was filled with kids wearing pants like mine.

I told my mother what happened. "Everyone is wearing the pants," I said. "They even call them *Victors*."

My mother just nodded her head in a knowing way. "Uncle Oscar would be so proud," she said.

Think About the Selection

1 Why does Victor have a weird dream?

2 How does Victor's mistake turn out to be a good thing?

3 What is Victor's problem in the story?

Story Structure

Copy this simple story map on a piece of paper and complete it.

Story Map for *Victor Sews*	
Main Character: Victor	
Settings: **1.** sewing class	**2.** Victor's home
Problem:	?
Beginning:	?
Middle:	?
End:	?

Falling Off a Log

by Anne Miranda
illustrated by Wayne Alfano

Strategy Focus

Can saving someone's life be as easy as falling off a log for Marta? As you read, try to **predict** what Marta will do each step of the way.

It had been only two months since Marta had moved to Ohio from Florida. Now she was at summer camp for the first time. She wasn't just away from home. She was away from her new home too! Everything there seemed so different and scary.

When Marta first saw the lake at camp, she stared at the brownish water. It sure wasn't anything like the clear blue water of the beaches back home!

"I'm supposed to swim in that?" she asked Susan. Susan was one of the five girls who shared Cabin 7 with Marta.

"Sure. Why not?" said Susan. Susan was fun and fearless. Marta wished she could be more like her.

"Because it's . . . cold and dark!" said Marta.

"Don't worry," said Susan. "You'll get used to it, once you're in."

"But I can't even see what's in the water," said Marta.

"Come on," said Susan. "Swim with me out to the float. It's as easy as falling off a log!"

That's what Susan said about everything. "As easy as falling off a log." Marta had never heard anyone use that saying in Florida.

But Susan had been right. Swimming to the float had been pretty easy. So had canoeing and diving. By the end of the first week, Marta started getting used to life at the lake. And Susan was becoming her best friend. Marta felt like she could do anything with Susan around.

That's why Marta agreed to go with Susan on a hike to an old cabin in the woods. Cody, one of the camp counselors, was going with a group of other girls.

Marta was excited the morning of the hike. But one look at Susan's face made her excitement instantly disappear.

"I can't go," Susan said. "I don't feel very well. You go. You'll have fun with Cody and the other girls."

"But — " Marta started to say.

Susan read her mind. "Don't worry," she smiled. "It will be as easy as falling off a log."

Marta rushed to the counselors' cabin. Cody was putting things into her backpack.

"Ready to go?" Cody asked.

"Susan's sick," said Marta. "Maybe we should wait another day."

"That's too bad, " Cody said. "But I've got a whole group of campers ready to go. I'll make sure that Nurse Thompson checks in with Susan."

Marta felt her stomach turn. "But Susan's my best friend," she started to say. "I do everything with her."

"You'll be fine without her," Cody said.

Marta swallowed and nodded her head.

Cody smiled and threw a few more things into her backpack. One of them was a small plastic box.

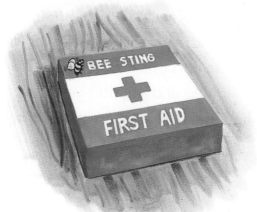

"What's that?" asked Marta.

"My bee sting kit," said Cody. "I'm allergic."

"You're a *what*?" asked Marta. "What's a *lergic*?"

"Not a *lergic*. I'm *allergic*. I have an allergy to bee stings," said Cody. "If I get stung by a bee I could die. I carry this kit all the time. I have to give myself a shot if I get stung."

Cody put on her backpack and headed out the door. Marta followed. They checked in with Nurse Thompson to tell her about Susan. Then they met up with the rest of the group and headed down the trail.

The hike seemed to take forever to Marta. She was tired when Cody finally stopped the group at the edge of a marsh.

"There it is," Cody said, taking off her backpack. She pointed beyond the marsh to the cabin.

Ellen Franklin, a girl from Cabin 12, asked, "How do we get there?"

Cody pointed to a thin bridge made of two logs lying side by side. "We just walk across that," she said.

The bridge didn't look safe at all to Marta.

"Ready to go?" Cody said.

Everyone jumped up and headed across the bridge. Marta could feel her stomach spinning like sneakers in a clothes dryer. "I wish Susan was here," she thought. "This really *will* be like falling off a log."

Cody could see that Marta was scared. "I'll go ahead of you to show you how," she said. "It's easy."

Marta watched as Cody slowly walked across the logs behind the other girls. Cody balanced herself like a tightrope walker. Marta didn't want to think about what was swimming in the dark water beneath her.

"Now it's your turn," Cody said when she got to the other side.

Marta swallowed and stepped onto the bridge. Her legs felt wobbly. She took six tiny steps and then stopped. She couldn't move another inch.

"I can't!" she gasped.

"Sure you can. It's easier than it looks," said Cody.

By this time, Marta wasn't listening. She had already crawled back to the other side.

"Come on, Marta!" said Cody. "You can do it."
But Marta wouldn't budge. Finally, Cody gave up.
"It's okay," she said. "I've got to join up with the
girls. We'll just take a quick look. You stay there. There
are some sandwiches in my backpack if you're hungry."

Marta nodded and sat down next to Cody's backpack. She was angry with herself. All the other girls had been able to go across. "I'd be able to do it if Susan were here," Marta thought to herself.

Marta figured the group would be back in a couple of minutes. But when fifteen minutes passed she started to get worried. "They better not leave me here," she thought.

Just then she saw Ellen running from behind the cabin. Ellen looked like she was crying.

"It's Cody," Ellen yelled. "She's sick! She can't breathe!"

Ellen ran across the log bridge and headed towards the trail.

"Come on!" Ellen cried. She disappeared down the trail, running full speed to get back to the camp.

Marta stayed put. She knew what was wrong. Cody must have been stung by a bee! And Cody had left her backpack with the bee sting kit on this side of the bridge.

Marta grabbed Cody's backpack and found the bee sting kit. With the kit in hand, she ran to the edge of the log bridge.

"I've got the bee sting kit," she called out. She hoped one of the other girls would hear her and come get the kit. But there was no answer.

Marta knew what she had to do. She took a deep breath and stepped onto the bridge. It shook as she took her first step. She took a look at the dark marsh water and felt sick. But she had to do it.

Marta slowly moved forward, inch by inch. When she got to the spot where she had stopped before, she started to back up. "But Cody could die!" she said to herself. "Just don't look at the water." It's what Susan would have said if she were here. Then Marta got down on all fours and slowly crawled across the rest of the bridge.

When Marta's feet finally landed on solid ground, she ran to the cabin. Cody was lying on an old wooden table. The other girls stood around her. They were all scared.

Cody was having trouble breathing, but she could still talk. "Thanks," she whispered, as Marta handed her the kit.

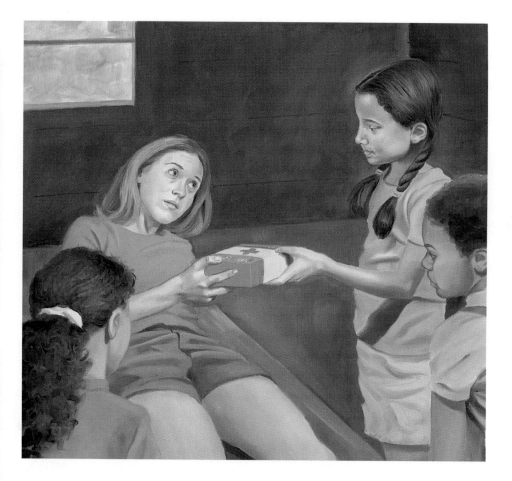

"Can you do it?" Marta asked.

Cody couldn't even answer. With her last bit of strength, she gave herself a shot. Then she just lay there for minutes.

Little by little, Cody started to feel better. Finally, she was well enough to start back to camp. Marta and another girl let Cody lean on them to walk.

When they got to the log bridge, Cody stopped. "Can you make it across?" she asked Marta.

Marta smiled and stepped onto the bridge. For some reason, it didn't scare her any more. She thought how proud of her Susan would be. "No problem," she said. "It's as easy as falling off a log."

Responding

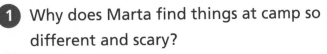

Think About the Selection

1 Why does Marta find things at camp so different and scary?

2 How does Marta feel about doing things with Susan?

3 What might Susan say to Marta after she hears about how Marta helped Cody?

What Will Happen Next?

Copy this chart. Write two other predictions about what might happen to Marta after the story's ending. Then tell why you think this.

What will happen next when. . .	Why I think this will happen.
Marta crosses back over the bridge: She will walk across and not be as afraid as before.	She finally made it across the bridge. She tells Cody, "It's as easy as falling off a log."
Marta gets back to camp: ?	?
Marta goes on another hike: , ?	?

BUCK LEONARD
BASEBALL'S GREATEST GENTLEMAN

by Tyrone Washington

ORESTE MIÑOSO, N. Y. Cubans   3rd Base   HERB SOUELL, Kansas City Mo
ROBERT HARVEY, Newark   RF   JOSEPH COLAS, Memphis Red
LUIS MARQUEZ, Homestead Grays   CF   WILLARD BROWN, Kan. City
LUCIOUS EASTER, Homestead Grays   LF   CLYDE NELSON, Cleveland Buck
LOUIS LOUDEN, N. Y. Cubans   C   QUINCY TROUPE, Chicago
WILLIAM CASH, Philadelphia Stars   C   SAM HAIRSTON, Indianapolis
MAXWELL MANNING, Newark   P   CHET BREWER, Cleveland

Do you know who Buck Leonard was? Chances are you don't. But you probably do know who Ken Griffey Jr. is — if you're any kind of baseball fan at all. You'd also know Griffey if you eat a certain cereal for breakfast every morning. But over fifty years ago, during the 1930s and 1940s, there were no black baseball players on cereal boxes. Back then, African American baseball stars like Buck Leonard were pretty much unknown to most fans.

Back in the 1800s, white and black players played on the same baseball teams. But in 1887, the National Association of Baseball Players said black players could no longer play on major league teams. And that was the way it stayed, for many, many years.

Black athletes played baseball in something called the Negro Leagues. In some ways, the Negro Leagues were like the major leagues. There were all-star games and world series. There were also many very talented players. But unlike the players in the major leagues, all the Negro League players were black.

Buck Leonard's name sits on top of the Negro National League All Star roster in this poster from 1946.

Satchel Paige

Oscar Charleston

Negro League players were never as famous as the major league players. But the Negro League had its stars. They were players who were just as good as, and maybe even better than, major league players. There were heroes like Josh Gibson, Satchel Paige, Oscar Charleston — and Buck Leonard.

Buck Leonard was one of the most admired players the Negro League ever had. He was known for his pleasant and easy-going way. He went to bed early, did lots of crossword puzzles, and had a friendly word for everyone. He was also known as one of the greatest gentlemen to ever play baseball.

And on the fields of the Negro Leagues, he made baseball history.

Buck Leonard in his Homestead Grays uniform

His full name was Walter Fenner Leonard. But people called him Buck. He was born in 1907 in the small town of Rocky Mount, North Carolina. His father, a railroad brakeman, died of influenza when Buck was a young boy. To support the family, Buck shined shoes at the railway station.

When he was sixteen, Buck worked full-time for a train company. At that early age, he was also a star of his hometown baseball team.

Buck soon began to play professional ball. He played first base for the Homestead Grays of Homestead, Pennsylvania, one of the best Negro League teams. He joined them in 1934.

The Homestead Grays in 1941. Buck Leonard is kneeling third from left in the front row.

Lou Gehrig

Buck's fans often compared him to Lou Gehrig, the famous New York Yankees first baseman. Both players were well-known for their polite manner. They were also big, powerful hitters who played in the shadow of even better hitters on their own teams.

Babe Ruth

Josh Gibson

Lou Gehrig was not quite as big a slugger as his teammate, Babe Ruth. No matter how hard Lou Gehrig worked, people always seemed to pay more attention to The Babe. Buck Leonard often played as well as his teammate, Josh Gibson. But no matter how well Buck played, Gibson usually stole the show. Gibson always managed to hit more home runs than Buck. He also hit them farther. Yet, like Gehrig, Buck didn't mind being out of the spotlight.

One thing was certain for both pairs of players: They made life hard for opposing teams.

Buck Leonard tags out a New York Cubans baserunner during a game in 1946.

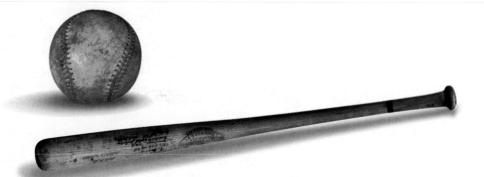

Buck Leonard was a tough, hard worker who played well, game after game. He once played with a broken hand. He broke it during the first game of a four-game series. Buck just taped up his bad hand and played to the end of the series.

Buck often played as many as three games a day! That's how things were for teams in the Negro Leagues. Major league teams might play double headers — two games in a day. But most of the time, major league players had it pretty easy, playing one game a day.

Buck also worked hard when he wasn't on the baseball field. Since the baseball season didn't last all year long, he'd make money doing different jobs. He might shine shoes or work on the railroad. He'd do whatever he could to support himself until the next baseball season started.

Negro League players didn't make as much money as major league players did, and they weren't as well known. During his first season with the Homestead Grays, Buck Leonard made $125 a month — much less than any major league player made. The Homestead Grays, like other Negro League teams, received very little attention in major newspapers. There was little opportunity for Buck to be a well-known, national hero.

Negro League All Stars in 1947

An even bigger problem for Negro League teams was the way the players were treated because they were black. Buck and his teammates were not allowed in most restaurants and hotels when they were on the road. That meant they sometimes had to sleep out on a baseball field or inside the team bus. At sunrise, the Homestead Grays would dust themselves off and get ready to play. But no matter what hardships they faced, Buck Leonard and the rest of Negro League players loved to play the game.

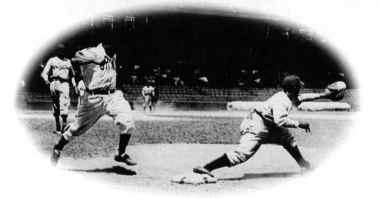

For seventeen seasons, Buck Leonard didn't just play baseball — he *shone*. Buck had one of the highest batting averages ever. To get a batting average, you divide the number of times a player gets a hit by the number of times he's at bat. A 1.000 would be perfect. Most players never hit over .300 in a single season.

Buck Leonard hit .341 over his whole career! In special games against major league teams, Buck hit .382 in all the games combined. That meant he got more hits off major league pitchers than he did off the Negro League pitchers. In 1947 he reached a high point, batting an amazing .410 average for the whole season.

In 1948, when he was 41 years old — old for a professional baseball player — Buck hit .395. Very few baseball players in any league — at any age — have ever hit that well.

Buck Leonard finishes one of his many home-run trots around the bases against the Newark Bears in 1943.

Buck Leonard takes one of his giant home-run swings in 1938.

Other players made up some tall tales about Buck Leonard. According to one of his teammates, Buck once hit a home run so far that made it rain. The ball cleared the bleachers, the back fence of the stadium, and several houses. When the ball hit a water tower, it rained for two weeks! These stories were based on Buck's amazing play. They showed just how much other ball players admired him.

In 1938, Buck Leonard almost got a chance at national stardom. He and Josh Gibson were invited into the office of Clark Griffith, who owned the Washington Senators. The Senators were a major league ball club. The two players could hardly sit still. Griffith had heard about how well Leonard and Gibson played. He asked if they would play for him. Of course, they answered yes!

It didn't happen. Griffith argued long and hard to get black players into the majors. But more powerful baseball officials shouted him down. Neither Buck Leonard nor Josh Gibson ever got a major league contract.

It wasn't until 1947 that the major leagues hired their first black player, Jackie Robinson. Robinson went to play for the Brooklyn Dodgers, where he became an instant hero to many. He was young and talented. He was able to take insults from people who wanted the league to be all white. Major league officials saw how well Robinson played the game and what a fine sportsman he was. His courage and self-control helped open the door for other black players to come into the major leagues. Little by little, things began to change.

Jackie Robinson was the first African American baseball player to sign a major league contract.

Monte Irvin and Larry Doby were two Negro League stars who crossed over to the major leagues after Jackie Robinson opened the door.

In 1952, Buck Leonard was finally invited to play in the major leagues. But by then he was 45 years old. Buck knew that he couldn't play as well as younger black players. So he said no. He knew that if he played poorly on a major league team, he might hurt other black players' chances of playing in the majors. To the end, Buck was a gentleman and a model of good sportsmanship.

Buck Leonard is presented with a plaque honoring his election into the National Baseball Hall of Fame.

In 1972, Buck Leonard finally got the honor he deserved. He was elected to the National Baseball Hall of Fame.

After his playing days were over, Leonard went back to the small southern town where he was born. He had started out life there as a shoeshine boy. He had become one of baseball's great heroes.

Buck Leonard passed away in 1997.

Responding

Think About the Selection

1 Why wasn't Buck Leonard as well-known as other baseball stars?

2 How was baseball difficult for teams in the Negro Leagues?

3 Give some supporting details that show that Buck Leonard worked hard off the baseball field too.

Main Idea/Supporting Details

Copy the chart on a piece of paper. Write two details that help support each idea.

Main Idea	Supporting Details
Buck's fans often compared him to Lou Gehrig.	1. Both were polite. 2. ?
Buck Leonard was a tough, hard worker.	1. ? 2. ?

Avid® Editing

Avid® Editing: A Guide for Beginning and Intermediate Users

Second Edition

by Sam Kauffmann

AMSTERDAM BOSTON LONDON NEW YORK OXFORD PARIS
SAN DIEGO SAN FRANCISCO SINGAPORE SYDNEY TOKYO

An imprint of Elsevier Science

Focal Press is an imprint of Elsevier Science.

♾ Recognizing the importance of preserving what has been written, Elsevier Science prints its books on acid-free paper whenever possible.

Library of Congress Cataloging-in-Publication Data
Kauffmann, Sam.
    Avid editing : a guide for beginning and intermediate users / Sam Kauffmann.—2nd ed.
       p. cm.
    Includes bibliographical references and index.
    ISBN 0-240-80541-0 (pbk : alk paper)
    1. Video tapes—Editing—Data processing. 2. Motion pictures—Editing—Data processing.
    3. MCXpress. 4. Media composer. I. Title.

    TR899 .K38 2003
    778.5′235′0285—dc21   2002192743

British Library Cataloguing-in-Publication Data
A catalogue record for this book is available from the British Library.

The publisher offers special discounts on bulk orders of this book.
For information, please contact:

Manager of Special Sales
Elsevier Science
200 Wheeler Road
Burlington, MA 01803
Tel: 781-313-4700
Fax: 781-313-4882

For information on all Focal Press publications available, contact our World Wide Web home page at: http://www.focalpress.com

10 9 8 7 6 5 4 3 2 1

Printed in the United States of America

For Katie, Allie, and Derek

*"Our deepest fear is not that we are inadequate.
Our deepest fear is that we are powerful beyond measure."*

— Nelson Mandela

Contents

Preface

A lot has changed since I wrote the first edition of this book during the summer and fall of 1999. Back then, Avid was the best known nonlinear editing system in the world. In many ways, it was just about the only game in town. Apple's Final Cut Pro was just a speck on the NLE horizon. Since then Avid has maintained its position as the leader in the film and television industry, but Final Cut Pro has become the most popular choice among students and independent film and video makers.

Recently Avid has made significant changes to its line of editing software, much of it in response to competition from Final Cut Pro. Few people ever claimed Final Cut was the best editing software around, but the price differential between it and Avid was substantial. But not any more; you can buy an Avid system, with all the bells and whistles, for not much more than the cost of a comparable Final Cut Pro system.

Why should you learn to cut on an Avid? Despite the competition, Avid is still the dominant player in the film and television industry. It is used to edit 85% of all feature films and 95% of all prime time television shows. And that's where the jobs are. Lots of people cut on Final Cut Pro systems, but more often then not, they're working on their own editing system, and so they don't do a lot of hiring.

One of the best things about Avid is that all the models, from the least to most expensive, share the same interface. You can learn to cut on the Xpress DV, then get a job on a Media Composer, and not need much time to get up to speed.

Although Avid wouldn't admit it, Avid editors owe a debt of gratitude to Apple and its Final Cut Pro system. The fact that you can now buy an Avid Xpress DV—a machine that contains almost as many features as a full-blown Media Composer—for under $2000 is due in large part to marketplace competition.

This book covers the Media Composer, Xpress, and Xpress DV. It teaches you all aspects of Avid editing, from basic and advanced editing, to creating titles and special effects. This book attempts to harness Avid's incredible power in as simple and straightforward a manner as possible. I won't show you every technique found in Avid's many manuals, but I'll show you all the ones you need to know.

I have many people to thank for their assistance, none more so than the many students I've had the pleasure of teaching during the past decade. There are too many to name, but all of them taught me as much as I taught them. My colleagues at Boston University have given me advice and encouragement throughout my teaching career, especially Bill Lawson and Mary Jane Doherty, who are inspired teachers and good friends. Bob Demers, Jamie Companeschi, and Jose Ponce all offered invaluable technical assistance and helped my students through difficulties whenever I wasn't there. They also shot one of the scenes on the enclosed DVD. I also wish to thank Nancy Maguire, Ray Carney, Jim Lengel, Steve Geller, Charles Merzbacher, Bob Arnold, John Augliera, Rich Folger, Dean Brent Baker, and Associate Dean Marilyn Root.

Special thanks to Matt Feury for all his help with the DVD, and to Michael Phillips, Tom Ohanian, Jodi Plasterer, and Amy Paladino of Avid. Thanks to Loren Miller, who first showed me how to cut on an Avid. Thanks to Don Packer, president of Finish Editorial, and Greg Dildine, the talented colorist there. Thanks to Wes Plate for helping me locate and correct several mistakes in the first edition. Also thanks to Michael Girard of Northeast Negative Matchers; Don Wilkins of the Berklee College of Music; Tony Dolan; Frank Capria; Adam Corey; Tony Gorman; Doug and Sandra Cress; Bob Jones; Jim Davidson; Hosea Gruber; Joanna Jefferson; Mary Choi; Brad Kimbrough; and my siblings, Margaret, Louise, and Bruce Kauffmann, who were my first friends and teachers.

Special thanks to Kate Shanaphy and Tim Eberle, who are Kate and Tim in "Wanna Trade." And thanks to Josh Wingate and Rachel Neuman, who play Peter and Michele in "Gaffer's Delight."

This book could not have been written without Kate Cress, who gave invaluable support and advice every step of the way.

Introduction

Although this book covers the Avid Xpress DV, the Xpress, and the Media Composer, I have put a lot of my emphasis on the Xpress DV. It's my belief that the majority of beginners will start their Avid experience on a Xpress DV system, and since this book's primary audience is the beginner, that's where I focus my attention. But I also believe that people who learn on the Xpress DV will soon be cutting on more advanced systems, and this book will show them how they can easily make that move. Writing a book that covers all three Avid systems is not as difficult as it sounds, because the interface for all three is practically identical.

Think of this as a textbook, workbook, and user manual all rolled into one. It is written so you can read it at home, studying a chapter's contents, or while sitting in front of an Avid, following the book's step-by-step instructions.

There are suggested assignments at the end of most chapters; they are there to encourage you to practice the techniques and skills explained in that particular chapter. Each chapter builds on the ideas presented in the previous chapter, so it's a good idea to practice one set of skills before moving on to the next.

I believe you will learn to use the Avid more quickly if you start by editing a short narrative scene, rather than a short documentary project. With a script for the scene in front of you, you know where you are going; you can then concentrate on how to get there. To get you started, I've enclosed a short scene for you to edit, entitled "Wanna Trade." It's on the DVD-ROM that comes with this book. Step-by-step instructions are provided in Chapter 1 to guide you through the editing process. A two-page script for the scene is included as well.

Ideally, your professor, instructor, or teacher will mount the scene onto the Avid so you can begin editing after the first or second class. If you will be mounting the DVD-ROM yourself, there are instructions in the section called "DVD-ROM Instructions" at the end of the book. If your instructor has material she or he is more comfortable with, then by all means use that material for the first assignment.

My goal is to get you editing as quickly as possible. The recording/ digitizing process is an important part of this book, but I've postponed it until Chapter 6. Once you've cut a scene, you'll find the intricacies of digitizing much more understandable.

There are two new chapters in this edition: Chapters 14 and 15. Chapter 14 explains how to create and edit 16:9 widescreen material. Since all of Avid's new models come with 16:9 capabilities, I wanted to cover these important features in this edition. Chapter 15 is devoted to script-based editing and the powerful tools that are a part of Avid's Script Integration. (Xpress DV users will need PowerPack to access Script Integration.)

So that you can practice the technique explained in Chapters 14 and 15, I have included a second editing exercise on the DVD-ROM—a scene entitled "Gaffer's Delight." It was shot on Super-16mm film and then transferred to videotape using a process called "full height anamorphic" in order to get a widescreen, 16:9 aspect ratio. It's complicated to load and edit, so wait until you reach Chapter 14 before you bring it in. This scene was covered by many different camera angles, involving several takes, making it a good candidate for Avid's Script Integration features. The script for the scene is included on the DVD-ROM so that you can bring the script into your Avid and then, following the instructions provided, attach clips to the action and dialog.

This edition will concentrate on software versions 3.0 and above for the Xpress DV, versions 5.0 and above for the Xpress, and versions 11.0 and above for the Media Composer. The first edition of this book adequately explains how to use Avid's software prior to these releases. Avid has made some major changes to the way the Avid works with the introduction of these releases, and I've written this latest edition in part to address those changes.

Xpress and Xpress DV are quite similar and I often use the generic term *Xpress* for both. When there are differences, I'll explain how they are different.

All three systems come on Windows and Macintosh platforms. I've used both Macintosh and Windows screens to guide you through the instructions. Mac and Window screens are almost identical. The main difference between cutting on a Mac and cutting on a Windows is the shortcut keys you'll use. On the Macintosh you'll often use the Command key, with its symbol ⌘. If you are using Windows, you'll use the Control (Ctrl) key instead. Windows users will also use the Alt key instead of the Macintosh Option key. That's it. That's about the only difference between the Mac and Windows versions.

One caveat. Competition from other nonlinear digital editing systems has forced Avid to offer powerful features on the Xpress and Xpress DV that were once only offered on the more expensive Media Composer. Given this healthy trend, you may find that a feature I describe as exclusive to the Media Composer is, in fact, available on the latest versions of Xpress and Xpress DV. So if you're cutting on an Xpress model, learn the Media Composer features contained in the book. You may use them sooner than you think.

Avid® Editing

Getting Started

THE EDITOR'S JOB

What does an editor do? Some say an editor's job is to simply take out the slow parts. Others say it's to follow the wishes of the director and to string together the best takes. Ask an editor what the job entails and he or she will say it's to breathe life into a film or video, or to find and expose its heart and soul. Ask that same editor at the end of a long and difficult project and you'll probably hear, "It's to make everyone else look good." All of these answers are true, yet none comes close to capturing the critical role the editor plays in any production. I think a great editor is like a great chef: Someone may hand the editor the ingredients, and even the recipe, but the editor puts those ingredients together in a way that fires the viewer's imagination, stokes the thought process, and stirs the passions.

There are thousands of tasks involved in editing a film or video, and thousands of decisions must be made along the way. All of them are important. Which take is best? Is the lighting and composition better in this shot or that one? Is the pacing of these shots too fast? Will cutting out the character's entrance make the scene more or less confusing?

Although the editor's primary job remains the same, the manner in which an editor works was transformed during the 1990s by the development of computer-based nonlinear editing systems (NLEs). The Avid was one of the earliest NLEs, and it is perhaps the best known system in the world.

Today, the transformation from analog editing machines to computer-based editing systems is practically complete. Only a tiny percentage of films and videos are still edited on analog machines. Compared with analog devices, computer-based systems make the editor's job much easier and faster. Yet these systems can also make an editor's job harder and take a lot longer to complete. It may seem like a paradox, but it's true.

Editing on a computer is much easier and faster than on an analog machine because nearly every task is executed with a single keystroke or the push of a button. Want to splice a shot into your project? Click one button and it's done. Want to make a shot two seconds longer? Click and drag a roller and it's done. Want a freeze frame? A few clicks of the mouse and it's just the way you want it.

Yet there is a price for all this speed. The Avid and the other popular computer-based systems are much more difficult to master than analog film or video systems. Today, when you buy an Avid, it comes with nearly 1500 pages of documentation. Because the Avid offers so many sophisticated tools, the editor is supposed to do things that were once handled by scores of other people. In the past, someone else designed and shot the titles, there was a team of sound and music editors, and a highly trained group of talented individuals created all of the special effects. Now a single editor is often the entire postproduction team!

Today's NLE editors are expected to be computer savvy, while possessing video engineering skills. Often an editor must set up, connect, and troubleshoot an incredible array of video decks, operating systems, audio drivers, and FireWire cards. So although it's true that a computer can make an editor's job easier and faster, it can also make the job more difficult and take longer.

An editor's job *has* gotten more difficult and complex, yet the rewards and satisfaction are greater as well. You, the Avid editor, have far more creative control over the project than at any time in the history of editing. You may have more to do, but you don't need much help getting the job done, and you can make sure everything looks and sounds just the way you want it.

AVID'S ROOTS

Many of the people who designed the first digital editing systems were filmmakers who found themselves doing a lot of videotape editing—and they didn't particularly like it. Still, there were things about video editing that they liked better than film editing. So they used the emerging power of personal computers to fashion a hybrid system that borrows the best from both worlds.

Film and Video: The Old Way

The main advantage film editing has always had over video editing is that it is nonlinear. You can remove a shot in the middle of the film and put it at the beginning—or vice versa. It takes time to do all that unsplicing and splicing of polyester tape, but you can make changes at any time to any part of your film. Videotape editing is more automated and faster. You push buttons on a machine to set editing points, and the machine makes the edits. But videotape editing is linear; you can't switch shots around as you can with film. In video editing, after viewing your production tapes, you decide which will be your first shot, which will be the second shot, and so on, and then you build your show one shot at a time. You do this by playing each shot on your source deck and recording the parts you want onto a second tape inside your record deck. If, midway through editing, you decide you want to change the order of shots, you must start over again.

Film editing is extremely flexible but slow. Videotape editing is faster than film editing, but making changes is much more difficult. When the Avid was designed, the idea was to combine the speed of video editing with the flexibility of film editing.

Working with Picture and Sound

Films are made using a process called *double system*. A film camera photographs the images at a rate of 24 frames per second. Twenty-four individual pictures make up 1 second of screen time. The sound is recorded on a separate tape recorder. The film is processed at the laboratory, and the sound is transferred to magnetic film stock. When films are edited on analog machines, like a KEM or Steenbeck, the sound and picture are kept separate. Because the film has sprocket holes and the magnetic sound track has sprocket holes, they can be played together in sync. After the sound and picture are placed in sync, an editor usually marks the film with a grease pencil to show where the film will be cut and then cuts the picture, and the same amount of sound, so that everything stays in sync. The parts of the shots that are not wanted are cut off, or trimmed, and hung on a trim bin.

Videotape runs at 30 frames per second, and both sound and picture are recorded on the same frame of videotape. Sound and picture are already locked in sync.

The Editing Process

To save wear and tear on the original film or video, both film and video editors have developed systems that enable them to do all of their creative work on a copy of the film or video, not on the original. After working on the copy, they make a clean master based on the work they did on the copy.

In film, a positive copy is made from the camera negative. This copy is called a *workprint*, and the editor does all of her or his work on this copy. It often gets dropped on the floor, hung on trim bins, marked with grease pencils, and cut into pieces by a splicer. None of the resulting dirt or scratches are of any real concern because it is a workprint, after all, and the camera negative is safely stored in a film laboratory's vault. After all of the editing decisions have been made, the camera negative is taken from the vault and the negative is conformed, or cut, to exactly match the workprint. The system works by use of latent numbers printed on the edge of the original negative film. These numbers are placed on the negative in ascending order every foot. When the negative is processed, with chemicals at the lab, those latent numbers—called *key numbers*—appear on the negative and are then printed onto the workprint. The job of conforming the negative to match the edited workprint is time consuming but fairly straightforward. The edited workprint serves as an exact guide to splice together the camera original so that eventually thousands of projection prints can be made for distribution to theaters all over the world.

In video, a different system is used, but the effect is basically the same. Instead of key numbers, videotape uses a system called *timecode*. As sound and pictures are recorded onto the videotape, unique numbers, the timecode, are placed onto the videotape as well. There are approximately 30 frames of video per second, and each frame has its own timecode number. Whereas film's key numbers are based on the length of the film, timecode is measured in time. The first frame on the videotape is designated as 00 hours: 00 minutes: 00 seconds: and 00 frames. Or 00:00:00:00. The next frame is 00:00:00:01. Because video is based on 30 frames per second, after 00:00:00:29 the next frame would be 00:00:01:00. Because all frames have their own unique address—the timecode—it is easy to keep track of them.

Production videotapes, the master tape shot in the field, would often be transferred to another videotape—the copy. Not only would the copy carry the images and sound of the master, but it would also carry the timecode of the master. The process of editing the copy is called *offline editing*. The video editor would edit the copy, and after she or he finished editing the entire show, the video editing machine would create an Edit Decision List (EDL) that simply listed all of the editing decisions—the places where the editor started a shot and ended a shot—listed by timecode. Now the master videotape could be put into an online video editing machine and, using the EDL, all the shots in the master would be selected, in the right length and in the right order, to make a finished video show.

AVID'S DIGITAL APPROACH

The Avid simply takes videotape, or film that has been transferred to videotape, and captures the images and sounds in digital form so that you, the editor, can access the material almost instantly. Because all of your pictures and sound are 0's and 1's, they are truly at your fingertips. There is no need to wind and rewind through 20-minute tapes to find a shot or to wind and rewind through 36-minute lab reels of film. If you're at the end of a 10-minute scene and you want to return to the beginning of that scene, simply push a button and you're there. You don't like what you did four cuts ago? Hit undo and it's undone.

Now that we have examined the Avid's roots, let's examine the computer hardware that houses the Avid software.

The Many Parts of Your System

Avid Xpress and Avid Media Composers are usually sold as turnkey systems; when you buy them from a certified Avid reseller, you get the hardware, the software, and all of the peripheral devices needed to run them. You turn the key and the Avid starts working. One of the reasons the Xpress DV costs so much less than an Xpress or Media Composer is that the Xpress DV is a software-only system. You buy the software from an Avid reseller, purchase the computer and peripherals, and put the system together yourself.

Because many people believe the job of configuring and connecting a computer system is a bit too daunting, several companies have sprung up to do the job for you, and they charge you extra for the service. In effect, you buy a turnkey Xpress DV system from them. What's nice about the turnkey approach is that you know whom to turn to if problems arise; however, you can save money by putting a system together yourself. If you are computer savvy on your platform of choice, or have a *really* good friend who is, then putting together your own system won't be a stretch. But if you're not comfortable putting boards into peripheral component interconnect (PCI) slots or hashing things out with a surly technical support person, then go with the turnkey system.

CPU

The Avid is like any other personal computer (PC) you may have used. At the heart of the system is the computer's central processing unit (CPU). For several years Avid's software would work only on the Apple Macintosh operating system. Now Avid models, from the cheapest to the most expensive, are found on a range of Macs and PCs. Whatever the system, the computer must have a fast processor, with substantial random access memory (RAM). Even the base systems require 256 megabytes of RAM. If you're buying the computer yourself, get the fastest processor you can afford. The Avid Website maintains a list of supported computers that are approved for the Xpress DV. Go to the page that lists the specifications: www.avid.com/products/xpressdv/specs.shtml.

You can buy computers that aren't supported but that have the same processor and RAM, but I think that's a recipe for trouble.

The CPU has an internal hard drive. On a Windows computer, it's the C: drive, whereas on a Mac it's the Macintosh HD.

The Avid software comes on one or more CD-ROMs and is mounted onto your internal or C: drive, just like a spreadsheet or word processing program. The process is almost automatic. You just load the CD, follow a few screen prompts, and everything's loaded within minutes.

Capture Boards

When you buy an Avid Xpress or Media Composer, it comes with a capture board called the Meridien board. The Meridien board can capture many different kinds of video signals, including analog and digital, and it can digitize the video at different resolutions.

The Xpress DV uses an IEEE 1394 capture board, often called iLink or FireWire, to bring in both video and audio media (Figure 1.1). It is specifically designed for digital video (DV) tapes. Unlike the Meridien, which can work with analog and digital tapes, an IEEE 1394 board handles only DV.

If you're putting together your own Xpress DV system on a Windows machine, you'll probably need to buy and then install an IEEE 1394 card inside one of the PCI slots attached to the CPU. I bought a PYRO digital video card for less than $70 and put it into one of the PC's slots. The new Macs come with a FireWire card already installed inside the CPU.

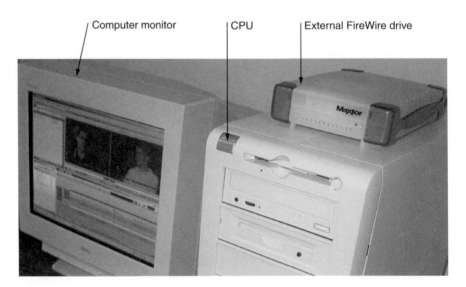

Figure 1.1   Xpress DV system on a PC with an external FireWire media drive

Media Drives

It's best if you put your digital media—your pictures and sounds—on an external media drive and not the computer's internal hard drive. Xpress and Media Composers are often hooked up to external drives that are connected to the CPU through a small computer system interface (SCSI) connector. Although expensive, SCSI drives are fast and capable of storing and playing several streams of uncompressed video.

Although the DV format is a high-quality video format that has been used to shoot feature films and network television shows, it is a compressed signal and doesn't have the same data stream requirements as uncompressed video. Consequently, Xpress DV systems can store their media on less expensive FireWire drives. FireWire drives run at different revolutions per minute (rpm); you should use a FireWire drive that runs at 7200 rpm.

In the past, all media drives were external to the CPU, but today many Xpress DV systems have internal FireWire drives, so the distinction between internal and external media drives is blurring. Xpress DV users with Powerbook Macs or portable PCs often put media on their computer's internal hard drive without a problem. PC users should make sure that they create a *partition,* so that the C: drive holds the Xpress DV software and a separate partition holds their media.

How large should your storage device be? Here, size does matter. Many people start with 60 Gigabytes and go up from there.

The Dongle

The Avid comes with a special key on a chain called a *dongle,* and you attach it to the CPU by inserting it into one of the universal serial bus (USB) ports in the back of the computer. Without the dongle, you can't turn on the Avid software. The dongle's sole purpose is to prevent software piracy.

Monitors

It used to be that the Media Composer was designed to work with two computer monitors and the Xpress was designed for one (Figure 1.2). Now it's your choice. Even the Xpress DV system supports two computer monitors. Some people switch back and forth: When they're on the road, they use a portable computer with its single monitor; when they're back in their home or office, they hook up a second monitor.

Speakers

Sound is a critical part of any film or video, and having good external speakers is of utmost importance. The turnkey systems come with speakers. If you're putting your own system together, don't try to save money here.

Figure 1.2   Avid with two computer monitors and a client monitor

The Client Monitor

An NTSC or PAL monitor (not a computer monitor) is critical to Xpress and Media Composer systems because you can alter the video signal into and out of the system. With DV systems, a client monitor may seem less critical because you can't alter the image coming into the system. But you can change it inside the Xpress DV, and knowing how the signal will look on a television screen once you put it back out to tape is important.

The television monitor has long been called a *client monitor* because it's the one the client is supposed to look at when the editor hits Play (Figure 1.3).

Look for a client monitor that can handle both 4:3 and 16:9 video.

Figure 1.3   An Xpress system using a single computer monitor and a client monitor

Uninterruptible Power Supply

When you spend thousands of dollars on a computer, you should consider buying an electrical backup device called an *uninterruptible power supply* (UPS). Because your work is important, and because you can't run a computer without electricity, common sense suggests that you plug the CPU, the computer monitor, and the media drives into this backup system, which provides a stable electrical current and will keep everything running in case of a power failure. The idea isn't that you keep editing, but rather that you use the backup power to save your work and then shut down your system. If you don't get a UPS, at least get a surge protector.

Input Devices

Xpress and Media Composer users can bring into the Avid a whole range of sound and picture material, so they'll probably have a variety of input devices. These devices might include a Beta SP videotape player/recorder, a DAT tape machine, and a VHS deck. You also might have a sound mixer to route the sound through. Just as these devices will help you bring sound and picture into the Avid, you will also use them to output the work you have created.

Xpress DV users will probably start out using their cameras to record tapes into their DV system. After a while, the need for a DV deck will become increasingly apparent. The Avid Website maintains a list of supported DV devices that work well with the Xpress DV. Go to the page that lists Xpress DV specifications: www.avid.com/products/xpressdv/specs.shtml. Click on "Cameras, Decks, and Transcoders." If the page moves (as they often do), search Avid's Website: www.avid.com.

The Sony DSR-11 is a great deck for the money. The Sony DSR-45 is another deck many people recommend.

Transcoders

The Xpress DV is designed for DV tapes; however, you can bring just about every kind of videotape into the Xpress DV if you attach a transcoder—otherwise known as a *media converter*. These units convert all sorts of tapes to IEEE 1394 DV. For instance, if you plug your Beta SP or VHS deck into the transcoder, it converts it to a DV signal and sends it, via a FireWire cable, to the media drive. Whatever the source tape once was, it's now a DV signal. Some DV decks can also serve as transcoders.

Avid Editing Workflow

Because the Avid is different from a film or videotape editing machine, the way you organize your work is also somewhat different. The recommended workflow sequence is as follows:

1. *Gather tapes and files.* First, gather together all the picture and sound elements that form the source material for your project. These may include the following:
   Videotapes: Digital Betacam, Beta SP, VHS, Hi-8, DVCPRO, DVCAM, or Mini-DV.
   Film: Currently there is no easy way to input film directly into the Avid. Film is first transferred to videotape. (We discuss this process at length in Chapter 17.)
   Audio: DAT tapes, CDs, Nagra production tapes, and sound on a videotape.
   Picture and audio files: Computer graphics, animation, pictures, and audio files.

2. *Create a new project.* When you start up the Avid software, it asks you to tell it which project to open. You might share an Avid with other students or other editors, all of whom are working on different projects. If you're beginning a new project, you would click the New Project button, name the project, and begin work on your new project.

3. *Digitize or record.* The Avid will open up the *Project window* for your new project. You would now begin to digitize or record all of your source material onto the media drives. As soon as you digitize something, the Avid creates two things: (1) a *media file*, which is the digital version of your picture or sound, and (2) a *clip*, which is a virtual copy of the media file. Because it's a virtual copy, you can see it, hear it, and edit it a thousand ways and not affect the media file—the digital picture and sound.

   Media files are stored on media drives—like the camera negative that's stored in the lab's vault. One media file is created for each track of video and audio. If you have video and stereo sound, the Avid will create three media files for that digital material. You don't edit or work with media files; you work with the clips. Think of the clip as a shot. You can edit the shot, duplicate the shot, and flip the shot, and all of those actions affect the clip, while the media file (the digitized picture or sound) stays safely on the media drive.

4. *Create bins.* When you digitize or record your source material, you organize it into *bins*. You might have a bin for all of the shots from tape number one and a second bin for all of the shots from tape number two. Bins are like folders on your home or office computer, but for people who are used to editing films, *bin* is a familiar name for a place to store material being edited. The Avid recognizes that you might be starting an ambitious project involving the creation of many bins, each holding hundreds of clips, and provides sophisticated search-and-find tools to help you locate just the shot you're looking for.

The steps listed previously are all about getting organized before you begin editing. If you're about to edit a feature film or an hour-long documentary, you'll appreciate how important the organizational steps are. Experienced feature film editors and documentary editors are among the most organized people on the planet.

Now that you have organized the material, it is time to edit.

5. *Edit*. When you open up a clip (think of an entire shot from head to tail) and select a part of it to be included in your project, you are making your first cut. The Avid calls any material that is cut together a *sequence*. You create a sequence by editing together clips. In traditional film editing, the editor starts by putting together an *assembly*, which includes all of the clips that might appear in the final film, spliced together in the right order. You could call your first sequence an "assembly sequence." Once you've assembled the material, the next stage is to create a *rough cut*, in which the clips are placed in the right order and trimmed to approximately the right length. You might call this a "rough cut sequence." Because the material is digital, sequences are easily duplicated. You might create a sequence on Tuesday, duplicate it on Wednesday morning, and start making changes to it. At any time, you can open up the Tuesday version for comparison. As you get to the end of your editing, you are working on what is normally called a *fine cut*. Shots are trimmed to give each scene the right pace and timing.

6. *Add titles and effects*. Once you have edited your sequence, you can easily add titles and effects to it. The Avid has tools for creating multilayered effects and titles. Titles can be created and added to a sequence in minutes. Some effects, such as dissolves, take only a few seconds to create. Once all of the titles and visual effects have been added, you have reached the stage called *picture lock*. No more changes are made to any of the picture tracks at this point.

7. *Do sound work*. Once you have reached picture lock, it's time to add the many sound effects and music cues that will create a rich and powerful sound track. The Avid can monitor between 8 and 24 tracks, and using built-in tools, you can make intricate sound adjustments to any and all tracks.

8. *Output your project*. Finally, the end of the Avid workflow takes place when the final edited sequence is sent out into the world. There are many output options, such as the following:
   • Record the finished sequence onto videotape.
   • Create an EDL for an online videotape editing session.
   • Create a film Cut List so that a negative cutter can conform the original camera film to the Avid sequence.

- Create a DVD.
- Turn your sequence into streaming files for posting on the Web.

With that overview behind us, let's turn on the computer, launch the software, and explore the workspace the Avid provides us. Your system may be set up in a slightly different manner than what is described here, but all systems are fairly similar.

TURNING ON YOUR AVID

The process for starting your system is pretty much the same whether you're on a Mac or using Windows. When the software is first loaded onto the system, a shortcut/alias is usually created and left on the desktop so that once everything is turned on, you simply double-click on the shortcut/alias icon to launch your Avid software (Figure 1.4).

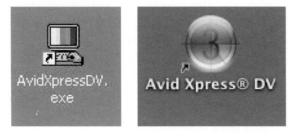

Figure 1.4   A shortcut (PC) and an alias (Mac) for launching the Avid software

The latest versions of the software often use a log-on name and password to determine who can use the software and how it is set up. If you don't have a log-on name and password, you can't get onto the system. Usually the first person to ever log onto the computer becomes the Administrator. The Administrator becomes the person in charge of the Avid, and she or he determines who can use it. If you're in a class or using someone else's system, you may need to ask the Administrator to assign you user privileges and a password.

To start the Avid:

1. Turn on the power to all of the devices that make up your system *except* the computer. That means the speakers, the external media drives, the deck or camera, and the client monitor. Wait 20 seconds for everything to spin up.
2. Press the Power key or button that turns on the CPU. Wait for the system to mount.
3. If there is a log-on process, type your username and password.
4. Double-click on the shortcut or alias for the Avid Media Composer or Avid Xpress application. Wait for the software to mount.

5. When the Avid Project window appears, click on the project you have been assigned. If Private is chosen, click on Shared. If it has been mounted, click on "Wanna Trade" (Figure 1.5).

6. Click OK. The project will open, showing you the Avid interface (Figure 1.6).

Figure 1.5   Project window

Figure 1.6   Xpress DV on a Macintosh laptop

THE AVID INTERFACE ON YOUR COMPUTER

Toolset Menu

Before we begin editing, let's make sure we're all using the same editing interface. If you're on a Media Composer, there's really only one editing mode, but the Xpress models have two editing modes: Basic and Source/Record. Go to the menu bar at the top of your computer screen and pull down the Toolset menu. Select the Source/Record Editing mode as shown in Figure 1.7. It's probably already set that way, but if not, let's all start off on the same foot. Just drag your mouse down the menu list and select it.

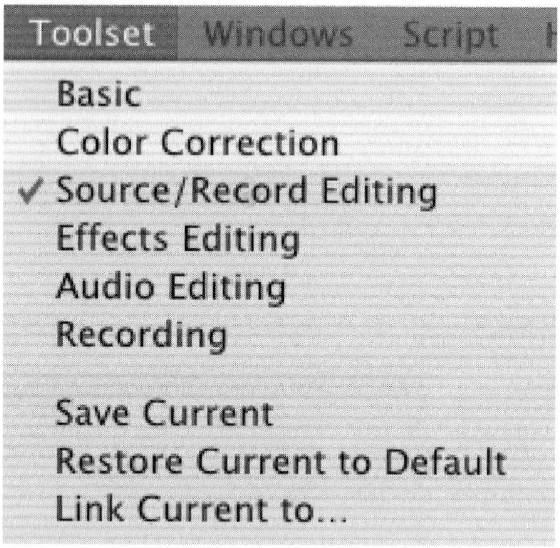

Figure 1.7 The Toolset menu

If the Xpress model you're using doesn't have a Toolset menu, then you'll be looking at your clips in a Pop-up Monitor, rather than in the Source Monitor.

The Xpress and Xpress DV are designed to work with just one computer monitor, which contains the Project window, containing all of your bins; the Composer window, containing the Source and Record Monitors; and the Timeline (Figure 1.8). You select clips in the bins and place them in the Source Monitor, on the left, which holds the clips that will be edited into the project. The Record Monitor, on the right, shows the edited sequence. The Timeline presents a visual representation of the clips in the sequence.

The Media Composer uses two computer monitors to do the same job. The monitor placed on your left is the Bin Monitor, and it contains the Project window and all of the bins (Figure 1.9).

Source and Record Monitors

An open bin containing clips

The Project window contains all the bins.

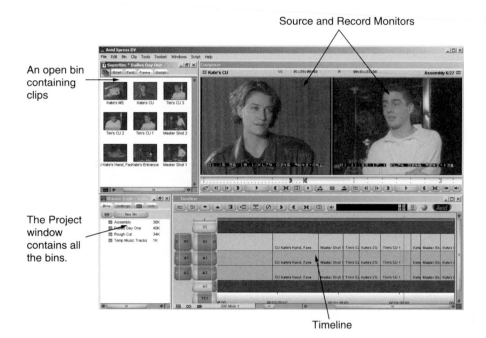

Timeline

Figure 1.8   Avid Xpress and Xpress DV

The project window contains all the bins.

Bins containing clips and sequences

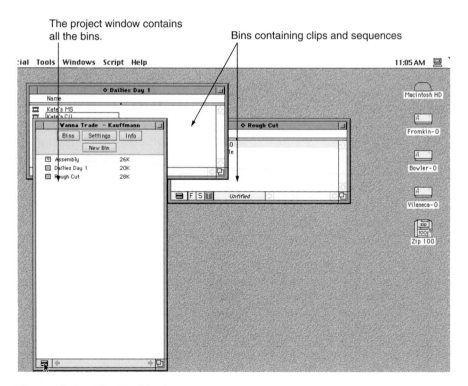

Figure 1.9   The Bin Monitor

The second computer monitor is called the *Edit Monitor,* as seen in Figure 1.10, and it contains the editing windows and the Timeline. All editing takes place here.

As the price of computer monitors has dropped, more and more Xpress systems are set up with two monitors, a Bin Monitor and an Edit Monitor, just like the Media Composer.

Now that you're looking at the Avid's interface, let's take a tour.

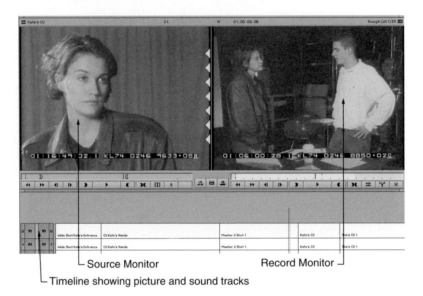

Source Monitor

Record Monitor

Timeline showing picture and sound tracks

Figure 1.10   The Edit Monitor

Project Window

The Project window is like a home page. It lists all the bins (Figure 1.11). It must be open for you to work on that project, so don't close the Project window until you're ready to quit for the day.

Open Bin icon

Unopened Bin icon

Figure 1.11   The Project window

Bins

You place the digitized material, the clips, into bins to help organize the material. You can name the bins anything you want. Common bin names are Tape 001, Tape 002, or Dailies Day One, Assembly, Sound Effects, Music. Whatever makes it easiest for *you* to organize your material, that's the best system.

On the Media Composer, one of the two computer monitors is devoted to bins and working with bins, whereas the other monitor is for editing. Some Xpress models have just one monitor, which does double duty.

If you double-click on the bin icon labeled Dailies Day One, the bin will open and you will see that it contains master clips and columns (Figure 1.12). This one shows columns for the clip name and the starting timecode.

The clip icon. Double-click on the icon and it will open in the Source Monitor.

Click inside the letters. They will be highlighted so that you can type a new name.

	Name	Start	
	Kate's Entrance - Wide Shot	01:16:02:06	
	Kate's Hands, Face - CU	01:17:04:08	
	Master Shot - Kate & Tim	01:19:45:02	
	Master Shot - Kate & Tim (PU)	01:21:35:20	
	Tim's CU Tk 1	01:22:22:02	
	Tim's CU Tk 2 (tape out)	01:24:00:11	
	Tim's CU Tk 3	01:25:44:11	
	Kate's CU	01:27:27:16	
	Kate's MS	01:29:02:08	

Figure 1.12   An open bin

Clips

The clips in the bin are the footage and sound—the shots from your source tape. The clip icon is on the far left. Next to it you see the name that I gave the clip, followed by important information about each clip. Clips don't take up hard drive space. Instead, each one is connected to the media file it represents. The media file is the actual digital picture and sound, and it resides on the media, or external, hard drive. The clip contains all of the timecode information (such as start and end timecode) about the media file.

Bin Views

You can look at the clips in the bin in several different ways.

- Brief View shows a minimal amount of information in column form.
- Text View looks like Brief View but can show many more columns of information.

- Frame View shows a picture of a frame from a clip.
- Script View is like Frame View, but there's space for you to write comments.

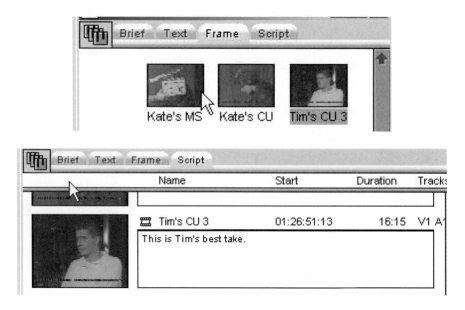

You can change your view simply by clicking the tab at the top of the bin.

SuperBin

In this mode, all of your bins can open in the same window. This saves screen space and keeps the screen from getting cluttered. Instead of double-clicking a bin icon in the Project window, you simply click once and it opens in the SuperBin. If you want to open another bin, instead of double-clicking it, you click once on that bin's icon, and it replaces the bin already there.

Source Monitor or Pop-up Monitor

When you double-click on a clip, it appears in the Source Monitor. This is where you determine what will be edited into your project.

Beneath the Source Monitor is a position bar with a position indicator, and beneath that is a toolbar with buttons (Figure 1.13). The toolbar contains buttons that carry out commands. Click a button with the mouse, and that command is executed. From left to right you'll see a button for creating a Motion Effect and buttons for moving backward and forward one frame at a time. You also have a button to place an IN edit mark, the Play button, and a button to place an OUT edit mark. There's a button to place both an IN and an OUT mark and a button that allows you to remove your IN and OUT marks.

Figure 1.13 The Source Monitor

On Xpress systems that don't have Source Monitors, clips appear in a Pop-up Monitor, which looks a lot like the Source Monitor. It has a position window, a position indicator, and a toolbar.

You close Pop-up Monitors to get them out of the way. Mac users close the Pop-up Monitor by clicking on the close box in the upper left-hand corner. Windows users click on the close button located on the upper right-hand corner.

Record Monitor

This monitor shows you what is in your sequence; it shows what you have created by editing clips together. Just like the Source Monitor, it has a position window, position indicator, and toolbar. Figure 1.14 shows the Source and Record Monitors together.

Source Monitor   Record Monitor

Figure 1.14   Source and Record Monitors

The Timeline

The Timeline shows a graphic representation of the shots in your sequence, in track form: V1, V2, A1, A2, A3, A4. The Timeline has Source and Record Track selectors, Scale and Scroll bars, and a blue position indicator (Figure 1.15).

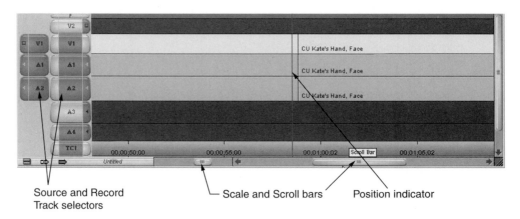

Source and Record   └─ Scale and Scroll bars   Position indicator
Track selectors

Figure 1.15   The Timeline

Commands

You will instruct the Avid to do what you want through commands. Some of the commands are offered as buttons below the monitors and some are hidden inside Fast menu buttons (often called *hamburgers* because of the resemblance). Click and hold the Fast menu and a palette appears. You can click and drag any palette and it will tear off, so you can place palettes anywhere you like. Once a palette is torn off, a click on the palette's close button will send it back inside the Fast menu. Many commands are also offered as keys on the keyboard.

When you click on a Fast menu button,
a palette of command buttons appears.

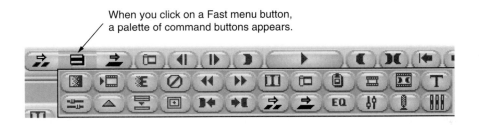

The Keyboard

The keyboard is an important part of Avid editing. Many of the most important editing commands can be executed by simply typing a key on the keyboard. The default or standard keyboard for the Xpress DV can be seen in Figure 1.16. Media Composer systems often come with a default keyboard like the one shown in Figure 1.17. As you can see, the two keyboards are similar.

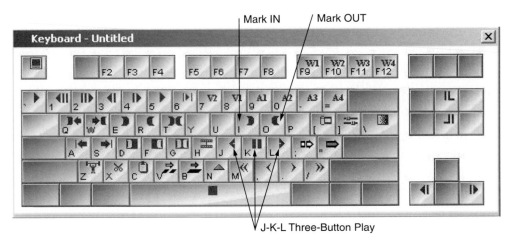

Figure 1.16 Xpress DV keyboard

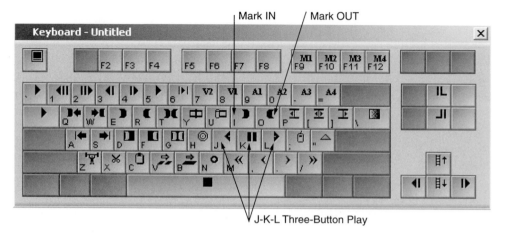

Figure 1.17   Media Composer keyboard

When you buy a Media Composer or Xpress system, you normally get a special keyboard, with the Avid command keys inscribed directly on the keys. Xpress DV users don't get special keyboards. Avid supplies stickers that you can apply yourself. Because all of these keyboard command keys are mappable—meaning you can change them to suit your own preferences—I recommend that you wait until you read Chapter 3 before you apply any stickers. For now, use these diagrams to show you where the command keys are located.

Three-Button Play

An extremely important keyboard combination involves the three letters on the keyboard J, K, and L. Press the L key to play your clip or sequence forward; the K key is like a pause button, and the J key will play the clip or sequence in reverse. By placing three fingers of your left hand (with the middle finger on the K key) on those three letters, you have a wonderful controller. Many people call this the *three-button play*. I urge you to get into the habit of keeping the left hand's three fingers on those keys at all times.

You can use these keys to play the sequence at different speeds. If you press the L key twice, it will play the clip or sequence at twice the sound speed. Click again and it will run at three times sound speed; again and you're running at 150 frames per second, or five times sound speed. Once more will bring you to 240 frames per second. Pressing the J key works the same way, only backward. If you hold down the K key while pressing either J or L, the Avid will creep in slow motion, backward or forward.

The Spacebar

The spacebar has always acted like a large Stop button. If you're playing a clip or a sequence, hit the spacebar and you'll stop playing. Brand new on Xpress DV 3.5, the spacebar is also a Play button. Just tap the spacebar and the clip or sequence will play. Tap it again and it will stop.

The I and O Keys

Similar to the J, K, and L keys, the I and O keys on the keyboard are particularly handy. When you press the I key you are marking an IN, telling the Avid where the start of your shot will be. When you press the O key, you are marking an OUT, telling the Avid where the end of the clip will be. Notice these two keys are right above the J, K, and L keys. Lift your middle finger off the K key and mark an IN. Lift your index finger off the L key and mark an OUT.

Other Important Commands

Examine the list of some of the most important commands and their symbols (Figure 1.18). Most are available on the keyboard, as buttons on the computer screen, or in a Fast menu.

Two of the most important commands are Undo and Redo. To undo an action, simply hold down the Command key (Mac) or Ctrl key (Windows) and press the letter Z. To Redo a previous action, hold down the Command key (Mac) or Ctrl key (Windows) and press the letter R.

> Command-Z (Mac) or Ctrl-Z (Windows)—Undo
> Command-R (Mac) or Ctrl-R (Windows)—Redo

You can go back and undo or redo up to 32 previous actions.

The expensive Avids come with special keyboards that have the command symbols painted on them, but the Xpress DV system doesn't. Memorize the keyboard keys listed here and you'll have the Avid commands down in no time. Really, these are about the only keys I want you to memorize. I want you to know, for instance, that whenever you want to remove both the IN and OUT marks, you'll press the G key.

Active Window

As you can see, there are several windows and monitors on the Avid screen. There's the Timeline, the Source Monitor, the Record Monitor, and the Project window. If you want to work within a particular window, you need to make it active. Many beginning Avid users get confused because they press a command button and nothing happens, or the command gets executed in

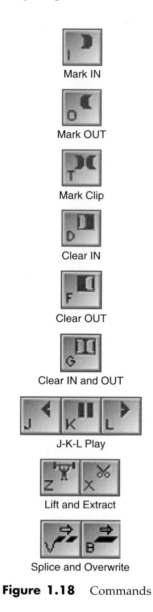

Figure 1.18   Commands

the wrong place. If you want to work in the Source Monitor, click on it first. The same is true of the Timeline or a bin window. All you need to do to make a window or monitor active is to click anywhere on it.

PRACTICE

There are many more commands and menus to discuss, and we'll get to all of them, but for now, let's practice what we've done so far by starting an editing session. Granted you'll be working at a handicap because you haven't been shown how to use many of Avid's most powerful tools, but you know enough to put together a rough cut of a scene. Just follow the instructions provided in the next section. They will guide you through your first edits and get you started. If you are cutting a scene other than "Wanna Trade," simply substitute your clip names for the clip names I provide in the instructions.

Before you make any edits, look at the script for the scene you'll be cutting to get an idea of action and dialog. If you are cutting "Wanna Trade," you'll find the script on pages 32 and 33. Most of the action has been shot from several camera angles. There's a master shot (MS) and a close-up (CU) of each actor. Some of the action has more than one take. Your job is to make the scene come to life and to choose among the choices the best parts. Examine the performances and determine which angle gives the audience the best vantage point for that part of the scene.

STARTING AN EDITING SESSION

The screen in Figure 1.19 shows the Xpress as it would look during an editing session. The Project window is in the lower left. The Dailies Day One bin is open, showing the clips that make up the "Wanna Trade" scene. One clip, a

Mark IN and OUT

Figure 1.19   Avid Xpress

close-up of Kate, has been opened in the Source Monitor. Several shots have been spliced into the Timeline, creating a sequence. The Record Monitor is on the right-hand side and shows what's in the Timeline. We're looking at a close-up of Tim because the position indicator in the Timeline is parked on that clip.

If you're using a Media Composer, the Project window and bins are all on the left-hand monitor, and the Edit Monitor holds just the Source and Record Monitors and the Timeline.

We'll start by loading clips into the Source Monitor. The Source Monitor is like a holding tank. Every time you double-click on a clip icon, it appears in the Source Monitor. The Source Monitor has a menu that shows all of the clips you have loaded into it. Click and drag on the name of the clip in the upper-left corner of the Source Monitor to see that menu and a list of all the clips that are held there. Drag down and release to choose another clip from the list, and that choice replaces the one currently in view.

Click and drag here to see the list of clips in the Source Monitor.

Kate's Hands, Face - CU

Clear Monitor
Duplicate
Clear Menu

√ Kate's Hands, Face - CU
Kate's Entrance - Wide Shot
Kate's CU

V1

Making Your First Cut

Follow the step-by-step instructions that will lead you through your first editing session.

1. In the Project window for "Wanna Trade" you'll see two bins: Dailies Day One and Assembly. Click once on the Dailies Day One bin icon. It should open in the SuperBin. If you double-click on the bin icon, it will open, but it won't go into the SuperBin. To get it to go into the SuperBin, you'll now have to double-click on the empty bin icon in the Project window (it's grayed to show it's already been opened).

2. Click once on the Assembly bin icon. It will appear in the SuperBin, replacing the Dailies Day One bin. In the Project window, click once more on the Dailies Day One bin icon. It will spring into view, replacing the Assembly bin.

3. In the Dailies Day One bin you will see several clips. You are probably in Frame View. Switch to Brief View. Switch to Text View. Try Script View. Click on the tabs at the top of the bin to switch views.

4. In the Dailies Day One bin, double-click on the clip icon for *Kate's Entrance—Wide Shot*. The clip appears in the Source Monitor or Pop-up Monitor. You can also place clips in the Source Monitor by dragging clips from the bin and bringing them across and then dropping them onto the Source Monitor.

5. You can play the clip by selecting the Play button under the Source Monitor, but I suggest you get into the habit of using the J, K, and L keys on the keyboard and practice playing the clips using those keys with your left hand. Hit J or L several times to go fast reverse or fast forward. Hold pause (K) while holding J or L to go backward or forward in slow motion.

6. To move quickly through the clip, drag the blue position bar inside the position bar window in the monitor.

7. Once you are familiar with the clip in the Source Monitor, choose your cut points. Mark an IN somewhere after the slate and mark an OUT after Kate is through searching for the papers on the desk. Either use the I and O keys or the Mark IN and Mark OUT command buttons in the Source Monitor as shown in Figure 1.20.

Mark IN and OUT

Figure 1.20

To make your first edit, click the Splice button.

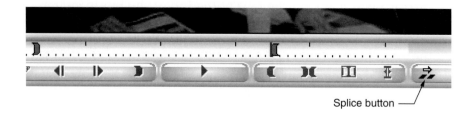

Splice button —

Now a dialog box may appear, asking you where you would like the "Untitled Sequence" to go. Select the Assembly bin and click OK. Presto! You have just created an "Untitled Sequence," and the Timeline will show you that the picture and tracks are spliced in your sequence.

In the Assembly bin, click on the "Untitled Sequence" letters (not the Sequence icon) so you can type a name, such as Assembly #1. If you're part of a class, add your initials so you can differentiate among others in the class. Make sure you do not close the Assembly bin. Your sequence will disappear if you do. If that happens, click on the Assembly bin icon and then drag the Sequence icon to the Record Monitor and it will go to the Timeline.

Practice navigating the Timeline by playing the shot at various speeds using the J, K, and L keys or by dragging the blue position indicator.

Adding Shots to Your Sequence

1. You are ready to cut in the next shot. The clip you want next shows a close-up of Kate's hands searching the papers on the desk. The shot then tilts up to a close-up of Kate's face. Go to the Dailies Day One bin and double-click on the *Kate's Hands, Face—CU*. You can either cut to her face or her hands—it's your choice.

2. Play through the clip so that you know what your choices are.

3. Click anywhere on the Timeline. Navigate along the Timeline, look-ing for a spot to cut this shot of her hands (or a close-up of her face) into the wide shot of her searching the desk. Don't worry about where you'll come back to the wide shot. Just concentrate on finding the IN point.

4. In the Timeline, place your IN where you will cut to the close-up. Do this by placing the blue position indicator at the correct spot and clicking on the Mark IN button, either on the keyboard or under the Record Monitor. This puts a Mark IN tag on the Timeline.

5. Click anywhere on the Source Monitor to make it active, find a point in the *Kate's Hands, Face—CU* clip where you think the cut will work, and mark an IN. Go to the very end of the clip and mark an OUT.

6. IMPORTANT: It takes three "marks" to make an edit, and you now have three—an IN and an OUT in the Source Monitor, and an IN in the Timeline. Count to make sure you have three.

7. Now you have two choices. You can select the Splice button or you can select the Overwrite button.

Splice and Overwrite

The Splice button inserts material into the sequence at the IN mark and pushes everything after that point to the right. The sequence gets longer. The Overwrite button replaces (writes over) what's already in the sequence with new material. In this exercise, I want you to press the Overwrite button.

8. First, check the Timeline's track selection buttons to make sure the source and record tracks for V1 and A1 and A2 are selected (colored in). Click on them if they are not. Now, press the Overwrite button. The extraneous part of *Kate's Entrance* has been replaced with the insert of her hands at the IN point you selected. Now play the entire sequence, to see if you like the way it works. If you don't like it, hit Command/Ctrl-Z (undo) and you will undo your last action; your overwrite is gone. Choose new edit points by clearing the IN or OUT in the Source Monitor, or the IN in the Timeline, and setting new marks.

9. When you cut an assembly together, you are normally overwriting—in effect placing a new shot over the tail of the last shot in the Timeline.

10. Now try cutting in a close-up of Kate's face (or her hands if you already cut in to her face). Drag or play along the Timeline until you find a new point for your IN. Then return to the *Kate's Hands, Face—CU* clip. To make sure it's the active window, click anywhere on the Source Monitor. Now choose an IN and an OUT point. Return to the Timeline, select it by clicking anywhere on it, and then mark an IN. Hit the Overwrite button. You should now have three shots in your Sequence.

11. If you want to cut extraneous picture and sound out of the Timeline, mark an IN and then an OUT in the Timeline. Make sure all your tracks are selected (highlighted, colored). To lift, hit the Lift button. To cut out and shorten the sequence, hit Extract. Hit undo (Command/Ctrl-Z) if there is a problem and try again after correcting it.

Lift   Extract

There are two takes of the Master Shot. One covers the whole scene and the other is a pickup. There are several takes of Tim's close-up. Kate has a close-up and a medium shot. Look at the performances, examine the choices, and continue cutting together the sequence.

Leave your shots a bit long, and we'll trim them up later.

ENDING AN EDITING SESSION

1. Make sure your sequence is in the Assembly bin, with your initials added as part of the name.

2. To close your project, click anywhere inside the Project window. That's the window that contains all of the bins. Hit Command/Ctrl-S to save all of your changes. Press Command-Q (Mac) or Ctrl-Q (Windows) to quit the program, or choose Exit from the File Menu or Quit from the Xpress DV menu.

3. Mac users: When you return to the main computer screen, go to Apple Menu and choose Shut Down.

    Windows users: When you return to the main computer screen, go to the Start Menu and choose Shut Down. In the dialog box, click OK.

4. When the computer shuts down, turn off the power to the deck or camera, the speakers and the NTSC monitor, and the external media drives.

Well done.

Script for "Wanna Trade"

The two-page, lined script for the scene "Wanna Trade" can be found on pages 32 and 33.

1   1A

1   INT. PHOTOGRAPHER'S STUDIO - NIGHT

A door slowly opens. Light pours into a darkened room. A
figure, in silhouette, enters cautiously. After a few steps
the figure is illuminated by moonlight coming from a high
window. KATE WINSLOW, attractive, in her mid-twenties, is
wearing jeans and a leather jacket. She turns on a desk lamp
and then crosses the studio in order to switch on a floor
1B lamp. She steps in front of a desk covered with papers and
begins rifling through it. Suddenly, TIM HARPER steps from
the shadows. He is a fashion photographer and looks the part:
handsome, sleek and self-satisfied.

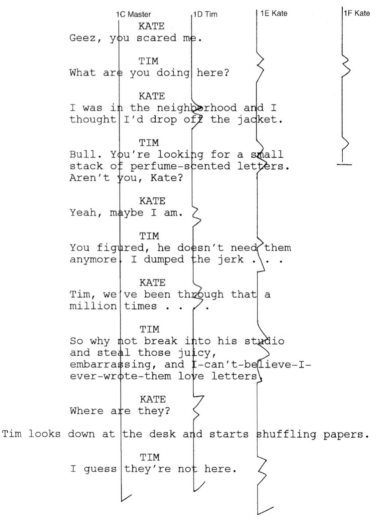

1C Master   1D Tim   1E Kate   1F Kate

           KATE
Geez, you scared me.

           TIM
What are you doing here?

           KATE
I was in the neighborhood and I
thought I'd drop off the jacket.

           TIM
Bull. You're looking for a small
stack of perfume-scented letters.
Aren't you, Kate?

           KATE
Yeah, maybe I am.

           TIM
You figured, he doesn't need them
anymore. I dumped the jerk . . .

           KATE
Tim, we've been through that a
million times . . .

           TIM
So why not break into his studio
and steal those juicy,
embarrassing, and I-can't-believe-I-
ever-wrote-them love letters

           KATE
Where are they?

Tim looks down at the desk and starts shuffling papers.

           TIM
I guess they're not here.

(CONTINUED)

2.

1   CONTINUED:

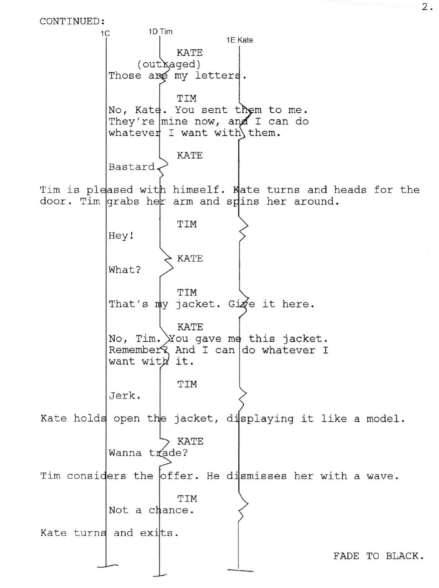

1C   1D Tim   1E Kate

KATE
(outraged)
Those are my letters.

TIM
No, Kate. You sent them to me.
They're mine now, and I can do
whatever I want with them.

KATE
Bastard.

Tim is pleased with himself. Kate turns and heads for the
door. Tim grabs her arm and spins her around.

TIM
Hey!

KATE
What?

TIM
That's my jacket. Give it here.

KATE
No, Tim. You gave me this jacket.
Remember? And I can do whatever I
want with it.

TIM
Jerk.

Kate holds open the jacket, displaying it like a model.

KATE
Wanna trade?

Tim considers the offer. He dismisses her with a wave.

TIM
Not a chance.

Kate turns and exits.

FADE TO BLACK.

2

Basic Editing

EDITING RULES

Unfortunately (or fortunately, depending on your perspective), there are no editing rules. That is not to say there isn't an aesthetic at work or that any ordering of shots is correct. If that were the case, a trained monkey would be as good an editor as Stephen Mirrione, who won an Oscar for *Traffic*.

So what makes an editor good? When you're editing a sequence involving several different shots, many skills and talents come into play. First, you must be able to choose from among the choices given to you. To make the right choices you must understand the script and not just the storyline, but also the subjects' or characters' needs. If you don't know what motivates a character or subject, you can't really determine which shot or which take will work best. You also must judge performance, composition, screen direction, blocking, camera movement, lighting, and sound, because all of those elements can help draw in your audience. The ability to judge the material is critical regardless of the nature of the program you are editing—be it documentary, narrative, commercial, or experimental.

Once you have picked from among the choices the material that will work best, you must cut it to the right length and attach it to the right shot. Once you think you have done that, the most important skill of all comes into play. To be a good editor you must be a good watcher. It sounds simple, but it's not. Good editors can stop being editors and quickly transform themselves into good viewers. You have to be able to erase from your mind all of your worries, hunger pangs, sore muscles, random thoughts, and anything else that could impede your concentration. Then you must really, really watch!

As you watch, you are asking yourself one question: Does it work? Hopefully, you'll know the answer to that question by the end of this book.

STARTING YOUR SECOND EDITING SESSION

Follow the instructions provided in Chapter 1 for turning on your Avid. When you launch your Avid software by double-clicking the shortcut or alias, you'll see the Select Project window, like the one in Figure 2.1.

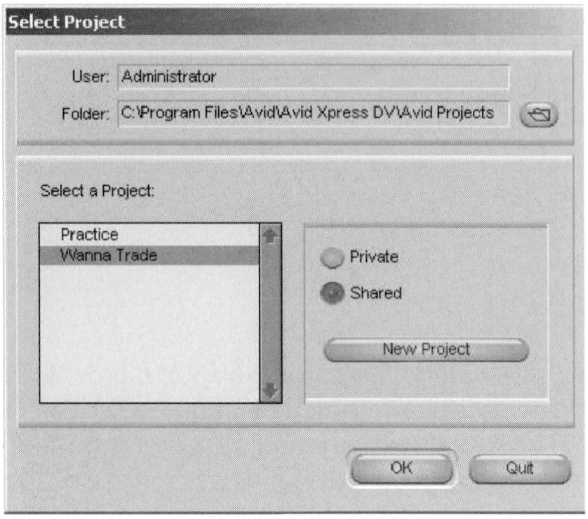

Figure 2.1   Select Project window

If you're working on "Wanna Trade," just click on it so that it's highlighted and press OK. If your instructor has loaded a different project for you, click on it and press OK.

When you reach the Project window, open the Dailies Day One bin and the Assembly bin. Find your sequence, which you created during your first editing session. You probably named it Assembly #1; perhaps you added your initials to distinguish it from others in your class.

There are two ways to get a sequence into the Record Monitor (the monitor on the far right). You can click on it and drag it to the Record Monitor, or you can double-click the sequence icon. It will load in the Timeline, and you are ready to continue.

What happens if you drag your sequence into the Timeline? If you're using a Media Composer, nothing happens, but if you're an Xpress user you'll create a new "Untitled Sequence." Things get confusing if you do that. Remember, to load a sequence so that you can continue to work on it, double-click the icon or drag it to the Record Monitor.

BASIC EDITING SKILLS

Let's review what we learned while cutting our first exercise at the end of the first chapter. Start by opening the bin containing your clips. SuperBin users will single-click on the bin icon, whereas those not using SuperBin mode will double-click. Now double-click on a clip to load it into the Source Monitor.

Marking Clips

Splice and Overwrite enable you to put your shots together in the order you want them to appear. They help you build your sequence. They may be the most important commands at your disposal, but to use them, you must first select the material you want to splice or overwrite into your sequence. You select this material by placing an IN where you want to start and an OUT where you want to end the shot.

Click anywhere on the Source/Pop-up Monitor to make it active. Use the J, K, and L keys to play through the clip, or click and drag the position indicator in the monitor's window. Once you are familiar with your clip, choose your cut points. Mark an IN and mark an OUT. You have just determined what will be spliced or overwritten into the sequence.

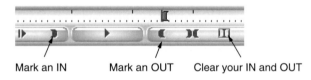

Mark an IN Mark an OUT Clear your IN and OUT

You can clear your marks by clicking the Clear IN and OUT button.

Instead of using the buttons under the Source Monitor, use the Mark IN and OUT command keys on the keyboard to set your marks. They are the I and O keys. It may be slower at first, but I think you'll find it faster in the long run.

Now you must determine where that material will go. Click anywhere on the Timeline to make it active. Play through the sequence. Using the keyboard, place a Mark IN.

Remember, it takes three marks to make an edit, and you now have three—an IN and an OUT in the Source Monitor, and an IN in the Timeline. Count to make sure you have three.

Now you have two choices: You can select the Splice button or you can select the Overwrite button.

Splice and Overwrite

Splice and Overwrite

The Splice button inserts material into the sequence at the IN mark and pushes everything after that point downstream. The sequence gets longer.

The Overwrite button replaces (writes over) what's already in the sequence with new material. Let's say your third shot, Kate's CU, is a bit too long. You can use overwrite to trim the end of the shot while putting in the fourth shot. In Figure 2.2 the tail of Kate's CU is a bit long. I place a Mark IN in the Timeline where I want the fourth shot to go. Overwrite will place Tim's CU right at the Mark IN and get rid of the tail of Kate's CU.

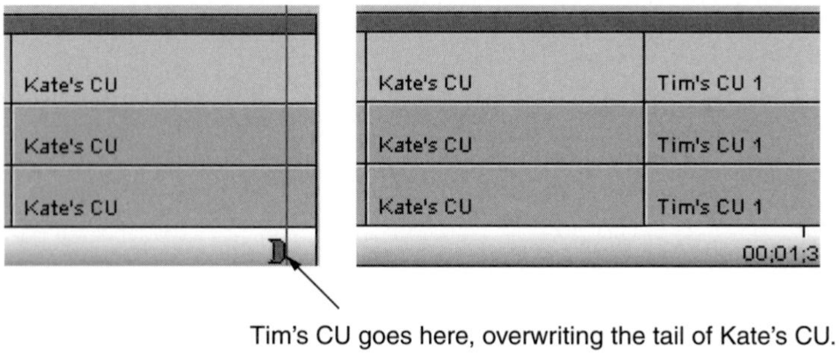

Tim's CU goes here, overwriting the tail of Kate's CU.

Figure 2.2

SOURCE MONITOR MENU

With the newer versions of the software, Xpress users have Source Monitors. Double-clicking on a clip's icon loads that clip into the Source Monitor. If you want to put more than one clip at a time into the Source Monitor, just shift-click and drag across a group of clips to the Source Monitor computer screen. Once clips have been loaded into the Source Monitor, they are available in the Source Monitor menu. Just press and hold the mouse on the clip name at the top of the Source Monitor screen. When the list comes down, drag and release on the clip you want to open in the Source Monitor. Figure 2.3 shows

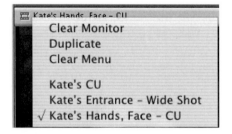

Figure 2.3

that three clips have been loaded into the Source Monitor. The check mark shows which one appears in the monitor.

The menu lists the clips in alphabetical order. One neat trick to remember is that if you hold down the Option (Mac) or Alt (Windows) keys, and then drag down the menu, you'll see the clips listed in the order you last used them.

THE TIMELINE

As mentioned in Chapter 1, the Timeline is a graphic representation of the shots in your sequence. It is one of Avid's most intuitive and user-friendly features.

Selecting and Deselecting Tracks

The Track Selector panels are on the left of the Timeline. When you have a clip in the Source Monitor or Pop-up Monitor, the Source Track Selector panel appears next to the Record Track Selector panel.

Before making any edits, always check to see which tracks are selected before splicing and overwriting. In Figure 2.4, if we were to try to splice the material in the Source Monitor into the sequence, the sound coming in on tracks A1 and A2 will not get spliced in. Why not? Because the Record Tracks selectors for A1 and A2 are *deselected*. To *select* the record tracks for A1 and A2, simply click on the track buttons.

If the record tracks are selected but the Source Track buttons are not, the source material won't get spliced or overwritten into the sequence either. Check your tracks before splicing or overwriting.

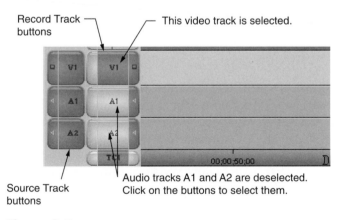

Record Track buttons

This video track is selected.

Source Track buttons

Audio tracks A1 and A2 are deselected.
Click on the buttons to select them.

Figure 2.4

Navigating the Timeline

It's easy to move around the Timeline: use the J, K, and L keys; use the mouse to drag the blue position indicator; or press any number of keyboard buttons that will move you to various frames or edit points. Two Xpress keys are particularly helpful:

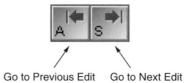

Go to Previous Edit   Go to Next Edit

Select the track whose cut points you wish to navigate. Press these buttons and you will jump to the cut points on the Timeline. If there is nothing on a track, such as V2, pressing these keys will take you not to the next cut point but to the head or tail of the entire sequence. Deselect any tracks that are empty, and only select the tracks whose cut points you want to see. To deselect a track, click on the Record Track button, as in Figure 2.4.

On the Media Composer the Fast Rewind and Fast Forward keys do the same thing.

Home and End

Click anywhere in the Timeline to activate it and then press the Home key, which you'll find on the keyboard. You'll jump to the beginning of the sequence. Hit the End key, just below it, and you'll jump to the end of the sequence. If the Source Monitor is active, Home and End work there as well. Laptop users will need to press and hold the Function (fn) key for the Home and End keys to work.

Moving with the Mouse

More often than not, you'll use the mouse to get where you want to go. The Media Composer lets you change the way the mouse behaves as you move around the Timeline. In Figure 2.5 you'll see two keyboard commands that are also available on the Command Palette (we'll discuss this in Chapter 3). The command activated by the N key is called *stepping* and the one activated by the semicolon key is called *shuttling*. Stepping (often called *jogging*) works just like the step-one-frame key. If you move the mouse to the left, the Avid steps to the left, and if you move the mouse to the right, it steps to the right. Shuttling feels a bit weird at first. In the shuttle position, the mouse acts like

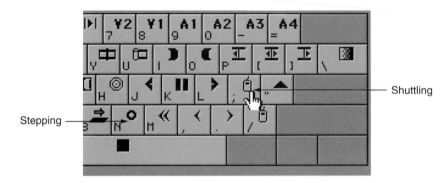

Figure 2.5   Media Composer commands

the shuttle control on a video editing system. The farther you drag the mouse left or right, the faster you move through the Timeline. To leave either shuttling or stepping, simply press the keyboard's spacebar. Some editors love these commands, but others hardly ever use them.

Snapping to Cut Points

So often when editing, you'll want to get to the end of a shot to mark an OUT or go to the head of a shot to mark an IN. But getting the position indicator to quickly land on the beginning of a shot isn't all that easy. If the position indicator in the Timeline isn't parked on the first frame, and you started splicing, you'll have little orphan frames hanging around. To quickly jump to the head of the clip in the Timeline, press the Command key (Mac) or the Ctrl key (Windows) while dragging the position indicator left or right. To quickly snap to the tail of a clip, press the Option-Command (Mac) or Ctrl-Alt (Windows) keys while dragging the position indicator left or right (Figure 2.6).

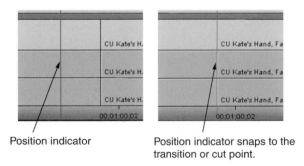

Figure 2.6   Snapping to transitions

- *Hold the Command (Ctrl) key* and drag the position indicator—you'll snap to the head, or first frame of a shot.
- *Hold Option and Command (Ctrl and Alt) keys* and drag the position indicator—you'll snap to the tail, or last frame of a shot.

Practice this technique until it's automatic.

The Timeline Fast Menu

The Timeline has a Fast menu, and it contains several options that allow you to change the Timeline's appearance and the view you have of your project. The Media Composer's Fast menu is extensive, allowing you to show or hide a great deal of information about your tracks. The Xpress Fast menu gives you fewer choices but still gets the job done.

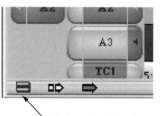

Click on the Timeline Fast menu to open.

One of the options available on both the Media Composer and Xpress is the ability to choose the color of your tracks in the Timeline. To change the default color, select the track(s) you want to change and then choose Track Color from the Timeline Fast menu by holding and dragging the mouse to a color you'd like to see (Figure 2.7). Release the mouse and your track(s) will show you your selection. Normally, I keep stereo tracks, which go together, the same color. I'll have one color for V2, another for V1, a third for my sync tracks, a fourth for my music tracks, a fifth for narration, and a sixth for sound effects.

Scaling and Scrolling the Timeline

There are times when you want to see the Timeline of the entire project, and there are times when you want to view just the section you're currently editing. Obviously, if you have a show that's an hour long, involving a thousand cuts, showing the entire Timeline isn't useful for editing purposes. All you'll see is black lines. For editing purposes, you'll want to look at a specific edit point, or five or six shots. The ability to zoom in and out is

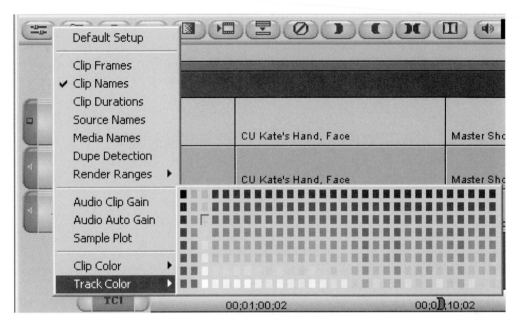

Figure 2.7   The Xpress Timeline Fast menu

obviously important. Once you've zoomed in, you may want to scroll ahead or back to another section of the project.

There are two bars along the bottom of the Timeline. The bar on the left contains the *Scale slider*. Drag the slider to the right and you're zooming in to look at just a few cuts—or even just a few frames. Try it and see. Drag it to the left and the Timeline compresses so you're looking at a much larger percentage of the sequence.

Scale slider and Scroll slider

The slider on the right is called the *Scroll slider*. You won't see it until you drag the Scale slider to the right. Then it appears because there are clips hidden from view. When you drag the Scroll slider to the right, it shows you a different section of the Timeline. When you drag the Scroll slider you are determining which section of the project is displayed in the Timeline.

The Xpress lets you use the keyboard's up and down arrows to zoom in (up arrow) and zoom out (down arrow). It's very fast.

Additional Timeline Controls in the Media Composer

The Media Composer has additional means of controlling the Timeline view. The Focus button expands the Timeline on the frame in the sequence where the position indicator is parked. Click on it once to expand, and then click it again to return to your view.

Fast menu   Focus button

The Timeline Fast menu gives you additional ways of controlling your view (Figure 2.8). There are keyboard equivalents for these commands, so you can quickly display different views of the Timeline with a few keystrokes. PC users should substitute Ctrl for Command.

Figure 2.8   Media Composer Fast menu Timeline controls

Name in Fast Menu	Keyboard Strokes	Timeline Result
More Detail	Command-]	Expands the Timeline.
Less Detail	Command-[	Shrinks the Timeline.
Show Entire Sequence	Command-/	Shows the entire sequence in the Timeline.
Zoom In	Command-M	Then, using the cursor, make a box around the area in the Timeline you want to examine and that area will fill the Timeline.
Zoom Back	Command-J	This works with Zoom In. It restores the Timeline view that was there before you zoomed in.

Practice changing the Timeline using all of the choices.

Enlarge or Reduce Tracks

You can make the tracks in the Timeline larger or smaller. This is handy when you're working with more than four tracks. With six tracks, it's difficult to fit them all in the Timeline unless you make some of them smaller.

To change a track's size, select the track and press:

Command-L (Mac) or Ctrl-L (Windows)—enlarge
Command-K (Mac) or Ctrl-K (Windows)—reduce

If four tracks are selected, all four tracks change size. If one is selected, only that one changes size. You can also place the mouse pointer at the bottom line of a track button. On the Xpress, the pointer changes shape and becomes a *resize track cursor*. Drag this cursor down and the track gets larger. Drag it up and the track gets smaller.

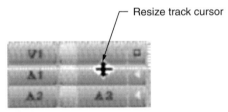

Resize track cursor

On the Media Composer you must hold down the Option key (Mac) or the Ctrl key (Windows) as you put the pointer on the bottom line of the track button. (Note that the Windows command is not the Alt key, as you'd expect, but the Ctrl key.)

The Xpress has a tiny "F" track just above the video track that displays individual video frames that represent the clips in your sequence. Enlarge the tiny "F" track and the frames become visible. Reduce that track and they disappear. Media Composer users can select the "Film" track from the Show Track submenu to display these frames. I'm hard pressed to provide an example of when you'd use this view. I really mention it so that if you inadvertently end up with these frames in your Timeline, you'll know what they are and how to get rid of them.

Track Monitor Icons

These curved buttons hold tiny monitor icons (Figure 2.9). The audio monitor icon looks like a tiny speaker, and the video monitor icon looks like a tiny screen. They show which tracks will be seen and heard. If the button on a track is empty, you won't see or hear anything. The exception is when you

Video Track Monitor icon. Both V2 *and* V1 will be monitored because the top video track has the monitor icon. If the monitor icon were on V1 we would not see anything on V2.

Audio Track Monitor icons

Figure 2.9

have more than one video track. If the top video track has the monitor icon, then all the video tracks beneath it will also be monitored.

Click on the box and the monitor icon indicator disappears. You won't hear (or see) that track. Click again and the indicator reappears and you'll hear (or see) the track.

Marking Clips in the Timeline

One of the most useful buttons at your disposal is the Mark Clip button (Figure 2.10). Often, you will be working on your sequence and see that you want to get rid of a shot. One way to do this is to work in the Timeline and mark an IN at the head of the clip and mark an OUT at the tail of the clip. But there's a much simpler way to do this:

1. Put the position indicator in the clip you want to mark (make sure all of the active tracks are selected).
2. Press the Mark Clip button.

Mark Clip

Figure 2.10   The Mark Clip button

The Mark Clip command can be found on the letter T on the keyboard or on the row of commands above the Timeline on most of the newer Xpress models.

You'll see an IN mark at the head and an OUT mark at the tail of the clip. The entire clip is highlighted. Note that if you have tracks that are empty of clips, and they are selected, Mark Clip will mark the entire sequence. Deselect all empty tracks first!

Now we're ready to master two important commands: Lift and Extract. But before practicing these commands on your sequence, let's *duplicate* it first, so if we get too excited by all of our lifting and extracting and totally mess it up, you won't care because the original is still in the bin.

DUPLICATING A SEQUENCE

The ability to save versions of your work is one big advantage digital editing has over analog editing. Get in the habit of doing this at the end of every session. Just include the day's date so you know which sequence is the most current one.

1. Go to the Assembly bin and find the sequence you've been working on.
2. Select it (click on the sequence icon and it will be selected) so that it is highlighted.
3. Go to the Edit menu and choose Duplicate or press Command-D (Mac) or Ctrl-D (Windows). You have created an identical copy of your sequence. The suffix ".copy.01." is added to it so that you can differentiate between the two versions.
4. Get rid of the suffix ".copy.01" and replace it with today's date.
5. Drag the new version into the Record Monitor (or double-click on the sequence icon). Now you have a new version to work with.

Name	Start	Duration
Assembly .Copy.01	00;00;30;00	59;
Assembly	00;00;30;00	59;

Lift and Extract

Now let's start exploring Lift and Extract, two commands that are important in helping us understand Avid editing. Because they are so important, you'll find them right on the keyboard; they are the letters Z for Lift and X for Extract.

Lift and Extract

Let's go to the third shot in the Timeline. In my sequence, it's Master Shot 1. For this exercise we'll be using the Mark Clip button to select the clip for lifting and extracting. Place the position indicator anywhere in the clip and then press the Mark Clip button.

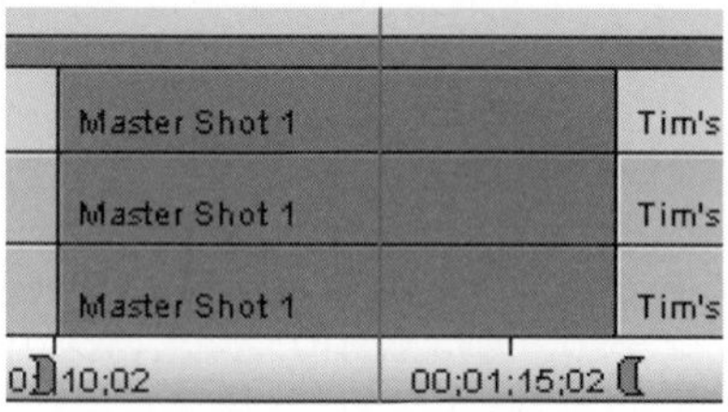

Now press the Lift button. The clip is gone and black *filler* is in its place (Figure 2.11). It's like black leader. Notice that when you Lift, the length of your sequence does not change. The Timeline is the same length.

Figure 2.11   The Master Shot has been *lifted* from the sequence.

Press Command-Z (Mac) or Ctrl-Z (Windows) to undo the Lift.

Now use the Mark Clip button to mark the Master Shot again. This time, hit the *Extract* button. Hey! The clip's gone and the Timeline has shrunk (Figure 2.12). This one can fool you sometimes because it happens so fast that you don't see it and you wonder if you actually did anything.

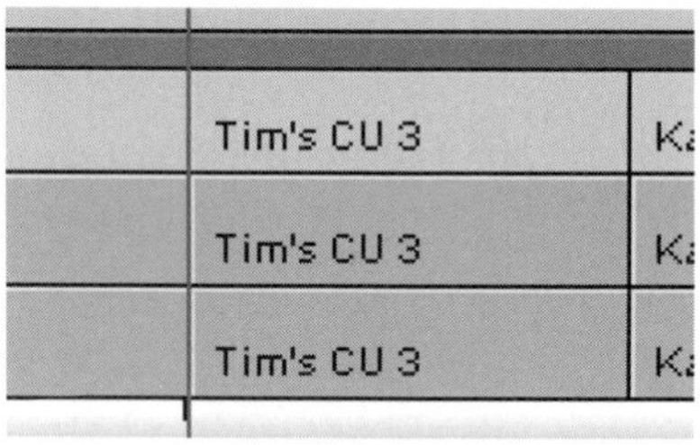

Figure 2.12   The Master Shot has been *extracted* from the sequence.

If you want the Master Shot back, press Command-Z (Mac) or Ctrl-Z (Windows) to undo the Extract.

Now try lifting clips and extracting clips with the video track (V1) deselected. You'll see that the Lift button will take away the sound, leaving the picture and black filler where the sound used to be. In this example, I have selected the audio tracks but not the video track, and then I hit the Lift button. The picture remains, but the sound has been replaced by black filler.

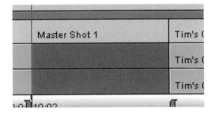

Lift works without a problem, but watch out for the Extract button! By extracting the audio and leaving the video clip in place, you shift all of the audio that comes after this clip!

Let's examine how Extract differs from Lift in this situation.

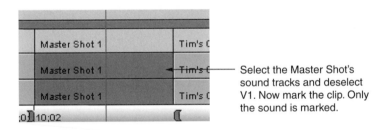

Select the Master Shot's sound tracks and deselect V1. Now mark the clip. Only the sound is marked.

As we've seen, if you *Lift* the Master Shot's audio, the audio is removed and replaced by filler. The audio downstream of this point isn't "pulled up" to fill in the space left by the missing audio because there's something there—the black filler. But with *Extract*, there is no filler. The audio rushes in to fill in the gap. Notice how Tim's audio moves into the gap caused when the Master Shot's audio is extracted, throwing everything out of sync.

This is not something you want to do. Because you extracted 184 frames of audio, while leaving the video in place, the audio becomes 184 frames out of sync everywhere after the extraction.

One nice feature of the Avid is that the Timeline shows you when you are out of sync and by how much. Plus and minus signs indicate the direction of the sync problem. The frame count indicates the extent of the sync problem.

Be careful when you Extract. It's a great tool, but only when all tracks are selected. Be prepared to use Undo to fix problems with Extract.

Trim Shots Using Extract

A common way to quickly trim the head or tail of a shot is to use Extract. Let's say the head of a shot that you cut into the sequence seems too long. Find the point where you want to cut it. Mark an OUT. Snap to the head of the clip (Command/Ctrl-drag the position indicator) and mark an IN. Hit *Extract* and the shot is trimmed to the desired length.

It Takes Three Marks to Make an Edit

This is a rather simple statement of fact, yet when you really understand it, it makes profound sense. Whenever you make a splice or overwrite, you need to make three marks. There are only four possible choices. Look at the choices in the following chart. So far, we have concentrated on the first one. In the Source Monitor you mark the material you want to edit into the sequence with an IN and an OUT, and then you mark an IN in the Timeline where you want it to go. You've got three marks.

Source Monitor	*Record/Timeline Mark*
1. Mark IN and OUT	IN
2. Mark IN	IN and OUT
3. Mark OUT	IN and OUT
4. Mark IN and OUT	OUT

Let's look at the other three choices. They are most often used with the *Overwrite button*, whereas choice 1 is used most commonly with the *Splice button*.

2. This is useful whenever you want to replace a shot (or audio) that you've already cut into your Timeline with a better shot. Let's say you've cut a shot of a smiling baby into your sequence. Once you play the sequence you see that it would make more sense to use the shot of a crying baby. You like the length of the shot but not the content.

So you simply mark the clip (use the Mark Clip button) in the Timeline and then find the clip of the crying baby in the bin. Play through the crying shot and mark an IN where you want the shot to begin. Now hit *Overwrite*. Now the shot of the smiling baby is replaced by the crying baby. The length of the sequence doesn't change. You've simply replaced one shot with another.

3. This is just like choice 2 except it marks the clip in the Source Monitor from the OUT rather than the IN. Think about it. You mark your clip in the Timeline that you want to replace. Then you find the shot you want to put in its place. Perhaps the end of the shot of the crying baby is what makes it special. So you use a Mark OUT, rather than a Mark IN. You've got your three marks, and now you hit Overwrite. The shot of the smiling baby is replaced by the crying baby. The length of the sequence doesn't change. You've simply replaced one shot with another.

4. When I drove a truck for a living, I was told that 99 percent of all trucking accidents occur when backing up. That's the reason why you'll seldom use choice 4. With this choice, the material is backed into the Timeline and can end up erasing material you want to keep; however, this choice is handy whenever you're laying in music. Let's say you have music and you know the point in the sequence where you want the music to end. You mark the music clip in the Source Monitor with an IN and OUT. Now you mark the point in the Timeline where the music will end with an OUT. You have your three marks. Hit Overwrite. You have backtimed the music into the Timeline.

Like a Mantra

It takes three marks to make an edit. Think about this simple sentence. Examine the choices. Imagine different situations where you would use each of them. Try them out. See what I mean? Profound.

Using the Clipboard

The Clipboard is one of the Avid's most useful tools. You can mark a section in the Timeline, with an IN and an OUT, and then place it into the Clipboard by pressing either Lift, Extract, or the Clipboard icon.

Unlike Lift or Extract, which removes the material from the Timeline, when you press the Clipboard icon the material stays in the sequence and a copy of it, including all of the audio and video tracks that you've selected, is saved to the Clipboard. This way you can take something you've done and place an exact copy of it elsewhere. You could even place it in another sequence.

To get material that you placed in the Clipboard, go to the Tools menu and select Clipboard Monitor (Figure 2.13). A Pop-up Monitor opens. Mark the material you want to cut into the sequence with an IN and an OUT, and then mark an IN in the Timeline. Now you can splice or overwrite the clipboard contents into the Timeline.

Figure 2.13

The Clipboard holds whatever you have stored there only until you press Lift, Extract, or the Clipboard icon again. Then, whatever was there is gone—replaced by the new material.

The Media Composer gives you a way to save Clipboard contents throughout your editing session by letting you hold the Clipboard contents in the Source Monitor as a clip, called "Clipboard Contents.n," which is available in the Source Monitor menu.

Undo/Redo List

As I noted, you can Undo your actions simply by pressing Command-Z (Mac) or Ctrl-Z (Windows). If you press the Undo command four times in a row, you can undo your four previous actions. There's an easier way to do this, however. Go to the Edit menu at the top of your computer screen and pull down the Edit menu. Drag down and then hold open the Undo/Redo List, like the one in Figure 2.14. You'll see a list of your actions. If you've been working for a long stretch, you may have up to 32 actions in the list. Find the one you want to Undo or Redo and select it from the list. Just remember that all previous actions—those actions above it on the list—will also be undone.

Who said you can never go back in time?

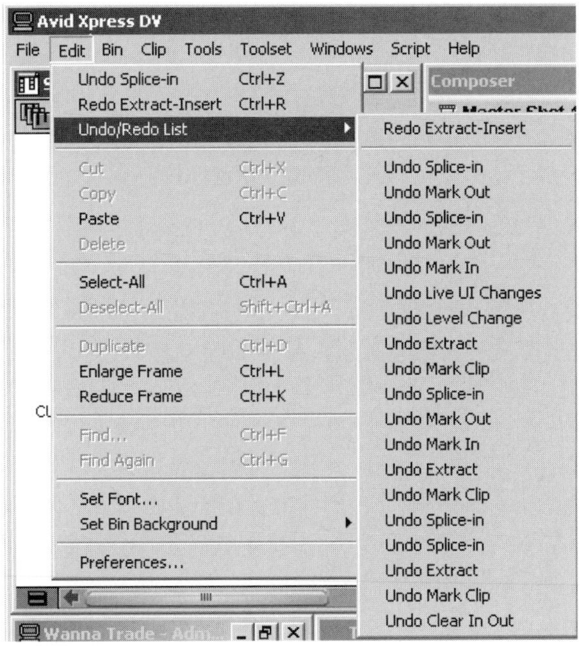

Figure 2.14

SUGGESTED ASSIGNMENTS

1. Duplicate your sequence. Change the name of the duplicate version to "Rough Cut" and add today's date.
2. Continue to work on the new version of your sequence until you have a rough cut of the entire scene.
3. Practice using all the commands discussed in this chapter.

3

The Project Window

Since we started this book, we've been working under the assumption that someone (your instructor or you) loaded material into the Avid system for you to edit. We have delayed the whole subject of starting a new project and recording/digitizing tapes. If you are under a tight deadline and must start a new project right away, then you'll want to proceed to Chapter 6. Once you've recorded your tapes, come back here to learn important information about the Project window. If you're in a class and are still working on the material your instructor provided or working with "Wanna Trade," so much the better; you can learn to use the Avid before embarking on the recording/digitizing process.

The Project window, as you'll recall from the first chapter, is like the home page of your project. To get you editing on the Avid as quickly as possible, we skipped some important information about the bins in the Project window; that information now needs our attention.

CREATING A BIN

In the Project window, there are several tabs and buttons. One says New Bin. Click on it, and a new bin is created (Figure 3.1).

Figure 3.1

Often, you will want to organize various categories of material, and the simplest way to do that is to create a new bin for each category. For instance, in addition to your video footage, you might have voice-over narration, music, animation, and titles. As you edit your footage, you might have a bin for your assembly sequences and one for your rough-cut sequences, and as your work progresses, you might have a bin for your fine-cut sequences.

Let's try creating a new bin and putting something in it.

1. In the Project window, click on the New Bin button, and a new bin will open. It will be titled "Wanna Trade Bin." The bin is named for the project. You'll want to give it a more helpful name, and the Avid knows this. Notice that the name is highlighted.
2. Simply type the name you want, such as "Rough Cut."
3. Now double-click the Assembly bin and click on the duplicate of your sequence in the Assembly bin, which you made while working on Chapter 2. Drag it into the Rough Cut bin.
4. You now want to change the name of the sequence from "Assembly" to "Rough Cut" and add the date—"Rough Cut v. 9/25." Just select it and type.

Remember, to duplicate a sequence, simply select it in the bin so that it's highlighted, and then press Command-D (Mac) or Ctrl-D (Windows) or select Duplicate in the Edit menu.

ALL ABOUT BINS

The bin is like your project's library and card catalog all rolled into one. We'll spend much of this chapter learning about bins because that's where everything begins.

Bin Views

Remember that there are four ways to view material in the bin: Brief View, Text View, Frame View, and Script View. Older versions of the software didn't have a Brief View. If you're working on a single monitor, where screen real estate is at a premium, Brief View is helpful because it takes up the least amount of space. Brief View provides you with just five columns of information: the name of the clip, the starting timecode, the duration of the clip in seconds, the clip's video and audio tracks, and whether the clip is online (meaning there is digital media on a media drive).

I use Text View the most because it lets me decide which pieces of information I want to see. In Text View there are about 30 columns to choose from, such as scene, take, camera roll, and videotape. It's particularly useful when you want to organize and search through a lot of clips. When you double-click a bin icon in the Project window, you get Text View. Frame View is often the default view when you're using SuperBins. This view is most useful when you're working on a documentary involving lots of different visual clips.

I hardly ever use Script View.

Selecting Clips

As with any Windows or Macintosh software, you can easily select more than one clip at a time by shift-clicking or lassoing. Command-A (Mac) or Ctrl-A (Windows) is particularly helpful because it selects all of the clips in two quick keystrokes.

Working in SuperBin Mode

SuperBin mode is a new feature for Avid, and it takes a bit of getting used to. It's a feature that came into existence once the Xpress DV moved onto portable computers. If you have only a single 15-inch screen to work with, you need a way to keep your bins from taking over your editing space. The concept is such a clever one that it has spread to all of Avid's products, including the latest Media Composers. For the Xpress DV user, SuperBin is active and available as soon as you launch your software. Other systems may need to make SuperBin the default mode. We'll learn to do that at the end of this chapter.

Let's look at what happens when I double-click the bin I recently created to hold my rough cuts. It opens in Brief View, just to the right of the project window. On a system using two computer monitors, you have plenty of room to move the bin around and place it wherever you choose. You can drag the size box to enlarge the bin. You can close the bin by clicking on its close box.

When you single-click a bin's icon in the Project window, it opens the bin into a special holding place—or SuperBin. You know right away when you're in SuperBin mode because the bin says SuperBin, and there's an icon showing bins stacked on top of one another (Figure 3.2). Because the default view in SuperBin mode is Frame View, that's what you'll get.

SuperBin icon ⟶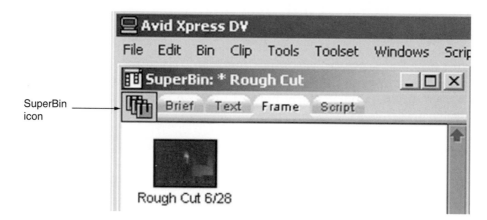

Figure 3.2   SuperBin

Try opening the Dailies Day One bin into the SuperBin. Just single-click on the bin icon and it opens in the SuperBin (Figure 3.3). If you want to see the Rough Cut bin, single-click on its icon in the Project window.

These two bins are open and in the SuperBin.

This bin is closed. Single-click on it and it will open in the SuperBin.

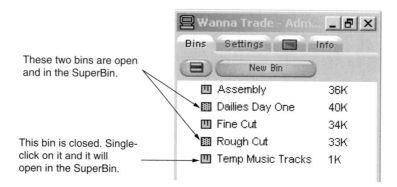

Figure 3.3   Single-click on any bin to place it in the SuperBin.

It doesn't matter if the bin is open or closed. Single-click on any bin in the Project window and it opens in the SuperBin.

If you want to open the bin on its own, outside of the SuperBin, that's easy: Just double-click on the bin icon in the Project window. To put it back into the SuperBin, double-click again. Remember, always use the Project window to open bins.

To review:

1. Single-click to place a bin in the SuperBin.
2. Double-click to open a bin on its own.
3. Double-click to move a bin on its own back into the SuperBin.

Changing the Default View

Frame View seems to be the default view whenever you place a bin in the SuperBin. That's fine if you're working on a documentary, but I find Text View or even Brief View to be more helpful when I'm working with a narrative project. Let's change the default view. Click anywhere on the SuperBin to make it active. Switch to Brief View by clicking on the Brief tab. Drag the resize box to line the SuperBin up against the Source Monitor. Now, go to the Toolset menu and choose Save Current. From now on, you'll be in Brief View (Figure 3.4).

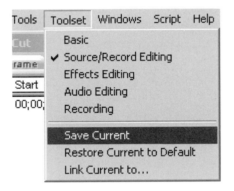

Figure 3.4

Bin Headings

We're living in the information age. Billions of facts are available to us through the Internet. It makes sense, therefore, to have all of the facts about your clips available as well. Double-click Dailies Day One to open it. Go to Text View, and drag the resize box or scroll along the bin box to see all of the columns. At the top of the bin you'll see columns listed, such as Name, Tracks, Mark In, Mark Out. There are about 30 column headings available to you, each providing specific information about each one of your clips. You'll notice that not all of the columns are displayed; many are hidden. To see all of the choices, go to the bottom of the bin and you'll see a Fast menu (looks a bit like a hamburger). Hold it and the Bin menu appears. (This is the same Bin menu found at the top of the computer screen.) One of the choices is *Headings*. Select it and you will get a dialog box like the one in Figure 3.5.

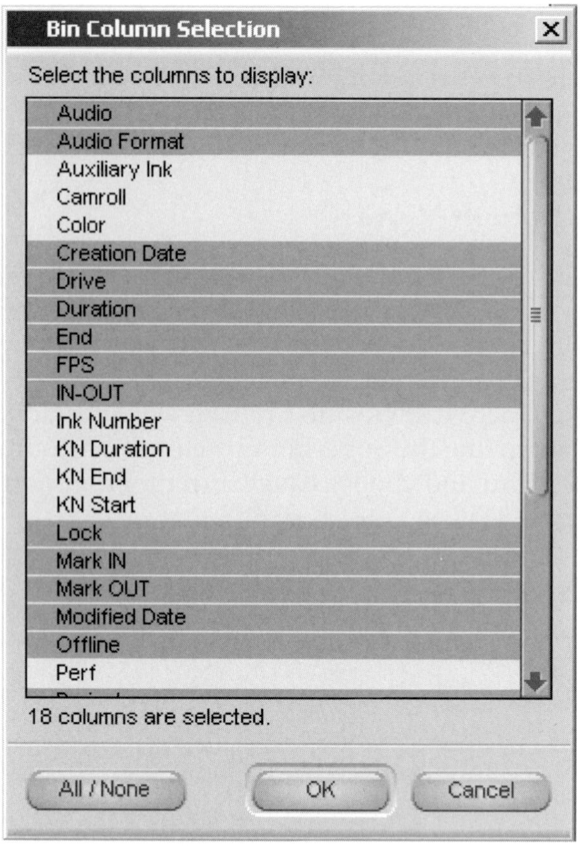

Figure 3.5

You can select or deselect headings by clicking on them. Some headings are more useful than others, and you'll want different headings at different stages of editing. Having all of the headings on display is more confusing than helpful. Select those you find useful and deselect those providing information you don't need.

Here are my choices for the early stages of editing:

Heading	Rationale for Use
Duration	It's helpful to know the length of a clip.
Start	Knowing the clip's starting timecode locates it on the source tape.
End	This is the clip's ending timecode.
Audio	This is the sample rate of the clip's audio.
Tracks	This lists the video and audio tracks that are part of the clip.
Offline	This is helpful whenever you've erased media files.

Other column headings (shown as follows) will be more helpful later on, so for now, don't select them for display.

Heading	Information Provided
Creation Date	The date and time the clip was digitized (or logged)
Disk	The location of the media file on your storage drives
IN-OUT	Length of the segment you have "marked" with edit points
Mark IN	Timecode of your IN mark
Mark OUT	Timecode of your OUT mark
Project	Name of the project

If you have additional software, such as Avid's FilmScribe software, other headings become available. We'll discuss those in Chapter 17.

To return to your bin, click OK.

Moving Columns

Now that you have the columns you want, you can arrange them in any order. Simply click on the column heading (the entire column is highlighted), drag the column to a new location, and release the mouse. I wouldn't change the position of the Name column because that's the most useful column and should be flush left, next to the icon. But you might want to set up your columns like this: Name, Start, End, Duration, Tracks, Video.

You can delete a column by selecting it and hitting Delete. It's still available under Headings.

You can jump from column to column with Tab, Shift-Tab, Return, and Shift-Return. In the Bin menu is a command that will align the columns if they are unevenly spaced.

Sorting

Another really useful command is *Sort*. When you select a column and then choose Sort from the Bin menu, the Avid will arrange the column's contents in either alphabetical or numerical order. You can also use the keyboard to sort. Press Command-E (Mac) or Ctrl-E (Windows).

Let's say you have a lot of clips in your bin, and you can't find the one you're looking for because you can't remember the name you gave it; however, you do know it came at the beginning of the source tape. Clips in the bin are usually sorted alphabetically by clip name, but because you can't remember the name, this column isn't helping you. You need to look at the names not in alphabetical order but by each clip's starting timecode.

Click on the Start column and choose Sort from the Bin menu—or use Command-E (Ctrl-E). The clips in the bin now appear listed according to the starting timecode. Now, when you look at the names, you'll probably find the clip you're looking for because it will be near the top of the list. To switch back to listing the clips by name, simply click on the Name column and choose Sort from the Bin menu, or use Command-E (Ctrl-E).

There are times when you may want to invert the order in which items appear. To sort in descending order, hold down the Option key (Mac) or Alt key (Windows) and then press Command-E (Mac) or Ctrl-E (Windows).

Frame View

Sometimes it's easier to edit material if you're looking at the choices as pictures rather than as columns of words and numbers. Frame View shows the clips in picture view.

Click on Frame at the top of the bin, and all of the clips will become frames from the clip.

- You can enlarge the frames by selecting Enlarge Frame from the Edit menu or by pressing Command-L (Mac) or Ctrl-L (Windows). Think of enLarge.
- You can reduce the size of the frames by selecting Reduce Frame from the Edit menu or using Command-K (Mac) or Ctrl-K (Windows).
- Repeat these commands, and the frames will keep getting bigger or smaller.

You can't enlarge or reduce just one frame; the command affects all of the frames in the bin. But you can change the frame of the clip you're looking at.

Look at Figure 3.6. We have a frame showing a slate with an open clapstick. The sticks don't give us much visual information about the clip. By selecting the frame (just click on it) and using the J, K, and L keys, you can play the clip. Whatever frame you stop on becomes the *reference frame*—the frame you'll see from now on. Depending on your version of

Figure 3.6

Avid's software, the J, K, and L keys might not work. If not, try pressing the number 1 (step 10 frames back) or the number 2 (step 10 frames forward) above the keyboard letters. The reference frame of Kate's CU was once a slate, but I advanced it so that the reference frame shows the actual composition of the clip, which is much more helpful.

You can also drag the clips all around the bin, putting them in any order. If things get messy, go to the Bin menu and choose Align to Grid.

Another useful Bin menu item is Fill Window. When you select it, the frames are positioned nicely in the bin window.

STORYBOARD TECHNIQUE

One of the features that people like to play with, because it seems so powerful and impressive, is called the *storyboard technique*. It works best in Frame View. Simply put, you make the bin large enough so that there is space at the bottom. Then drag the clips in the order you think they might appear in the final version, creating a storyboard. A storyboard looks like a comic strip in a newspaper.

Xpress users can create an instant rough cut by selecting the clips in a storyboard (shift-click or lasso them) and then dragging them to the Timeline and releasing them. If you are a Media Composer user, you can create an instant rough cut by selecting the clips in your storyboard (shift-click or lasso them) and then pressing and holding the Option key (Mac) or Alt key (Windows) as you drag them to the Record Monitor. To be honest, this is something that looks good and impresses people, but you'll hardly ever use it.

But, hey, let's try it. If you already have a sequence in the Timeline and you don't want to mess it up, start a new sequence.

Starting a New Sequence

You will often want to start over again—to try something new or different. The Avid makes it easy to do this.

Go to the Clip menu (top of your screen). You'll see the first choice is New Sequence. Select it and you'll have a new, untitled sequence. If you have several bins open, a dialog box will appear asking you into which bin you'd like the new sequence to go. Choose one, such as Rough Cut bin.

Now go into the bin and give a name to the "Untitled Sequence."

Creating a Storyboard

In Frame View, drag any three clips to the bottom of the bin, forming a storyboard (Figure 3.7). Now shift-click on the three clips and drag them into the Timeline (Xpress) of your newly created sequence. Media Composer users press the Option key (Alt key) and drag them into the Record Monitor.

The problem with this technique is that the entire clip is now in your Timeline. You will need to edit each clip. Frankly, it's much easier to mark sections of the clip in the Source Monitor and then splice or overwrite what you've selected into the Timeline. So, this feature looks cool and shows off the Avid's drag-and-drop power, but it isn't that useful.

Cops Ride Casspir   Pola Trucking   People wave

Lasso to here

Figure 3.7

Drag-and-Drop Editing

Unlike storyboard editing, drag-and-drop editing is useful and is often one of my students' favorite techniques. Unfortunately for Media Composer users, it's found only on the Xpress and Xpress DV models. This is an amazingly quick way to put together an Assembly or Rough Cut. Create a New Sequence, as outlined previously.

Go to the Source Monitor and mark an IN and an OUT in any clip. Now, place the cursor anywhere inside the monitor window. Click and drag the clip to the end of the Timeline and drop it (let go of the mouse button). Presto, it gets spliced onto the last clip in the Timeline.

As you do the drag part in the Source Monitor, you'll see the Source Monitor do this weird thing where all these white lines appear. Don't worry. Just keep dragging. You can actually drop the clip on any transition point in the Timeline, and when you let go, the clip is spliced right there. Xpress users, try this technique. It's amazingly fast. Just click, hold, and drag clips from the Source Monitor to the Timeline.

SUBCLIPS

You may have clips that are overly long. Perhaps when you digitized a tape, you kept several different shots together in one long master clip. For example, you might have a single clip that includes a wide shot of a man climbing a ladder, a close-up of his face, and a shot of a crowd of people watching him. You realize that it would make editing easier if each shot were separated from the others. You can do this by making subclips. It's easy.

To create a subclip:

1. Double-click on the clip to place it in the Source Monitor.
2. Play the clip and mark the IN point and then mark an OUT point.
3. Press and hold the Option key (Mac) or Alt key (Windows), then click and drag the picture from the Source Monitor to the bin in which you want to store the subclip.
4. Drop it in the bin.

Notice a couple of things. When you hold down the Option or Alt key and click and hold on the clip in the Source Monitor, the mouse pointer turns into a hand. Once the subclip is in the bin, you'll see that the subclip has the same name as the clip it came from but with the addition of *sub n*. *N* is the number of times that the master has been subdivided. Also notice that in Text View the subclip icon is like a mini-clip icon (Figure 3.8).

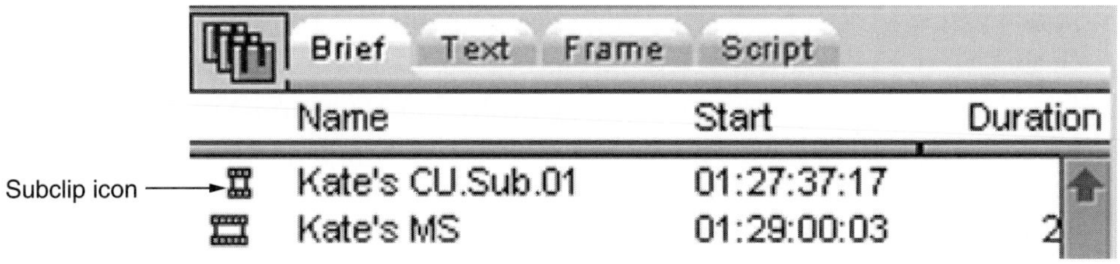

	Brief	Text	Frame	Script	
	Name		**Start**		**Duration**
Subclip icon →	Kate's CU.Sub.01		01:27:37:17		↑
	Kate's MS		01:29:00:03		2

Figure 3.8

In our example of the man climbing the ladder, we would create three subclips. We'd create the first by marking the IN and OUT points of the man climbing the ladder. The second one would be created by marking the IN and OUT points on the close-up of his face. The last subclip would come from the footage of the crowd. Now rename each subclip so that you can easily find those shots.

During editing, subclips behave exactly like clips.

DELETING SEQUENCES AND CLIPS

You can delete just about anything you've created. You do this by working in the bin. Say you wanted to delete a sequence. Just click on the sequence icon and press the Delete key on the keyboard. Because you don't want to accidentally delete something important, the Avid will immediately bring up a dialog box—kind of an "Are you sure?" prompt just like the one in Figure 3.9. The dialog box provides a list of things you can delete. If you've selected a sequence, the sequence button is checked. Click OK.

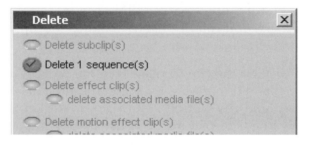

Figure 3.9   Deleting a sequence

You'll probably delete a lot of sequences in the course of your work. Let's face it, not everything is worth saving. But think twice before you delete a master clip. Remember that a master clip is "the shot." It's your footage or sound. It has two parts: the master clip itself, which contains all of the timecode information, and the media file, which is the digitized material on the hard drive.

If you have selected a master clip for deleting, the buttons will not be checked. You have to click inside the button to check off your choice. You can either delete the master clip, the media file(s), or both. This is an important decision! Let's look at why we might want to delete any part of a master clip.

Let's say you select a clip in one of your bins and press the Delete key. Figure 3.10 shows the dialog box that appears.

Here are your choices:

1. If you want to get rid of the shot because it's worthless, you'll never use it, and you want to permanently remove it, then check *both* boxes: *Delete master clip(s)* and *Delete associated media file(s)*. The clip and its media file are deleted. Yes, the footage still exists on your source tape, but the Avid doesn't know anything about it. Check both boxes if you want to get rid of a shot.
2. If you are running out of storage space and you need to make room for other material, delete the associated media file but not the master

Figure 3.10 Deleting a master clip

clip itself. In this case click *only* the box *Delete associated media file(s)*. The actual footage gets erased from the media drives, but all of the information about the clip, including editing choices about the shot, remains with the Avid. If you used the shot in a sequence, all of that information is still there. Whenever you look for that clip you'll find it in the bin, but a "Media Offline" tag will appear in Frame View. To get your clip back, you'll need to redigitize it, which is fairly simple. The neat thing about the Avid is that once you redigitize that clip, not only is it restored in the bin, but it will also reappear everywhere that it has been cut into a sequence.

3. The third choice isn't a choice at all. You'd almost *never* want to check the *Delete the master clip* by itself. If you did, you'd be using up space on your hard drive with material you couldn't use because the Avid couldn't find it.

Getting Folders

On the left-hand side of the Project window you'll see a Fast menu. Pull it down and you'll see a list of commands. If you're editing a large project, involving scores of tapes, you may need to store bins in folders so that the Project window isn't an unruly mess. Just select New Folder from the Fast menu, and when it appears in the Project window, name it and drag into it the bins you want it to hold (Figure 3.11).

We've examined the Bin and the Bin menu in considerable detail because it's at the heart of nearly everything you do with your clips. The other important part of the Project window has to do with Settings.

Creates a folder to store bins

Figure 3.11

SETTINGS: HAVE IT YOUR WAY

The folks from Tewksbury, Massachusetts (Avid's headquarters) have created an editing system that you can configure and rearrange in so many different ways that it's mind-boggling. Some critics say there are too many choices and too many ways of doing the same thing, and all of those choices have turned what was supposed to be an intuitive and fun-to-use editing machine into something else. I can understand where the critics are coming from. The Media Composer is a mature system, in terms of computer life cycles, and it has gone through many changes. We're already at version 11.x and counting. Whereas the Avid has gained lots of features along the way, it hasn't lost many, and, as any kid knows, if you keep adding blocks to your tower, it can grow out of control.

Because this book is primarily for beginning users, I'm showing you only what I think you need to know to create outstanding films or videos. If I included every trick or feature, you'd be overwhelmed. The Settings window is one area where you can easily feel swamped. Still, setting the Avid up to suit your editing style is one of the Avid's best features.

Let's explore just a few of the ways the Avid can be set up. We'll explore this topic in greater detail later in the book, but for now, we'll just get our feet wet.

Kinds of Settings

If you go to the top of the Project window and click on the Settings button (Figure 3.12), the Settings window appears.

Figure 3.12

There are three different kinds of settings: User settings, Project settings, and Site settings. User settings are ones that you control and that reflect your editing preferences. Project settings are specific to a project, and if a change is made, the change affects all of the editors on that project. Site settings establish the default settings for the Avid.

In the middle of the Project window is a pull-down menu listing all of the different users (Figure 3.13). You'll see your name at the top of the list. The Users menu is interesting. Up until now, you've been using the default settings. As you begin to select settings under your name, those settings will stay with you every time you open the project under your name. Kyra Smith might select different settings, and her choices will be brought up each time she launches the project. You can even create several different usernames. You might, for example, want the Avid to have a certain look for client screenings that's different from the look it has when you're engaged in heavy-duty editing. Log in under a different username, such as "Client Screenings." Any changes to the way the Avid is set up will be saved under Client Screenings.

Figure 3.13

On the left of the Settings window you'll see a Fast menu, which lists the settings options: Active Settings, All Settings, and Base Settings. For now, select All Settings.

Beneath the Settings window you'll see the main scroll list. If you want to see more of the list, drag the size box or scroll down the long list of settings.

Almost every feature on the Avid can be altered to suit your preferences. The scroll list shows you the Avid features you can change. To make changes, double-click on the setting whose parameters you want to change, and a dialog box with several choices or options will open (Figure 3.14). Simply type in the changes, or check a box, and click OK.

Double-click on the bin name to see the options.

Figure 3.14

There are more items on the Media Composer scroll list than on the Xpress scroll list because you can configure the Media Composer in more ways.

We're not going to go through each item on this scroll window because we don't need them all yet. We'll get to some items later in the book. As you become more familiar with your Avid, I recommend that you go through all of the items. By then you'll be able to make informed choices. For now, let's open up some of the items that are most useful at this stage in the learning process.

Bin Settings

When you double-click on the name "Bin" in the Settings list, the dialog box in Figure 3.15 opens. These choices provide you with options for backing up and saving your work.

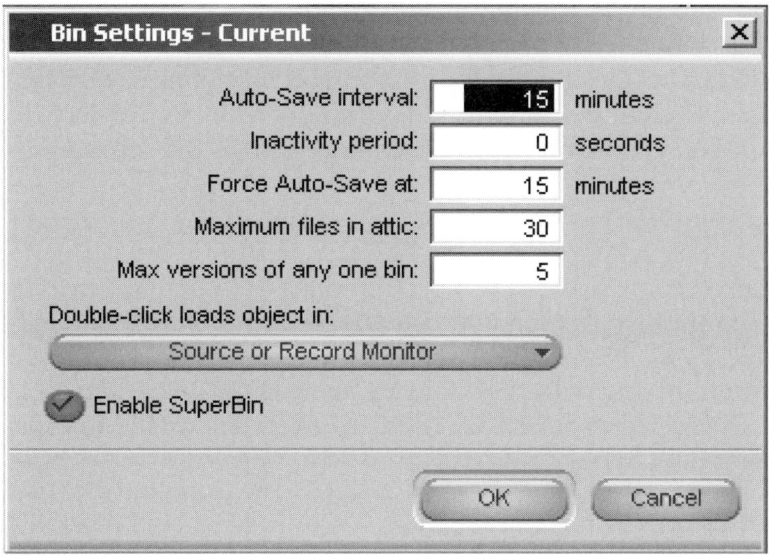

Figure 3.15

Your work is important, and any bugs or glitches that suddenly crash the system and wipe away your morning's work could be upsetting. To avoid such a calamity, the Avid has an auto-save feature. You determine at what time interval the auto-save kicks in. Depending on your system and the complexity of the work you're doing, auto-save can take a few seconds and seem like a real interruption. So auto-saving every 15 minutes seems about right. There is also a feature called Inactivity Period so that the Avid will wait before it saves if you are really editing like crazy. Genius should not be interrupted. Change it to 10 seconds, and it will wait until you've paused in your work for 10 seconds before beginning the auto-save. But what happens if you never pause that long? That's where force auto-save comes in. It will interrupt you to force a save no matter what you are doing. Try 20 minutes.

You can always save manually. Remember Command-S (Mac) or Ctrl-S (Windows).

The *Attic* is appropriately named. It's a place on the computer's internal drive where the old versions of your project are stored. The Avid sends your work to the Attic whenever you, or it, executes a Save. The Attic stores a certain number of files, and when that number is reached, the Attic begins discarding the oldest files in favor of the newest. That's what the last two choices are about. We'll go into more detail about the Attic later.

The pull-down menu item "Double-click loads object in" gives you the choice of loading clips and sequences directly into the Source or Record Monitor (default) or opening them as Pop-up Monitors. Make sure "Source or Record Monitor" is selected.

Here is where the "Enable SuperBin" choice can be found. If you're working with a single computer monitor, you'll probably want to check this button. If you have two monitors, you might want to deselect this option. Remember, you can always come back and change the setting.

Interface

When I started using Xpress DV 3.0, I found the default interface depressingly dark and lugubrious, so I made substantial changes. The first time I launched Xpress DV 3.5, I found that the interface was much brighter and more colorful. If you're happy with the way your computer looks, skip all this. If you don't like the appearance of your Avid, double-click on the Interface setting, and a dialog box, like the one in Figure 3.16, opens.

One setting you might like to select is "Automatically Launch Last Project at Startup." This saves you time if you're working on only one project and don't want to be bothered with having to pick from the choices when you launch the Avid software. Click on the button to make it happen.

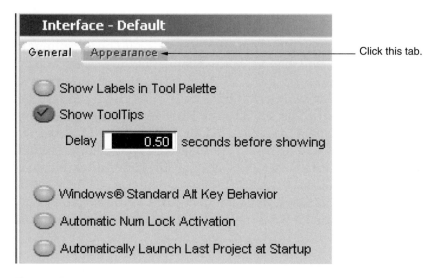

Figure 3.16

Now let's change the way the Avid looks on your computer. Click the Appearance tab. Figure 3.17 shows you some of the choices available to you.

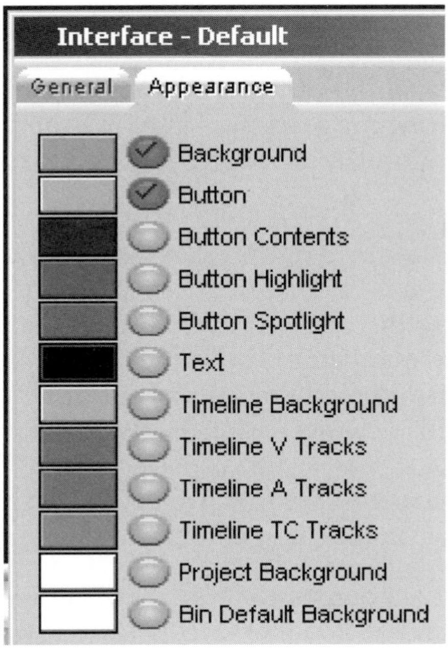

Figure 3.17

I didn't change a thing on my Xpress DV 3.5 on the Mac, but I made several changes to DV 3.0 on Windows because the interface was too gloomy. I started by brightening the Avid's background. I clicked on the gray box and a color chart appeared. I selected a lighter gray, as in Figure 3.18.

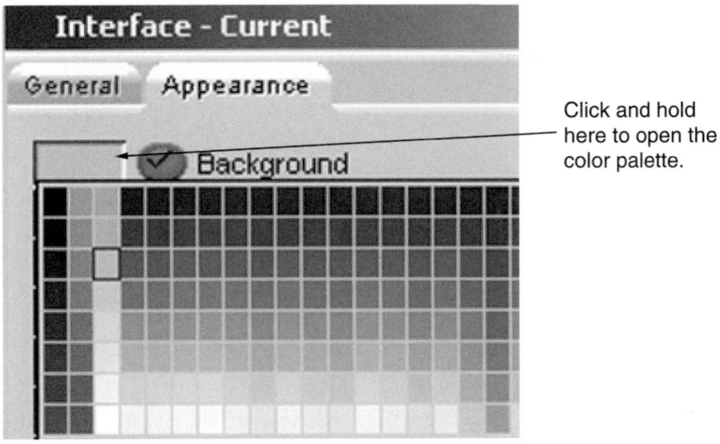

Click and hold here to open the color palette.

Figure 3.18   Changing the background

I changed only two other appearance settings. I picked a light blue for all of the Buttons on the Avid, and I picked a lighter shade of gray for the Timeline Background. To have your changes take effect, you must click on the button so that a check mark appears, and then you must choose Apply at the bottom of the dialog box.

You can go wild with all of these settings. Personally, I don't want too many bright colors staring me in the face late at night or early in the morning, but have it your way. You can always go back and change them again.

Keyboard Settings

In the old days, the commands on the Xpress keyboard could not be changed. The ones you got were the ones you were stuck with. Not anymore. Now all Avid keyboards are mappable. You can change every single key.

Not only can you place any of a hundred different commands on any key, but you can also place items found in any of the pull-down menus onto keyboard keys.

Let's make some changes. But first, we're going to make a duplicate of the Default settings and then make changes to the duplicate rather than the default.

1. Click on the Keyboard setting so that it's highlighted.
2. Press Command-D (Mac) or Ctrl-D (Windows).
3. Click on the space just to the right of the name, and in the box type "Default" in one and "Mine" in the other.

Now double-click on the "Keyboard Mine" to open it. A picture of the keyboard opens. Now go to the Tools menu and select the Command Palette (Figure 3.19).

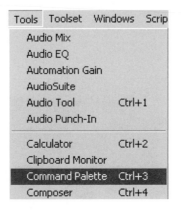

Figure 3.19

You'll see that all of the command buttons have been organized according to their function and are accessible by clicking on one of seven tabs. In Figure 3.20 I have opened the "Other" Command Palette by simply clicking on the "Other" tab. Explore the different tabs. At the end of this chapter, as a handy reference, I have included a screen capture for all seven tabs found on the Xpress DV. The commands are almost identical to the ones found on the Media Composer.

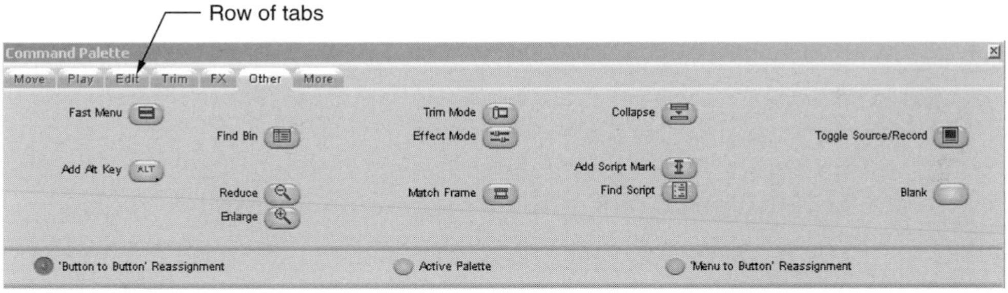

Figure 3.20

Now what I'm about to propose may seem heretical, but instead of adding commands to the keyboard, the first thing I'm going to ask you to do is to remove commands from the keyboard. I'm a firm believer in J-K-L play. I want you to place three fingers of your left hand on the keyboard and use those keys to play, as well as to mark IN and OUT with the I and O keys. Well, it sometimes happens that your fingers land on the wrong keys. Two keys just to the right of the J, K, and L keys can be particularly troublesome.

These are the Segment Mode keys, and although we'll use them a lot later on, for now they can cause problems if you press them by accident.

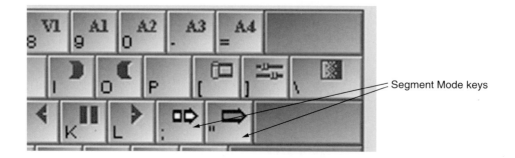

Segment Mode keys

So, to prevent an accident, we're going to remove them. Go to the "Other" tab in the Command Palette and look for the blank button.

To replace a keyboard key, make sure the radio button next to "Button to Button Reassignment" is red. Now simply drag the blank button on top of the yellow arrow key and release—it's gone. Now repeat this process and put the blank button on top of the red arrow key, so the result looks like Figure 3.21.

See? That was easy. Let's try another one.

Go to the "More" tab. Drag the top "Add Locator" button (it's red) to the F5 key. You won't need this yet, but we'll use it later in the book.

The Segment Mode keys are gone.

Figure 3.21

Add Locator ⬭ 0

Add Locator ⬭ 0

Add Locator ⬭ 0

Well, you get the idea. I don't want you to make any more changes just yet. Let's wait until you're more familiar with all of the commands and can decide which ones you will want to use most frequently.

By the way, the Command Palette works like a giant Fast menu. You can open it from the Tools menu, click on a tab, and then click on the "Active Palette" button. Now press any command, and it is executed.

Let's go back to the Project window. To make the changes we've made to the keyboard active, we need to do one more thing. Click the mouse in the area just to the left of the "Keyboard Mine" setting so that a check mark appears. If at any time you want to go back to the default keyboard, just click the Default setting.

✓ Interface

Keyboard   Default

Click here to
activate a   ──────▶ ✓ Keyboard   Mine
setting.

✓ Media Creation

Changing Command Buttons

The Avid lets you change any of the command buttons on the computer monitor. The process is basically the same as changing the keyboard commands. You go to the Command Palette in the Tools menu, and then you drag commands to the buttons you want to change or replace. Look at the buttons on the toolbar beneath the Record Monitor. The ones on the Xpress DV look like this:

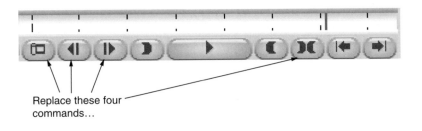

Replace these four
commands...

I propose we make some changes. Open the Command Palette and go to the Edit tab. Drag the Lift and the Extract buttons onto the Step-One-Frame buttons. The step buttons are useful keys, but the left arrow and right arrow keys, next to the numeric keypad, do the same thing. Next drag the Mark Clip button onto the button that looks like a roll of 35mm film. Finally, we're going to replace the Mark Clip button that's already on the Record Monitor and put in its place a command called "Match Frame." You'll find it in the Other tab.

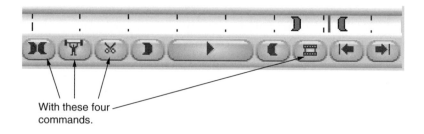

With these four commands.

With this setup, it's easy to Mark clips and then Lift or Extract them. You don't need to move your fingers off the J, K, and L keys to reach the keyboard's Z or X to execute them. We'll learn about the Match Frame command in a later chapter, but trust me, it's a useful key to have in front of you.

The Media Composer's Composer Settings

The Avid Media Composer lets you change the look of the Composer window, which contains both the Source and Record Monitors. Double-click on the Composer settings and a dialog box will open. The latest version gives you tabs that organize the choices.

For now, we're interested in just two items: The first item is called "Second Row of Info," and the second is called "Second Row of Buttons." They are in the Window tab. Click in the empty boxes to select them. Now click OK. Return to the Bin window (press Bins at the top of the Project window) rather than the Settings window, and examine the changes to the Composer window. Notice that you now have a second row of information at the top of the window and a second row of command buttons at the bottom of the Source/Record Monitors.

You'll notice that some buttons are empty, or blank. You can map command buttons from the Command Palette to these keys (or to any key for that matter).

Wait until you're further along in this book before you map any more command buttons. By then you'll have a better idea of which commands you like on the keyboard and which ones you'd rather click with the mouse.

SUGGESTED ASSIGNMENTS

1. Create a new bin. Name it.
2. Duplicate your sequence. Change the name of the duplicate version to today's date.
3. Place this version of your sequence into the new bin.
4. Examine your clips in Frame View, Brief View, Text View, and Script View.
5. Delete the duplicated version of the sequence you just made.
6. Open the Headings list and change your headings.
7. In Text View, move the columns around.
8. Sort the columns using various headings.
9. Reverse the selections.
10. Open a clip and make a subclip of a portion of it.
11. Open the Settings window.
12. Scroll through the list and examine various settings.
13. Duplicate the Keyboard setting and name it.
14. Use the blank button to remove the Segment Mode keys.
15. Media Composer users, add a first and second row of buttons in the Composer setting.

COMMAND PALETTE COMMANDS

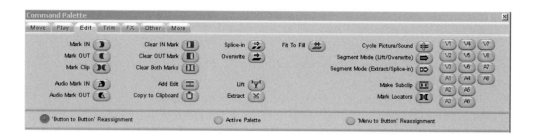

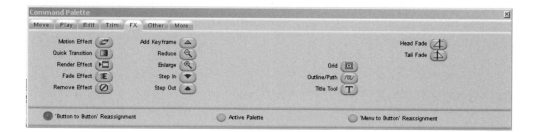

4

Trimming

Whenever I'm teaching a class on editing, one of the questions students often ask me is, "How do you know how long to hold a shot?" The first time I was asked that question I gave the worst possible answer. I said, "I don't know. (beat) You just know."

I've given the question a bit more thought since then. Sometimes it's obvious how long to hold a shot. If the shot is of a specific action, you've got to hold the shot until the action is finished. For example, if someone is putting a cake into an oven, you don't want to cut before the cake is safely on the cooking rack. But everyone knows that. The ones that are tricky involve the length of a cutaway, or how long to hold on a person who is talking, or how long to hold a static shot or a reaction shot. My students know there is no one answer, just as they know there are no rules. What they are really asking is: How do you learn timing?

The answer to that question goes back to watching. You make the cut the way you think it should be, and then you watch it. And you watch it again, and you pay attention to the timing. Is the cut too fast? too slow? confusing? Does it increase the energy of the scene or drag it down? You try adding and shortening the shot, until it's just right.

This is where digital editing machines, and especially the Avid, are light-years ahead of analog systems. The Avid has a special feature called *Trim Mode*. In Trim Mode you can quickly and easily lengthen or shorten the shots in your sequence. This tool has made the Avid famous, and it's the main reason an Avid will make you a better editor. Not only is it easier to shorten or lengthen shots, but you can also make those changes while you are watching! Remember, the key to being a good editor is having the ability to really watch. In Trim Mode, you can cut and watch at the same time. Sounds incredible, and it is.

TRIM MODE

Most of your editing with the Avid takes place in the Timeline, and that's particularly true of Trim Mode. Trim Mode takes place at the cut points. Some editors call them *transitions*. On the Timeline, these lines show where one shot ends and the next shot begins.

Getting into Trim Mode

To enter Trim Mode, drag the blue position indicator to the cut point, or transition, you want to work on and click the Trim Mode key on the keyboard.

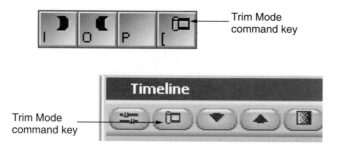

Because it is so useful, the Trim Mode button is located on the Timeline toolbar (Xpress). In the Media Composer, it's also on the bar at the bottom of the Timeline, next to the Edit Mode button (Figure 4.1).

Figure 4.1

To help explain what happens when trimming, people talk about the A-side and B-side of the transition. The A-side is the outgoing shot, and the B-side is the incoming shot. Because we have a sequence involving two actors, we'll place Kate's CU on the A-side and Tim's CU on the B-side, so you'll be sure of what you're looking at in Figures 4.2 and 4.3.

When you press the button, two things happen. First, the Composer monitor changes to a split screen, and you see a different set of tools appear in the toolbar. You see the last frame of the A-side (Kate's CU) and the first frame of the B-side (Tim's CU). Second, you will see colored rollers appear on either side of the cut point in the Timeline. You are seeing the Trim Mode display.

A-side. This is the last frame of this segment, often called the Tail.
B-side. This is the first frame of this segment, often called the Head.
Composer
00;01;25;12

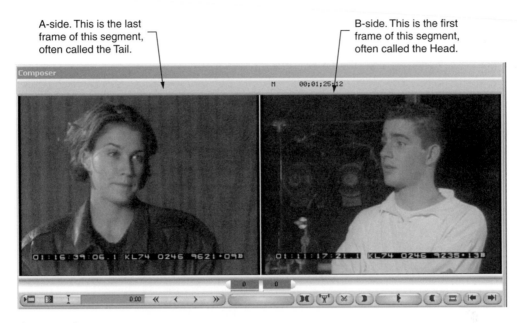

Figure 4.2 Trim Mode display

Kate's CU
Tim's CU 1
Kate's CU
Tim's CU 1
20;02
00;01;30;02

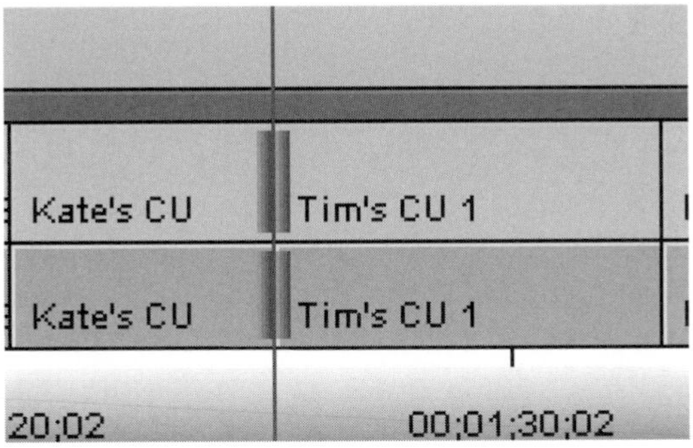

Figure 4.3 Rollers appear on either side of the transition point for all selected tracks.

Media Composer Trim Modes

There are actually two trim modes in the Media Composer: Big Trim Mode and Small Trim Mode. Big Trim Mode is just like the Trim Mode on the latest versions of Xpress and Xpress DV. Small Trim Mode looks and behaves a lot like the old Xpress Trim Mode. The Record Monitor splits in two, giving you incoming and outgoing frames.

Because it will simplify instruction, I suggest that Media Composer users stay with Big Trim Mode, which is the default setting.

Lassoing the Transition

There's a faster way to enter Trim Mode: Click the mouse pointer in the gray area above the tracks and to the left of the transition you want to work on. Drag down, left to right, encircling the transition including all of the tracks, and let go (Figure 4.4). You are instantly in Trim Mode. Lassoing the transition is the fastest method because you don't need to select the tracks. It's the method you should practice most often. Remember, be sure to place the mouse above and to the left of the transition point.

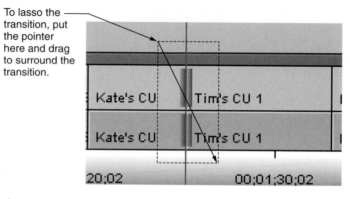

To lasso the transition, put the pointer here and drag to surround the transition.

Figure 4.4

Be careful that you don't lasso an entire clip. If you do, you'll enter Segment Mode (see Chapter 8) and the entire clip will be highlighted. The Avid behaves quite differently in Segment Mode. If you inadvertently enter Segment Mode, click on whichever Segment button is highlighted at the bottom of the Timeline (Figure 4.5). You'll be back in Edit Mode. Now try lassoing just the transition.

Now that you know how to get into Trim Mode, you need to be able to get out of Trim Mode.

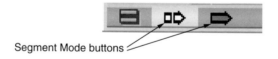

Segment Mode buttons

Figure 4.5

Leaving Trim Mode

Any one of these methods will take you out of Trim Mode:

- Press either one of the step-one-frame buttons (the left and right arrow keys).

- Press the Edit Mode button (Media Composer—see Figure 4.1).
- Press the Trim Mode button again (Xpress).
- Click the mouse in the Timecode track (TC1) at the bottom of the Timeline.

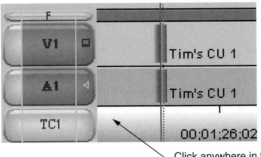

Click anywhere in the Timecode track, and you will leave Trim Mode. The position indicator will jump to the spot you clicked.

I prefer to click on the Timecode track to get out of Trim Mode. I usually click to the left of the transition I just trimmed. That way the position indicator jumps to the spot where I clicked, and I'm ready to watch the transition I just trimmed.

There are two kinds of Trims: Dual-Roller Trim and Single-Roller Trim.

Dual-Roller Trim Mode

Dual-Roller Trim is the default Trim Mode. When you press the Trim button, or lasso a transition, you go into this mode.

In Dual-Roller Trim Mode:

- The overall length of your sequence remains the same.
- You lengthen the A-side while shortening the B-side.

or

- You shorten the A-side while lengthening the B-side.

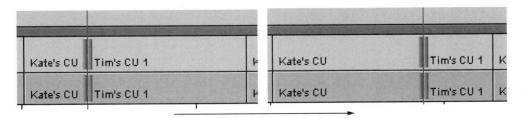

As you can see from the two screen captures, Kate's CU has been lengthened, whereas Tim's CU has been trimmed. If Kate's CU was lengthened by 40 frames, Tim's CU would be shortened by 40 frames.

Trim Frame Keys

If you look at Figure 4.6, you'll see several Trim Frame keys. The < and > keys are single-frame trim keys. They will trim the shot by one frame. The << and >> keys will trim the shot by 10 frames. In Dual-Roller Trim Mode the direction of the arrow tells you which side will have the frames added and which side will have the frames removed.

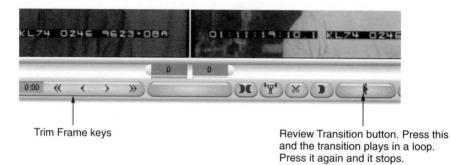

Trim Frame keys

Review Transition button. Press this and the transition plays in a loop. Press it again and it stops.

Figure 4.6

Let's look at a specific cut and see what happens as we Dual-Roller Trim. Here Kate is finishing her dialog, and Tim is beginning to say his dialog.

- If you press the > key you are adding one frame to the tail of Kate's CU, while taking one frame off the head of Tim's CU.
- Press the > key *five times*, and you will add five frames to the tail of Kate's CU, while taking five frames off the head of Tim's CU.
- Click the < key. Now you are trimming Kate's CU by one frame, while lengthening Tim's CU by one frame.
- The << and >> keys add or trim by increments of 10 frames.
- The boxes above the trim keys keep track of the frames you have moved.

Review Transition Button

After you have trimmed in either direction, press the Review Transition button, and you'll see how the scene looks with the new transition points. This button will review the scene as you just cut it, in a continuous playback loop. Press the button again, and you'll stop the loop and return to the Trim Mode display.

Frame Counters

The frame counters show you how many frames you have trimmed. If you press the trim keys that point left (<<, <), the numbers will be negative. If you press the trim keys pointing right (>, >>), they will be positive numbers.

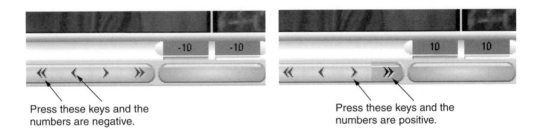

Press these keys and the numbers are negative.

Press these keys and the numbers are positive.

In the screen capture on the left, the << key was pressed once. In the screen capture on the right, the >> key was pressed once.

Let's say you're working on the part of the scene where Kate asks Tim for her letters.

KATE

Where are they?

TIM

I guess they're not here.

Imagine that when you spliced it in, you cut Kate too soon—she barely gets her last words out before you cut to Tim. And imagine that when you cut to Tim, you cut it too long, so we're waiting and waiting for Tim to answer. What you want to do is add frames to the tail of Kate—lengthen her shot—and shorten the head of Tim's shot.

In Dual-Roller Trim Mode, it's easy. To get into Trim Mode:

1. Go to the transition.
2. Lasso the transition point, including all of the audio track, or press the Trim Mode key.

Let's say the cut is off by 20 frames.

1. Click *twice* on the trim-by-10-frames key >>, and you'll be adding 20 frames to the end of Kate's shot while taking away 20 frames from Tim's shot.
2. Press the Review Transition button.

Now, watching the cut, you see that Kate finishes her line, and Tim isn't waiting so long to speak.

To get out of Trim Mode, do one of the following:

• Press the Trim Mode button again (Xpress).
• Press the Edit Mode button (Media Composer).
• Press either one of the step-one-frame buttons.
• Click the mouse in the Timecode track (TC1) at the bottom of the Timeline.

Dual-Roller Trim has the advantage of keeping all of your tracks in sync. Why? Because whenever frames are taken from a shot, the exact number of frames are added to the neighboring shot.

Undo in Trim Mode

Undo and Redo work in Trim Mode. For instance, if you click the > key and you want to get back to zero, just press Command-Z (Mac) or Ctrl-Z (Windows). If you made several trims, keep pressing Undo until you're back where you started (0 in the frame counters).

Trim by Dragging

You don't need to click on the trim keys at all. Once you are in Trim Mode, you can simply click on the rollers at the transition point and drag the rollers to the left or right!

Try it. It's not as precise as clicking the Trim keys, but it really gives you a sense of how the rollers work. Notice that the frame counter boxes keep track of how many frames you've dragged left or right.

If you drag the rollers so far that you reach the end of the shot, you'll hear a beep and see a small red marker in the frame to indicate that you can't roll any farther because there are no more frames to extend.

Single-Roller Trim Mode

This is the Trim Mode you will use most often to trim your shots. I use it a lot more than Dual-Roller Trim, but because Dual-Roller Trim is the default mode, we started there. Let's sum up Single-Roller Trim Mode and compare it with Dual-Roller Trim Mode.

With Single-Roller Trim Mode:

- The overall length of your sequence *will* change.
- You lengthen or shorten the A-side.
- You lengthen or shorten the B-side.

Let's work with Single-Roller Trim Mode.

As you can see in Figure 4.7, when you enter Single-Roller Trim Mode, there is only one roller, and it falls on one side of the transition point. Here we are working on the B-side, the head of Tim's CU.

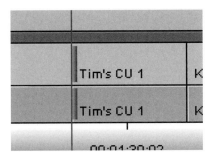

Figure 4.7

Getting into Single-Roller Trim Mode

You enter Single-Roller Trim Mode the same way you enter Dual-Roller Trim Mode:

1. Click the Trim button or lasso the transition. You're now in Dual-Roller Trim Mode.
2. Place your mouse in the Trim Mode display and click on the A-side picture (left). The rollers move to the A-side in the Timeline.
3. Place your mouse in the Trim Mode display and click on the B-side picture (right). The rollers move to the B-side in the Timeline.

We clicked on Tim's picture in the Trim Mode display (Figure 4.8), and the rollers jumped to his side of the transition. Now, if we drag the roller to the left, we will make Tim's shot longer. If we drag the roller to the right, we will make Tim's shot shorter.

In the diagram in Figure 4.9 you can see we have lengthened Tim's shot by moving the rollers left. We move Tim's rollers simply by clicking on one of his rollers and dragging it to the left, or we could click on the trim frame keys: << and <.

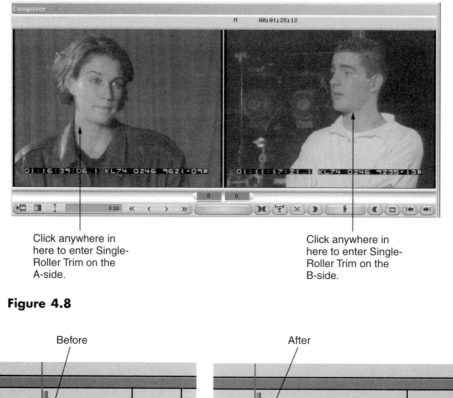

Click anywhere in here to enter Single-Roller Trim on the A-side.

Click anywhere in here to enter Single-Roller Trim on the B-side.

Figure 4.8

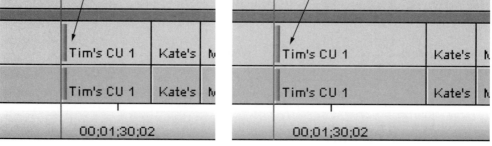

Drag the rollers to the left.

Figure 4.9

Let's examine these Trim Frame keys, while looking at Figure 4.9:

- The << and < keys will make Tim's shot longer.
- The > and >> keys will make Tim's shot shorter.

It took me a while to figure out how the Trim Frame keys worked with single-roller trims. Remember, when you're in Single-Roller Trim Mode, all of the Trim keys affect just one side, in this case the B-side—Tim's.

If we now click on Kate's picture in the Trim Mode display, the rollers will jump to the A-side. All of the Trim Frame keys now affect Kate's shot.

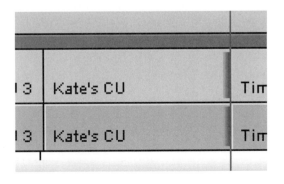

Figure 4.10

Look at these Trim Frame keys as you look at Figure 4.10:

- The << and < keys will make Kate's shot shorter.
- The > and >> keys will make Kate's shot longer.

Examine Figures 4.9 and 4.10 and the explanations that go with them. You must understand the relationship between the direction the rollers travel and the effect that has on a shot's length before you go any further.

TRIM PRACTICE

Before you learned how to use Trim Mode, you used Splice and Overwrite to lay down the shots, leaving them long to begin with. If you wanted to shorten a shot, you marked an IN and an OUT in the Timeline and used Extract to shorten the shot. If you wanted to lengthen the shot, you spliced in more. Now that you have Trim Mode at your disposal, the way you edit changes significantly. If you see that a shot in the Timeline is too short or too long, it's so easy to cut it to just the right length.

Let's say you are playing your sequence, and you see that the tail of Kate's shot is much too short. When you spliced it in, you marked it at the wrong point, and you've clipped part of her last word of dialog. You need to lengthen the shot.

Action	Result
Go to the transition and lasso it.	You're in Trim Mode.
Click on Kate's picture in the Trim display.	You're in Single-Roller Trim Mode.
Click the >> Trim key.	You've lengthened Kate by 10 frames.
Click on the Review Transition button.	The new cut point plays in a loop.

As you watch it, you see that adding 10 frames wasn't quite enough.

Action	Result
Click on the Review Transition button.	The looping stops.
Click on the > button three times.	You've added three more frames (13 total).
Click on the Review Transition button.	The new cut point plays in a loop.

When you watch it, you see that the new transition point works. Now you want to get out of Trim Mode.

Action	Result
Click on the Review Transition button.	The looping stops.
Click in the Timecode track.	You're out of Trim Mode.

Changing from Single-Roller to Dual-Roller Trim Mode

If you're in Single-Roller Trim Mode and you want to be in Dual-Roller Trim Mode, simply move the mouse to the Trim Mode display and click on the line *between* the outgoing and incoming frames. (You don't have to click exactly on the line. A bit on either side will work.)

Media Composer Trim Keys

The Media Composer has three keyboard keys not found on the Xpress. These three keys—the P, [, and]—will change the Trim Mode to Single-Roller Trim A-side, Dual-Roller Trim, and Single-Roller Trim B-side, respectively. You have to be in Trim Mode before they'll work.

Adding Tracks for Trimming

If you get into Trim Mode and notice that one or more of your tracks doesn't have rollers, it's probably because the Track Selector box wasn't selected. To add rollers to that track, simply click on the track selector.

Adding and Removing Rollers

Once in Trim Mode, you sometimes want to add a roller or remove a roller so that you're working with some tracks and not others. A quick way to add or delete rollers is to hold down the Shift key while clicking your cursor on the transition point you want to change (Figure 4.11).

- Shift-click on a roller to remove it.
- Shift-click on a transition to add a roller.

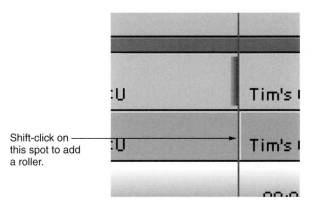

Shift-click on this spot to add a roller.

Figure 4.11

ADVANCED TRIM MODE TECHNIQUES

Assuming that you're comfortable with trimming as explained in this chapter, and you want to work even faster and with more precision, let's look at a couple of advanced techniques.

Trimming While Watching

We talked about the important role that watching plays in every phase of editing. There's a very simple technique that involves trimming a cut while watching it:

1. Get into Trim Mode.
2. Choose a side that you want to work on, either the A-side or the B-side.
3. Press the Review Transition button.
4. While the transition is looping, hit the trim frame key(s) <<, <, >, or >>.

When you're just starting this exercise, you'll want to hit the trim-by-10-frames >> or << keys so that you can see a big change. What happens is that the Avid makes the trim and then shows you what the new transition point looks like. You can keep hitting the trim keys until the cut looks right. You can go in either direction, depending on what works. Go ahead and try this.

For example, let's say you're trying to fix the head of Tim's shot to give him just the right amount of pause before he speaks (Figure 4.12).

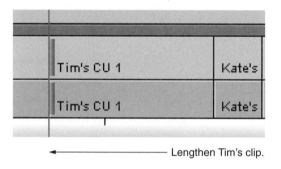

Lengthen Tim's clip.

Figure 4.12

Say you press the Review Transition button and then click the << key, lengthening his shot by 10 frames. As the loop plays, you see it needs even more, so you press the << key again. Now you've added 20 frames and realize it's close, but it still needs to be lengthened a bit more. Now press the < key five times. Now you like the length of the shot. When you press the Review Transition button to stop the loop, you'll still be in Trim Mode.

Look at the frame counter under Tim's frame in the Trim Mode display. It will display 25. You added a total of 25 frames to the head of Tim's shot. But notice it is −25 (minus 25). Why? Whenever you go left the numbers are negative, even though you added to Tim's shot.

How many frames you add and remove doesn't really matter. What matters is that the shot is now working. And it's working because you trimmed and watched, trimmed and watched, trimmed and watched—until you got it right.

Trim One Side, Then the Other

It often happens that after you've finished cutting one side, it becomes apparent that the other side needs to be trimmed. Without leaving Trim Mode, simply click on the other frame in the Trim display and the rollers will jump to the other side. Now press the Review Transition button and use the Trim Frame buttons to trim the other side.

If you want to shorten the tail of Kate's CU, you would press the << or < button (Figure 4.13). Let's say the transition point was way too long to begin with. Kate finishes her line, and then she just stands there. Click the << key three times, and you've trimmed 30 frames (a second) off Kate. You see that's too much. Click the >> once, and now you've put 10 frames back on. You've now shortened her shot by 20 frames. As you continue to watch it in playback, you can fine-tune the cut by using the trim-by-one-frame buttons (< and >) until the cut looks right. Say you decide to put back two more frames (press > twice) for a total of 18. You have shortened Kate's shot by 18 frames.

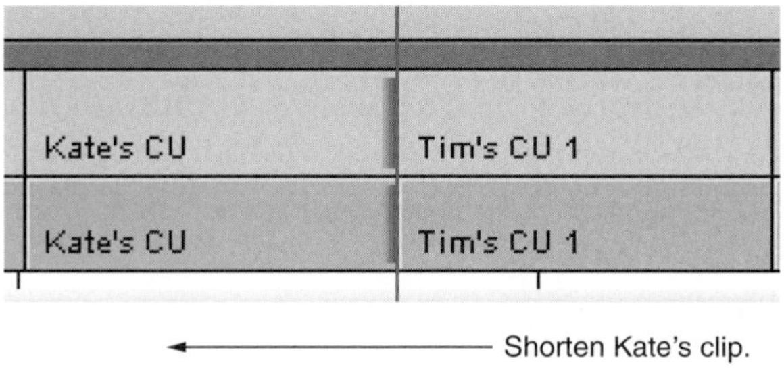

Shorten Kate's clip.

Figure 4.13

Now, without ever having left Trim Mode, you've worked on both sides of the transition, and the frame counters will show you what you've done. They would look like this:

Why? Because you trimmed Kate's side by 18 frames and you added to Tim's side by 25. They both are negative numbers because in both cases we dragged to the *left*—left to shorten Kate, and left to extend Tim. I don't like the way the Avid does this. I think that if you add to a shot it should be a positive number. If you shorten a shot, it should be a negative number. Someday.

Using the Keyboard, Not the Mouse

You can use the trim keys in the Trim Mode display by clicking on them with the mouse; however, it's faster to use the trim keys that are on the keyboard, which do the same thing (Figure 4.14). As the transition point loops around, you press the trim keys with your fingers, while keeping your eyes on the screen. Watch and trim, watch and trim, until the shot works.

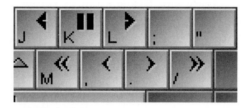

Figure 4.14

Trim Settings

In Chapter 3 we learned about Settings. Both the Xpress and Media Composer give you the ability to shorten or lengthen the amount of time the loop takes whenever you press the Review Transition button. Go to the Settings window and double-click on Trim. A dialog box appears (Figure 4.15).

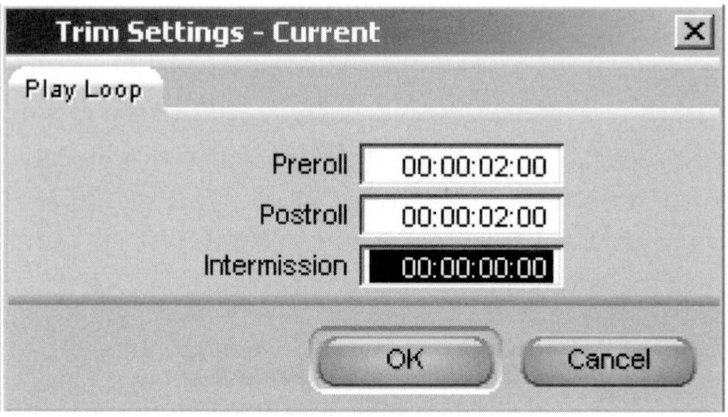

Figure 4.15

The default length is 2 seconds of preroll (the A-side) and two seconds of postroll (the B-side), with no pause at the end of the loop (intermission). You can change this to whatever length works best for you. I like 2 seconds when I'm trimming picture and sound, but if I'm working on just sound, I like to hear the changes I've made with the trim keys more quickly. So then I change the settings to 1 second for both preroll and postroll. I don't like an intermission, or pause, but you might like a second to gather your wits, so type in 1 second and see if you like the pause.

Dragging to a Mark

Earlier we discussed dragging the rollers to extend or shorten a shot. By simply clicking on the rollers, you can drag them left or right. This is less precise than using the Trim Frame keys; however, if you combine dragging with a Mark IN or a Mark OUT, then it can be efficient. Use this technique when you know where you want to go with the trim.

Before you go into Trim Mode, play your sequence. If you find a shot that needs trimming (or extending), you can place a Mark IN, if it's to the left of the transition, or a Mark OUT, if it's to the right of a transition. Then, enter Trim Mode. Now hold down the Command key (Mac) or Ctrl key (Windows), click on the roller, and drag it to the mark (Figure 4.16). The Avid stops precisely on the mark.

This works with either Single-Roller or Dual-Roller Trim Mode.

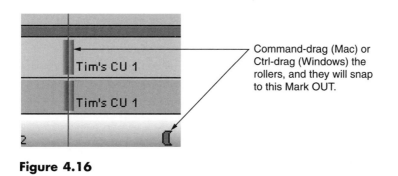

Command-drag (Mac) or Ctrl-drag (Windows) the rollers, and they will snap to this Mark OUT.

Figure 4.16

Picture and Sound Overlaps

Just about everyone knows what a straight cut looks like. When the picture and sound end at the same point, you have a straight cut. When you splice in the next shot, it too is a straight cut. So far, we've worked with straight cuts, but it often happens that the best place to cut the picture isn't necessarily the best place to cut the sound. When a picture and its sound are cut at different points, you have an overlap. Some editors call these overlaps *L-cuts*.

Let's say you have spliced two shots together, and you love the way the dialog flows from one person to the next, but you're not really happy with the picture cut point. If there were a law that said you had to have straight cuts, you'd be stuck. But there isn't and you're not. You decide to create an overlap. This is where Dual-Roller Trim Mode excels.

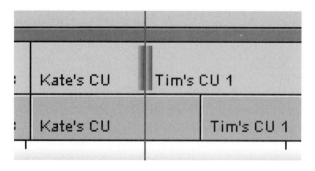

Figure 4.17

Let's say we have Kate finishing her line and Tim about to say his line. What you decide to do is to remove 30 frames of Kate's picture and replace it with 30 frames of Tim's picture (Figure 4.17). The sound stays where it is.

1. Enter Trim Mode by lassoing just the video track at the cut point. You are now in Trim Mode with the dual rollers on V1 but not on the sound track.
2. If you do get rollers on the sound track(s), remove them by clicking on the Track Selector box. They're removed.
3. Drag the rollers 30 frames to the left or press the trim-10-frames key << three times.
4. Press the Review Transition button to see how it works.

When the overlap is made, you have Kate talking, then before she finishes talking we see Tim listening over her words, and then Tim talks. Tim's picture has overlapped Kate's sound.

Here's another example:

Say you have a three-shot sequence. First you have a shot of a woman sitting at her desk, telling a man she must leave to catch a plane. Then you have a medium shot of the woman putting papers in her briefcase. Then you cut to a shot of the woman walking through a busy airport. When you spliced them together, you used straight cuts. The pictures are cut perfectly, but you realize that the sequence of shots would have more power if we heard the sound of the airport come in over the shot of her packing up her briefcase.

How? Simple. Get into Dual-Roller Trim Mode, and deselect the video track so that the rollers are only on the sound track(s). Then drag the dual rollers on the sound track to the left. You'll be replacing some of the woman's office sounds with the sound of the busy airport.

When the audience first hears the airport noises breaking into the shot of her in her quiet office, they may be momentarily confused, but that confusion creates a bit of suspense, which is quickly resolved when the picture of her walking through the airport comes onto the screen. Sound overlaps like this are used quite often to set up the next scene. How much should you overlap the sound? Try about three seconds of overlap, and then trim from there.

Removing an Overlap

After working on a transition and creating an overlap, you might decide that in fact a straight cut would work better. A quick way to turn an overlap back into a straight cut is to Command-drag (Mac) or Ctrl-drag (Windows).

1. Get into Trim Mode.
2. Select the track that has been overlapped, and deselect the track that is already a straight cut.
3. Hold down the Command key (Mac) or Ctrl key (Windows) while you drag toward the straight cut. The trim will snap to the transition point.

A word of caution: You always want to create overlaps using Dual-Roller Trim. Because you are working with one track and not the other, Dual-Roller Trim Mode keeps everything in sync. If you use Single-Roller Trim and trim one track and not the other track, you will immediately go out of sync.

Creating overlaps is Dual-Roller Trim's main purpose. I use Single-Roller Trim for adjusting the length of my shots.

SYNC PROBLEMS IN SINGLE-ROLLER TRIM MODE

This is a good time to examine what happens when you use Single-Roller Trim Mode on one track and not on the other(s).

In Figure 4.18, I went into Single-Roller Trim Mode, but only the video track was selected. The trim action affected only the picture. Without thinking, I trimmed anyway and dragged the roller to the left. Thus I lengthened

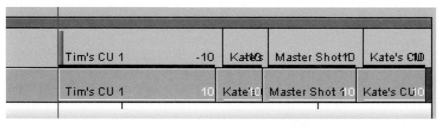

Video track was lengthened by 10 frames.
Audio track was not lengthened.

Figure 4.18

Tim's picture by 10 frames. Because the audio was not trimmed, the clip went out of sync. Tim's audio is now 10 frames shorter than his video and thus out of sync by 10 frames. As you can see, anything downstream of this transition point will also be out of sync by 10 frames. Kate's CU wasn't trimmed, but because Tim's is out of sync, her clip is thrown out as well. Remember, to keep picture and sound in sync, you must cut the picture *and* sound at the same time. When you add picture, you must add sound.

To get back in sync, we must either trim 10 frames of Tim's picture or add 10 frames to Tim's audio. Let's add 10 frames to Tim's audio.

When you're out of sync, you need to go into Single-Roller Trim Mode to fix the problem. Now we need to click on the A1 track and deselect the V1 track. The single-roller will jump to trim Tim's audio. Remember, we want to lengthen his audio by 10 frames. We can use one of several methods:

- We can hit the << frame key once (10).
- We can drag the roller to the left and watch the frame counter until negative 10 appears.

ENTER TRIM MODE ON SELECTED TRACKS

It often happens that you want to enter Trim Mode on an audio track. Perhaps you want to create an L-cut (sound overlap) by trimming the audio track instead of the video track, but you can't lasso just the audio track without lassoing the video track as well. Yes, you can click on the Track Selector buttons to deselect the tracks where you don't want rollers, or you can shift-click on the specific rollers you don't want, but all that's time consuming. There is an easy way to do this.

Hold down the Option key (Mac) or Alt key (Windows) and then lasso just the track(s) you want, and it works beautifully. Examine Figure 4.19. Here I'm lassoing not the video and audio tracks, but just the audio track. This won't work unless I *first* hold down Option key (Mac) or Alt key (Windows). Press Option or Alt and then lasso the transition from the middle of the track above.

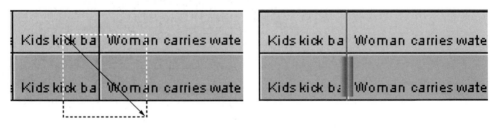

Figure 4.19

Now I can create a sound overlap by dragging the rollers either way. I stay in sync because I'm in Dual-Roller Trim Mode. Practice this technique. We'll use it often when working with multiple audio tracks, or when we have several video tracks in the Timeline.

THE TILDE KEY

There's a special key at the top left of the keyboard (next to the 1) called the Tilde key (~). It acts like a superplay button. When you press it, your clip or sequence will play. But it also works as a Review Transition key in Trim Mode. I often use it instead of pressing the Review Transition button on the Trim Mode display.

TRIM MODE REVIEW

We've spent a lot of time discussing Trim Mode, devoting an entire chapter to its many advantages and features. Let's review some of the hows and whys of Trim Mode.
Getting into Trim Mode:

- Lasso the transition.
- Drag the position indicator to the transition and press the Trim Mode key.

Getting out of Trim Mode:

- Press the Trim Mode button again (Xpress).
- Press the Edit Mode button (Media Composer).
- Press either one of the step-one-frame buttons.
- Click the mouse in the Timecode track (TC1) at the bottom of the Timeline.

Switching Trim Modes:

- To go from Dual-Roller Trim Mode to Single-Roller Trim Mode, click either the A-side or the B-side frames in the Trim Mode display.
- To go from Single-Roller Trim Mode to Dual-Roller Trim Mode, click the frame line between the A-side and B-side frames.

Add Rollers and Delete Rollers:

- In Trim Mode, shift-click on the transition side where you want to add a roller.
- If there is a roller you want to remove, shift-click on it and it will be removed.

Drag the Rollers:

- Click and drag the rollers left or right.
- Command-drag (Mac) or Ctrl-drag (Windows) to IN or OUT marks.
- Command-drag (Mac) or Ctrl-drag (Windows) to transition points.

Trim While Watching:

1. In Trim Mode, press the Review Transition key to have the transition go into a loop.
2. Use the Trim Frame keys <<, <, >, and >> to trim as you watch.

ADVANCED TRIM WHILE WATCHING

We talked about the importance of trimming while you watch. One technique you might try uses the Mark IN and Mark OUT buttons. This is particularly useful if you have left the shots a bit long and now want to trim the sides up.

Get into Trim Mode by lassoing a transition. Choose the A-side, B-side, or Dual-Roller Trim. Now press the Review Transition button. While you watch the transition loop go around, press the Mark IN if you're trimming the A-side, or the Mark OUT if you're trimming the B-side. Notice that the cut point changes to the exact frame you marked. You've got to try it a few times to get the hang of it.

SUGGESTED ASSIGNMENTS

Although Trim Mode is a fantastic feature, it isn't always intuitive. Study this chapter and then practice, using all of the many techniques discussed.

1. Make a duplicate of your sequence and give it today's date.
2. Practice getting in and out of Trim Mode.
3. Practice Dual-Roller and Single-Roller trims, trimming and lengthening the A-side and the B-side, and creating picture and sound overlaps.
4. Practice dragging the rollers.
5. Practice trimming while you watch, using the trim keys.
6. Practice adding and deleting rollers.
7. Using Trim Mode, create a fine cut, with sound overlaps where appropriate, of "Wanna Trade," or whatever assignment you have been editing to date.

5

Menus

In this chapter we're going to take a look at the various menus and menu commands the Avid provides, including those at the top of the computer screen and those found on the monitor screens. We'll discuss each command, point out the ones you'll use most often, and explain when you will find them most useful. But before we begin, let's talk about screening the sequence you've been editing of the scene "Wanna Trade." If you edited a different scene for your first project, it doesn't matter because we'll be exploring the whole process of screening your work. Your last assignment involved using Trim Mode to fine-cut the scene. Now it's time to get some feedback.

SCREENING A WORK IN PROGRESS

Most editors place a high value on screening their work while they are still editing it. Call it a rough-cut or a fine-cut screening, but whatever name you give to it, it's a screening of your work in progress. You've spent a lot of time and energy cutting the material; you've given it your very best, but usually you've been working in a vacuum. What you're looking for now are fresh eyes and ears. You want an audience (it can be one or two people or a classroom full of fellow students) to give you feedback. Nothing teaches you more about your work than screening it in front of an audience. Sometimes screenings are painful, sometimes they are exhilarating, but they are always useful.

Whenever possible, I like to start off small, with an audience of just a few people. I like to split my attention between the audience and the screen. If something isn't working, I usually know it by feeling the attention (or lack of attention) the audience is giving to a particular section. After you've screened the footage, start your inquiry as wide as possible, and then work toward the specific. Take notes! If the audience members aren't all that forthcoming, ask them questions. How did it work? Were you confused about what was going on? What emotion did it evoke? If it's a narrative piece, you might ask about the actors' performances. Which actor did they like best? Because you're working on a digital machine, you can quickly go to any section to review it. If your project is longer than 10 minutes, there's probably a lot to talk about in terms of structure, pacing, character development, and dramatic tension. With a scene as short as "Wanna Trade," you can probably move on to an analysis of specific editing problems. At this stage you're trying to find places where your audience tripped over things that didn't work.

If you're lucky, the audience will give you feedback that's right on the money:

Audience member:	When Tim searches the desk, pretending to look for the letters, I didn't like the cut from the master shot to Tim's close-up.
You:	Why not?
Audience member:	I couldn't see what he was doing.

That's specific. Or someone might say that she thought a cut seemed awkward, or an actor remained on the screen for too long before you cut to the next shot. More times than not, especially if your audience knows nothing about video or filmmaking, they won't tell you what tripped them because they honestly don't know. In those instances, you have to play detective and figure out what's going wrong. It's not easy, but it can be rewarding. I've often found that when people who don't know much about editing say something doesn't work, the problem isn't where they think it is; it's usually before that.

If they can't tell you what is bothering them, but they feel a bit confused, I suggest you slow down the beginning. Make sure the audience is grounded at the start. Once they know who's doing what, then you can speed things up.

Whatever you do, don't argue with your audience. You might be the expert on the project you're cutting, but they're the experts on their feelings about it. If they criticize your work and point out shortcomings, it's human nature to be defensive. I've never met anyone who *liked* being criticized. But if you argue with them, you're missing the point of the screening, which is to learn what is working and what isn't. You don't have to take any of their suggestions. If you think they're way off base, so be it. Toss out your notes and find another audience.

Sometimes you leave a screening embarrassed. The suggestions were so good you feel embarrassed that you didn't see the problems yourself. Other times you feel grateful because you identified a problem, know how to fix it, and can't wait to get back to work. Then there are the times when you realize there are lots of problems and it's depressing to think how far you have to go. Those are the days when, if possible, you take the afternoon off and go for a long walk. Once in a while, people will pat you on the back, shake your hand, and tell you it's brilliant. But unless you get raves from everyone, you'll probably head back to work, fix the problems, and try to schedule another screening with another group with fresh eyes and ears.

MENUS

Pull-down menus are at the heart of the Macintosh and Windows interface. On the Avid a lot of choices and commands are located on the menus. Sometimes an item is grayed out, meaning it isn't available. You'll need to select something or do something for it to come into play.

Different Avid systems have different pull-down menus. Menus change as Avid software is upgraded. Xpress Avids have fewer menu functions than Media Composers. Given all of the different Avid systems and software upgrades, there's really no way to keep up with all of the changes in a guide-book like this one.

Even so, I believe it's useful to examine the many menu commands in some detail. All Avids share about 90 percent of the same commands, and these commands tell us a great deal about how the Avid functions. By going over each command, you can learn a lot about the work you'll soon be able to do. Some commands are geared for advanced users, and we won't go much beyond the brief description provided here. Others are so important to our daily use of the Avid that we'll review them often and in great detail in later chapters.

Because the book you're reading is probably yours—you paid for it and own it—I suggest you use a highlighter pen and highlight a command the first time you use it. That way, the ones you use will be highlighted, and the ones you don't use won't get in your way. When you want to look up a command, you'll quickly look at the ones you use, and your eyes can skip over those you don't. Over time you'll use most of them, but it might be interesting to see how many you never use.

As you can see, some of the commands have keyboard equivalents. Either drag down the menu and select an item or memorize the keyboard equivalent and type it instead.

I've included menus from the Media Composer and the Xpress DV. In most cases, the Xpress DV menus are from a Mac and the Media Composer menus come from a PC. The only real difference, other than their appearance, is that shortcut commands on a Macintosh use the Command key, ⌘, and Windows machines use the Control key, Ctrl.

AVID XPRESS DV MENU

We'll use only two of the items from this menu (Figure 5.1). The first is Hide Avid Xpress DV, which we'll use whenever we want to hide the Xpress on the Mac. This menu item acts a lot like Minimize on a Windows PC, and we'll use it whenever we need to view the desktop. We'll also use the command Quit Xpress DV. We'll use this whenever we want to exit the Avid program.

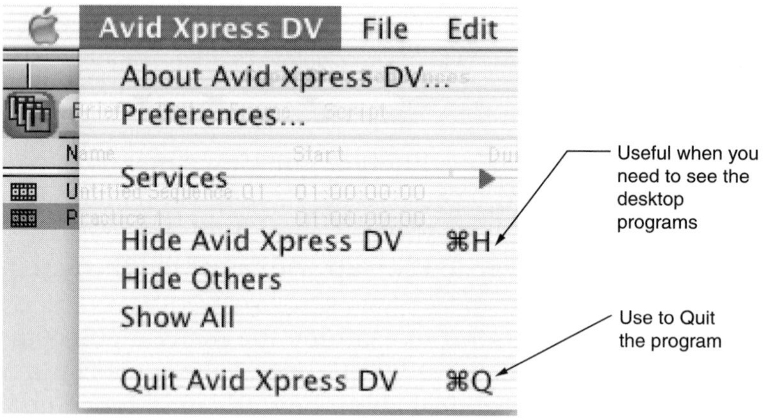

Figure 5.1

FILE MENU

If you've used just about any software on a Windows or Macintosh computer, you're already familiar with most of these File commands (Figures 5.2 and 5.3). Open, Close, Save, Print—they're all standard. The rest are very Avid specific.

New Bin: Creates a new bin. In the past, we clicked on the New Bin button on the Project window. Avid gives you many ways to do the same thing.

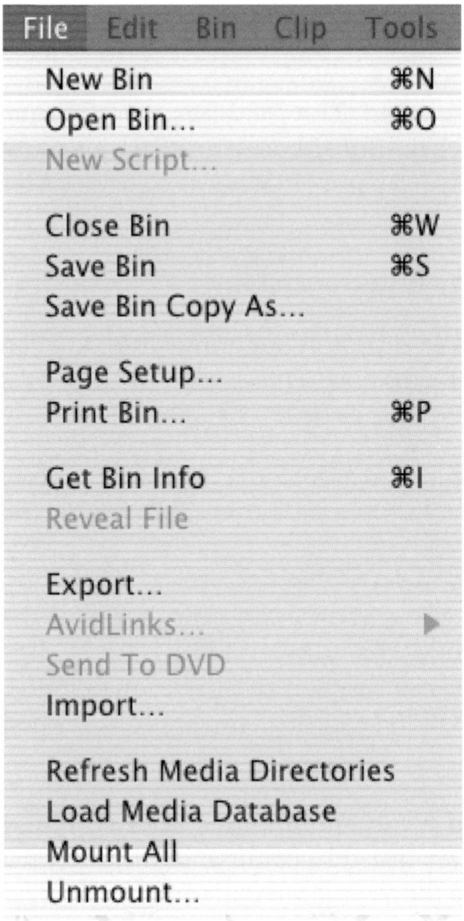

Figure 5.2 Xpress DV File menu

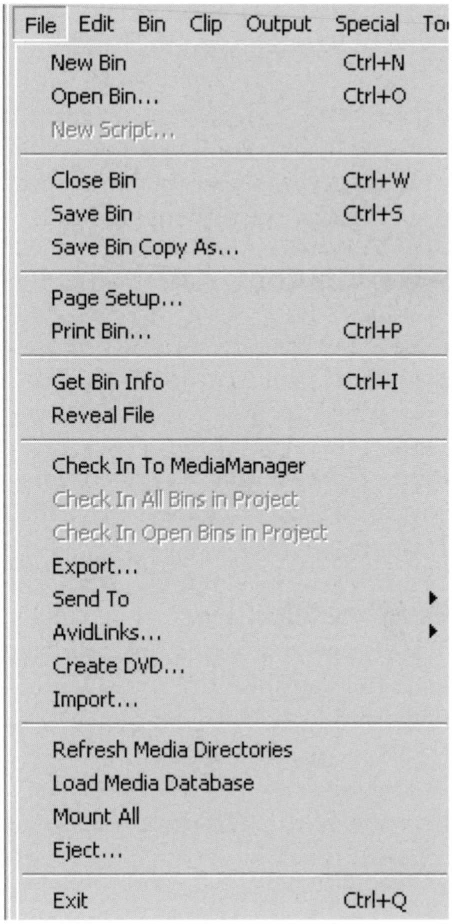

Figure 5.3 Media Composer File menu

Open Bin: In fact, this is more than it seems. If a bin is selected, and you choose this, the bin opens. But you'll probably just double-click on the bin to open it. This command does more than just open a bin, however. When you select this menu command, you're presented with a dialog box. That dialog box taps into all the bins on all the projects on the Avid. Let's say you want to take a clip of music from another project and use it in this project. Select Open Bin and then navigate through the computer's hierarchical menus until you find the bin you want. Open it and you can open a music clip from another project and put it into your current project.

New Script: This command works with the Script Integration feature, which we will discuss at length in Chapter 15.

Close Bin: This command closes the active bin. We usually click on the close box in the corner of the bin itself.

Save Bin: This saves any bin that is selected. The Avid has an auto-save function that automatically saves your work. But if you want to make sure you save what you just did, then type Command-S (Mac) or Ctrl-S (Windows), or select this menu item.

Save Bin Copy As: This saves a copy of the open bin.

Page Setup: If you have a printer hooked up to your computer, you can print out a lot of different items and information. This command opens a dialog box so that you can determine the page setup.

Print Bin/Frame: This opens a dialog box that lets you choose what you would like to print on your printer: an active bin, a frame of a clip, or the Timeline.

Get Bin/Clip Info: This tells you the name and the start timecode for the clip you have selected and information about the number and length of clips in your bin. To tell you the truth, I rarely use this command because it also places items in the Console, and I try to avoid the Console, which is designed for Avid programmers.

Reveal File: This is a rather advanced command and one you won't use often. If you select a master clip, you can use this command to go to the computer's Finder level to locate the media file associated with that master clip.

Check in to MediaManager: This item, and the next two, relate to Avids that are connected together and share media across a network. The MediaManager lets you share files between systems.

Export: Because Avid deals with digital information (1's and 0's), almost anything that can be digitized can be brought in or sent out as a file. The Avid allows you to bring in and send out many kinds of files: picture files, animation files, and audio files. When you export, you send out digital information you have created in the Avid. Perhaps you have sound that needs cleaning up; you have camera noise or an irritating hum. You could export the sound clip as an audio file and give it to a sound engineer, who could filter out the offending hum or camera noise.

Import: Import is the flip side of Export. You use Export to send files you created in the Avid to other computers. You use Import to bring all sorts of files into your Avid. You could import digital photographs, digital audio, animation you created in After Effects, or titles you created in Photoshop. The list of importable files is extensive. We'll spend some time learning how to export and import later in the book.

Refresh Media Directories: If you remove a media drive from the Avid or delete a lot of media files, you will want to let your Avid figure out what's still available. You do this by refreshing the media directories.

Load Media Database: The media database is like a card catalog that keeps track of what's being put on and taken off the external drives. The Avid doesn't keep the entire database in memory all the time. After certain actions, some of your sequences might be offline—the images or sounds don't play—and you'll see that the media is listed as "Media Offline." When you load the Media Database, the Avid may find the missing offline material.

Mount All: This command mounts, or makes active and available, all of the media drives attached to your Avid.

Eject/Unmount: This opens a dialog box that allows you to select drives or disks for ejection or unmounting.

Exit: This command closes everything currently opened, including bins and monitors, and quits the Avid application software. You are returned to the computer desktop.

EDIT MENU

The Edit menu (Figures 5.4 and 5.5) contains some commands that are similar to those found on other common software types, so again, much of this will be familiar to you. Cut, Copy, Paste, Undo, Redo, and Duplicate are commands I'm sure you've used before. They behave a bit differently here, but probably as you would expect.

Undo: You are no doubt already a devoted user of this command. The Avid gives you 32 levels of Undo. You can go back and change actions that you took up to 32 actions ago.

Redo: Redo replaces the action that you undid. Just as handy as Undo.

Undo/Redo List: This list outlines your last 32 actions (either Undo or Redo). Instead of working through all of them, one at a time, to reach the

Edit	Bin	Clip	Tools	To
Undo				⌘Z
Redo				⌘R
Undo/Redo List				▶
Cut				⌘X
Copy				⌘C
Paste				⌘V
Delete				
Select–All				⌘A
Deselect–All				⇧⌘A
Duplicate				⌘D
Enlarge Frame				⌘L
Reduce Frame				⌘K
Find...				⌘F
Find Again				⌘G
Set Font...				
Set Bin Background				▶

Figure 5.4   Xpress DV Edit menu

Edit	Bin	Clip	Output	Special	Tool:
Undo					Ctrl+Z
Redo					Ctrl+R
Undo/Redo List					▶
Cut					Ctrl+X
Copy					Ctrl+C
Paste					Ctrl+V
Delete					
Select–All					Ctrl+A
Deselect–All					Shift+Ctrl+A
Duplicate					Ctrl+D
Enlarge Frame					Ctrl+L
Reduce Frame					Ctrl+K
Find...					Ctrl+F
Find Again					Ctrl+G
Set Font...					
Set Bin Background					▶

Figure 5.5   Media Composer Edit menu

one you want, with this list you can search the list and then select the action you want to change. Remember that all previous actions back to that point—those actions above it on the list—will also be changed.

Cut: If you select material in the Timeline by using a Mark IN and a Mark OUT and then choose Cut, the selected material is removed and immediately goes into the Clipboard. Cut works just like Extract.

Copy: If you select something by using a Mark IN and a Mark OUT and then choose Copy, the selected material is copied to the Clipboard, where it is stored until you Paste it in somewhere. This is a great way to get audio from one area of the sequence, copy it to the Clipboard Monitor, and then put it somewhere else.

Paste: This command places whatever is in the Clipboard at the blue position indicator or at a Mark IN in the Timeline.

Clear/Delete: This works just like the Delete key. It opens a dialog box for deleting clips from a bin or tracks from the Timeline.

Select-All: This is a terrific way to quickly select all of the things you're working on. You can select all of the clips in a bin or select all of the tracks in the Timeline.

Duplicate: We already practiced this in Chapter 2. There will be many times that you want to duplicate sequences. Just select the sequence you want to copy and hit Command-D (Mac) or Ctrl-D (Windows). Rename the copy and you can make changes to the new version, while holding on to the previous version.

Enlarge Track/Frame: This enlarges tracks in the Timeline. It also enlarges frames when you're working in the bin in Frame View.

Reduce Track/Frame: This reduces frames in Frame View or reduces tracks in the Timeline. You'll use this frequently.

Find: This is just like Find in most word-processing programs, but it is used to find clips in the Timeline or text you've attached to a locator. Great if you have a Timeline with hundreds of clips.

Find Again: This command repeats the previous Find command.

Set Font: You can customize the way things look on the screen, including the font used in bins and certain windows. Not very useful, unless you have nothing to do with your free time.

Set Bin Background: Like Set Font, this command is for those who want to make their bins and Composer window look "different." Waste of time, if you ask me.

Preferences: This opens the Settings window, allowing you to change settings, such as bin settings, keyboard settings, and so on. I prefer to click on the Settings tab in the Project window.

BIN MENU

Now we arrive at the pull-down menus that are not like those found on most word-processing programs (Figures 5.6 and 5.7). We'll begin by examining all of the commands shared by the Xpress DV, Xpress, and Media Composer.

Bin	Clip	Tools	Toolset	
Batch Record...			Composer	
Batch Import...				
Consolidate...				
DV Scene Extraction...				
Relink...				
Change Sample Rate...				
Headings...				
AutoSync(tm)				
AutoSequence(tm)				
Custom Sift...				
Sort Again			⌘E	
Show Sifted				
✓ Show Unsifted				
Set Bin Display...				
Reverse Selection				
Select Offline Items				
Select Media Relatives				
Select Unreferenced Clips				
Align to Grid			⌘T	
Fill Window				
Fill Sorted				
Select Unrendered Titles				

Figure 5.6 Xpress DV Bin menu

Bin	Clip	Output	Special	Tools	Toolset	Wind
Go To Capture Mode					Ctrl+B	
Headings...						
Hide Column						
AutoSync(tm)						
Group...					Shift+Ctrl+G	
MultiGroup...						
AutoSequence						
Send Selected Clips...						
Custom Sift...						
Sift Selected Items						
Sort					Ctrl+E	
Show Sifted						
✓ Show Unsifted						
Set Bin Display...						
Launch In Native Application...						
Reverse Selection						
Select Offline Items						
Select Media Relatives						
Select Sources						
Select Unreferenced Clips						
Loop Selected Clips						
Align Columns					Ctrl+T	
Align Selected to Grid						
Fill Window						
Fill Sorted						
Select Unrendered Titles						
Check In Bin To MediaManager						
Update from MediaManager...						

Figure 5.7 Media Composer Bin menu

Then we'll discuss those commands on the Media Composer that you won't find in the Xpress DV and the Xpress.

The main difference between the Media Composer and the Xpress is one of scope. The Xpress does nearly everything the Media Composer does but presents you with fewer options to accomplish the same task. You can usually get there with the Xpress, but perhaps not as quickly or easily.

Keep in mind that the Bin menu is made up of commands that act on things you'll find in a bin. It seems obvious, but sometimes we overlook the obvious. Often, you need to have a bin open and selected for these commands to be available.

Batch Record/Batch Digitize: This opens a dialog box that leads you through the process of recording/digitizing selected clips. Because the Xpress DV is designed for DV tapes, which are already "digitized," the word "Record" replaces "Digitize." Normally you use this command after you have logged a lot of clips. You've set the IN and OUT timecode for the clips, but you haven't digitized them. By invoking Batch Record/Digitize, you can go to lunch while the Avid digitizes each of the selected clips. (In the Media Composer, this command is in the Clip menu.)

Batch Import: Some projects contain a lot of imported files, such as graphic and animation files. Before Batch Import, graphic-intensive projects were at a severe disadvantage because any file that was changed, or came in at a different resolution, would have to be reimported individually and then manipulated individually. Batch Import makes it much easier to make changes to files and then bring them back into the Avid.

Consolidate: Consolidate has two functions. It allows you to send media files to the drive of your choice, which means you can better organize your media files. It also helps you remove material that you digitized but no longer need, enabling you to reclaim a large amount of space on your hard drives. When you consolidate a sequence, you are telling the Avid to keep all of the media from the clips that went into the sequence and to throw out all of the media from the clips that didn't get edited into the sequence. You don't want to consolidate until you've made a very fine cut. You might fine-cut the first half of your project and consolidate that half to free up a lot of drive space to enable you to digitize all of the footage you need for cutting the second half. (In the Media Composer, this command is in the Clip menu.)

DV Scene Extraction: Whenever you stop and start a DV camera, a marker is put down on the tape. Therefore every single shot in your tape has been tagged. This command helps you break all of those shots on your videotape into individual "clips." You can make a master clip of the entire tape—or the portion you're interested in recording—and then use DV Scene Extraction to break each individual shot into subclips, automatically. This saves no space on your media drive, but it's a really fast way to break what you have into distinct clips.

Relink: The connection (link) between the master clip and the media file is sometimes broken. The clip appears offline, even though you know the media file is on the drive somewhere. In this case you need to relink the clip to the media file. (In the Media Composer, this command is in the Clip menu.)

Change Sample Rate: When you record audio from a digital source, like a DV tape, that audio's sample rate was determined by the camera. It might be at 32kH, 44.1kH, or 48kH. If you're recording material from different tapes coming from different cameras, you may find that the audio on those tapes was recorded at different sample rates. You can edit material containing different sample rates and then, in the bin, you can choose this command to determine one sample rate for the entire sequence. This is important when putting your sequence out to tape.

Headings: We've already discussed this command in Chapter 3. It opens a dialog box that lists all of the possible columns, listed by headings, that are available to you. You select the ones you want and deselect the ones you want hidden from view.

AutoSync: This is especially handy when you're working on film projects. Film is recorded double-system, meaning the sound is recorded on a tape recorder and not by the film camera. You digitize the picture, then the sound. The sound and picture are then placed in sync in the Avid. Once they are in sync, they can be locked together so that sync breaks appear whenever sync is broken.

AutoSequence: If the original videotape had no audio, as with a film-to-tape transfer, you could bring in the sound, sync it up, and then use this command to put the in sync audio back onto that videotape.

Custom Sift: This command opens a dialog box in which you set various options and parameters for sifting through a bin to find clips you want to locate. You can sift by name, creation date, tape, duration, and so on.

Sort/Sort Again: We spent some time in Chapter 3 discussing this command. It enables you to choose a column in a bin and sort all of the clips alphanumerically by that chosen column. After you have sorted, it will change to Sort Again.

Show Sifted: During sifting, this command displays only those items in a bin that met the sift criteria. All others are hidden from view.

Show Unsifted: This command restores the unsifted items for viewing.

Set Bin Display: This command presents a dialog box that lets you determine which items you want displayed in the bin. There are many choices. You're familiar with only a few. The choices are as follows:

- Master clips (you know all about these)
- Subclips (you know about these)
- Sequences (you know all about these)
- Sources (lists the tapes the material comes from)
- Effects (dissolves, wipes, etc.—we'll learn about these)
- Motion effects (freeze frames, slow motion—we'll learn about these)
- Rendered effects (we'll learn about these)

If you checked off all of the choices, your bin would be packed with too much information, making it hard to find the sequences, clips, and subclips you need. When we learn about effects, titles, and motion effects and start creating them, we'll sometimes want to see them displayed in the bin.

Reverse Selection: This is a handy command. Let's say you select a clip in a bin. It becomes highlighted. If you click on this command, your selection is reversed. The clip you selected is deselected, and all of the other clips in the bin are selected. Let's say you want to select all of those clips that are close-ups. And let's say that of the 40 clips in the bin, two are wide shots and the other 38 are close-ups. Shift-click on the two that are wide shots, and then on Reverse Selection—all 38 close-ups are selected. The two that are wide shots are deselected. You reversed your selection.

Select Offline Items: Later on we'll learn about logging and recording/digitizing clips. When you're recording, you're often looking for clips that are offline—meaning they have no media files because they haven't been recorded, just logged. It makes your life easier to be able to go to a bin, select this command, and have all of the offline clips selected.

Select Media Relatives: This enables you to select a sequence or a clip and then have the Avid highlight all of the objects related to it. Let's say you've finished the final sequence and you want to make sure you used all of the shots available to you. Click on the sequence and then on Select Media Relatives; the Avid will highlight every clip that was used in the Sequence. For this to work, you need to be able to see two bins at once. If you're working with SuperBins, double-click on the bin containing your sequence(s) and select a sequence. Then single-click the bin containing your clips so that you can see both bins at once. Now choose this command to see the media relatives.

Select Unreferenced Clips: This command works like the flip side of Select Media Relatives. Select a sequence and then choose this command. It shows you all of the clips in the bin that have *not* been used in the sequence. For this to work, you need to be able to see two bins at once. If you're working with SuperBins, double-click on the bin containing your sequence(s) and select a sequence. Then single-click the bin containing your clips so that you can see both bins at once. Now choose this command to see the clips you haven't used.

Align Columns: When you are in Text View, this command puts the columns in nice, neat rows. When you are in Frame View, this command changes to Align to Grid.

Align to Grid: When you are in Frame View, this command aligns all of your frames to a grid.

Fill Window: When you are in Frame View, this command distributes all of the frames evenly inside the window.

Fill Sorted: You can't sort in Frame View because there are no columns to sort; however, if you sort a bin in Brief or Text View, you can get into Frame View, select this command, and have the clips appear in Frame View according to how you sorted them in the other views.

Select Unrendered Titles: Titles often need to be rendered (created) by the computer before they play in real time. This command shows you all of the titles that have not been rendered.

ITEMS FOUND IN MEDIA COMPOSER BIN MENU AND NOT IN XPRESS BIN MENU

Go to Capture Mode: This command opens up the Digitize Tool you'll use for digitizing material.

Group: This is an advanced feature. You can take clips that were shot with different cameras, or on different days, and group them together into one clip. Once they are grouped, you can use Avid's MultiCamera editing features. Let's say you grouped four clips into one group. In Quad Split mode, for instance, the Source Monitor shows all four clips. You can see all of the choices and then cut into your sequence whichever one works best. It's a quick way to build a montage of different shots or to edit together various shots of the same action.

MultiGroup: This is also an advanced feature used primarily for editing big-budget situation comedies. It's similar to Group Clips, except that all of the different camera shots covering the scene must have identical timecode. Shots from the different cameras are grouped together so that they act as one clip, staying in sync and playing together. You can then tie together several Group Clips. Both Group and MultiGroup are designed so that an Avid editor can "switch" between camera angles as she edits the show, just as a television director would use a switcher when producing a live show.

Send Selected Clips: This command allows you to send clips to another Avid on a network.

Select Sources: This command selects (highlights) all of the source clips that make up a selected object.

Align Selected to Grid: When you are in Frame View, this command aligns all of those frames you have selected to a grid.

Check in Bin to MediaManager: This command relates to Avids that are connected together and share media across a network. The MediaManager lets you share files between systems.

Update from MediaManager: This command relates to Avids that are connected together and share media across a network. The MediaManager lets you share files between systems.

CLIP MENU

In my opinion, the Clip menu is a bit of a misnomer because many of the commands here don't really have much to do with actual clips (Figures 5.8 and 5.9). I think these commands have a lot more to do with the Timeline, but here we go. I've listed all of the menu items common to both the Xpress and the Media Composer first, and then I've listed the items found only on the Media Composer.

New Sequence: Whenever you want to create a new sequence, use this command. Often, you'll begin a new sequence by simply splicing a marked clip to the Timeline. Whenever you do, you'll automatically begin a new sequence. Using the menu command is a more formal way of doing it.

New Video Track: This command creates a new video track on the Timeline. Later, when we create effects and titles, we'll want to put them on a new video track, such as V2, so that picture images can be combined.

Figure 5.8   Xpress DV Clip menu

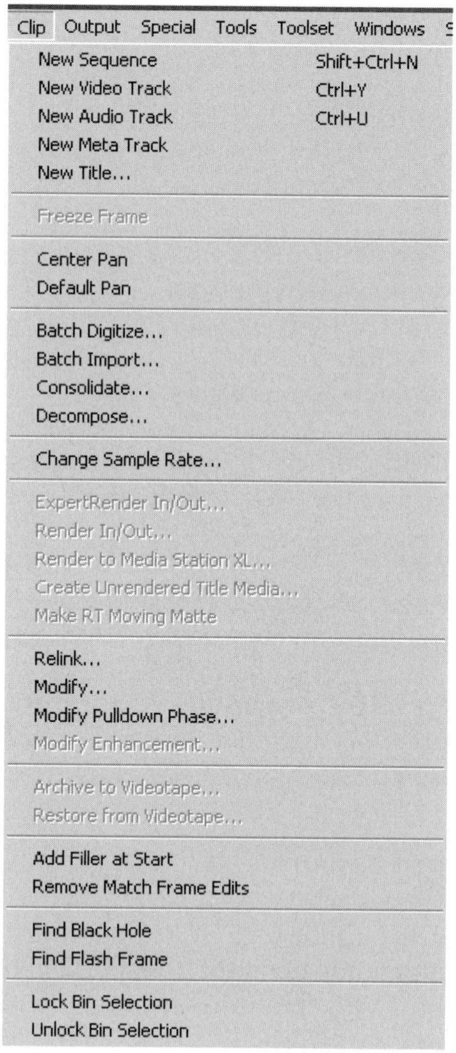

Figure 5.9   Media Composer Clip menu

New Audio Track: The Avid can play between 8 and 24 tracks of audio simultaneously. If you add music, a narration track, and several sound effect tracks to your dialog tracks, you can easily need six or seven audio tracks. This command instantly creates a new track on the Timeline.

New Title: This command opens the Title Tool, which we'll use to create titles.

Freeze Frame: This command opens a list of freeze-frame lengths: 1 second, 5 seconds, 10 seconds, and so on and creates the freeze frame of your choice.

Load Filler: This opens a Pop-up Monitor that contains black filler. For filmmakers, it's like grabbing a roll of fill that you then splice onto your tracks to create a pause or to replace picture or audio. Let's say you want to put 30 frames (1 second) of black between the end of one scene and the beginning of the next. Choose Load Filler. In the Pop-up Monitor, mark an IN, go 29 frames, and mark an OUT. Then mark an IN on the Timeline where you want the fill to go. Select all of your tracks and hit Splice. It acts just like any clip, except that this one has only black. (The Media Composer places this command in the Monitor menus. We'll examine these Monitor menus at the end of the chapter.)

Audio Mixdown: Currently, the Xpress can monitor only eight of your audio tracks. But what if you have 10 tracks? Before outputting to tape, you could "mix down" (combine) three of the 10 tracks onto one track. Now you have eight tracks. (In the Media Composer, this command is in the Special menu.)

Video Mixdown: The same explanation and rationale given for audio mixdown applies here. The problem with mixdowns is that if your media is deleted, you can't recreate the mixdown. (In the Media Composer, this command is in the Special menu.)

Expert Render at Position (In/Out):   Effects often need the computer to create a combination of media. This creation of new media is called *rendering*. If the effect isn't too complicated, the Avid can often play it in real time, without having the computer create new media. This is nice because you can see if you like the effect and want to use it before you commit any media space on your drives to the effect. Sometimes the Avid can't play the effects in real time, and they will need to be rendered for you to see them. With this command, the Avid will look at the effects you have on several tracks and decide which of them need to be rendered for all of them to play together. Instead of rendering them all, the Avid will "intelligently" render only those that need to be rendered.

Render at Position or Render In to Out: Eventually, you'll need to render all of the effects if you want to send it out into the world. If you have just one effect to render, you place the position indicator on that effect and choose Render at Position. If you have several effects that need to be rendered, you'll mark an IN before the first, and an OUT after the last, and then you'll choose Render In to Out.

Render On-the-Fly: If you have combined several effects, or if you have effects that are complex, the Avid might not be able to play them unless you render them; however, you can coax the Avid into showing you the effect before it's been rendered by turning on Render On-the-Fly. The effect(s) won't play in real time, but with Render On-the-Fly selected, you can see the effect by dragging the position indicator through the Timeline. It's a fudge, but this is often preferable to rendering the effect. (In the Media Composer, this command is in the Special menu.)

Re-create Title Media: Media Composer and Xpress users often edit projects at a low resolution, because it saves hard drive space, and then redigitize the final sequence at a much higher resolution for output to tape. Titles created at a lower resolution won't play. To get them to play at the new resolution, you'll need to select Re-create Title Media. Now you have your titles in the higher resolution. Xpress DV users may take titles offline and then need to re-create them at a later time.

16:9 Monitors: This configures the Source and Record Monitor for the widescreen aspect ratio. We'll discuss this command at length later in the book.

Digital Cut: The Avid can be connected to sophisticated analog and digital video decks for recording the final, completed sequence onto tape. When you use the Digital Cut Tool, the Avid controls the videotape deck and records your sequence to tape using timecode.

Modify: This command allows you to change important data about a clip that has been logged incorrectly. For instance, you might mistakenly log a tape as having two audio tracks, when in fact there is only one usable audio track. You can select the clips you logged in the bin, and then, using the Modify command, deselect one of the audio tracks. Now, when you go to record/digitize the tapes, you won't be forced to record two audio tracks. Once a clip has been digitized or recorded, this command will no longer work.

Modify Pulldown Phase: When working with film that has been transferred to videotape, you can use the matchback feature on the Avid to keep track of the original film's key numbers. You sometimes need to modify the information about the way the film frames were transferred onto the video frames. We'll explore this topic in Chapter 17.

Add Filler at Start: This command adds a second of filler at the start of a new sequence. Handy.

Remove Match Frame Edits: We'll get to what are more often called *add edits* later in the book. With this command you can mark an IN and then an OUT and remove add edits from your sequence.

Lock Tracks/Lock Bin Selection: This command enables you to lock one or more tracks. It's especially handy as you get to the end of your editing phase and don't want a lot of work dislodged inadvertently. A padlock symbol appears in the Track Selector box in the Timeline. When working in bins, this lets you lock bins so that they can't be changed.

Unlock Tracks/Unlock Bin Selection: This command unlocks the tracks or bins.

ITEMS FOUND IN MEDIA COMPOSER CLIP MENU AND NOT IN XPRESS CLIP MENU

Center Pan: When we get to the chapter that discusses audio, we'll spend time on panning, but basically sound is said to come from the left speaker, to be centered on both speakers, or to come from the right speaker (and anywhere in between). This command centers the sound on all of the clips you select.

Default Pan: Returns you to the default pan setup.

Decompose: This one is a bit gruesome sounding, but it is a powerful feature, especially when you up-rez to an online resolution. When you edit your project, you'll no doubt be editing at a low resolution to save space on the media drive. Then when you want to output the final sequence, you will redigitize the clips in the final sequence at a much higher resolution. On the Xpress, this redigitizing process takes place in one way. With Decompose, you're free to set up the process in any of a hundred ways. For instance, you might want to sort your clips by tape. Decompose allows you to do this. You can then up-rez the last tape first or in any order you wish.

Relink: The connection (link) between the master clip and the media file is sometimes broken. The clip appears offline, even though you know its media file is on the drive somewhere. In this case you need to relink the clip to the media file. (This command is in the Bin menu on the Xpress).

Archive to Videotape/Restore from Videotape: The Media Composer lets you back up clips and sequences to videotape as a way of archiving what is important to a project. If you take that project off the Avid to work on a different project, putting the first project back online 6 months later is quick and easy.

Find Black Hole: If you have any black fill between video segments in the Timeline, this command will take you to it so you can make sure the fill is intentional and not a mistake. Use this command right before you send the final sequence to tape.

Find Flash Frame: This command will take you to any video clip in the Timeline that is shorter than 10 frames (the default setting) in length so you can check to make sure this "flash" is intentional and not a mistake. Use this right before you send the final sequence to tape.

OUTPUT MENU (MEDIA COMPOSER ONLY)

The Xpress doesn't have an Output menu (Figure 5.10), but it has most of the same capabilities.

Figure 5.10   Media Composer Output menu

Digital Cut: The Avid can be connected to sophisticated analog and digital videotape recorders (VTRs) for recording the final, completed sequence onto tape. When you use the Digital Cut Tool, the Avid controls the VTR and records your digital cut to tape, using timecode. (This command is in the Clip menu on the Xpress).

FilmScribe: This opens Avid's film matchback software. When you do a film project on an Avid, the film negative is transferred to videotape and then digitized for editing on the Avid. You edit the sequence, and then you get a Cut List, which tells you how to match the Avid sequence to the film negative. We'll discuss this topic at length in Chapter 17. If your Xpress DV has the Filmmaker's Toolkit, you have FilmScribe; however, unlike the Media Composer, there is no menu item. Instead, you must find the application on the computer's internal drive and launch it.

EDL: This opens a tool that organizes the generation of an Edit Decision List (EDL). Many projects that originated on high-end videotape are not "finished" on an Avid. The Avid is instead used to make all of the editing decisions. Then the final master copy of the project is made by taking the original videotapes to an online video editing suite. There the editors assemble the show based on the EDL the Avid generates.

You can create an EDL on the Xpress DV, but it involves going to an application on the computer's internal drive and launching the EDL Manager. It's the same EDL Manager that the Media Composer uses, but having it available as a menu item makes opening it a lot easier.

SPECIAL MENU (MEDIA COMPOSER ONLY)

The Xpress doesn't have a Special menu, and some of the items found here aren't found on any of the other Xpress menus, which has mostly been the case up to this point (Figure 5.11). Many of these commands are, well, special. I guess if you apply the logic at work here, then if the Xpress had them, they wouldn't be special.

The Xpress is an incredibly powerful machine, especially given how much less it costs when compared with a Media Composer. That being the case, Avid has to make sure the Xpress doesn't have all the bells and whistles that are included on the Media Composer, because if it did . . . you get the picture.

Figure 5.11   Media Composer Special menu

Site Settings: The Avid can be set up in a variety of ways, depending on user preferences and the project demands. Most of the choices are made in the Settings window, where items are listed as user or site settings. This opens the Site Settings window.

Bin/Composer Settings: This command opens the Settings window for whichever window is active.

Restore to Default: This command restores whatever setting you have selected to the default settings. Open the Settings window. Click a setting to highlight it, and choose this command.

Audio Mixdown: Depending on the model, most Media Composers can monitor 24 audio tracks. But there may be instances when you want to combine or "mix down" two or more audio tracks. (This command is in the Clip menu on the Xpress).

Video Mixdown: Certain projects demand sophisticated graphics involving many video tracks. It's often helpful to combine several tracks into one track, using this command. The problem with mixdowns is that if your media is deleted, you can't re-create the mixdown. (This command is in the Clip menu on the Xpress).

Read Audio Timecode: The Avid can read the longitudinal timecode recorded on any audio track and display that information in the bin. Select the clips and then choose this command. A dialog box opens, giving you choices about how this will be accomplished.

Restore Default Patch: In the Timeline, patching involves routing source audio to the record track of your choice, rather than to the default track. For instance, you might want music that is coming in on source track A1 to go onto record track A5. To do this, you patch the tracks. This menu command ignores your patching and restores the default patching setup.

Sync Point Editing: This command activates a special type of overwrite editing based on sync points. You can line up a point in the Source Monitor (one sync point) and have it overwrite at an exact point in the sequence (the second sync point). This is often used when editing rock videos.

Show Phantom Marks: We spent a lot of time going over the rule that says, "It takes three marks to make an edit." In fact, whenever an edit is made, there are really four marks: IN and OUT on the source and IN and OUT on the record. You don't set the fourth mark—it's just there. The fourth mark is called a *Phantom Mark,* and when you choose this command, the Media Composer will display all four marks in the source or record window.

Render On-the-Fly: If you have combined several effects, or if you have effects that are complex, the Avid might not be able to play them unless you render them; however, you can coax the Avid into showing you the effect before it's been rendered by turning on Render On-the-Fly. The effect(s) won't play in real time, but with Render On-the-Fly selected, you can see the effect by dragging the position indicator through the Timeline. It's a fudge, but this is often preferable to rendering the effect.

Fast Frame Display: This one is tricky to explain. On Avids that are capable of running projects at 24 frames per second, like a feature film, those projects are digitized as frames made up of two interlaced video fields, but they are played in the Avid not as frames but as single fields. Using this command, you can see the entire frame, rather than only one of the two fields. It won't play as a frame, but when you park the position indicator, you can see a frame.

MultiCamera Mode: When clips have been grouped together and created into a grouped clip, they can be cut by switching between the different camera angles or shots. This is called *MultiCamera editing*. There are three displays available when using MultiCamera editing. This command calls up one of the choices.

VTR Emulation: If you have the right cable, you can have an external videotape editing system play your sequence. An external edit controller takes control of the Avid and plays the sequence as if it were just another source video in a videotape deck. That way you could have multiple source tapes, including the Avid sequence, edited together onto a master videotape.

TOOLS MENU: XPRESS AND MEDIA COMPOSER

The Xpress and Media Composer share many of the same tools, so the Tools menus for each are similar. I have placed the two menus side by side (Figures 5.12 and 5.13) for purposes of comparison. As we go through each command, I'll state whether it is found on both or on one or the other. You'll notice the order that some commands appear in the Xpress menu is a little different from on the Media Composer's menu. When an item is found on both menus, I follow the Xpress DV's Tools menu lineup.

New Deck Controller: (Media Composer only) This command opens a tool for controlling a videotape deck. You can screen footage from your source tapes without having to open the digitize tool.

Audio Mix: This is an important tool. When it opens, you see what looks like a mixing board with volume and pan sliders. You can adjust volume and pan by dragging the sliders. You can make changes to individual clips, segments of the Timeline, or an entire track in the Timeline.

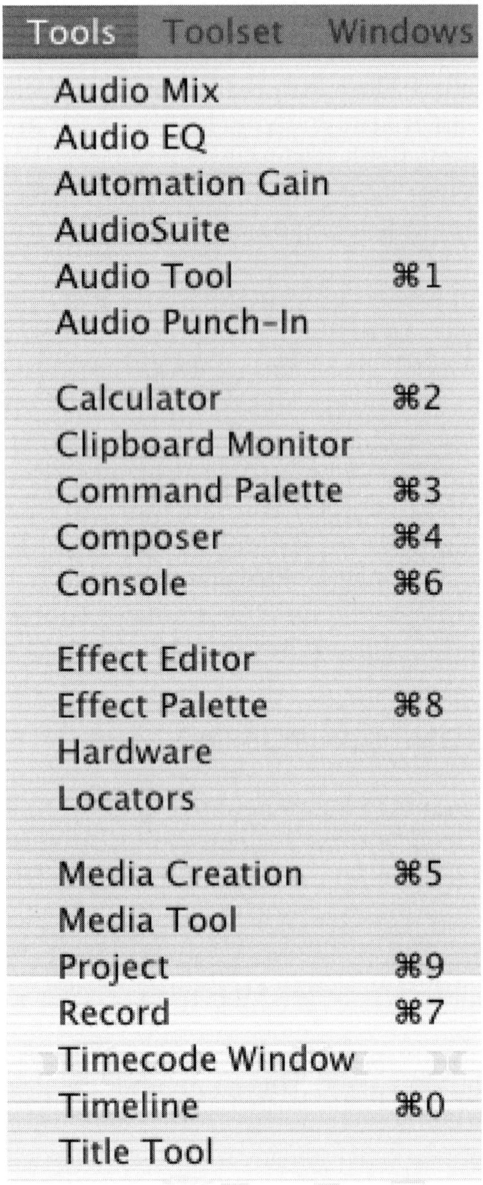

Tools	Toolset	Windows
Audio Mix		
Audio EQ		
Automation Gain		
AudioSuite		
Audio Tool	⌘1	
Audio Punch-In		
Calculator	⌘2	
Clipboard Monitor		
Command Palette	⌘3	
Composer	⌘4	
Console	⌘6	
Effect Editor		
Effect Palette	⌘8	
Hardware		
Locators		
Media Creation	⌘5	
Media Tool		
Project	⌘9	
Record	⌘7	
Timecode Window		
Timeline	⌘0	
Title Tool		

Figure 5.12   Xpress DV Tools menu

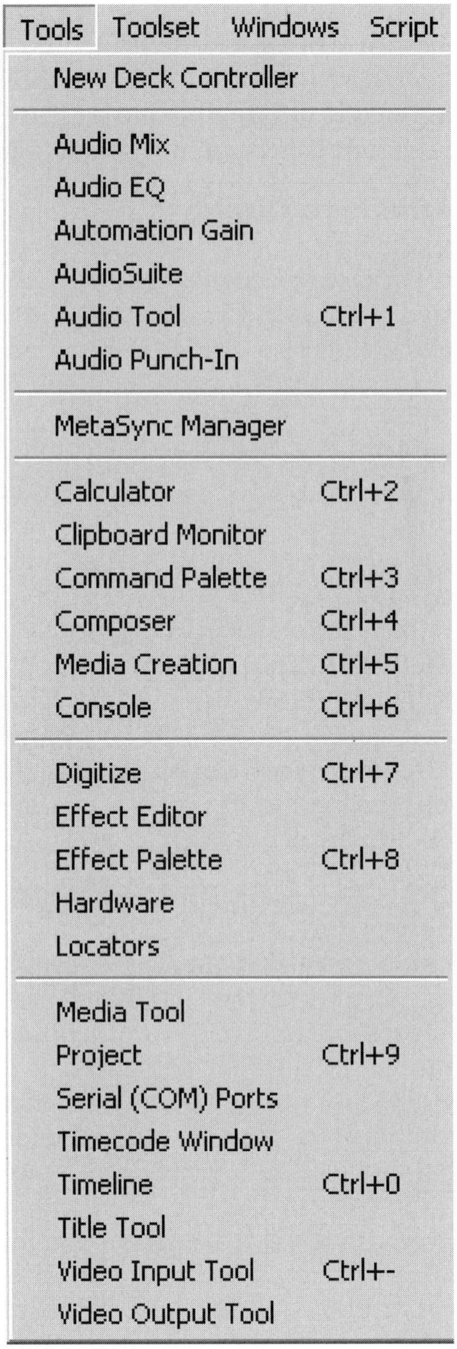

Tools	Toolset	Windows	Script
New Deck Controller			
Audio Mix			
Audio EQ			
Automation Gain			
AudioSuite			
Audio Tool	Ctrl+1		
Audio Punch-In			
MetaSync Manager			
Calculator	Ctrl+2		
Clipboard Monitor			
Command Palette	Ctrl+3		
Composer	Ctrl+4		
Media Creation	Ctrl+5		
Console	Ctrl+6		
Digitize	Ctrl+7		
Effect Editor			
Effect Palette	Ctrl+8		
Hardware			
Locators			
Media Tool			
Project	Ctrl+9		
Serial (COM) Ports			
Timecode Window			
Timeline	Ctrl+0		
Title Tool			
Video Input Tool	Ctrl+-		
Video Output Tool			

Figure 5.13   Media Composer Tools menu

Audio EQ: This opens a tool that enables you to adjust the equalization of individual audio clips in the Timeline. By changing the low, middle, and high frequencies, you can alter or improve your sound.

Automation Gain: This tool looks a lot like the Audio Mix Tool, but it allows you to actually mix your tracks on the fly. As you play the sequence, you can change volume levels, and the ramps you create as you raise and lower the volume sliders are marked by key frames. When you look at the Timeline, you'll see a visual representation of your level changes.

AudioSuite: This command opens a tool that gives you access to audio processing plug-ins, such as pitch processing and reversing of audio.

Audio Tool: This command brings up a tool that is like a digital VU meter. It measures the strength of the incoming or outgoing audio signal(s). For instance, when you digitize a tape with an audio signal, you'll use this tool to make sure the levels are correct.

Audio Punch-In: This command opens a tool that allows you to record audio directly to the Timeline. It is used primarily to quickly add voice-over narration.

MetaSync Manager: (Media Composer only) Metadata is a new buzz-word that here refers to extra material embedded in a video or DVD, such as subtitles, close-captions, or links to the Internet. This command opens the tool that lets you place this metadata on the Avid's Timeline.

Calculator: This opens a special calculator that helps you figure out different film and video durations. For instance, you could enter a duration in timecode numbers and then calculate the number of feet and frames it would equal in the 35 mm film format.

Clipboard Monitor: Several actions, such as Lift, Extract, and Paste, as well as clicking the Clipboard button, will send whatever has been marked in the Timeline to the Clipboard Monitor for temporary storage. This command opens the Clipboard Monitor. Once it's opened, you can splice or overwrite any or all of the Clipboard's contents into the Timeline.

Command Palette: All of the commands available to you are contained in the Command Palette; there are more than 100 commands from which to choose. You can map any of them to the keyboard and create a custom keyboard, and you can map them to the Source and Record row of command buttons. The palette looks like a file cabinet with tabs for categories of commands: Move,

Play, Edit, Trim, FX, 3D, Mcam, Other, More. Click on the tab for the category you want, and you'll see all of the command buttons.

Composer: This activates the Composer Monitor window.

Console: This opens the Console window, which gives you detailed information about your system, including your ID number and model. It provides information about bin objects and the sequence in the Timeline. It also provides a log of error messages, which you might read to an Avid technician who is trying to help you solve a problem over the phone.

Digitize: (Media Composer and Xpress only) This opens a tool that is used to control the digitizing process. When opened, it looks a lot like the working face of a video deck, with buttons for playing, fast-forwarding, and rewinding tapes. We'll devote a lot of time to this tool in the next chapter. This is basically the same as "Record" on the Xpress DV.

Effect Editor: This tool opens the Effect Editor, which you use to adjust a visual effect's parameters. We'll examine it in detail in Chapter 10.

Effect Palette: This tool opens a palette from which you can select all of the various visual effects available to you.

Hardware: This tool gives you information about the computer hardware that makes up your Avid. This tool also shows you how much space is available on your various disk drives. Open it and you'll see all of your drives, with a bar graph next to each one that shows the amount of the drive that is filled and the amount that is currently available.

Locators: Locators are like little colored labels that you can place on any track in the Timeline. They help you flag important points. You can even write yourself notes. This tool opens a window that shows you where all of the locators are in your sequence and gives you the ability to look at them in different ways.

Media Creation: This command opens a dialog box in which you can tell the Avid how you want to handle all of the media you bring into the Avid. You can set the resolution of all of your video or choose a drive for storing both audio and video. You can also use it to determine the resolution of titles and motion effects you create in the Avid and on which drive you would like to store your titles and motion effects.

Media Tool: This tool looks a lot like a bin in Text View. It lists all of the project's media files.

Project: This command makes the Project window the active window.

Record: (Xpress DV only) This opens a tool that is used to control the recording process. When opened, it looks a lot like the working face of a video deck, with buttons for playing, fast-forwarding, and rewinding tapes. We'll devote a lot of time to this tool in Chapter 6.

Serial Ports: (Media Composer and Xpress only) This command opens a tool through which you can designate the use of the CPU's serial ports (the modem port and printer port). You could use the tool to assign an Avid Media Reader to a printer port, while a videotape deck is assigned to the modem port.

Timecode Window: This opens a window that can display up to eight lines of timecode information. If you click on the window, a pop-up menu appears, giving you options such as IN to OUT, sequence duration, and remaining time.

Timeline: If you inadvertently close the Timeline, or find you don't have a Timeline, select this command and a Timeline will appear.

Title Tool: This opens the tool that we'll use to create titles. This command does the same thing as "New Title" in the Clip menu. They are identical.

Video Input Tool: (Media Composer and Xpress only) When you are digitizing video, you open this tool to monitor and change the incoming video signal. We'll discuss this tool at length in Chapter 6. Because it brings in video digitally, as ones and zeros, the Xpress DV does not have this tool because you cannot change the DV signal.

Video Output Tool: (Media Composer and Xpress only) This opens a tool for measuring and calibrating the video output signal. This is important whenever you are recording your sequence onto videotape. Xpress DV does not have this tool.

TOOLSET MENU

This menu is new to the Avid line, starting with Xpress DV 3.0, Xpress 5.0, and Media Composer 11.0 (Figures 5.14 and 5.15). It represents Avid's desire to have all models share the same interface and to make it faster and easier to switch among common editing tasks.

In the past, many Avid users took advantage of Avid's powerful user controls to customize the Avid so that it would perform a variety of tasks in a particular way. For instance, an editor might open various tools, place the tools in a particular spot on the computer monitor, and tell the Avid to

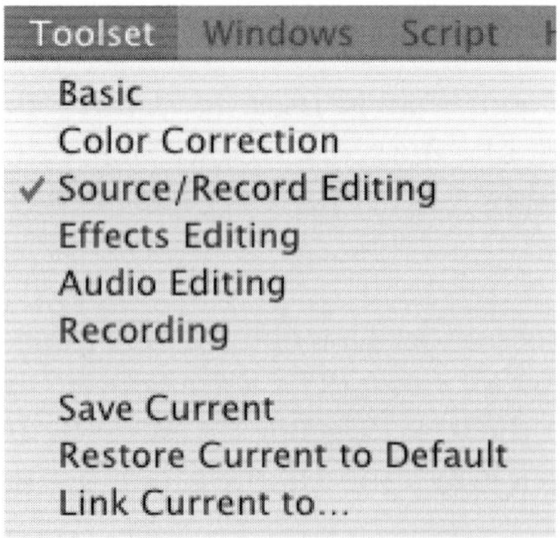

Figure 5.14   Xpress DV Toolset menu 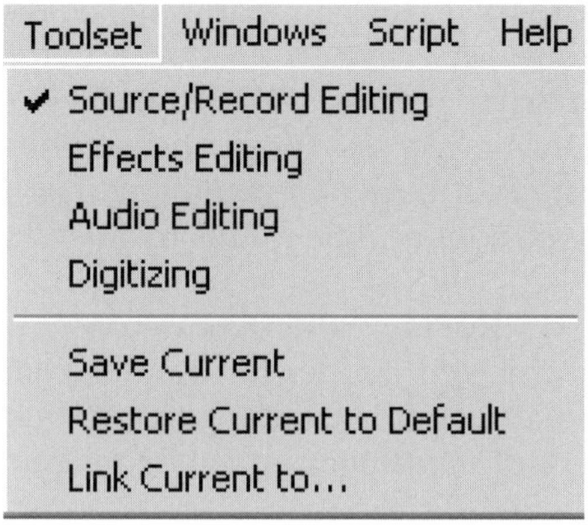   **Figure 5.15**   Media Composer Toolset menu

memorize that configuration. The final step was to assign a single keyboard stroke to instantly recall this setup. The problem was, you had to be a fairly advanced Avid user to know how to do all this. Now Avid has made this power available to all Avid editors. Simply select the Toolset menu item for a particular editing task, and the computer screen instantly displays most, if not all, of the tools you'll need.

What's even better is that you can make changes to the way a particular Toolset works and save your changes with ease.

Basic: This removes the Source and Record Monitors. When you double-click on a clip, it goes into a Pop-up Monitor and not into the Source Monitor. This is the way the Xpress and Xpress DV used to work. The Media Composer always uses the Source and Record Monitors, so it doesn't have a Basic choice.

Color Correction: This opens a tool that allows you to make detailed adjustments to the color of a clip. This tool was originally found on only the most expensive Avid systems and is just now finding its way to the lower-priced models. Surprisingly, the Xpress DV was one of the first systems to get it.

Source/Record Editing: This gives you a Source Monitor and Record Monitor. It's the mode we have been using throughout this book.

Effects Editing: When you select this menu item, the Effects Palette Tool opens, showing you all of the visual effects available to you. The Effect Editor opens as well. The Effect Editor lets you change the way each individual effect works. You might add a border to an effect, change the transparency of an effect, or move the effect around within the Record Monitor. In fact, the Record Monitor changes as well. It no longer shows you the sequence. We'll spend a lot of time working in this mode in Chapter 10.

Audio Editing: This opens the Audio Mix Tool. From the Audio Mix Tool, you can easily open other tools to alter or improve the quality of your sound. Because you are working with clips in the Timeline, you don't need the Source Monitor, just the Timeline and the Record Monitor, so the Source Monitor disappears.

Recording/Digitizing: When you select this editing mode, the Record/ Digitize Tool opens so that you're ready to begin recording or digitizing tapes into the Avid.

Save Current: This lets you change the way the Toolset items are configured and save the changes. This command makes it easy to have it your way. For instance, when I'm in Source/Record Mode I like to have Text View be the default view. So, I simply change the bin view from Frame to Text, and then select Save Current. From then on, that's the way Source/Record will work for me.

Restore Current to Default: Any changes you make to the default setup, using Save Current, gets wiped away if you select this command.

Link Current to: In Chapter 3, we spent some time discussing Settings. We changed the color of the Timeline background, we changed the keyboard settings, and we changed the bin settings. We also learned to duplicate settings and to call the original setting "Default" and the new setting "Mine." With "Link Current to" you can have various settings, name them, and then connect those settings to particular Toolset modes.

WINDOWS MENU

I don't use the Windows menu much. I don't usually want to close all of my bins, and Home is one of those commands that seems to change the appearance of my Avid in ways I don't like.

Close All: This closes all of your bins. If you have a sequence loaded in the Record Monitor, it will disappear, as will your Timeline. I never use this command because I don't like what happens when I use it.

Home: This works on whatever window is active. I don't like having my Timeline or Source and Record Monitors messed with, so I avoid this command. If you do happen to select it, and don't like what you see, go to the Toolset menu and choose Source/Record Editing.

SCRIPT MENU

Script Integration is based on the style of editing commonly used on feature films. It's one of Avid's most powerful features and needs an entire chapter to adequately explain. We'll tackle all of its many features in Chapter 15.

HELP MENU

The Avid offers an online reference tool, in the form of a directory listing hundreds of items. If you're stuck and can't figure out how to do something, scroll through the entries until you find Avid's explanation.

TRACKING AND MONITOR MENUS

Above the Source/Pop-up Monitor and Record Monitor there is a bar that displays information about your project. It also contains pull-down menus. Try selecting and dragging the different menus to see what information they display and the options you have for displaying the information.

Tracking Menu

The Tracking menu provides information in timecode format about your clip or sequence. There's one for the Source Monitor, which gives information about the clip, and one for the Record Monitor, which gives information about the sequence. This tracking information is updated continuously as you play either the source material or the sequence. When you drag and select one of the choices from the menu, that choice will be displayed in the tracking information display, above the monitor. In Figure 5.16, the I/O has been selected, and the check mark confirms the choice. Let's look at all of the choices.

Mas: This displays what is called the *master timecode* at the point where the position indicator is currently located. Let's say a sequence's starting timecode is set at 00;00;00;00. As you can see in Figure 5.16, we are stopped

Figure 5.16 Tracking menu

at a frame that is 1 minute, 6 seconds, and 23 frames after the first frame of the sequence.

Dur: This displays the total duration of the sequence (or clip).

I/O: This displays the duration between your IN and OUT marks. Very handy.

Abs: This number displays the running time of the sequence, from the first frame to the position indicator.

Rem: This displays the time remaining from the position indicator to the end of the sequence.

TC: These are the timecode numbers for the various tracks in the Timeline at the point where the position indicator is located.

Clip Name: This provides a submenu of the clip names for each track in the Timeline at the point where the position indicator is located.

None: With this chosen, no tracking information will be displayed.

Monitor Menu

Both the Source and Record Monitors have a Monitor menu (Figures 5.17 and 5.18). Just click on the name of the clip in the Source Monitor or the name of the sequence in the Record Monitor to open the Monitor menu.

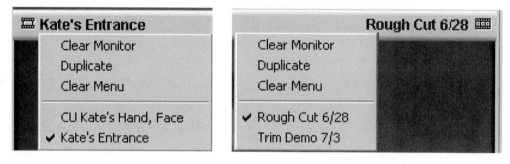

Figure 5.17 Source Monitor menu   **Figure 5.18** Record Monitor menu

Clear Monitor: This clears the clips or sequences from the monitor. The monitor screen goes black, and the Timeline is empty; however, all of the clips or sequences are still loaded.

Duplicate: This duplicates the clip or marked segment.

Clipboard Contents: (Media Composer only) When you save something to the Clipboard, it appears as a Pop-up Monitor when you select Clipboard from the Tools menu. The Media Composer also places it here. It is available as a source clip.

Add Comments: (Media Composer only) You can add comments to a clip, and they will appear in an EDL, as well as in the Timeline if Comments is selected.

Load Filler: (Media Composer only) This loads filler into the Source Monitor. On the Xpress, this feature is located on the Clip menu.

Clear Menu: This removes all but the current sequence or clip from the Monitor menu.

Clip/Sequence List: Below the Clear Menu item, you'll find a list of all the shots in the Source Monitor or all the sequences that have been loaded into the Record Monitor.

Whew! We have spent considerable time and energy trying to digest the scores of commands located in the pull-down menus that are at the heart of Avid editing. We now have a much better sense of the Avid's rich working environment, and we've had a preview of the work we'll be doing from here on in. We also know where we can find the commands we'll need to do different sorts of tasks. You may never use some of these commands, whereas others will be in your repertoire continually. Whenever keyboard equivalents are listed in the menu, try learning them, because they will speed up your work considerably.

MAPPING MENU ITEMS

You can place any command located on any menu onto any key on the keyboard or onto any of the command buttons. Holding down the Shift key on the keyboard opens up lots of unassigned keys that can be used to hold menu commands. Let's try it. We're going to place the Clip menu item "Render In/Out" on the Shift-R key. We won't use this item until we get to Chapter 10, when we have effects to render.

1. In your Timeline, mark an IN and an OUT (this makes the menu item "Render In/Out" active).
2. Open your keyboard in the Settings window—the one we created in Chapter 3.
3. Get the Command Palette from the Tools menu.
4. Select the Menu to Button Reassignment box on the Command Palette—it doesn't matter which tab you select. Notice the mouse cursor looks like a white menu.

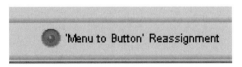

5. On the real keyboard, hold down the Shift key. Now click on the R-key on the keyboard on the computer monitor, so it turns lighter—almost white.
6. From the Clip menu, select Render In/Out. You'll see something jump down to the keyboard.
7. Close the Command Palette.

The initials RI should appear on the Shift-R key. Again, we won't need this tool until we get to Chapter 10. You can close the keyboard now.

Remember, you can place any menu item on any button or keyboard key. Let's wait to map other menu commands until we're more familiar with all of the menu items.

SUGGESTED ASSIGNMENTS

1. Hold a screening of your edited scene, taking notes of the various suggestions.
2. Duplicate the sequence.
3. Make changes to the new version of the sequence.
4. Compare your old version with the one that is based on the feedback you received.

6

Recording/Digitizing

Now that we've finished cutting "Wanna Trade," it's time to move on to new material. It is my suggestion that you now work on documentary footage or a public service announcement (PSA). Avid used to supply footage for a PSA about saving the rain forest, and if that's available, this is a good time to work with it. If it's not available, any documentary footage with voice-over narration and music will work. Many of the techniques we will introduce in the next few chapters work nicely with visual footage and narration. A script-based, dramatic scene with sync dialog, like "Wanna Trade," is great for introducing you to the Avid basics, but as we move on to more complex tools, documentary material is best for showing off these features.

STARTING A NEW PROJECT

When you double-click on the Media Composer or Xpress icon, you are launching the Avid software. Soon the Avid brings up a dialog box that asks you to let the Avid know which project you will be editing (Figure 6.1). One column lists all of the projects that are currently in postproduction on the machine. Some Avids offer a second column, listing all the different editors on the machine. There will be a New User button, and you can register as an editor by clicking on the button and typing your name.

If you are going to start a new project, one that the Avid has never dealt with before, you must first decide if you want others to be able to work on this project (Shared) or if you want to restrict access (Private). Once you've made that decision, you press the New Project button. A dialog box appears, giving you a chance to name the project and to provide the Avid with information about the type of project you'll be starting (Figure 6.2). The name of the project is often the title or working title; you just type the name. Before clicking OK, check to make sure that the other choices are correct. Is it a PAL

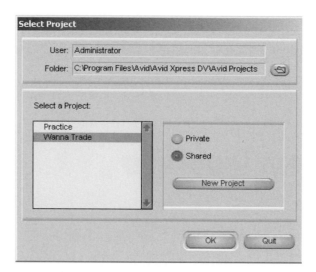

Figure 6.1 Select Project dialog box

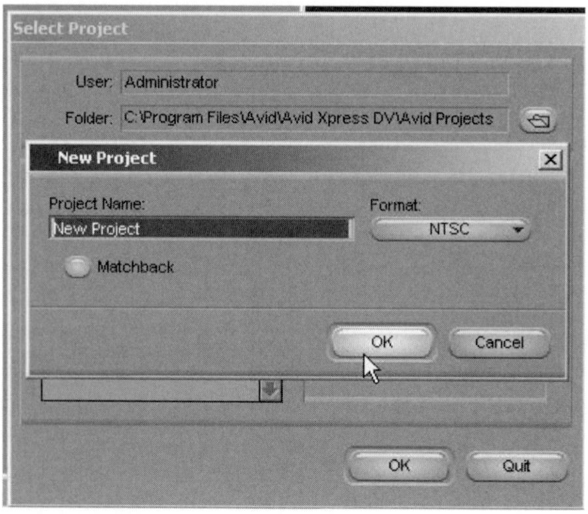

Figure 6.2

or NTSC project? If you're working in the United States, it's NTSC. PAL is a television system common in Europe and many other parts of the world. There are many important differences between the two formats; the Avid can accommodate either one, as long as it knows with which it is dealing.

Depending on your version of Avid software, you might have other boxes to check. For instance, some Avids are equipped with *matchback* software for those editing 16 mm or 35 mm film that has been transferred to video. The Avid can generate a list that describes where to cut the original film. We will discuss this process at length in Chapter 17. Some Media Composers can run at 24 frames per second, to match the running speed of a feature film or a 24P high-definition television (HDTV) project. If your Avid has that capability, it will be listed as an option here.

Once all of the boxes are selected, click OK. You are returned to the Select Project window, and you select the newly created project and click OK. Now the Avid brings you to the Project window for that project. From now on, this new project will appear in the Select Project window.

GETTING YOUR TAPES INTO THE COMPUTER

To take advantage of all of the Avid's digital editing capabilities, you must first get your material into the Avid. How this is accomplished depends on two factors: the tape format you've used and your Avid's video capture board.

Tape Formats—Digital and Analog

The videotape world is divided into two parts: digital videotape and analog videotape. In the analog world, Hi-8 and S-VHS are popular formats. VHS is still in use, and there are millions of VHS decks in homes throughout the world. Betacam SP is a high-quality analog format, which has long been an industry standard for professional video. During much of the 1980s and 1990s, most television news and documentaries were shot on Betacam SP, but the world is rapidly moving from analog to digital tape.

There are several professional digital videotape formats. I won't list them all, just several of the more popular ones:

Digital Betacam
D-1
D-5
DV, including: Mini DV
                  DVCAM
                  DVCPRO
DVCPRO50

Digital Betacam became the format of choice in the mid-1990s because of its high quality and reasonable cost. Today, people are starting to choose from among the high-definition digital formats, such as HDCAM.

The DV Format

The growth of the digital video (DV) format is fairly astounding. Introduced in 1995, it has taken the world by storm. Although it was originally seen as a "pro-sumer" format, professionals quickly adopted it for use in demanding situations, when they couldn't bring in large, heavy gear, and they discovered it could handle everyday tasks as well. DVCAM and DVCPRO offer better quality than mini DV, and given a choice, you should always pick them over mini DV. They run the tape faster, and the tracks that hold the digital data are wider. Feature films, network television programs, and nightly news stories have all been shot using the DV format.

That's not to say that the DV format's quality is equal to a professional format such as Digital Betacam. Almost all of the digital formats involve some form of compression. DV systems compress the video signal using a compression ratio of 5:1 versus Digital Betacam's 2:1. DV's sampling ratio (comparing the luminance with the color ratio) is 4:1:1 (NTSC) compared with Digital Betacam's superior 4:2:2. But for the price there is no comparison. The DV format wins hands down.

VIDEO CAPTURE BOARDS

The kind of *video capture board* inside your Avid determines the kind of tapes you can bring into your Avid. If you have an Xpress DV, you're using an IEEE 1394 capture board (FireWire/iLink), and it is designed to handle DV tapes. With FireWire, you aren't digitizing because you're bringing in a signal that is already digital. So instead of digitizing your tapes, you are recording them to the Avid. To bring in other kinds of tape into your Xpress DV you can purchase a transcoder, also called a *media converter*, which converts other formats to DV. You could bring in an analog tape, such as VHS or Beta SP, or a digital tape, such as Digital Betacam. Keep in mind that whatever format you bring in through a transcoder will have the specifications of DV. A number of decks can function as transcoders.

The *Avid Broadcast Video Board* (ABVB) was the most popular board through 1999. It has been supplanted by the *Meridien board*. The ABVB can digitize either analog tape or digital tape. What makes the Meridien board so special is that it can easily digitize analog *and* digital signals. You can just as easily digitize a Beta SP (analog) tape as a Digital Betacam (digital) tape.

The latest versions of the Avid Media Composer and Xpress have as an option a standard IEEE 1394 (FireWire) connection, so you can now bring a DV project into a Media Composer or Xpress without losing image quality. Before this, neither the ABVB nor the Meridien board could easily handle DV tapes.

CONNECTING YOUR EQUIPMENT

To record/digitize the picture and sound, you need to run cables from your tape deck to your Avid video and audio capture boards. Most likely, the cables have been connected for you. All you need to do is turn on the power to the deck, boot the Avid, and insert your tape. But let's take a minute to examine the cables going from your deck to your computer's CPU.

With the Xpress DV, you need concern yourself with only one cable—the FireWire cable. This cable will control the deck, or camera, and carry both the digital picture and sound. The same cable is used later to send the digital signal out of the Avid to your camera or deck for putting your finished project out to tape. You plug one end of the FireWire cable into the FireWire connection on the back of your computer and the other end into the video deck or camera.

If you're using a transcoder to bring in tapes from formats other than DV, you'll run the FireWire cable from the transcoder to the computer. But now you'll have additional cables to hook up, including audio and video cables that run from those tape decks to the transcoder.

Media Composer and Xpress editors using the Meridien or ABVB boards usually have a fair number of cables to connect. Let's say you're using a standard analog videotape deck, such as a Beta SP deck or VHS deck. Let's start with the audio. On the back of the tape deck there are connections for Input and for Output. Because we are sending the signal from the tape deck to the Avid, you would connect the audio cables to the deck's Output. These audio cables could go either into a mixing board, and from there to the Avid's Audio In for digitizing, or directly to the Avid's Audio In.

The video signal from the tape deck could come in one of two forms: (1) The video signal's luminance (brightness) and chrominance (color) could be combined as one signal, called a *composite* signal; or (2) the video signal could be split, so that one channel holds the luminance (Y), and chrominance is separated into red (R-Y) and blue (B-Y) signals. This system is called *component*. Component video is a professional signal, whereas composite video is associated with consumer products such as Hi-8, S-VHS, and VHS. If you were using a Betacam SP deck, you would take the cable marked Video In (because the video signal is going in to the Avid's video capture board) and plug its three BNC connectors into the tape deck's three Video Output connectors.

If you have a Meridien board, an external Input/Output (I/O) box makes the connections much easier. On the back of the box there are connections for component and composite, as well as for S-video and serial digital video. Those who have purchased the DV option would have a FireWire connection as well.

Media Composer and Xpress users have one more cable to hook up; it's called the *Serial Deck Control cable*, often called the *serial control*. You connect this cable to the videotape deck's nine-pin D connector, usually labeled Remote or Remote In/Out. The other end is usually connected to the CPU's modem (eight-pin DIN) or printer port. Once this cable is connected, you can play, fast-forward, rewind, and even eject tapes using the Digitize Tool on the Avid.

The Xpress DV doesn't need this cable because the same FireWire cable that brings in the picture and sound also gives the Avid control of the camera or video deck.

IMAGE RESOLUTION

In some ways, Xpress DV editors have an easier time starting a new project because they don't have to deal with the issue of image resolution. They will edit the material at the same image resolution that it was shot. Media Composer and Xpress editors must decide whether to bring the video signal in at the highest resolution (most beautiful image quality) or at some resolution that sacrifices image quality. One key factor in making this decision is storage space on their media drives.

If you have a lot of source material—hours and hours of tapes—and you want to have all of the footage available to you, then you will be willing to sacrifice image quality. Usually you do this knowing that after you finish editing, you can redigitize the finished sequence at the highest image quality. If you have a lot of storage space on the media drives, and only several minutes of material, then you may decide to digitize the material at the highest resolution to save time.

When the Avid digitizes video, it usually *compresses* the signal. Compressing your video is a bit like packing a suitcase; you can't get it all to fit, so you start tossing things out. If you have a big suitcase (media drive), you don't have to toss much out. But if you have a small suitcase, those wild paisley shirts might not make the trip. When you compress a video signal, you keep a certain percentage of the signal and throw away the rest. Obviously the more signal you throw away, the worse the image looks, but the greater the savings in storage space. Because each frame of video is made up of two fields, one way to save storage space is to digitize only one field. Avid offers single-field resolution (one of the two video fields is tossed out) and two-field resolution (both fields are digitized).

The Meridien board describes image resolution as a ratio (Figure 6.3). A ratio of 1:1 is full, noncompressed video. A ratio of 20:1 indicates a lot of compression. Choosing a ratio of 15:1s would mean you could store the most footage possible on the drives because not only is there a lot of compression, but one of the two video fields is missing.

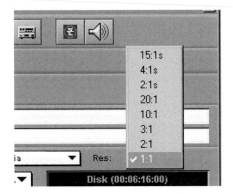

Figure 6.3   Resolution choices offered on an Avid with a Meridien board

Let's look at the following chart to see how resolution affects storage space on the media drive. The numbers in the table come from an Avid specifications sheet for the Meridien board.

Minutes per Gigabyte (GB) with 2 audio tracks

15:1s	4:1s	20:1	10:1	2:1	1:1
32.1 min.	10.5 min.	14.1 min.	7.9 min.	1.9 min.	0.8 min.

If you digitized your material at 20:1, and you had a 54 GB storage system, you could digitize more than 12 hours of material; however, if you brought your footage in at 1:1, you could digitize less than 45 minutes of material.

Digitizing Strategies

One thing to consider is that you can mix resolutions, as long as they are compatible. By that I mean you can mix two-field resolutions (such as 20:1 and 2:1) in the same Timeline, and you can mix all of the single-field resolutions in the same Timeline (such as 15:1s and 4:1s), but you can't mix single-field with two-field resolutions. The one exception to this is the 1:1 noncompressed resolution. You can't mix that with anything.

For instance, 2:1 is amazingly high quality. You might use that as your finishing resolution. You might bring in all of your source tapes at 20:1 and all of your graphics at 2:1. Then, when it is time to redigitize the final sequence, you don't need to reimport any of the graphics—they are already at 2:1. You'll simply redigitize all of the clips used in the final sequence, bringing them from 20:1 to 2:1.

Xpress DV Storage Issues

Because the IEEE 1394 signal isn't converted—it stays as a 5:1 compressed digital stream throughout—you can't bring your tapes into the Xpress DV at a lower resolution. The whole process of digitizing the video signal at a low resolution to save drive space and then redigitizing, at a much higher resolution, just those clips used in the final sequence is not an option. DV's compression of 5:1 may seem like a lot of compression, but the DV system uses an extremely clever and sophisticated way of picking what to toss out and how to encode what's left. Because you can't compress the signal any further—you can't choose a resolution such as 20:1 the way an Xpress or Media Composer editor can—storage space is a real issue. DV takes up 216 Megabytes per minute, so with that in mind, let's look at the following chart to see how much drive space (approximately) you'll need for your projects.

30 minutes	60 minutes	2 hours	6 hours	12 hours
6 GB	12 GB	24 GB	72 GB	144 GB

The good news is that FireWire drives are inexpensive compared with the SCSI drives needed to handle the 2:1 and 1:1 ratios used in the Xpress and Media Composer systems. You can purchase a pair of 80 GB FireWire drives for less than $500. You can also use SCSI drives to store your DV signal, but you don't have to.

AUDIO

The latest versions of Avid's software handle three different types of audio files: SD2, WAVE, and AIFF-C. Sound Designer II (SD2) is a sound format for Macintosh computers, and WAVE is a Windows-based format. Audio Interchange File Format, often called *AIFF-C*, works well with either system. That's the audio file format you should choose in the Audio Project Settings window whenever you begin a new project because it's the easiest to format to move to another application or system.

Audio Sampling

When analog audio is digitized, the signal is sampled and then converted to digital information. *Sampling* means that not all of the sound is converted, but a representative sample of it is. The more samples that are taken, the better the fidelity, or faithfulness, to the original analog signal. When you're bringing in audio from an analog tape, such as a Beta SP, the Avid gives you a choice about which sampling rate you would like to use. The choices are 32 kHz, 44.1 kHz, or 48 kHz. Compact discs use 44.1 kHz as their sample rate, so you can see that 48 kHz is high quality.

With digital tapes, the sample rate is determined by the camera. Many digital cameras let you choose the sample rate before you shoot, so set it on the highest rate available. Don't assume it's set on the one you want.

In the Avid's Settings window, you can select the sample rate for your project or tape. If you're bringing in an analog tape, I suggest you use 48 kHz. With digital tapes you want to choose the sample rate of the tape you'll be recording. These days, that's probably 48 kHz. To set the sample rate, double-click on Audio Project Settings in the Settings window (Figure 6.4), and select your sample rate. Xpress DV users, examine Figure 6.4. Make sure the Sample Rate Setting is correct and the Input Source is set at OHCI, not Line In or Internal microphone.

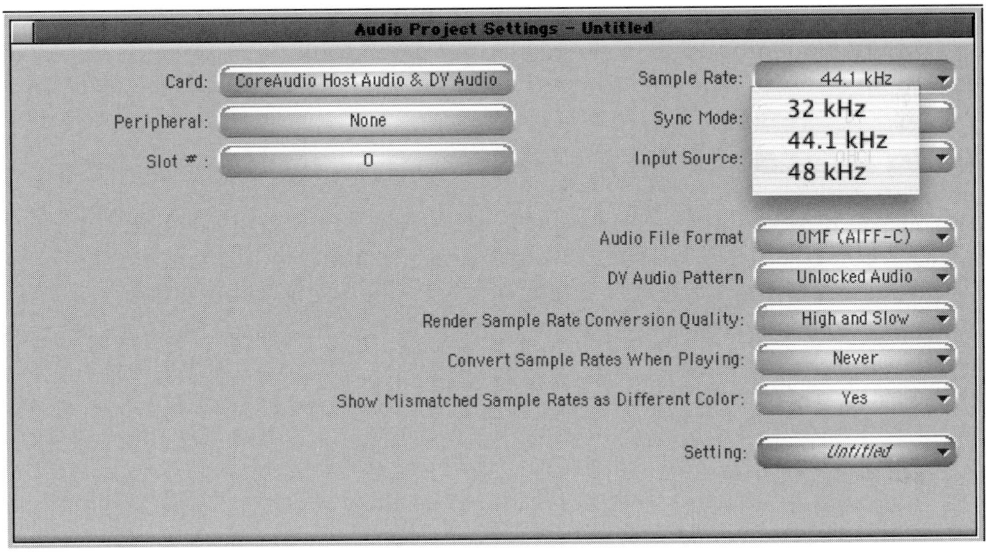

Figure 6.4

Sound takes up a fraction of the storage space needed by video—really it's almost insignificant—so you don't have to worry about running out of media drive space whenever you digitize sound.

GETTING ORGANIZED

After you have gathered together your source tapes and decided on an appropriate resolution, you should come up with a system for naming the tapes. In a way, you might want to consider your system of naming tapes even before you start shooting, so the name you give the tape in the field is the same name you give it when digitizing. One of the worst mistakes you can make when digitizing is to give two tapes the same name.

Your naming system need not be complicated. My suggestion is that whenever you begin a new project, you simply call the first tape *001*. The second tape is *002*. Because the Avid knows which project you are working on, you don't have to include the project name with the tape. So you need not type Wanna Trade 001. Just 001. Keep it simple.

Remote/Local

Most decks have a switch or button labeled "Local/Remote." In Local mode, you can press the deck's controls to play, stop, and rewind the tape. In Remote mode, you no longer have control of the deck's functions, but this is the mode the Avid will need to control the deck. Media Composer and Xpress users, make sure you place the deck in Remote.

Many DV decks have this switch, but the Xpress DV's Record Tool can operate in either Local or Remote.

Xpress DV—Connecting a Camera or Deck for the First Time

Avid uses a Texas Instrument–designed Open Host Controller Interface (OHCI)–compliant IEEE 1394 driver. Normally, you would want to turn on all external devices, such as camera or decks, before you boot the Avid, but that sometimes causes the wrong driver to try to jump in. Start the Xpress DV before you connect a *new* camera or deck. Then, once the Xpress DV software is up and running, plug the FireWire cable into the camera or deck and turn the device on. A dialog box appears, telling you to turn the camera or deck off and then turn it back on. This installs the right driver. Once the camera or deck has been turned off and is back on, click OK. The dialog box closes and you're connected to the right driver.

Organizing Your Bins

Before you begin the actual digitizing process, you must decide into which bin your newly digitized material will go. On film projects, many editors prefer to organize their bins according to what was shot on a given day. All of the tapes from the first day of shooting would go into a bin called *Dailies—Day 1*. On a video project, it makes sense to have a bin for each camera tape. So tape 001 goes into a bin called *Tape 001*. Begin by creating a bin into which clips from the first tape will go. Just click the New Bin button at the top of the Project window, and a new bin will be created. Click on the name the Avid gave it (the name you gave the project) and type Tape 001 or Dailies—Day 1.

Remember, before you open the Record/Digitize Tool, open the bin you want the material to go to and close any other bins that may be open. Make sure the deck you are using is set to *Remote* and not Local. Remote gives control of the deck to the Avid.

OPENING THE RECORD/DIGITIZE TOOL

Open the Record/Digitize Tool either by selecting it from the Tools menu or, better yet, by going to the Toolset menu and choosing Record/Digitize. The Media Composer's Digitize Tool may have more audio track buttons than an Xpress, but they are almost identical. Examine the Record/Digitize Tool's user interface (Figure 6.5). Parts of it look exactly like a video deck. Other parts are logical renditions of the actions they perform.

The buttons on the deck control are self-explanatory. You have buttons for fast rewind, fast forward, stop, pause, play, step one frame backward, and step one frame forward, as well as a slider that acts like a shuttle control. There's even an eject button. There are little triangles for opening and closing sections of the Tool.

LOG OR DIGITIZE

The Record/Digitize Tool has two modes of operation: one for logging the shots and one for digitizing them. When you *log* your tape, you are choosing the shots you want to digitize, marking IN and OUT points, but not digitizing them. Many editors log each tape first and then digitize those clips they selected. Why? Basically it's better to divide your tasks. Concentrate first on selecting the shots to be digitized and then later on performing the digitizing task. In some cases you may find it's better not to log, but to digitize each

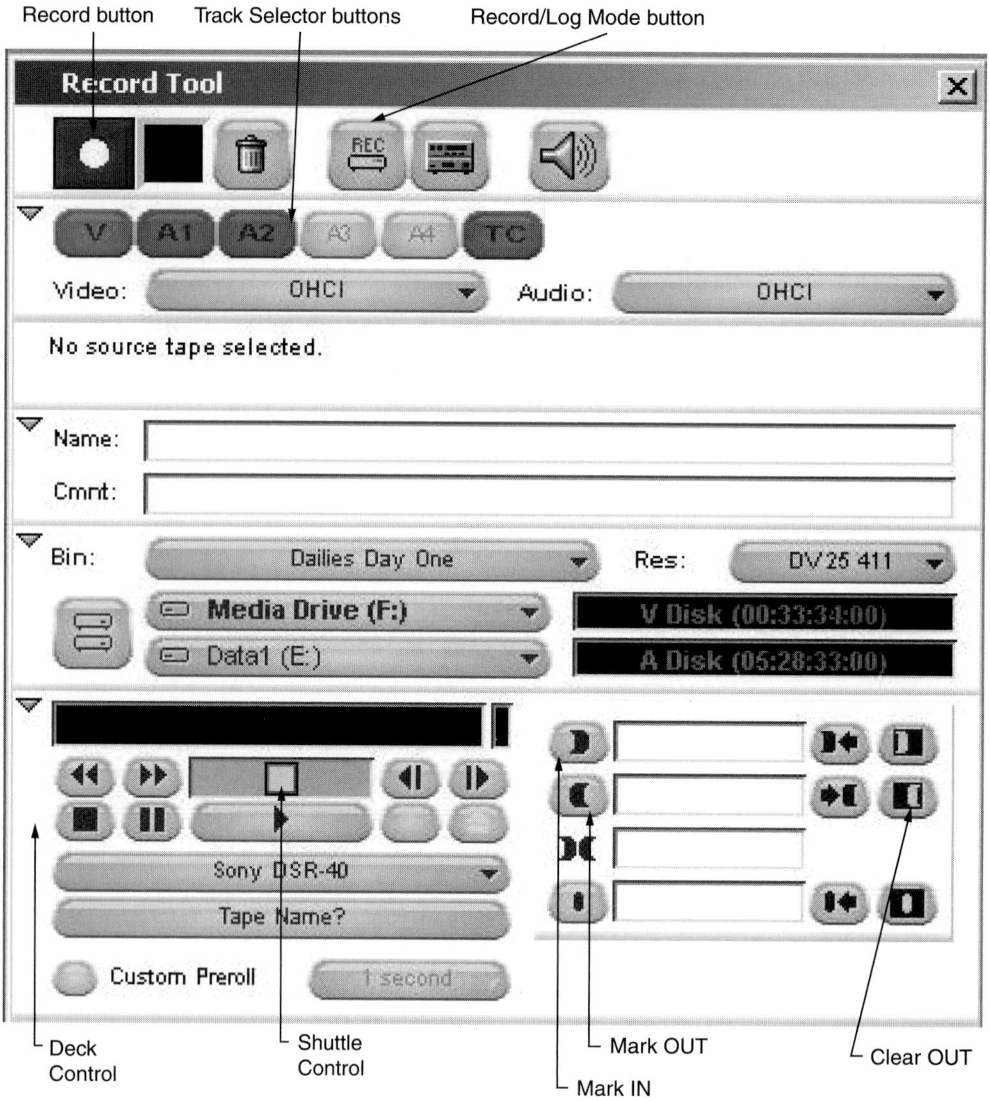

Record button   Track Selector buttons   Record/Log Mode button

Figure 6.5   Record/Digitize Tool

shot on the tape as you come to it. For instance, you may find that the field audio is uneven and one level won't work for the entire tape. In that case you may need to change your audio levels as you digitize each clip, one at a time.

Let's go through the options on the Record/Digitize Tool and set it up to record from a DV tape and to digitize from a Beta SP tape. Both tapes contain picture and two tracks of audio.

CONFIGURING THE RECORD/DIGITIZE TOOL

1. *Select the tracks.* As you can see in Figure 6.6, the video track is selected (V), and the audio tracks A1 and A2 have also been selected. Make sure the timecode (TC) track is selected as well.

Figure 6.6

2. *Select the target bin.* If there are several bins open, the Avid might select the wrong bin.
3. *Select the resolution.* With Xpress DV, your only choice is DV 25. Media Composer and Xpress users go to the resolution pull-down menu and pick from the choices (see Figure 6.3).
4. *Select a target drive.* Your instructor may have assigned you a drive. If not, you'll want to use the drive that has the most space. Go to the drive window (Figure 6.7) and drag down to select the assigned drive or the drive with the most space. That drive is always the darkest drive.

    Make sure that you don't record or digitize any media onto your System (C:) drive (Windows).

Figure 6.7   Drive window

5. *Select Log Mode or Record/Digitize Mode* (Figures 6.8 and 6.9). Press the Log/Record selector button to switch from Record Mode to Log Mode, and vice versa. When you press the button, the tool will switch to Log Mode. Notice that the pencil icon shows that you are in Log Mode.

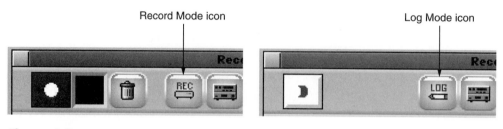

Figure 6.8   Record/Digitize Mode   **Figure 6.9**   Log Mode

6. *Select the type of video signal.* If you're using a Media Composer or Xpress, then you need to open the video tool and select the video signal of your tape. Click on the Video Tool button.

You'll see a window called *Input*. It's a pull-down menu that lists the types of video signals your system can handle. A Meridien system would list Component, Composite, S-Video, and Serial Digital (Figure 6.10). Choose the correct one, depending on the signal you are going to digitize.

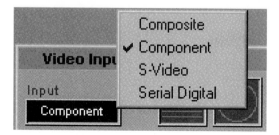

Figure 6.10

The Beta SP tape we are going to digitize is component video, so we'll select Component from the Input window. (If you are digitizing a VHS tape, the signal would be Composite.) Once you have selected Component, you may close the Video Tool by clicking in the tiny Close box.

7. *Insert your first tape into the camera or deck.* A prompt will appear, asking you either to select the tape's name, if a name has already been entered, or to give the tape a new name. Because we haven't named any tapes, you will click on the New button and then type the name 001.

Once you have typed the name, you'd think that you could click OK, but you can't. After typing, you have to click on the tape's icon to highlight the tape name before you can click OK (Figure 6.11).

Now you should have control of the tape through the deck controls on the Record/Digitize Tool. Hit the Play button on the Record/Digitize Tool and the tape plays. Hit the Rewind button and it rewinds. Notice how the tape's timecode appears in the Timecode window, just above the deck controls. You can use the J, K, and L keys as well. You can even shuttle the tape at faster-than-normal speeds by pressing J and L several times.

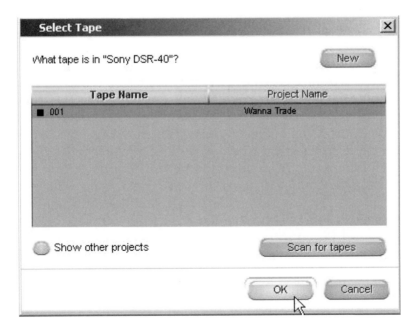

Figure 6.11

IF THE AVID SAYS "NO DECK"

If for some reason your Avid doesn't recognize that a deck or camera is attached, go to the pull-down menu just below the Play button and select Check Decks (Figure 6.12). That should force the Avid to recognize the camera or deck you're using. If that doesn't work, and you've checked to make sure everything is properly connected and you've gone through the checklist of items provided previously, try Auto-configure. Sometimes this wakes the Avid up. Auto-configure forces the Avid to provide you with a generic deck. On the Xpress DV it's called *Generic DVDevice*. This should work.

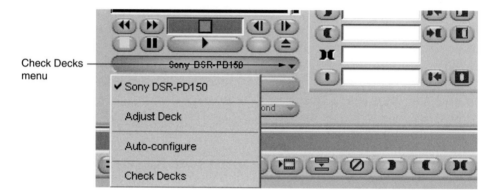

Figure 6.12

WHAT SHOULD HAPPEN

If everything is working correctly, when you press the play button, Xpress DV users should see their tapes play in the Record Monitor. The sound should come out of the speakers inside the computer or the speakers attached to the computer. If you are using a client monitor with an Xpress DV, the picture (and sound) coming from the client monitor will not play in sync with the picture and sound coming from the computer's Record Monitor. Don't be alarmed. The client monitor is hooked up to the video deck, *not* to the Avid, and it takes time for the Avid to buffer the signal. You'll see that once you have recorded the clip into a bin, the sound and picture will play together in sync in the Source and Record Monitors.

Xpress and Media Composer users won't see anything in the Record Monitor as they log or digitize. Instead, their images will play in the client monitor, which gets its signal from the Avid and not from the video deck (as in the Xpress DV system). With the Xpress and Media Composer, the picture in the client monitor and sound coming from the external speakers will be in sync because the computer is sending the signals to both.

Once the clips have been digitized into the Xpress or Media Composer, they will play in the Source and Record Monitors and client monitor. One of the nice features of the Meridien capture board is that whenever you play something in the Source and Record Monitors, it will play in sync with the client monitor. The Xpress DV system can't do that. There's always a delay.

TWO COMMON PROBLEMS

If you're having a problem, remember to select the V1 and/or A1 and A2 tracks on the Record/Digitize Tool. If they are not selected, you won't see or hear anything!

Avid editors digitizing on a Media Composer or Xpress, don't forget to check the correct video input (see Figure 6.10). Remember, in the Video Tool select Component, Composite, S-Video, or Serial Digital. If you aren't getting anywhere, and you've selected the V1 and audio tracks, check this.

XPRESS DV EDITORS—GO TO THE RECORDING PROCESS

Xpress DV users don't need to worry about setting video or audio levels (the next section), so they can proceed to "The Recording Process" on page 156. Aren't they lucky? Or, they can join the rest of us and find out about setting video and audio levels.

SETTING VIDEO AND AUDIO LEVELS

When you digitize video or audio, you want to bring in the signal at its optimal level. You don't want to digitize the audio at a level that is too low, so it's barely audible, or too high, so it overmodulates and breaks up. And you don't want to bring in the video signal so that the picture is too dark or the colors look terrible. To help you bring in the signals at the right levels, the Avid provides you with two tools: the Video Tool and the Audio Tool. You can get these tools from the Tools menu, but they are also on the Digitize Tool deck. Because the Audio Tool is easiest to use, let's start with it. Simply press the speaker icon at the top of the Digitize Tool, and the Audio Tool appears.

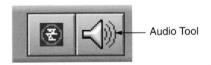
— Audio Tool

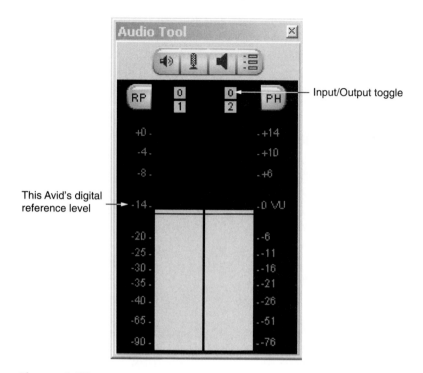

Figure 6.13   Audio Tool

The tracks should be set to I for input. If they are set to O for output, as shown in Figure 6.13, just click on the Input/Output toggle, and they will change to I.

Audio Levels

Setting audio levels on the Avid is similar to setting levels on a tape recorder. The Avid has a Peak Level Meter, which uses green bars instead of a needle to show signal strength and includes both a digital scale (on the left) and an analog VU scale, measuring in decibels. As the tape plays, watch the levels.

Play your tape. If the tape has *color bars* and a *tone* (1000 Hz) at the head of the tape, you should use that tone to set your levels. If there is no tone, play the tape until you come to a sound that best represents what was recorded in the field, and use that as a reference.

If your tape has a 1000-Hz tone, set it to the Avid's reference level. On the one I'm using, it's –14. Other Avids may be set at –20 dB. The reference level is the digital dB signal that's equal to 0 dB on the analog (right-hand) side. That's where the tone should fall.

Your tape deck may be connected to a mixing board, and that's how you adjust the levels. Or you may have some sort of sound panel with knobs to adjust your levels. Depending on your system, you now raise or lower the strength of the signal so that the audio will be digitized at the correct levels.

Once you have set your audio levels, you can move the Audio Tool to the side so that you have room for the Video Tool, or you can close it altogether.

Video Settings

Setting video levels is more complicated than setting audio levels. With video levels you are concerned about the *luminance*, or brightness of the signal, and the *chrominance*, or color of the signal. I'm not going to go into too much detail on this topic because it is beyond the scope of this book. Basically, if the picture looks good, then leave the settings as is; however, if the color is off, or the image appears too light or dark, you can change the levels by adjusting the sliders on the Video Tool.

Let's examine the Video Tool (Figure 6.14). Click on the Video Tool button at the top of the Digitize Tool or select it from the Tools menu.

By clicking on the Waveform Monitor and the Vectorscope icons, you can bring up the Avid's version of these two important tools that are used to measure your signal. The Waveform Monitor measures the luminance of your signal, and the Vectorscope measures the chrominance of your signal.

The standard way to set proper video levels is to play your tape's color bars with the Video Tool open and then adjust the sliders until the Waveform

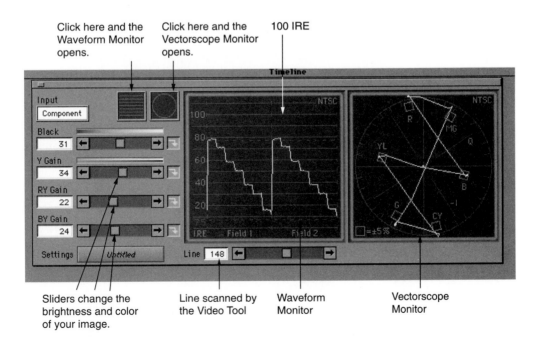

Figure 6.14 Video Tool

Monitor and Vectorscope display the "correct" pattern of lines. As you move the sliders, you'll see the pattern of white lines move and change. There are different types of color bars, but the most common bars in the NTSC world are SMPTE Bars. While playing the SMPTE Bars on your tape, you adjust the luminance of your signal by setting the Line Setting to Line 247 and then moving the Y Gain slider until the bars on the Waveform Monitor reach the 100 IRE line.

You adjust the color of your signal by moving the Line Setting to Line 148 and then moving the RY Gain and BY Gain sliders until the six color vectors fall within the target boxes on the Vectorscope.

We could fill chapters about the correct usage of Vectorscopes and Waveform Monitors. For now, if your tape has bars, try moving the sliders while playing with the color bars and observe the changes that take place. I wouldn't suggest this if the Avid didn't give you a nice feature. See the downward-pointing green arrows (Figure 6.15) next to the Waveform Monitor? As you move the sliders from the factory preset level, the arrow turns gray, showing that the preset levels have been changed. To return to the factory preset levels, simply click on the arrow and the Avid returns the slider to the factory preset level, indicated by the green color. You're back where you started.

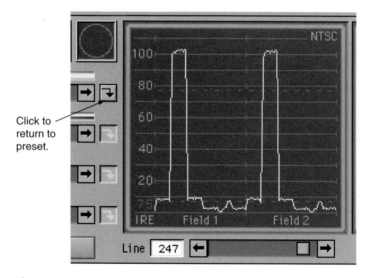

Click to return to preset.

Figure 6.15

THE RECORDING PROCESS

There are three ways to capture your material. We'll examine all three. Keep in mind that your J, K, and L keys work with the Record Tool's deck controls to play, pause, and play at faster-than-standard speed.

Logging

In this method, you log the clips first and then digitize them after they have been logged. With this method, you first go through your tape and select the shots you want to record/digitize by marking IN and OUT points.

1. To get into Log Mode, click the Log/Digitize Mode button. You know you're in Log Mode when the pencil icon appears in place of the red Digitize button.
2. Play the tape using the deck controls. When you come to the first clip you want, go to the beginning and mark an IN. Notice that the timecode of the exact spot you chose is displayed in the window next to the IN marker (Figure 6.16).

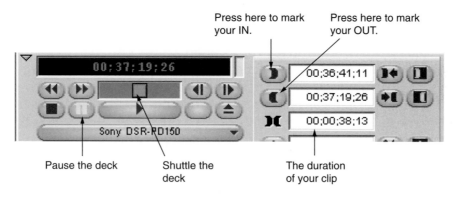

Press here to mark your IN. Press here to mark your OUT.

Pause the deck   Shuttle the deck   The duration of your clip

Figure 6.16

3. Now play the tape until you come to the end of the clip you want. mark an OUT. The timecode for that spot is displayed, as well as the duration of the clip, listed in the IN to OUT window.
4. Pause the deck. Hit the Pause button or "K" on the keyboard.
5. Enter a clip name. Use names that best describe the shot. If the shot is of a man on a ladder, name the clip "Man on Ladder." You can add comments as well.

Name: Man on Ladder
Cmnt: Nice lighting
Bin: Tape 001

6. Now press the Pencil icon, and the shot will be logged in the bin. Several of the latest versions of the Avid will pause the deck or

camera as soon as you mark your OUT, giving you time to type a name for the clip. After you press the Pencil icon, it will start playing the tape again. If you need more time and want to stop the Avid, press the pause button or the spacebar.

7. Repeat steps 1 to 6 to log all of your shots.

Batch Digitizing Your Logged Clips

Once you have logged all of the clips on the tape, you're ready to *batch record/digitize*. Do not log another tape until you have recorded all of the clips on this tape.

1. Select all of the clips in the bin. Hit Command-A (Mac) or Ctrl-A (Windows) to select all of the clips, or lasso the clips, or Shift-click all of the clips, or go to the Edit menu and choose Select All.
2. If you're on a Media Composer, go to the Clip menu and select Batch Digitize. If you're on an Xpress or an Xpress DV, go to the Bin menu and select Batch Record/Digitize.

A dialog box will appear. Because you have no media, it doesn't matter whether you check the button "Offline media only," but later on you'll want this box selected, so get in the habit of checking it. Then click OK.

The Avid will rewind the tape to the first clip, find the IN point, roll back a few seconds for preroll, and then begin recording/digitizing. It will stop when it reaches your OUT point. After digitizing the first clip, it will go to the IN of the second clip on the tape and record it. You can watch the bin and see the progress the Avid is making as it records each clip.

Recording/Digitizing Each Clip As You Mark It

If you have only a couple of clips from a tape or you need to change audio levels or video levels because different sections of the tape need different kinds of correction, recording/digitizing each clip as you mark it is the method that will work best for you. With this method, you mark the clip and then digitize it before going to the next clip.

To get into the Record/Digitize Mode, click the Log/Record Mode button. You'll know you're in Record Mode when the big red Record button replaces the pencil icon.

Now:

1. Play the tape using the deck control, and mark an IN.
2. Play the tape using the deck control, and mark an OUT.
3. Hit the large Record/Digitize button, and it will flash red as it digitizes the clip.
4. Name the clip in the bin.
5. Repeat the previous steps to digitize all shots.

You can abort the recording process while it is in progress by clicking on the Trash icon.

To save time, you can actually type the clip's name without waiting for the digitizing to end. Just start typing as soon as the Record button flashes. When the clip has been recorded, the name you typed will appear in the bin. Press the Tab key to enter comments.

Recording/Digitizing "On-the-Fly"

When you use this method, you don't bother using the Mark IN or Mark OUT controls. You simply digitize various portions of the tape as you play it.

To get into the Record Mode, click the Log/Record Mode button. You'll know you're in Record Mode when the big red Record button replaces the pencil icon.

Now:

1. Play the tape using the deck control, and press the large Record button as you approach the material you want (the IN). The red button will flash to show you that it is recording material.
2. When you reach the end of the segment of the tape you want (the OUT), press the large Record button again.
3. Repeat the previous steps to record all of the material on the tape.

You can abort the recording process while it is in progress by hitting the Trash icon.

If you use this Recording/Digitizing on-the-fly method with material that has timecode, the Avid will provide IN and OUT points determined by the point on the tape where you pressed the Record/Digitize button to start or stop the digitize process.

I often use this Recording/Digitizing on-the-fly method whenever my IN point is too close to a timecode break. The Avid often needs 5 seconds of preroll to batch record a clip. If there aren't 5 seconds, the Avid chokes when trying to preroll. So I play the tape, wait until the Avid is across the timecode break, and then I press the Record button.

DIGITIZING MATERIAL WITHOUT TIMECODE

Without timecode the Avid can't control the deck, and it can't remember IN and OUT marks if no timecode exists. That doesn't mean the Avid can't digitize the tape, it just means that the material will not have timecode associated with it. For instance, the Avid can't control a Nagra 4.2 tape recorder or a VHS or 8 mm deck, and it can't control cameras hooked directly to it, unless they are DV cameras and you have a FireWire connection on your camera and computer. But you can still bring that material into the Avid. The problem is that if the media file is ever lost or erased, there's no way to batch digitize the clip and retrieve it.

Let's say you shot footage on a Hi-8 camera. You can connect the camera to the Avid by connecting the Avid's yellow CV In cable (Composite Video) to the camera. If you need an adapter, such as a BNC connector, on one end and your camera's Video Out connector on the other, go to Radio Shack and they'll probably have it. While you're there, you may need to pick up audio connectors so that you can send the camera's audio into your mixing board or Audio In.

Now bring up the Digitize Tool (Figure 6.17). Because the Avid can't control the camera or deck, you need to configure the tool a bit differently.

Deck Control button

Figure 6.17

Press the Deck Control button and you'll notice that a "you can't do that" line appears across the picture of the deck. Once in this mode, the Digitize Tool changes appearance. Your deck controls disappear. To name the tape, press the Tape Name button at the bottom of the Record/Digitize Tool. It's probably flashing. The Tape Name dialog box appears, and you give the tape a name.

Because you are not bringing in timecode, the TC track is missing from the Record/Digitize Tool. But make sure the correct video and audio tracks are selected. Because the Avid can't redigitize this footage at a higher resolution after editing (because there's no timecode), you'll want to bring the footage in at a high resolution, such as 2:1 or 1:1. (Xpress DV users have only one resolution, so it's not an issue.)

If you're capturing a videotape, bring up the Video Tool and switch to Composite Video. Your only choice is to record on-the-fly. You can't mark IN or OUT points. Instead, play the tape using the camera's (or deck's) controls. When you reach a section you want, hit the Record/Digitize button and begin the recording process. When you reach the end, hit the button again. Now go in the bin and name the clip. Keep doing this until you've captured all of the material you want.

Once the material is digitized, it behaves just like any other digitized material. In fact, the Avid will provide fake timecode as it records the material. Don't be fooled. The numbers have no relation to your video or audio.

SOME USEFUL SETTINGS

In Chapter 3 we discussed settings. It may have been helpful if I had talked about several useful settings that pertain to recording and digitizing at the beginning of this chapter, rather than at the end, but I really didn't want to overwhelm you with information. When I first learned how to use the Avid, I found this whole business a bit confusing, so I'm sensitive to the quantity of information involved. But perhaps you're a quicker learner than I am. Let's look at some useful settings. Remember, in the Project window, click on Settings and then double-click on the name of the setting you want to change. Here are some recommendations:

Audio: Select "All Tracks Centered." Dialog and narration should be centered. Music should be Left and Right. If you are bringing in the spoken word, this is the setting you want. If you're bringing in music, change it back to "Alternating L/R."

Audio Project: Select the sample rate of the tapes you're going to record or digitize. Pull down the Audio File Format menu and select OMF (AIFF-C). This gives you more flexibility if you want to move your audio files to another system.

Media Creation: Under the Record tab, select your media drive and then select "Apply to All." This way, all of your master clips, titles, and motion effects will go to your media drive.

Video Display Settings:
- Select "DV Device supports digital video input." If you have a client monitor, select "Send video to DV device."
- Select "High Quality (fewer simultaneous effects)." Otherwise the image looks out of focus on your Source and Record Monitors.

Record:

- General tab, select "Force unique clip names." This makes sure you don't end up with five clips having the same name.
- General tab, deselect "Pause Deck While Logging."

The last one, "Pause Deck While Logging," is deselected because I don't like having the deck pause while I'm logging. When I log, I like to mark an IN. Then I play the tape and as I approach the end of the shot, I keep clicking on the Mark OUT button—many times. The OUT point will keep changing as the shot plays and I keep clicking. Then, even if I set the last OUT just past the shot, there's no need to rewind and mark an exact OUT because my last click was close enough. With "Pause Deck While Logging" selected, I can't do that. As soon as I press the first OUT mark, the deck pauses. It drives me crazy. I want to keep changing my OUT and then, when I'm satisfied, stop the deck myself.

You can change any of these settings at any time. There are many other settings, but that's enough for now. We'll get deeper into the Settings window in later chapters.

SUGGESTED ASSIGNMENTS

1. Create a new project, create a new bin, and then open the Record/Digitize tool.
2. Name your source tape.
3. Media Composer and Xpress users, set the video levels using the Video Tool. Set the audio levels using the Audio Tool.
4. Record five clips from the tape by marking IN and OUT points and then digitizing. Name the clips in the bin.
5. Log five clips into the bin. Now, batch record/digitize the clips into the bin.
6. Record/Digitize five clips on-the-fly. Name the clips in the bin.

7

Sound

THE IMPORTANCE OF SOUND

Many videomakers and filmmakers don't realize just how important sound is to the success of a project. "It's a visual medium," is the common wisdom handed down as gospel. Well, half right is better than all wrong.

I've organized several film festivals and served as a judge at others, and although I've often been amazed by the stunning cinematography on display in student projects, just as often I've been dismayed by the poor quality of the sound. I think what separates a student project from a professional project is the lack of care that students give to their sound tracks.

On most films and videos, the only sound you care about during shooting is the sync sound—the dialog or words spoken by the subject(s). A good sound recordist works really hard *not* to record the ambient sounds (e.g., the traffic, people in the background, footsteps). Yes, ambient sounds are vitally important, but you add them during editing.

If, for example, you record the hum of an air conditioner on your dialog track, it's very difficult to remove; however, if you turn the air conditioner off just before shooting, you have much clearer dialog. If the air conditioner's hum is important to the story, you can always tape the hum separately and add it to your scene during editing. That way you can adjust the relative levels of the dialog and air conditioner.

Most sounds are added to films and videos after the picture and dialog have been edited. This stage is often called *picture lock*. Once picture lock is reached, sound editors begin finding and creating the sound effects that were kept out during shooting. Often, sound editors must invent sounds. What does a dinosaur sound like? What sound does Darth Maul's laser sword make? Sound designers and sound editors like Walter Murch (*The Conversation, Apocalypse Now*), Cecelia Hall (*Witness, Top Gun, Wayne's World*), and

Gary Rydstrom (*Terminator 2, Jurassic Park*) deserve as much credit for the success of the films they've worked on as the cinematographers who shot the films because so much of the emotional impact comes from the sound track. Film is shot. Sound is built one layer at a time during editing.

Although the Avid is known for its ability to cut pictures, you'll soon realize that's only half the story. The Avid gives you tremendous control over your sound tracks. Take advantage of that capability. It'll make a huge difference in the success of your work.

TRACK MONITORS

The tiny speaker-shaped icons next to the Track Selector boxes show you that a track is being monitored. These are called *Track Monitors*. If you click on a Track Monitor, the icon inside it will disappear, indicating that you won't hear any sound from that track. To get the icon back, simply click in the Track Monitor and the speaker reappears. Examine Figure 7.1.

Figure 7.1   Track Monitor icon for A1 is present, while A2 is turned off.

Monitoring Only One Track

Let's say you are monitoring eight tracks and you hear a sound glitch, but you aren't sure which track it's on. You think the problem is on the narration track A1, but you aren't sure. One way to monitor just A1 is to deselect all of the other Record Track Monitors; however, if there are eight of them, that's a pain. There's a fast way of monitoring one track.

- Hold down the Command key (Mac) or Ctrl key (Windows) and click on that track's monitor. The indicator box turns *green* to show that this is the only track "on." All of the other tracks are off (Figure 7.2).

This will turn green and solo the track.

Figure 7.2

To return to monitoring all of your tracks, simply click in the Track Monitor and it will no longer be soloed. You can solo more than one track by Command/Ctrl-clicking multiple Track Monitors.

The Hollow Speaker Icon

If you look at Figure 7.3, the speaker icons for track A1 and A2 are hollow. They're also gold, although it's a bit hard to pick that up from the black-and-white screen capture. The speaker icon for track A3 is neither hollow nor gold.

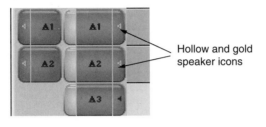

Hollow and gold
speaker icons

Figure 7.3

The tracks with the hollow (and gold) speaker icon are special. Those are the tracks you are listening to when you play the sequence at speeds faster than normal (30 fps) or when you "scrub" your audio.

AUDIO SCRUB

"Scrubbing" the audio is a technique used to concentrate on a particular piece of audio. You scrub it. There are two types of audio scrub: smooth audio scrub and digital audio scrub. Smooth audio scrub is simple:

- Hold down the K key (pause) while pressing the L key (forward). You hear what's on the hollow icon tracks in slow motion. It works backward as well. Use the J key.

Digital audio scrub involves sampling a frame of audio. Because it's sampled, the pitch and speed don't change.

1. Select the tracks you want to scrub.
2. Press the Caps Lock key or hold down the Shift key.
3. Step forward or backward by clicking the Step-one-frame forward or Step-one-frame backward button, or drag the position indicator forward or backward.

This is great for locating a specific sound that will become your cut point. Say you're searching in the Timeline for the first frame of a hammer striking a nail. Click on the Caps Lock button and press the Step-one-frame forward button. (Pretend it's five frames away.) Step, step, step, step, step—*CRUNCH.* Ah, there it is.

Selecting the Tracks for Scrubbing

Now, let's say the hollow icons are on tracks A1 and A2, and the sound you want to scrub is on tracks A3 and A4. To move the hollow speaker icon to track A3, simply hold the Option (Alt) key and then click on the A3 speaker icon. A3 is now the track with the hollow icon. Now, Option (Alt)-click on A4. Remember: Option-click (or Alt-click) on the speaker icon(s) you want to scrub.

ADDING AUDIO TRACKS

In the later stages of editing, you will want to add sound effects and music to your sequence. Those sounds need their own sound tracks; you don't want them messing up your sync dialog tracks. To create additional tracks:

- Go to the Clip menu and select New Audio Track, *or*
- Press Command-U (Mac) or Ctrl-U (Windows).

SCROLLING YOUR TRACKS

Whenever you have more tracks than can be viewed in the Timeline, a scroll bar appears on the right-hand side of the Timeline so that you can scroll up and down to see different tracks. I often resize the tracks I'm not working with, making them smaller, so I can see more tracks without having to scroll.

PATCHING AUDIO TRACKS

When you want to splice or overwrite a shot of video, it usually goes onto the V1 track. Your sync sound—the sounds that come with that video—usually goes onto A1 or, if you have stereo sync sound, onto A1 and A2.

If you're bringing in music or sound effects, you don't want them to go onto A1 or A2 because they'll replace your sync sound. Music, sound effects, and narration are additional sound elements, and they need to go onto additional audio tracks.

Let's say you have a stereo music cue that you want to add to the scene. You want it to play underneath the dialog. You need to create two additional tracks, A3 and A4, and *patch* the audio onto A3 and A4. When you put a music clip into the Source Monitor, you'll see the source tracks A1 and A2 appear in the Timeline, parallel to record tracks A1 and A2.

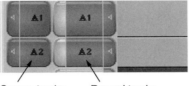

Source tracks   Record tracks

If you splice the music into A1 and A2, you throw your dialog out of sync. If you overwrite it, you erase your dialog. Instead, you create two additional tracks, A3 and A4, and patch the tracks so that your music will get spliced onto them.

To patch: Click and hold the mouse on the first source track that you want to patch. In the example provided here, it's source track A2. Drag the mouse from A2 on the source side to A4 on the record side. You'll notice that as you hold down the mouse and drag, a white pointer arrow appears and points to A4, and when you release the mouse, the source track (A2) moves down to line up with your record track on A4 (Figures 7.4 and 7.5). Try it.

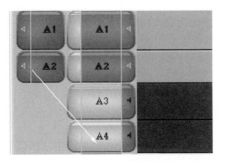

Figure 7.4

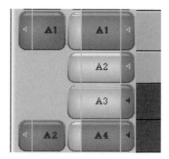

Figure 7.5

Do the same thing with A1. Move it to line up with A3. Now when you splice or overwrite, that's where your music will go—onto A3 and A4, not A1 and A2.

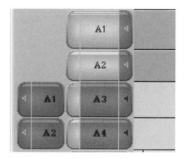

DELETING TRACKS

You sometimes need to delete one or more tracks. Perhaps you've created more tracks than you need, and the extra tracks just take up space on the computer screen. To delete a track, deselect all of the other tracks and select just the one you want to delete. Press the Delete key on the keyboard. A dialog box will ask if you are sure you want to do that, and you click OK. If you make a mistake and inadvertently delete an important audio track, don't worry. Just press Command (Ctrl)-Z to undo the action. Deleting tracks works with video tracks just as well as with audio tracks.

CHANGING AUDIO LEVELS

When you digitize your audio, the sound levels aren't always perfect. Often, you need to raise or lower the levels once you start editing. Changing levels becomes especially important when you begin to add audio tracks and mix several sounds together. For example, you wouldn't want your music to drown out the actor's voices or to have unintelligible narration because the sound effect track is too loud. The Avid provides several tools to help you control the sound levels of your tracks so that they work well together. Just imagine what it would sound like if you had 12 audio tracks and you couldn't change any of the levels.

AUDIO MIX TOOL

The first tool we'll look at is the Audio Mix Tool (Figure 7.6). You can open it by going to the Tools menu, or go to the Toolset menu and select Audio Editing. If I am going to change the level of a clip in the Source Monitor, I'll get it from the Tools menu. If I'm going to work on clips that are already in the Timeline, I'll get it from the Toolset menu.

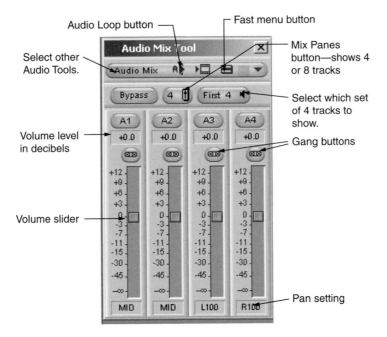

Figure 7.6   Audio Mix Tool

The Audio Mix Tool looks like a standard mixing board, with volume sliders for each track of audio. In Figure 7.6, you see we have only four tracks. If you are monitoring eight tracks, you have the option of looking at all eight by clicking on the Mix Panes button that shows four or eight tracks. To save screen space, you can keep it to four tracks and change the four you are viewing.

The Audio Mix Tool can be used to change the volume of clips in the Source Monitor or clips that have been edited into the Timeline.

- To change the volume of a clip, place it in the Source Monitor and then raise or lower the slider.
- To change the volume of a clip in the Timeline, click on the Timeline (or the Record Monitor) and place the position indicator on the segment you want to change.

Now simply raise or lower the slider(s) to change your levels (Figure 7.7).

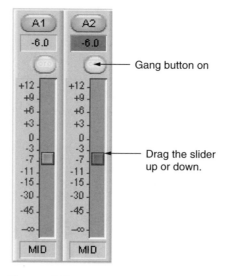

Figure 7.7

Usually I don't change levels until I've edited the clips into a sequence. The sound levels are usually good coming in, and the only reason I want to change them is to change the way they work with other tracks and within the sequence as a whole. Before I change a clip's volume, I want to see how it works with the other clips. The one time I do change the levels of a clip in the Source Monitor is when I've brought in sound from a CD. (This is explained in Chapter 13.) Sometimes those levels can be quite hot and need adjusting before cutting them into the Timeline.

When adjusting clips in the Timeline, you'll notice that you are affecting the level only for the clip on which the position indicator sits. The entire track is not affected by the changes. This makes sense, when you stop to think about it, because often you want to raise one actor's level, while keeping another actor unchanged.

Mixing Tool with Audio Tool

I often have both the Audio Mix Tool and the Audio Tool open at the same time so that I can see the true audio levels as I make changes. Just get the Audio Tool from the Tools menu and place both tools together on the screen so they're easy to see. If you like the arrangement, go to the Toolset menu and select Save Current, and they'll open together whenever you select Audio Editing from the Toolset menu.

Speed Tips

A couple of tricks can speed up the adjustment process. Let's say that A1 and A2 are stereo narration tracks, and you want to lower both of them at the same time. Click on the gang buttons for A1 and A2 (they'll turn a bright green), and as you click on one slider, the other moves up and down with it (see Figure 7.7).

Let's say you want to go back to 0 dB. Sure, you could drag the slider back to 0, but that's time-consuming. Simply hold down the Option key (Mac) or the Alt key (Windows) and click on the slider button. The level will jump back to 0 dB.

Panning

The window at the bottom of each track is for *panning* the audio. Panning is a technique used whenever you have more than one channel of sound coming from more than one speaker. When you set the pan you are determining how much of the sound will come from the left speaker, how much from the middle (both speakers equally), and how much from the right speaker. To set the pan, click on the window, and a horizontal slider will appear. Drag it left or right (Figure 7.8).

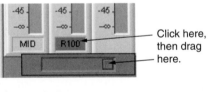

Click here, then drag here.

Figure 7.8

Option-click (Mac) or Alt-click (Windows) on the Pan button, and it will jump to MID, the center pan position.

Audio Clip Gain

As you use the Audio Mix Tool to change levels on your clips in the Timeline, the Avid gives you a way to graphically see the decibel level at which you have set each clip. This Timeline view is called *Audio Clip Gain,* and you get it from the Timeline Fast menu. Audio Clip Gain also shows you which clips have been changed.

Select the tracks in the Timeline that you want to see, and then go to the Timeline Fast menu and select Audio Clip Gain (Figure 7.9). Media Composer users, go to Audio Data in the Timeline Fast menu and choose Clip Gain. Horizontal lines appear in the Timeline showing the clips that have been changed.

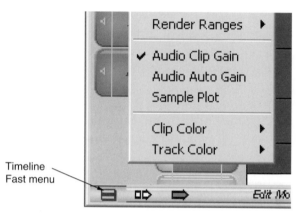

Figure 7.9   Audio Clip Gain

If you enlarge the audio tracks by selecting the track and pressing Command-L (Mac) or Ctrl-L (Windows), or by stretching the track with the mouse, decibel reference lines appear (Figure 7.10). As you can see, I have enlarged this audio track to twice its normal size. Decibel lines appear, and you can now see that I have raised the volume on Tim's clip to 4.0 dB. If you look closely, you can see that I dropped Kate's volume on her close-up to just below –3.0 dB. When the tracks are sized normally, you don't see the lines indicating decibel levels, but if you enlarge the tracks, the lines and numbers will appear.

Normally, you enlarge your tracks to this size only when you are making critical sound-level adjustments and you want to see the relationship between your setting and the 0 dB line.

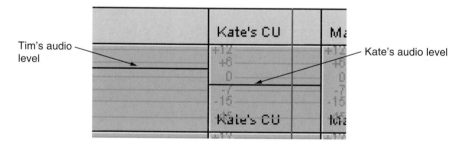

Figure 7.10

Changing Volume and Panning on Multiple Clips

You will often want to change the pan or volume throughout the sequence, or a large portion of the sequence, rather than making changes to individual clips. Open the Audio Mix Tool.

To affect pan or volume levels for a segment of a track(s) in your sequence:

1. Select the track(s).
2. Mark an IN inside the first clip; mark an OUT inside the last clip.
3. On the Audio Mix Tool, click on the track button for that track (Figure 7.11).
4. If you are changing more than one track, click the track button and gang button for each track to gang the tracks together.
5. Raise or lower the Volume slider or the Pan slider.
6. Go to the Audio Mix Tool Fast menu and drag down to Set Level On Track—In/Out or Set Pan On Track—In/Out.

Figure 7.11

If you want to affect the entire track, rather than the area inside your marks, don't place any marks. Instead do the following:

1. Select the track.
2. Remove any IN and OUT marks.
3. On the Audio Mix Tool, click on the track button for that track (see Figure 7.11).
4. If you are changing more than one track, click the track button and gang button for each track to gang the tracks together.

5. Raise or lower the Volume slider or the Pan slider.
6. Go to the Fast menu and drag down to Set Level [or Pan] On Track—Global.

There are a few things to remember when using the Audio Mix Tool. Because center pan is the standard for dialog and narration, the Avid allows you to set the pan before you bring the material in. In the Project window, select Settings. Audio is at the top of the list. Double-click it. Select "All Tracks Centered."

The Media Composer also provides a way to center pan using a menu item. Set IN and OUT marks and then go to the Clip menu and select Center Pan.

Although the Audio Mix Tool is ideal for making changes to entire clips or large segments of your audio, Avid provides a second tool, called *Audio Auto Gain*, so that you can really fine-tune your audio. With Audio Auto Gain, you can make many volume changes within a clip.

AUDIO AUTOMATION GAIN

This tool is also called *volume rubber-banding*. Instead of using a slider to change the level of an entire clip, this tool uses key frames to set and adjust levels *within* a clip.

There are several ways you can use this feature: (1) You can set the key frames manually; (2) you can play the sequence and let the Avid place key frames as you move the sliders; or (3) you can attach a fader. The Avid supports several models. An external fader allows you to use your fingers to move multiple sliders, rather than having to use the mouse to make volume changes on the Avid interface's sliders.

We'll use the manual method first. From the Timeline Fast menu, deselect Audio Clip Gain and select *Audio Auto Gain*. Now select the track(s) with which you want to work.

A thin, gray line will appear across the selected tracks.

Placing Key Frames Manually

Place the blue position indicator in the Timeline where you want to make audio changes. Then hit the N key on the Xpress keyboard, the double quote (") key on the Media Composer keyboard, or the Key Frame command button.

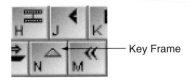

A key frame appears in the Timeline. Because both tracks, A1 and A2, are selected, key frames appear in both simultaneously. Move the blue position indicator in the Timeline farther along the Timeline, and hit the Key Frame key again. Another key frame appears.

Using the mouse, move the pointer to the second key frame. Notice that the pointer changes into a hand. Now drag the key frame down, vertically in the Timeline (Figure 7.12). You have created a volume ramp. Play the section in the Timeline and listen to the volume change.

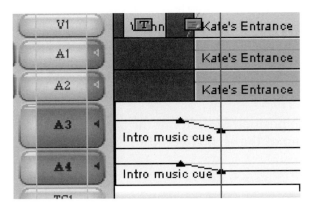

Figure 7.12 Key frames

When working with stereo tracks, you often want to create volume ramps on both tracks simultaneously. Simply select both tracks, and the key frames you place will appear in both tracks. All of the actions you give to one track's key frame(s) will affect those on the other track.

You may find that you have placed the key frame in the wrong place. You can easily move your key frames so that they affect the sound at a precise point.

To move a key frame:

1. Hold the Option key (Mac) or Ctrl+Alt keys (Windows).
2. Click the mouse on the key frame you want to move, and drag it to the new spot.

Now add two more key frames farther down the clip in the Timeline, and drag the fourth key frame—this time *up*. You have created an audio dip.

To delete a key frame:

1.   Bring the mouse pointer over the key frame(s) you want to remove and click on it. The mouse turns into a hand.
2.   Press the Delete key on the keyboard.

Sometimes the Avid gets confused and thinks you are trying to delete an audio track, and you'll get a message asking you if you want to delete a track. Click No, and repeat the above steps. To remove multiple key frames, select IN and OUT points, and delete any key frame in the marked area.

Placing Key Frames Automatically

As mentioned, you can place the key frames automatically. This method imitates the way a mixer in a mixing studio works. From the Tools menu, select the Automation Gain Tool (Figure 7.13). This looks complicated, but it is actually easy to use. You can use this tool to place key frames on all of the clips on a track. You can mix as much, or as little, as you like. If you're not happy with what you're doing, press the Trash icon to stop the recording. If, after you're through, you don't like what you've done, press Undo and it's all erased.

1.   Place the position indicator at the beginning of your tracks or at the beginning of the section you'd like to change.

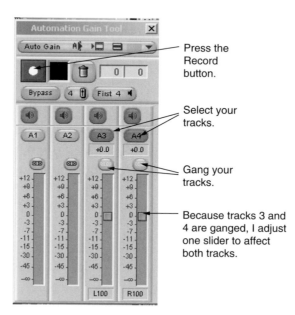

Figure 7.13

2. Open the Automation Gain Tool from the Tools menu.
3. Select the tracks in the Automation Gain Tool.
4. If you want to work on two tracks at once, like stereo tracks, gang them.
5. Press the Record button.
6. As the position indicator plays through the Timeline, raise and/or lower the track's slider with your mouse.
7. Press the Record button to stop.

If, after you have placed key frames in the Timeline, you deselect Audio Auto Gain from the Timeline Fast menu, the key frames disappear, but a single, small red key frame sits on the clip to show that key frames are in place.

EQUALIZATION

On most sound mixing boards, there are dials you can turn to boost or cut (decrease) various frequencies—low, midrange, high—to alter or improve the sound. Such alteration of frequencies is called *equalization* (EQ). For example, if a voice is too bass sounding, you can cut the low frequencies and boost the midrange frequencies.

The Avid has a tool that enables you to do the same thing. The EQ Tool is in the Tools menu. The EQ Tool affects clips in the Timeline.

From the Tools menu, choose Audio EQ. A window appears (Figure 7.14).

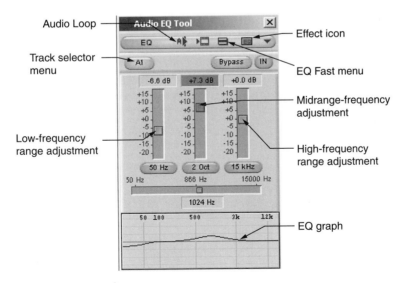

Figure 7.14

Setting the EQ

The sliders enable you to emphasize (boost) or deemphasize (cut) the low, midrange, and high frequencies. The horizontal slider allows you to change the shape and placement of the parametric curve. This adjustment allows you to locate the frequency that you most want to boost or cut. Watch the EQ graph to see the changes.

There is an Audio Loop button, which will play the sound in a continuous loop and allow you to hear the changes you make as you adjust the sliders. There is also an IN button, which gives you the opportunity to turn off the effect of the EQ so that you can tell how your changes compare with the original sound. Are you making the sound better or worse? Click once and it turns gray, indicating that no EQ is taking place. Click again and it turns yellow, indicating that the effect is on.

Steps in applying EQ:

1. Select the track(s) you want to change.
2. If it's a single clip, place the position indicator on the clip. If it's more than one clip, identify a portion of the track(s) with IN and OUT marks.
3. Click the play loop.
4. Drag the sliders to select values. If it's a single clip, you're done.
5. If you have placed IN and OUT marks, stop and then choose Set EQ In/Out from the EQ Fast menu.

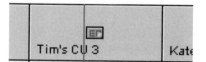

You can also use the EQ Fast menu to remove the EQ (Figure 7.15). Or you can use the Remove Effect button located on a Fast menu Command Palette. Click on the effect in the Timeline and then press the Remove Effect button.

— Remove Effect button

EQ Templates

Avid has several EQ templates that fix common audio problems. You can apply, but not change, any of these EQ templates.

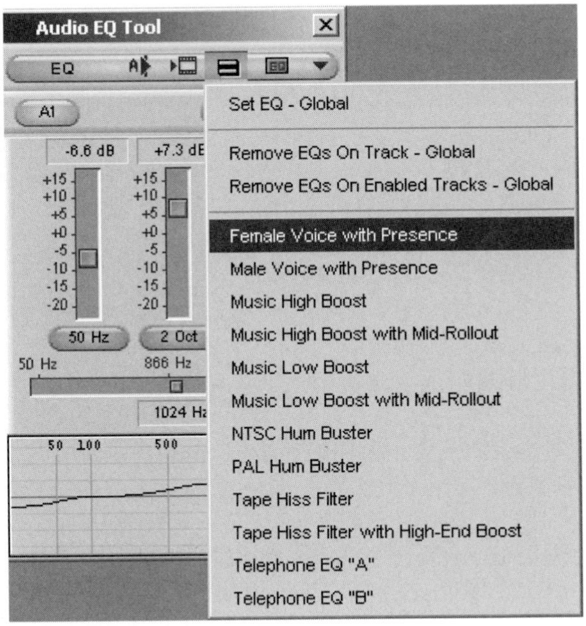

Figure 7.15

1. Put the position indicator on the audio clip in the Timeline that you want to change.
2. Choose the template from the EQ Fast menu. The EQ effect will be placed on the clip.

One way to learn how to equalize your sound is to examine the graphs that these different templates produce. Look at the frequencies that are boosted and cut. Examine the point where the center of the parametric curve is located. These EQ templates cover most of the problems you'll encounter. Use them as a jumping-off point for fixing your sound. It's true, you can't change them, but you can re-create them and then make adjustments to fit your own set of problems.

Saving Your EQ Effect

You can also save an EQ effect so that you can use it later on in your project. Once you have the effect set up the way you want, simply click and drag the *icon* (Figure 7.16) to whichever bin you would like it saved to. Try it. It's easy to do. Once it's in the bin, you can name it.

Now simply click and drag it from the bin to Tim's other clips in the Timeline, and they'll have the same EQ applied to them.

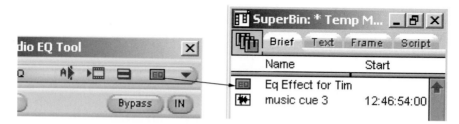

Figure 7.16 Drag the EQ icon to the bin.

When to Use the Different Audio Tools

Here's how I work with my audio tools. I use the Audio Mix Tool to set the overall levels of my clips. I'll select Audio Clip Gain from the Timeline Fast menu. Then I'll go into the Timeline, put the position indicator on Kate's CU, and raise or lower it with the slider. Then I'll do that with the next clip that needs adjustment. I might find that a whole section is too low, and then I'll mark an IN and then an OUT in the Timeline. Using the Audio Mix Tool menu, I'll choose Set Level On Track—In/Out (see Figure 7.11).

Now, let's say I don't like the way something sounds. Kate's voice seems muffled, or there's too much sibilance, or there's a hum I don't like—then I'll use the EQ Tool.

The last tool I use, after I've set levels and EQ, is the Audio Auto Gain Tool. If I want an audio ramp, because I have music or sound effects that I want to bring down or up, I'll go to the Timeline Fast menu, deselect Audio Clip Gain, and select Audio Auto Gain. When I see that gray line, I place key frames, using the N key on the keyboard. Then I raise or lower key frames to set a ramp up or down.

If I have a section of music that needs a lot of adjustment, I'll use the Automation Gain Tool. While I'm listening and watching the picture, I'll record my level changes and let the Avid set all of those key frames automatically.

What's important to note is that the levels you set with the Audio Mix Tool are memorized and kept. If you then add key frames, manually or automatically, those changes are added onto the settings you've already made.

I don't like to have both the Audio Clip Gain and Audio Auto Gain views selected at the same time. You can have both of them present, but I think the Timeline gets too confusing that way.

Remember, do your gross adjustments first, using the Audio Mix Tool; then work on the quality of the sound with the EQ tool; and then fine-tune the levels with the Audio Auto Gain.

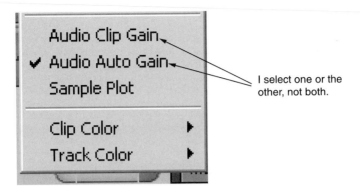

I select one or the other, not both.

What Level is Correct?

When editing my sequence together, I will try to have normal conversation fall within the –30 dB to –14 dB range on the digital scale. Loud sounds will then have ample headroom, peaking at –4 dB for the loudest shout or bang. But I won't let any of my levels get higher than that. Place your average sounds at the reference level, and let your loud sounds use the headroom, but never let anything get higher than –4 dB.

WAVEFORMS

The audio *waveform* is a visual representation of your audio's signal strength, or amplitude. The Avid's Timeline has the ability to show you the waveform of your audio. This feature provides a handy way of finding specific sounds and "seeing" where to trim your sound.

If you're using an Xpress, first go to the Timeline Fast menu, deselect Audio Clip Gain and/or Audio Auto Gain, and select Show Sample Plot (Figure 7.17).

If you're using a Media Composer, go into the Timeline Fast menu and select Audio Data. In the submenu, deselect Clip Gain or Auto Gain and choose Sample Plot.

Figure 7.17

The Avid will draw the waveform. The speed with which the sample plot is drawn depends on your Timeline view and the number of tracks selected. Once the waveform is drawn, you can see where your sounds begin and end. This can be helpful when you're fine-tuning your audio. As you can see in Figure 7.18, the Timeline has been expanded so we can see music beats.

Figure 7.18

A couple of commands can help you better see the waveforms:

- To make your tracks larger, use enlarge track—Command-L (Mac) or Ctrl-L (Windows).
- To make the waveform itself larger, use Command-*Option*-L (Mac) or Ctrl-Alt-L (Windows).

Waveforms are helpful whenever you're trying to edit complex sounds, such as music. For example, let's say you wanted to lengthen a music cue because it ends a bit too soon. You can easily do this by copying a section of the music into the Clipboard, opening the Clipboard Monitor, marking the section, and then cutting it into the Timeline at the end of the music. Now the music is extended. The waveform shows you where the beats are in the music. Use those beats to make your marks and edit points. Try it.

USING TRIM MODE TO FINE-TUNE THE AUDIO

I often do my audio work using Trim Mode. Let's say you have a lot of narration that you've cut into your sequence, and the narration track is a bit noisy. When the narrator speaks, you don't hear a hiss, but as soon as he or she stops talking, you can hear a hiss or hum on the track.

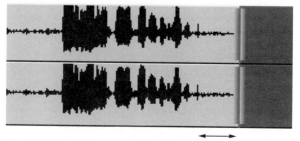

Use Dual-Roller Trim to get rid of this noise.

You want to clean the track up. The best way to do this is to enter Dual-Roller Trim Mode and cut the narration so that the only segments left in the Timeline are those that contain the voice and not the "silent" bits, which are actually noisy.

OTHER AUDIO TECHNIQUES TO FIX PROBLEMS

When you're working on a cut in Trim Mode, you'll sometimes hear a glitch in the audio, but it's so close to the transition point that you aren't sure which side of the transition has the sound glitch. As you play the transition, the sound loops around. Try this: Press the Go to Mark IN key (Q on the keyboard). The loop will play on the outgoing clip but not the incoming one.

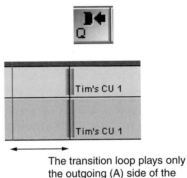

The transition loop plays only the outgoing (A) side of the transition.

To hear just the incoming, or B-side, of the transition, press the Go to Mark OUT key.

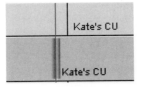

This technique enables you to locate spurious sound glitches. Once located, you can often erase them by using the Dual-Roller Trim to create a sound overlap. Let's say there was a glitch on the outgoing audio, five frames from the transition. The dialog is finished, but a table got bumped. You might be able to replace the glitch on the outgoing clip with five frames of good sound on the incoming clip. Create your overlap, and the bump is gone.

Using the Clipboard to Fix Audio

If we continue with the example of the sound glitch on the outgoing clip, what do we do if the sound on the incoming clip isn't a good match and the Dual-Roller Trim makes the sound even worse? Here's where the ability to copy and paste comes in handy. We can easily mark the area where the glitch is located and, using Lift, get rid of it. But you can't have *nothing* on your soundtrack. You need to replace what was cut out with some sort of room tone, or ambient sound, to fill in the blank spot.

Measure the size of the gap by looking at the Record Monitor menu's I/O. Say it's 11 frames. Now go find 11 frames of ambient sound that will fit in. Now we locate 11 clean frames up ahead in another clip. We mark the frames of sound we want (select the audio track and deselect picture track), and hit the Clipboard icon (on the keyboard, it's the letter C). The sound is copied to the Clipboard.

Go to the Tools menu and open the Clipboard Monitor. Now click on the Mark Clip button to set an IN and OUT, and overwrite the sound into the hole in your Timeline.

Add Edits

Sometimes you want to make an abrupt change in the audio level inside a clip. Let's say you have a scene where music is playing on a CD player in the living room, and you cut to a scene in the kitchen. You hear the music at a normal level in the shot of the living room, but when you cut to the kitchen, its level should drop with the cut. The best way to do this is to split the music clip into two clips, so you can set different audio levels for each segment. To do this you use the *Add Edit* button.

An Add Edit is an artificial edit point made between continuous frames. To a filmmaker it would be like an unintentional splice. Yet this cut, or break, between two frames in a clip is intentional. Put the position indicator on the frame in the Timeline where you want the break to occur. Hit the Add Edit button. On the Xpress keyboard, it's the H key. Media Composer users will find it on the Fast menu. You may have already pressed it by accident and found little Add Edit marks in your Timeline.

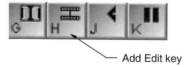

— Add Edit key

In the Timeline, an Add Edit looks like an equals sign (=) that's been stamped at the transition point. Now you can go into the Audio Mix Tool and set different sound levels in the same clip.

As you can see, the music clip has been split into two, and the second half has the audio volume set below that of the first half.

You can delete Add Edits, but not if you have different settings on either side of the Add Edit. If that's the case, you need to remove the change.

To Delete an Add Edit:

- Enter Trim Mode at the Add Edit and press the Delete key on the keyboard.

TIMELINE VIEWS

You can set up your tracks in the Timeline—the color of the tracks, the size of the tracks, whether you see Waveforms—and save those settings. All you have to do is fix the tracks just the way you want, then move your mouse all the way to the bottom of the Timeline, next to the Scale bar, and click and hold on the "Untitled." A pop-up menu comes up, and you can choose Save As. In the dialog box, type a name, such as Edit Mode, and click OK.

Now let's set up a different view. Set up your tracks to show the Sample Plot. Notice the Edit Mode name changes to look like it's italicized. Click on the Edit Mode name and choose Save As. When the dialog box comes up, name it Sample Plot or Waveform.

You can also make changes and then instead of creating a new view, you can replace a view with a new one. Select the one you want to change, make changes, then update by holding down the Option key (Mac) or Alt key (Windows) and clicking on the Timeline name. You'll see "Replace."

Select the view you want to replace from the list, and the replaced view will hold on to the changes.

MEDIA COMPOSER: REARRANGE TRACKS

Media Composer users have the ability to rearrange Timeline tracks. This means you can move the timecode track (TC1) from the bottom of the stack of tracks and put it anywhere you want. Because this is such a useful track—I use it all the time to get out of Trim Mode—I like to move it up so that it's just below the V1 track. This is especially handy when I have three, four, or more audio tracks. Once I've moved it up, so it's always visible, then I make this setup one of my Timeline views.

Hold down the Option key (Mac) or Ctrl key (Windows), click on the track button that you want to move, and drag it with the mouse to wherever you want it to go. The only track I ever care to move is the TC1 track, and I move it up to just below V1.

SETTING UP YOUR TRACKS

In the traditional analog film editing style, the editor would cut the entire film using, for the most part, only two tracks! That's because the KEM or Steenbeck is capable of playing only two or three tracks at a time. Most of the sound was added after the picture was cut. Once the film's editor reached picture lock, the sound editors would then take over and build whatever music and sound effects tracks were needed to give the film its emotion and tone.

After the tracks were built, the film was mixed at a traditional mixing studio, using magnetic dubbers to play the magnetic film tracks in sync with the picture. A cue sheet, which is a paper diagram showing the location of the sounds on each track, would be prepared before the mix, and the mixer would use that as a sort of road map. Usually, the tracks would be set up in a specific order, so that when the cue sheet was made it would read, from left to right on the page, like this:

Narration Tracks   Dialog Tracks   Effect Tracks   Music Tracks

A simple mix might involve seven tracks. You might have one track of voice-over narration, two tracks containing dialog, two sound effects tracks, and two music tracks. A complicated mix, involving lots of sound effects and music cues layered on top of each other, might need 24 tracks.

With the Avid, it's easy to add tracks, but you should consider how your tracks are laid out. Because analog filmmaking spans the entire 20th century, the techniques that served it so well and for so long are often worth emulating, even in this digital age.

In the Avid's Timeline, the tracks go one on top of another, flowing left to right. If you have narration, it should go onto the topmost audio track—A1. Reserve the next two tracks for dialog. The sound effects come next. Finally, your music tracks go at the bottom of your Timeline. If you have no narration, the topmost tracks will contain dialog.

We've examined many of the important techniques and tools at your disposal, all of which will help you create clean, clear sound. Perhaps the most important advice I can give you is this: Wait to add sound effects and music until as late in the editing process as possible. Editors who are new to the Avid often create complex sound tracks much too early in the editing process, making even the simplest change an onerous task. Tell the story first, by cutting the picture and sync sound. Then build your other tracks, laying down the sound effects and music cues that will give tone and emotional content to your project.

SUGGESTED ASSIGNMENTS

1. Move the hollow speaker icon to different tracks.
2. Enlarge all of your sound tracks.
3. Make individual tracks smaller.
4. Add two additional audio tracks.
5. Splice sound into these new tracks by patching.
6. Adjust the volume of your tracks using the Audio Mix Tool.
7. Change the pan on three of your clips.
8. Select Audio Auto Gain from the Timeline Fast menu, and place several key frames on a clip. Create volume ramps.
9. Move the key frames in the Timeline.
10. From the Timeline Fast menu, leave Audio Auto Gain and go to Waveforms. Try cutting audio, using the waveforms as cutting guides.
11. Place an EQ template onto a clip in the Timeline.
12. Create an EQ effect for several clips in the Timeline and apply it using IN and OUT marks. (Remember, go to the EQ Fast menu and choose Set EQ IN to OUT.)
13. Save an EQ setting by placing it in a bin.
14. Create a Timeline View.

8

Advanced Editing

As we've noted on several occasions, the Avid is a complex editing system, loaded with features that give the editor tremendous flexibility. For the most part, we've stuck to the basics to limit the amount of material you must grapple with to get the job done. Now we'll examine more advanced features, some of which are unique to nonlinear digital systems.

SEGMENT MODE EDITING

Segment Mode editing gets at the heart of nonlinear editing. For those of you with a background in film editing, this won't seem all that special because you've been doing it on your Steenbeck or KEM all along. For those of you who are tape editors, however, this is the mode you've most often dreamed about. With Segment Mode editing, you can move clips around in the Timeline, changing the order of the shots in your sequence. The speed with which you can shift around whole segments of your project will astound you.

Let's say you realize that the first shot in your sequence should actually be the third shot. Enter Segment Mode, click on the shot in the Timeline, and drag it to the new position. Presto!

Segment Mode editing isn't really all that advanced of a feature, but I've held off introducing it because it's much more useful to an editor working on a visual montage or working with documentary footage than it is to an editor cutting a narrative scene. When we were editing "Wanna Trade," you didn't have many opportunities to change the order of your shots, but now that you're working on a documentary, or some other reality-based material, you'll find yourself wanting to move shots around.

There are two Segment Mode buttons, and they appear at the bottom of the Timeline on all Avid systems (Figure 8.1). The yellow arrow that

Extract/Splice button ————   ———— Lift/Overwrite button

Figure 8.1

appears to be missing its midsection is the Extract/Splice button, and the thick red arrow is the Lift/Overwrite button.

Before we go any further, notice the similarities and differences between the Splice and Overwrite keys and the two Segment Mode keys (Figure 8.2). When I was first learning the Avid, I often clicked the wrong one, and it took me a while to figure out what I'd done.

Splice and
Overwrite keys   Segment Mode keys

Figure 8.2

Extract/Splice Segment Mode Button

When you click on the Extract/Splice button, you'll enter Segment Mode.

Extract/Splice ———▶

To let you know you're in Segment Mode, the background color on the segment key at the bottom of the Timeline will lighten. If you then click on a clip (segment) in the Timeline, the clip is highlighted. If the clip has picture and sync sound, you normally want to move both of them together. To select the sound clip, hold down the Shift key and click on the sound. Now both are selected, as shown in Figure 8.3.

Let's say we want the shot called "Ext-Pool," which is the third shot in this sequence, to become the second shot (Figure 8.3). We want to move it so that it comes after "Burning Hills." To move the clip, click on it and then drag it to the spot where you want it to go. As you drag, a white outline will appear around the clip to show you it is moving.

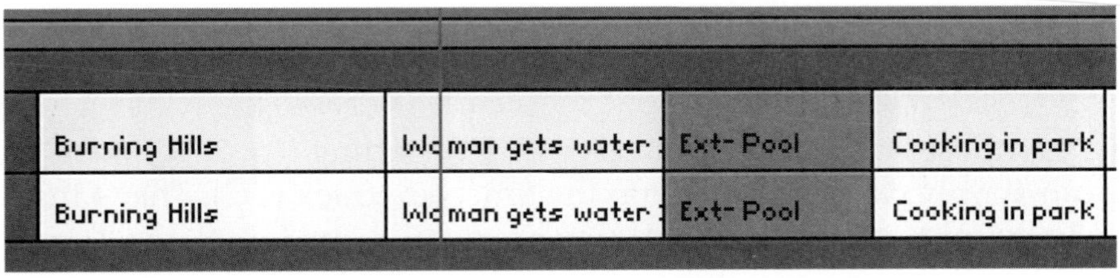

Figure 8.3

Xpress users, when you drag your segment, it snaps to cut points or to the blue position indicator. Media Composer users must press and hold either Command or Option-Command (Mac) or Ctrl or Ctrl-Alt (Windows) to make the segments snap to head and tail cut points, respectively.

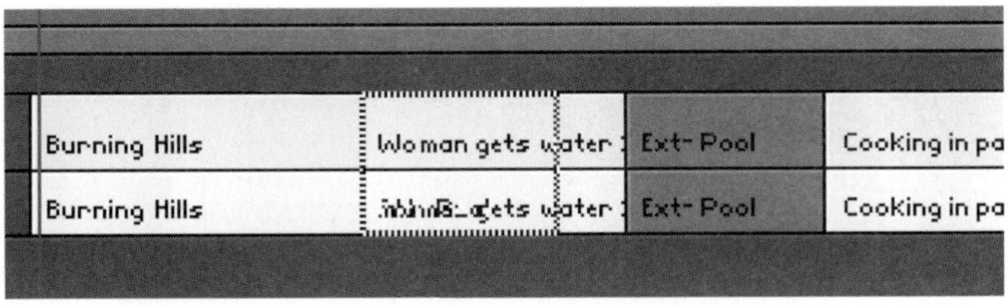

When you release the mouse, the clip moves to the new location.

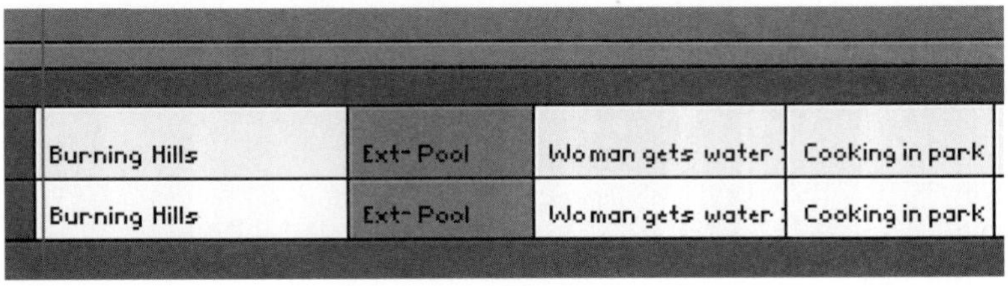

As you can see here, "Ext-Pool" is now the second shot in the sequence. What was the second shot becomes the third shot. Because you're moving segments, the length of the sequence remains the same, and everything stays in sync. You can drag shots in either direction.

When you move a segment in the Media Composer, the Source/Record Monitor changes from the normal display to a four-frame display, showing you the tail and head frames of the shot you are moving and the head and tail frames of the shot in between. Avid calls this display *Segment Drag Quads*. I call it confusing.

You can suppress it by holding down the Shift key as you drag the segment. For a more permanent solution, go to Settings in the Project window and select Timeline Settings. Deselect "Show Segment Drag Quads."

To leave Segment Mode:

• Click on the segment button.

Media Composer users have a simpler way of getting out of Segment Mode. They can simply click anywhere on the timecode track (TC). That's the same way you get out of Trim Mode. I suggested to Doug Hansel, the Xpress DV chief designer, that he add this feature to Xpress DV. We'll see what kind of influence I have.

Lift/Overwrite Segment Mode Button

This button is a little less helpful, and you'll use it less often when moving shots around. When you click on the Lift/Overwrite button (red button) and drag your segment, it moves the segment you've chosen (fine) and overwrites the segment it lands on (not so fine). That's not usually what you want to do.

Look at the example provided (Figure 8.4). Here we selected "Ext-Pool," using the Lift/Overwrite button (red).

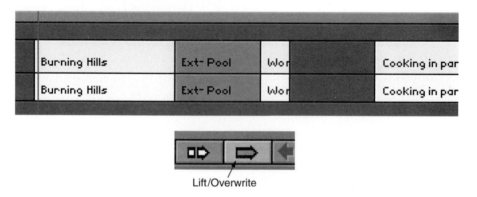

Lift/Overwrite

Figure 8.4

Examine what happens when we use Lift/Overwrite to drag "Ext-Pool" to the same spot as we did using the Extract/Splice segment button. The shot is lifted from its old position, leaving blank fill in its place, and is moved to its new position. But instead of pushing "Woman Gets Water" to the third spot, it erases (overwrites) most of the clip.

Obviously this is not what Lift/Overwrite Segment Mode is used for, but it is important, particularly when you want to move blocks of sound quickly. Let's say we are working on a sequence involving a series of shots that are explained by voice-over narration. When you first cut in the narration, it doesn't flow as nicely as you might like. The narrator's sentences are too close together, so you decide to spread the narration out. Here's where the Lift/Overwrite Segment Mode button excels.

In the example in Figure 8.5, I want to move the narration on A1 toward the head of the visual on V1. I place the position indicator where I want the head of the narration to land.

Figure 8.5

Next I click the red segment button, click on the narration segment, and drag it to the position indicator.

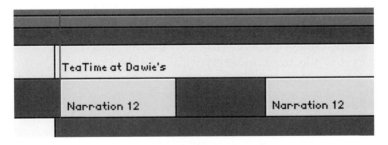

When I release the mouse, the block of narration is right where I want it, and nothing has been thrown out of sync (Figure 8.6).

Figure 8.6

Another handy trick involves the use of the Lift/Overwrite segment button with the Trim keys. Press the red segment button, select the block of audio you want to move, and press the << or < Trim key to slide the segment of sound toward the head of the sequence, or the > or >> Trim key to slide the sound toward the tail. Try it. It is quite precise.

Lift/Overwrite Segment Mode is also great for moving titles around. We'll try this in Chapter 9.

Moving Sound to Different Tracks

You'll also use the Lift/Overwrite segment button whenever you want to move a sound (or picture) clip that's on one track onto another track. In Figure 8.7, the sound for "TeaTime" is on A3, and I want it to go onto A2, just below the narration track. It's easy.

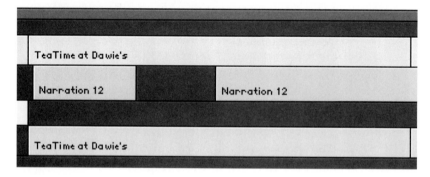

Figure 8.7

1. Click the Lift/Overwrite segment button.
2. Click on the sound segment you want to move.
3. Drag it to the track where you want it to go to.

Again, a white outline will form around the box to show that it's moving and where it's moving to. The result, as shown in Figure 8.8, is what you expected (and hoped). To keep the track from sliding horizontally and going out of sync, hold down the Control key (Mac) as you move the track vertically. Windows users, hold down the Shift+Ctrl keys as you drag.

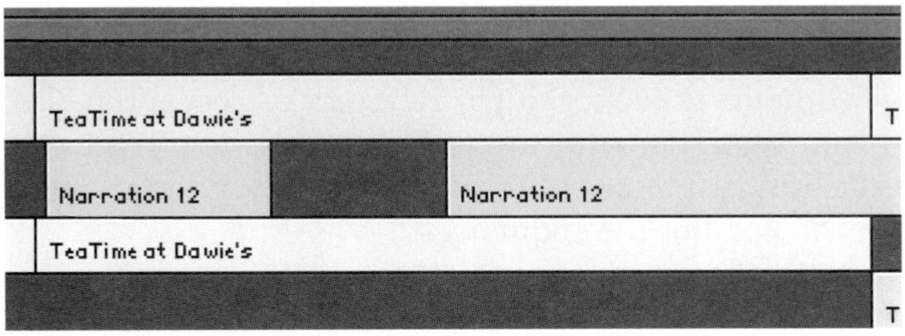

Figure 8.8

Lassoing to Get into Segment Mode

You've probably already done this by accident. As you know, you go into Trim Mode by lassoing a transition from left to right. If, instead of lassoing a transition, you lasso a segment, you'll go into Segment Mode.

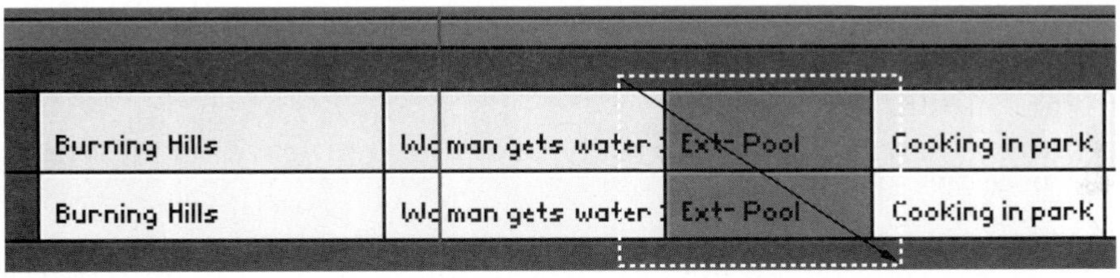

Which Segment Mode will you enter when you lasso a segment? The button selected is the one you used last. If you want the other one, just click on it. Lassoing is a great way to select several clips at once. Lasso all of the clips you want.

You can move more than one segment at a time. For instance, you may want to take the fourth and fifth shots and move them to the beginning of your sequence. You could press a Segment Mode button, click on a segment, and then shift-click to get all four segments selected (two picture and two sound), or you could lasso them all in one quick move. Although in the example here I'm moving only two segments, you can move 30 or 50 segments at once.

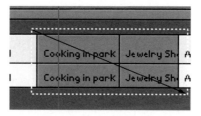

You will sometimes be working on a larger project and realize that scene number 5 would work better at the beginning of the project. Scene 5 might encompass 20 clips. Just lasso the entire scene, click Extract/Splice, and drag all 20 clips to the head of the sequence.

To sum up the Segment Mode buttons:

- Use Extract/Splice to move shots around in the Timeline.
- Use Lift/Overwrite to move blocks of sound in the Timeline.

Delete Segments with Segment Mode

You can delete segments of your project without marking IN and OUT points. Go into Segment Mode and shift-click or lasso the segments you want to delete. Then press the Delete key on the keyboard. The material is deleted.

- Extract/Splice will remove the material and close the gap. The Timeline shrinks.
- Lift/Overwrite will remove the material and leave a gap with black fill.

This is faster than marking IN and OUT points and using the Lift or Extract button, especially with multiple segments. Let's review this concept. Remember that in Chapter 2 we explored the Lift and Extract buttons. You marked an IN in the Timeline and then marked an OUT. The *Extract* button removed the marked material and filled in the gap, whereas *Lift* removed the material and left black fill. The Segment Mode buttons can do the same thing. In fact, if you hit Command-X (Mac) or Ctrl-X (Windows) instead of the Delete key in Segment Mode, the material is removed and saved to the Clipboard.

If you use a Segment Mode button to select the clips, Extract and Lift don't work. You must use the Delete key or Command-X (Mac) or Ctrl-X (Windows).

Remember, in Segment Mode:

- If you select clips with the Segment Mode buttons, you must use either the Delete key or Command-X. What happens depends on which Segment Mode you are in:

 Will extract.

Will lift.

TRIMMING IN TWO DIRECTIONS

Once you begin to add additional tracks to your sequence, using Trim Mode can get a little tricky. For instance, say we have a clip on V1 of people voting in the first free election in South Africa. Your narration describes the action on A1, and your sync track is on A2. You're happy with the way the narration works with the picture and sync track, but let's say you need to trim the head of the clip because the sequence is running too long. I've placed red markers, called *locators*, on all three tracks to show what happens if you trim the voting clip without adjusting your narration track (Figure 8.9).

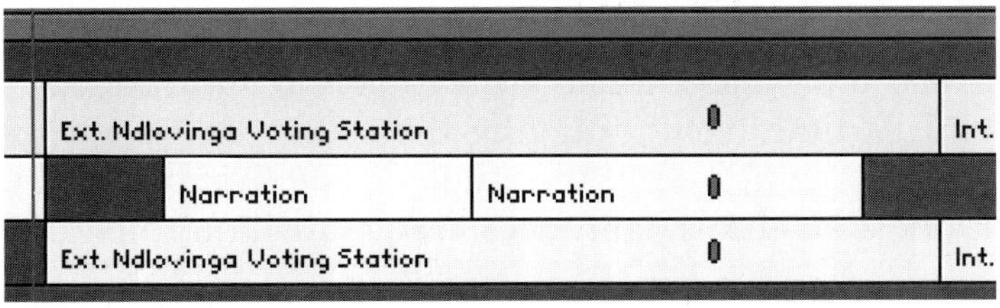

Figure 8.9 Before trimming

In Figure 8.10 we have trimmed 30 frames off the head of the Voting Station picture and sync track. Track V1 and A2 have been shortened by 30 frames, whereas A1, containing the narration, has remained the same length.

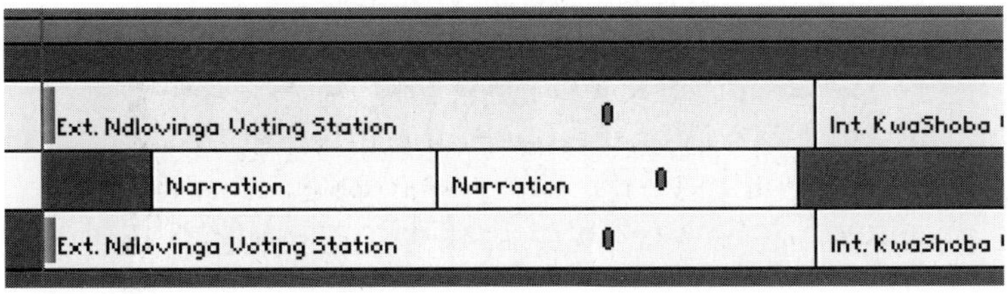

Figure 8.10 After trimming

Everything is thrown off. You say, "Well, trim 30 frames off the narration and everything will be in sync." But we can't, because if we trim the head of the narration, we'll be cutting off the narrator's words! The solution is *trimming in two directions*. The Avid realizes this is a common situation and allows you to trim in the black, or filler area, to keep tracks aligned. Watch.

By placing a Single-Roller Trim on the other side of the narration track, as shown in Figure 8.11, where there is fill and not voice, and then trimming, the Avid takes 30 frames of black fill off the narration track while it takes 30 frames off the "Voting Station" clip. All of the tracks are still aligned. As you can see, the arrows go in two different directions. We are trimming in two directions.

Ext. Ndlovinga Voting Station   0   Int. KwaShobc
Narration   Narration   0
Ext. Ndlovinga Voting Station   0   Int. KwaShobc

——————————→ Drag roller to the right to trim the "Voting" clip by 30 frames.
Narration fill is shortened by 30 frames.

Figure 8.11

We can use the Single-Roller Trim to *add* to the head of the "Voting Station" clip. This time we're dragging the rollers to the left to extend the clip by 30 frames. Again, we put the Single-Roller Trim on the black fill side of the narration. (Remember, shift-click on a transition to add a roller.)

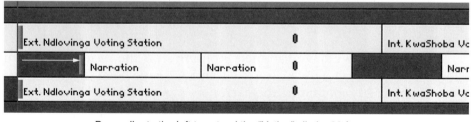

←—————————— Drag roller to the left to extend the "Voting" clip by 30 frames.
Narration fill is lengthened by 30 frames.

It took me a while to get the hang of trimming in two directions. Just remember that once you have the clip you want to trim, for the other tracks to stay in alignment downstream of that trim you have to add or subtract from every track, or else you throw everything out of sync. Here's another example (Figure 8.12), showing many tracks having their black fill adjusted, so that the picture clip can be trimmed.

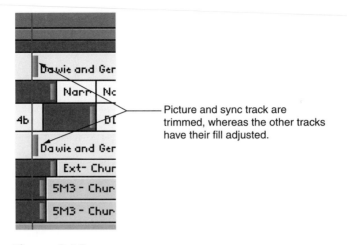

Picture and sync track are trimmed, whereas the other tracks have their fill adjusted.

Figure 8.12

Watch Point

The transition the Avid shows you in the Trim Mode window when you click on the Review Transition button is called the *watch point*. It's easy when there are only two tracks and everything is straight cut, because then there is only one transition to watch. But whenever you have transitions that aren't in a straight line, the Avid can select only one of the transitions to show in the Trim Mode window. The last track selected for trimming is the one that becomes the watch point. This isn't necessarily the one you want to watch, however. Look at the location of the position indicator in the example in Figure 8.13. It's on the roller for a sound effect. But the whole reason you're making a trim is to adjust picture and sync track. That's where you want the watch point to be.

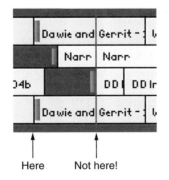

Here   Not here!

Figure 8.13

To fix this situation, simply click the mouse on the roller at the transition you want. The position indicator jumps to that transition, and the watch point moves to the correct spot. Remember, the last transition you select is where the watch point will fall.

Practice this technique. See what happens when the watch point is wrong. Move the watch point so that the transition you want to trim is shown in the Trim Mode display.

MATCH FRAME

Sometimes when you're working in the Timeline, you want to see which clip a shot in the Timeline comes from. Or, you're wondering what comes before or after the section you spliced in. A quick way to open the entire clip is to hit Match Frame. Immediately, the entire clip will appear in the Source Monitor. Go to the Source/Record Monitor's Fast menu to find the command.

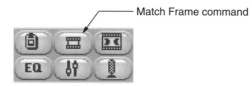

Match Frame command

Place the position indicator on the clip in the Timeline and press the Match Frame button. (I usually place it at the head or tail of the clip.) Match Frame finds the source clip for whichever track is selected and opens it in the Source Monitor, with a Mark IN showing you the exact frame you've marked with the position indicator in the Timeline. If you want to find the source clip for a clip of narration, make sure that's the track selected. If it's a picture, then make sure you select the video track.

SLIPPING AND SLIDING

Slip and *Slide* are power editing features that affect clips in the Timeline. They are unique versions of Trim Mode. These two features didn't come to the Xpress until late in 1999, with software version 3.0.

Slip

Slip is particularly handy. Say you have spliced a section of a master clip into the Timeline, and after playing the sequence, you see that the section of the clip you used just isn't right. Maybe you put your IN and OUT marks in the Source Monitor a bit too early. Without Slip, the only way to fix this would be to mark the clip in the Timeline and choose a new IN in the Source Monitor. Press Overwrite, and you've replaced the clip with a different section of the clip. If it still isn't right, try it again.

With Slip, you don't need to go back to the Source Monitor. You can change the clip in the Timeline. What you're doing is changing the IN and OUT at the same time. Think of Slip as working a bit like a conveyor belt. The whole belt is the master clip, and the portion of the belt you're seeing in the Timeline is the section you've spliced in.

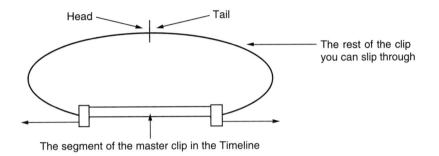

You can change the section that's in the Timeline with Slip. As you slip through the footage, the length of the clip in the Timeline remains the same. When you slip, you are adding frames to the head of the clip in the Timeline, while trimming the tail by the same number of frames. Or you can trim frames from the head of the shot, while adding the same number of frames to the tail of the shot.

Dragging the rollers left reveals material that comes before what's in the Timeline—you're slipping toward the head. Dragging the rollers right reveals material that comes after what's in the Timeline—you're slipping toward the tail.

To get into Slip Mode:

- Press the Trim button and then double-click on the clip in the Timeline.
- Lasso the clip from the right to the left.

Single-trim rollers will jump to the cut points. The Source and Record Monitors will change to four screens (Figure 8.14).

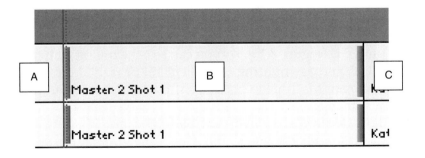

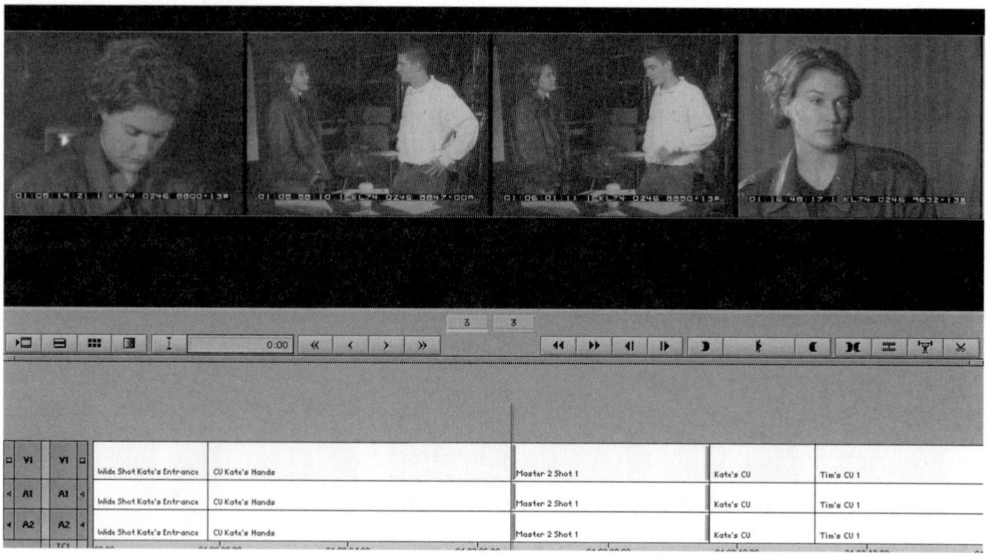

Figure 8.14

The two inner screens are the head and tail frames of the clip you are slipping—Master 2 Shot (Clip B). The far-left screen is the tail frame of Clip A, and the far right is the head frame of Clip C. The frames of Clip B (Master 2 Shot) will change as you slip it. The frames of Clip A and C will not change at all.

You can use the Trim keys (<<, <, >, and >>) to move the clip, or click on and drag either roller. The frames that appear in the two inner screens will change as you slip.

Getting out of Slip is just like leaving Trim Mode. To leave Slip Trim:

- Click on the timecode track.
- Press the Trim Mode button (Xpress).
- Press the Edit Mode button (Media Composer).

Slide

Slide is the inverse of Slip. It doesn't change any of the frames in the clip you're sliding (Clip B); instead, it moves Clip B along the Timeline. Here we are sliding Tim's CU (Figure 8.15). As you can see, the rollers jump to the other side of Tim's CU, and as you drag the rollers left or right, you move the clip to a different spot on the Timeline. Tim's CU doesn't change, but the shots on either side of it change.

You might think you'd never use Slide because it's hard to imagine why you'd want to move a clip in this way. I mean, imagine sliding a clip along the Timeline, as we have in Figure 8.15. You'd lose all control of your shots.

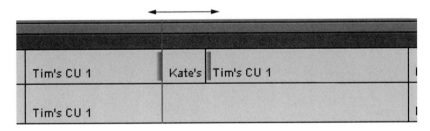

Figure 8.15

Think instead about using Slide with a cutaway. Ah, now we're getting somewhere. Examine Figure 8.16. Here we have Tim's CU, in which Tim is explaining in detail how Kate's letters are now his and he can do whatever he wants with them. Let's say we want to see what Kate thinks of all this. We want to break up Tim's little speech with a cutaway of Kate, looking a bit disgruntled. So we overwrite just her picture somewhere over Tim's CU. But where should it go? Using Slide, we can move it along the Timeline until it's placed perfectly.

Figure 8.16

Slide can also be used to move audio clips, such as segments of narration, or titles on V2, to a new position on the Timeline, but Lift/Overwrite Segment Mode does that job fairly well.

To enter Slide Mode:

• While holding down the Option key (Mac) or Shift+Alt keys (Windows), lasso the clip from right to left.

To get out of Slide:

• Click on the timecode track.
• Press the Trim Mode button (Xpress).
• Press the Edit Mode button (Media Composer).

MEDIA COMPOSER AND XPRESS

J-K-L Trimming

This is one of the greatest editing innovations of all time, but it's not yet available on the Xpress DV. In fact, it just came to Xpress users. There are Avid editors out there who love it so much that they'll pay thousands of dollars more to get it. I can understand why. Some people call this trimming on-the-fly. You don't use the trim keys << and >>. You trim as you play, using the J, K, and L keys in Trim Mode.

Let's first try J-K-L Trimming by working on the A-side or B-side of a transition, but not both.

1. Lasso a transition and then get into Single-Roller Trim Mode.
2. Press the J or L keys. Your transition(s) will lengthen or shorten as you watch.
3. When you see the frame where you want to end the trim, press the K key or the spacebar.

When you first try this, things can get confusing, so slow things down by pressing and holding down the K key, and then J or L.

1. Hold the K key while pressing J or L to glide slowly backward or forward as you shorten or lengthen your clip(s).
2. When you reach the frame where you want to end the trim, release the K key.

Most people love this function so much that they're hooked forever.

Now try J-K-L Trimming in Dual-Roller Trim Mode. You'll notice that only one side of the Trim Mode display will play in real time. The other side will catch up once you stop. Whichever side has the green line just below the counters is the one that plays in real time (Figure 8.17).

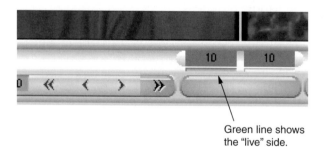

Green line shows
the "live" side.

Figure 8.17

Just move the mouse over the other window (don't click on it) to choose which side you want to see play. The green line shifts to the other side.

There is a way to get both sides to play in Dual-Roller Trim Mode. Go to the Settings window, and double-click Trim. Select Dual-Image Play. With this selected, both the A-side and B-side should play in the Trim Display window at the same time. Depending on your Avid, however, and the resolution of the images you're editing, you may find that playing both sides at once uses so much computing power that your Avid needs you to slightly reduce the size of your Source/Record Monitors. If you get an error message telling you the Avid needs you to resize the monitor, just drag the lower right-hand corner of the Record Monitor toward the center of the screen and make the size of the monitors a bit smaller.

Replace

This is another handy feature that has arrived on the Xpress only recently. It's not yet available on the Xpress DV, but it will get added someday.

Replace does what you'd expect: It replaces material in the sequence with other material of your choosing. Let's say you have placed a clip in the Source Monitor, marked an IN and an OUT, and spliced it into the Timeline. Looking at it, you think another take would work better. Without Replace, you would have to find the new take and overwrite it into the Timeline. Replace is different. Unlike Overwrite, Replace doesn't need IN and OUT marks. It can use the location of the blue position indicators to do its work. I realize this is a new concept, so let's take a closer look at it.

Let's say we have footage of two people swimming. What's shown in the picture in Figure 8.18 is taken from "Swim Take 1." You cut this into the Timeline. When you review the sequence, you think Take 2 might be better, because when the woman lifts her head out of the water, we see more of her face in Take 2.

Figure 8.18

The most important action is the woman touching the wall and lifting her head, so I put the position indicator on that frame in the Timeline.

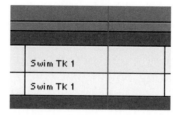

Then I go to the Source Monitor and get "Swim Take 2" (Figure 8.19). I play through the clip until I find the spot where she's lifting her head out of the water. I leave the position indicator there. Now I hit the Replace command, located in the Source/Record Fast menu.

Figure 8.19

I have now replaced "Swim Take 1" with a clip of the same length taken from "Swim Take 2," but the part of "Swim Take 2" that is overwritten is based on the location of the position indicators. The woman's head will lift out of the water at the same point in the sequence as it did when Take 1 was there. In this case, we are matching the action while replacing.

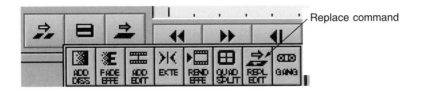

Replace command

What's special about Replace is that it can replace sound and picture even if there is an overlap edit! It replaces sound based on the amount of sound used in the Timeline, even if there's more sound than picture (as might happen with an overlap) in the Timeline.

This command can also be useful if you want to try to replace a section of bad sync sound. Let's say there was a loud background noise during one take. The second take isn't as good visually, but it has cleaner sound. If the take isn't very long, you can mark a word in the Timeline with the position indicator, then place the position indicator on the same word from the second take, which you've placed in the Source Monitor. Now hit Replace, and you should have pretty good sync. If the clip is too long to hold sync, try placing Add Edits around the bad spot of audio in the Timeline, so you're just replacing a word or two, rather than lots of lines.

If you don't find the Replace command in a Fast menu, go to the Command Palette, click on the Edit tab, and place the command inside a Fast menu.

SUGGESTED ASSIGNMENTS

1. Go into Segment Mode by clicking the Extract/Splice button. Now move a clip (shift-click to get sound) toward the head of your sequence.
2. Undo.
3. Move it again, but this time suppress the four-frame display by pressing the Shift key (Media Composer only).
4. Undo. Leave Segment Mode.
5. Go into Segment Mode by clicking the Lift/Overwrite button. Move a clip to the head.
6. Undo. Leave Segment Mode.
7. Get into Segment Mode by clicking the Lift/Overwrite button. Move a clip of audio using Trim keys. Undo.

8. Lasso three clips to get into Segment Mode.
9. Practice trimming in two directions.
10. Set the watch point to show the clip you want to "watch" in the Trim Mode display.
11. Select a video track and hit Match Frame.
12. Deselect the video tracks and select an audio track. Hit Match Frame.
13. Get into Slip Mode and slip a clip.

Media Composer and Xpress Users

14. Use Replace to change a clip in the Timeline, using the position indicators to replace the material in the Timeline with the material in the Source Monitor.
15. Practice J-K-L Trimming.

9

Titles

There are many different kinds of titles, and they serve different functions in a production. There's the main title of the show, and there are the opening and closing credits, identification titles (lower thirds), subtitles, and copyright information. When you think about it, you really can't finish a project without adding titles.

The Avid used to come with a less-than-functional Title Tool, but that has changed. Now even the basic Xpress has a Title Tool that can handle almost all of your title needs. Titles can be simple, such as white letters over a black or colored background, or complex, involving moving titles over a moving video image.

Usually, you add titles when you're nearing the end of the editing phase. If you're still making a lot of changes to your sequence and you cut titles in, they can easily get out of sync and drift away from the images they belong to—and it's a real pain to put everything back together. Trust me on this one. Wait to add titles as late in the editing process as possible. Because we're through editing "Wanna Trade" and possibly another short assignment, you can go back and add titles to them.

OPENING THE TITLE TOOL

If you're planning to add a title over a video image, normally you park the position indicator on that image in the Timeline and then open the Title Tool. That way, the background of your choice becomes the background that the Title Tool shows you. To open the Title Tool, go to the Clip menu and select New Title. The Title Tool will open, and you'll see the Title window (Figure 9.1).

Video background

Safe action area

Safe title area

Title

Toolbar

Figure 9.1   Title Tool

CHOOSING A BACKGROUND

If you don't want a video image as the background for your title, click on the Color Background window (Figure 9.2). The green V will turn black. Black is the default background color, but you can hold the pointer in the Color Background window and a Color Picker will appear. Move the mouse through the colors to select the one you want for your background. You can also use the eyedropper to pick a color.

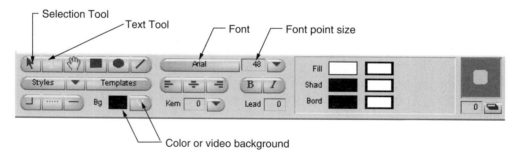

Selection Tool

Text Tool

Font

Font point size

Color or video background

Figure 9.2

CREATING YOUR FIRST TITLE

Creating titles is fairly straightforward. I'm going to create a title to go over a specific shot of Nelson Mandela greeting voters. I click on the V so that the video image appears in the Title Tool window. To type the letters, make sure the T for *Text Tool* is green. If not, click on the T to make it active. Now click on the image where you'd like the text to land. The cursor becomes an I-beam. As you type, the text will appear and flow to the next line. Don't worry—just type your text. You can delete letters, edit letters, type additional letters—basically do all of the functions provided by most word-processing programs.

Selection Tool

On some systems, Arial is the default font, and 48 is the default font point size. You'll find that 48 is often too large. Once you're finished typing, click on the *Selection Tool* (it's next to the Text Tool) so that the arrow turns green. Now click on the title. A box with selection handles appears around the title. Change to another font simply by clicking on the font button and selecting a different font from the list. You can also select a different point size.

The selection handles also allow you to change the size of the box that the words fall into. If your words wrap around to a second line and you want them to all fall on one line, drag the right-hand selection handle—the one that's in the middle—all the way to the safe title line. Now drag the left-hand selection handle all the way to the safe title line. You'll see that your words have more room, so they fall onto one line. Click on the center choice (not flush left or right), and your title will be perfectly centered. Now you can click and drag the entire title to a different area of the frame. In Figure 9.3, I've dragged my title to the part of the frame often called the *lower third*, where most identification titles are placed.

Selection handles: Drag this right or left to affect word wrap.

Figure 9.3

Use the Text Tool to type the letters; use the Selection Tool to make changes to your title. I'm choosing Tahoma for my font and a point size of 36. This will allow the words "Nelson Mandela" to fit nicely on one line. *Kerning* allows you to change the spacing between letters. Select the text you want to kern, and pull down the Kerning menu or type a number into the box. Negative numbers tighten the spacing. Positive numbers loosen the spacing. *Leading* changes the spacing between lines of text.

SHADOWS

You can add a *drop shadow* or *depth shadow* to your titles. Shadowing can often make the letters stand out from a busy background. To add the shadow in Text Mode, click and drag across the words to select them. Or, in Selection Mode, click on the title so that the handles appear. Then go to the Shadow Tools.

By toggling the Drop and Depth Shadow button, you change from one type of shadow to the other (Figures 9.4 and 9.5). By clicking on the shadow in the box, you can use the cursor to drag the shadow in any direction and increase or decrease the depth of shadow you'll add to your letters. The number will change in the Shadow Depth Selection box to indicate how much shadow you are creating. Here, I've set the direction so that the shadow appears to the upper-right of the letters, and at a depth of 14. Really, 14 is a bit too much, but by exaggerating the effect you can see the difference better.

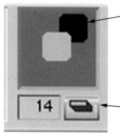
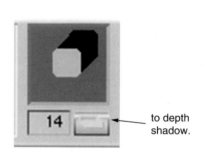

Drag the shadow to set the direction and amount of shadow.

Toggle this button to go from drop shadow. . .

to depth shadow.

Figure 9.4

Drop shadow

Depth shadow

Figure 9.5   Drop shadow and depth shadow

You can also click on the Shadow Depth Selection box and type a number and press Enter or Return.

SAVING TITLES

Titles aren't saved automatically. You must save a title in a bin to use it. Go to the File menu and select Save Title as . . .

A dialog box will open, letting you select the bin that the title will be saved to, the hard drive partition, and the resolution. After clicking OK, the title will be saved in the bin you selected. If you're finished creating titles, go to the File menu and select Close. If you want to keep creating titles, choose New Title in the File menu.

CUTTING TITLES INTO YOUR SEQUENCE

You can't edit titles directly into the sequence from the Title Tool. Once you've saved your title and closed the Title Tool, you must find the title in the bin. The icon for a title is different from the icon for a clip. The Avid treats titles a bit differently from regular clips. All titles are *effects*. An effect is something that needs computer power to make it appear on your screen. Here I've located the title in the bin (Figure 9.6). Double-click on it. It will appear in the Source Monitor just like any other clip.

With the title in the Source Monitor or Pop-up Monitor, you're ready to splice it into your sequence. But wait. Where will it go? Because this title is supposed to be superimposed over the video of Nelson Mandela, we need to open a second video track. Go to the Clip menu and choose New Video Track. V2 will appear in the Timeline. Now you must patch the source track to the V2 record track, as shown in Figure 9.7.

Once you make the patch, V2 will be highlighted, and V1 will not. Make sure the Video Monitor icon is on V2. Remember, the Avid will monitor all of the video tracks at or below the track with the Video Monitor. If the icon stays on V1, it won't monitor any tracks above it.

Name	Start
[T] Title:Thabo Mbeki	00;00;30;00
[T] Title: Soweto Housing	00;00;30;00
[T] Title: Nelson Mandela.01	00;00;30;00

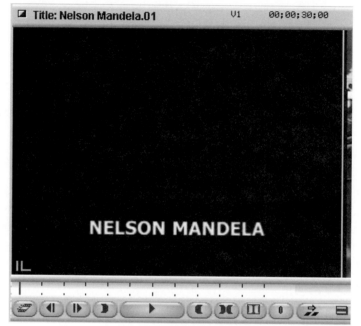

Figure 9.6

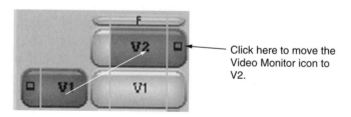

Click here to move the Video Monitor icon to V2.

Figure 9.7

Now you're ready to cut the title in using "three marks make an edit." There are a few things you should know before you make the edit.

The Avid generates about two minutes of title material every time you create a title. Because that's far more than you'll ever need, don't make your

IN on the first frame in the Source Monitor. Instead, go in about 60 frames and then mark your IN. That way you can have fades and Trim available. Mark an IN and OUT and then look in the Source Monitor tracking menu to check the I/O of your marks. Three seconds is a good length for most short titles. Now go to the Timeline and mark the IN where you want to cut the title into the sequence. It's best to use *overwrite* instead of Splice. Because this is the first clip you'll put on the V2 track, it doesn't matter now, but later on, when you add titles to a track that already has titles, only Overwrite will keep those titles from getting pushed out of place.

As you can see, the title has been placed in the Timeline above the shot it will be superimposed over.

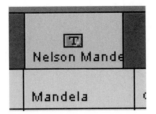

There's a tiny ball on the Title icon, telling us that the title is *unrendered*. An unrendered effect is one in which the effect, in this case a title, has not been created inside the computer. The title and its color, shadow, point size, and so on have not been turned into one whole entity. When you render a title or an effect, you create a new thing—a media file on your media drive.

Media Composer and Xpress systems often come with title and effect capabilities that surpass those found on the Xpress DV. Those Avids will play the title even though it has not been rendered. As soon as you cut in the title clip, you can see the title whenever you hit the play button. You'll see an orange dot on your title in the Timeline, signifying that it will play in real time, even though it has not been rendered.

Xpress DV RealTime Effects Button

Xpress DV users don't always have these same title capabilities as Media Composer and Xpress users. For instance, you can't see your titles in the default mode. Look at the Timeline toolbar and you'll see that the RealTime Effect toggle button is blue (it looks like a ball). That's the default color.

RealTime Effect toggle button

Avid knows you need to see how the title plays in your sequence, so it gives you several ways to look at your titles.

Go to the Clip menu (Special menu for Media Composer) and select Render On-the-Fly (Figure 9.8). Now you can see the title in the Record Monitor when the position indicator lands anywhere on it.

Clip	Tools	Toolset	Windows	Script	He

New Sequence	Shift+Ctrl+N
New Video Track	Ctrl+Y
New Audio Track	Ctrl+U
New Title...	

Freeze Frame
Load Filler

Audio Mixdown...
Video Mixdown...
ExpertRender at Position...
Render at Position...
✔ Render On-the-Fly

Figure 9.8

The second method is to click on the RealTime Effect button (blue); it will turn green. Now your titles play in real time, even though they're not yet rendered.

To review, Xpress DV users, to see your titles:

1. Select Render On-the-Fly from the Clip menu.
2. Click on the blue RealTime Effect button in the Timeline toolbar so it turns green.

What's the big deal? We'll get deeper into this topic in the effects chapter, but for now, the simple explanation is that you can't send your sequence out to tape if the RealTime Effect button is green. It has to be switched back to blue, and once you do that all of your titles have to be rendered before you can record your sequence to tape (a topic we'll explore in Chapter 16).

There are a lot of different computer configurations out there, and not all of them have the ability to play complicated titles and effects in real time. If you find that your computer chokes, stutters, or flashes as it tries to play your titles, you may want to render them, even if the RealTime Effect button is green.

Just remember that rendering can take a long time and interrupt the flow of your work. The rendered title also takes up additional space on your hard drive. So it's worth waiting to render until right before you're ready to go to tape. You might change your mind and not want the title anymore. If you've rendered it, you've taken up media drive space for nothing.

We'll get into rendering in more detail in the next chapter, but if you must render a title or several titles, here's how.

Rendering Your Titles

To render a single title:

1. Select the track containing the title.
2. Place the blue position indicator on the T icon in the Timeline.
3. Go to the Clip menu and choose Render at Position, or
   Click the Render Effect button in the Fast menu between the Source and Record Monitors.
4. When the dialog box appears, choose a target disk for the "pre-compute."
5. Click OK.

Render Effect button

If you have several titles that need to be rendered, it's easier to render them all at the same time.
To render multiple titles:

1. Click the Track Selector to choose the track(s) holding titles you want to render.
2. Mark an IN before the first title and an OUT after the last title.
3. Go to the Clip menu and select Render In/Out.

Adjusting Your Title's Length

If it turns out that the title is on the screen a bit too long, use Dual-Roller Trim to trim the head or tail of the title. If it's not on the screen long enough, use Dual-Roller Trim to extend the tail of the title.

Adding Fades to Your Title

The title I created looks fine, but after watching it I decide I don't like that it pops in and out on the screen. Let's add a half-second fade to the start and end of it.

1. Click the Track Selector to choose the track holding the title.
2. Place the position indicator so that it's inside the title clip in the Timeline.
3. Click the Fade Effect button in the Fast menu between the Source and Record Monitors.

Fade Effect button

A dialog box appears like the one in Figure 9.9. Type in the number of frames you want for your fade (15 frames) and click OK.

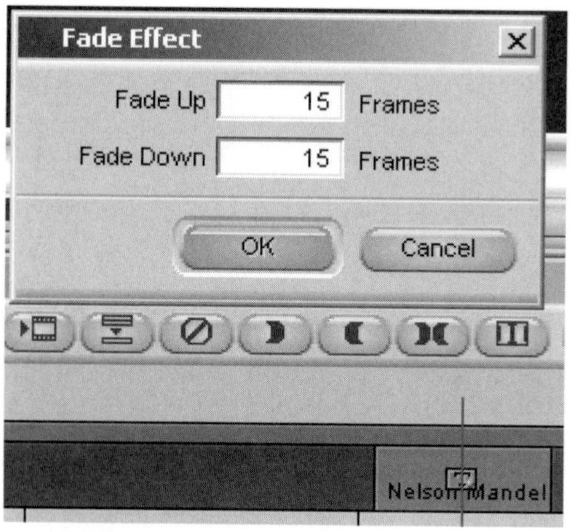

Figure 9.9

You won't see any indication in your Timeline that the Fade Effect is in place, but you'll see the results when you press Play.

That's it. We've created a title with drop shadow, placed it in the lower third of the frame, saved it to a bin, opened it, cut it onto a new video track, and added a fade. There's a lot more you can do with the Title Tool.

COLORED TITLES

You can change the colors of the letters, the color of the shadow, or both. You can even create a blend so that, for example, a title starts out dark and becomes lighter as it progresses. (Because this book is in black and white, you're going to have to practice the techniques on your Avid to see the colors.)

To turn a white title into a title containing color, select it with the Select Tool or, if you're in Text Mode, select the words by dragging. Now click on the Fill window (Figure 9.10). Press and hold the mouse on the Fill window, and a Color Wheel or Color Picker appears.

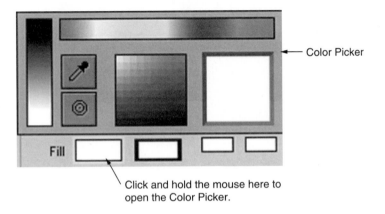

Color Picker

Click and hold the mouse here to open the Color Picker.

Figure 9.10

Drag through the colors until you select the color you want. Or you can click on the eyedropper and click inside the video frame to choose any color already inside the frame.

In Figure 9.11 I've selected the color red to "fill in" the title letters.

Figure 9.11

You can also select a color for the shadows. They don't have to be black. Select the title in the window, and then click and hold on the shadow window (Figure 9.12). The Color Picker appears, and you drag through the choices until you select the one you want. Here I've selected a light red for the shadow. I've exaggerated the shadow by choosing a depth of 7 so that the change is more pronounced (Figure 9.12). Here I have a white title with red shadow.

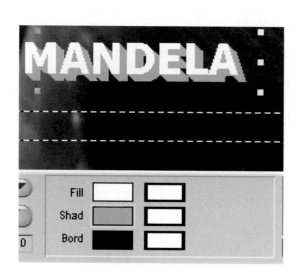

Figure 9.12

BLENDING A TITLE

Let's say the video background shifts from bright to dark so a white title won't show up in the bright areas, and a dark title won't show up well in the dark areas. You can create a blend so that the title changes from one color to another color. When I click on the Fill window (Figure 9.13), two small windows appear to its right. Click and hold on the left window and select a dark color. Click and hold on the right box and pick a lighter color. Your choices appear in the respective box, and the mixture of the two appears in the Blend Direction box. You can change the direction of the blend by dragging the mouse inside this box. I've selected a dark gray in the left-hand box and white in the right-hand box.

Figure 9.13 shows the resulting title. Notice how the letters go from dark gray to white over the width of the title.

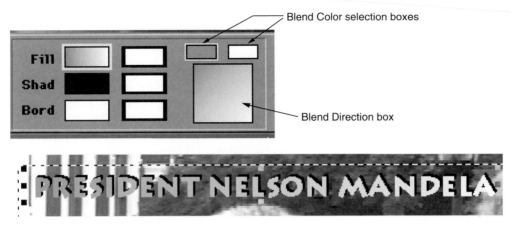

Figure 9.13

CREATING TITLE STYLE SHEETS

After doing a lot of work to set up the title just the way you like it, it would be nice not to have to reinvent the wheel the next time you create a similar title. Fortunately, the Title Tool has a Save As feature, which lets you create a *Style Sheet* so that you can set the same title parameters to any new titles you create.

To create a Style Sheet:

1. Click on the title or object you want to save as a Style Sheet so that it becomes a selection, and the arrow lights up in the toolbox.
2. Press the triangle next to Styles so that the Save As box appears.

3. Choose Save As.
4. The Style Sheet dialog box appears.
5. Make sure that the parameters reflect your choices.

6. You'll see the name of the font style in a box. Type over this, substituting a name, such as "Lower Thirds" or "Credits."
7. Click Done.

Once you have created a style, your Style Sheets appear in the Save As window.

To apply a style, simply type a new title and then go to the Styles menu and select your choice. The same parameters will be applied to the new title.

SOFT SHADOWS

When you place shadows on the letters, they have a hard edge to them. Sometimes giving the shadow less definition improves its appearance. In the Title Tool, select a title that has shadowing and then go to the Object menu at the top of the computer screen. This menu and the Alignment menu appear only when the Title Tool is open. Select Soften Shadow—it's the last item at the bottom of the Object menu. As soon as you select it, a dialog box appears, like the one in Figure 9.14.

Figure 9.14

Type in an amount. The range is from 4 to 40. Try 5, and then press Apply. You'll see the amount of softening in the title's shadow. If you like what you see, press OK. If not, change the value and press Apply again until you're happy with the look.

GLOWING TITLES

Another look you can give your titles is to make them glow. The title will appear to be surrounded by a haze of color. To create a glow effect, you will use the same tools we used to create Soft Shadow titles—only you'll use them a bit differently.

Open the Title Tool and type the text. Using the Selection Tool, position the text where you want it. Make sure the title has no shadow value. If there is a number in the Shadow Depth Selection box, click on it and type 0 and press Return or Enter. Now go to the Shadow box and select a color. Try a light yellow or light red. I know it seems strange to pick a color for a shadow when there is no shadow, but have patience. Now, go to the Object menu and select Soften Shadow. Try typing in a value of 10. Press Apply to preview the look. Figure 9.15 shows the effect I got. It's difficult in a black-and-white screen capture to show off this feature, but you can see that there is a softness coming around and through the letters.

Make sure there is "0" depth shadow and that you have selected a color in the Shadow box.

Figure 9.15

DRAWING OBJECTS

The Title Tool has drawing tools with which you can create boxes, circles, lines, and arrows of various shapes and colors. The title in Figure 9.16 uses white letters and a bit of drop shadow and has a red line below the letters to add emphasis. I created the line using the Rectangle Tool and just dragged the selection handles to make a long, thin line.

Figure 9.16

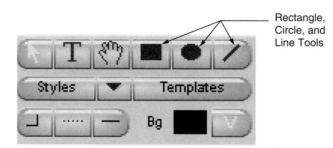

To give the red rectangle a more rounded look, I selected it, and then I went to the tool that changes the corners of all objects.

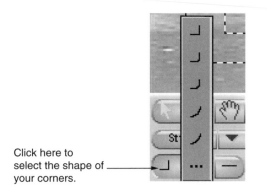

Click here to
select the shape of
your corners.

Delete Key

If you create a title or draw an object and you don't like it, just select it with
the Selection Tool and press Delete. You can also use Undo.

TITLES WITH OBJECTS

To give you an example of some of the other things you can do with these
tools, I've created a title that I want to superimpose over a shot showing
swimmers in the ocean off Durban, South Africa (Figure 9.17). The white
letters don't show up as well as I'd like, so I'm going to create a colored
rectangle, which I'll place behind the title. First I'll select a color for the
rectangle by clicking in the Fill and choosing an aqua-blue color. Next I select
the drawing tool that creates boxes (and rectangles). Because I want the
rectangle to have rounded corners, I select the curved corner with the Corner
Selection Tool. When I drag the pointer across the Title window, a blue rectangle with rounded corners appears.

Figure 9.17

Using the Selector Tool, I drag the rectangle on top of the title "Durban
Waterfront." The title is no longer visible. I know—that's not good. But I'm
not finished.

Now, I go up to the Object menu (Figure 9.18). I select Send To Back. This places the object that is in front—the blue rectangle—behind the title.

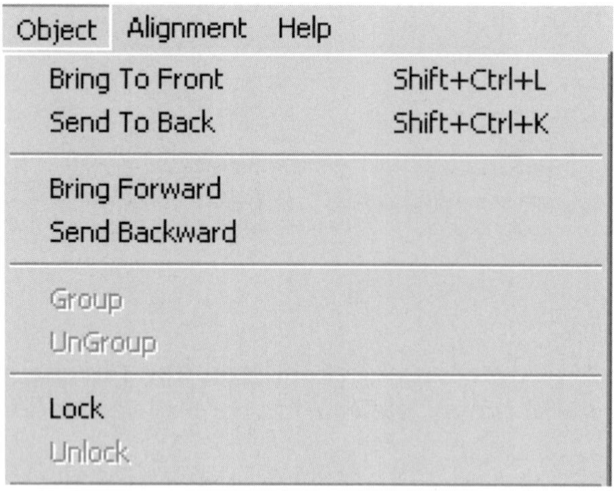

Object	Alignment	Help	
Bring To Front			Shift+Ctrl+L
Send To Back			Shift+Ctrl+K
Bring Forward			
Send Backward			
Group			
UnGroup			
Lock			
Unlock			

Figure 9.18

Now that's more like it. Our title is a lot more visible now that a blue rectangle surrounds it (Figure 9.19).

Figure 9.19

GROUPING AND LOCKING

If I were satisfied with this look, I'd *Group* the title and rectangle, and then *Lock* them together. To group, choose the Selection Tool and, while pressing the mouse, drag the cursor around the objects to be grouped. Then select Group from the Object menu (see Figure 9.18). To lock them, select the object that is now a group, and choose Lock from the Object menu. Now you can't make inadvertent changes to your creation.

TRANSPARENCY

I'm not happy with the title and its blue rectangle. I think the rectangle would look better if it were less opaque, so that some ocean showed through. To set the transparency of an object, select the Transparency Tool for the object that you want to affect. The Transparency box is right next to the Fill box.

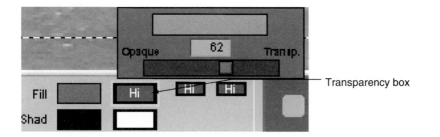

In this example, I've selected the Transparency box for the Fill, which affects the transparency of my blue rectangle. To make the blue box more transparent, I must first place it in the foreground. I choose Bring To Front from the Object menu. Then I click and hold on the Fill Transparency Tool. A slider appears, and as I drag it to the right, the blue rectangle will become more transparent. It now has a HI (high) degree of transparency. I need to send it to the back, using the Object Tool. Now that I'm satisfied, I'll group and lock it.

ALIGNMENT MENU

There's a second menu available once you've opened the Title Tool; it is called the *Alignment menu*. You'll see that it has many items that help you position selected objects inside the frame. Using the selection tool, practice using the various alignment choices available in the pull-down menu.

LINES AND ARROWS

There are tools for creating arrows and lines of various thickness. These work with the Line-Drawing Tool and can be changed and manipulated just like the rectangle we created using the Drawing Tool. Select the line thickness or

arrow shape, and then click on the Line Tool and drag across the Title Tool
to create a line or arrow.

OTHER BUTTONS

The Video Placement Tool is one tool I'd suggest you avoid using for now.
It doesn't move objects within the frame; it moves the entire frame.

On the Media Composer and Xpress toolbar, there are two buttons for
creating rolling ("R") and crawling ("C") titles.

ROLLING TITLES

Filmmakers have always called a title that moves from the bottom of the screen
to the top of the screen a *crawl*. The many credits that appear at the end of
films are usually handled by a lengthy crawl. Avid calls them *rolling titles*.
They're not that difficult to create. The one oddity is that the speed with
which the title "rolls" is determined by the size of the clip in the Timeline.
To make the crawl go faster, you trim the clip. To make it go slower, you
extend its length (size) in the Timeline. Unfortunately, Xpress DV doesn't yet
have rolling or crawling titles, but I bet the day will come soon.

To create a "rolling title":

1. Select a background (black or video) by putting the position indica-
    tor over black or a shot in the Timeline.

2. From the Clip menu, choose New Title.
3. Click on the Text Tool.
4. On the far right of the Title Tool, click the "R" button—it turns green.
5. Choose your font and point size, and click the text alignment box for "centered."
6. Type the text. As you type, the text might word wrap. Don't worry. Just keep typing. Press the Return key at the end of each line of text.
7. Get the Selector Tool and drag the handles to the left and right to make the text wide enough to prevent word wrap.
8. If the text goes onto more than one page (screen), drag the scroll bar that appears on the right-hand side of the Title window to scroll through the text.
9. Select Close from File menu.
10. Save the title:
    • Select the target disk and bin.
    • Don't save with Fast Save.
11. Click OK.

The title is saved as a clip in a bin.

Cutting in Rolling Titles

Double-click on the title so it opens in the Source Monitor. Mark an IN at the very beginning of the Source Monitor and an OUT at the very end. Now go to the Timeline and mark an IN where you think you'd like the title to go. Usually it's at the very end of your sequence. Now splice the rolling title into the Timeline. You may find you have this huge title that is miles long. Simply lasso the tail to get into Trim Mode and drag the roller to the left. This will shorten the title and speed it up. Another technique is to mark an IN in the Source Monitor. Now estimate the amount of time you think the rolling title should last. If it's 15 seconds, go to your Timeline and place an IN and an OUT about 15 seconds apart. Now overwrite the rolling title.

It may seem strange, but you actually use Trim Mode to adjust the speed of your rolling (or crawling) title. Lasso the tail of the rolling title and drag the roller to the left to speed up the title (and make it shorter). Drag the roller to the right to slow it down (and make it longer).

CRAWLING TITLES

Avid calls a title that move across the screen horizontally a *crawl*. The text runs along the frame from screen-right to screen-left.

You create crawling titles the same way you create rolling titles, but you click on the "C" instead of the "R." You'll need to use the Selector Tool handles to keep the letters from word wrapping. For example, let's say you wanted the following title to crawl across the screen:

"New England Patriots win the SuperBowl. First time in club's history. Watch the News at Eleven for highlights."

To get this text to crawl as a single line, you'll need to drag the Selector handle to the far right so that the text doesn't word wrap, as this sentence does. To get the crawl to come true—that took a miracle.

ADVANCED TITLES

We're going to discuss more advanced titles at the end of the next chapter, after we have learned about Avid's visual effects. Having an understanding of the way the Avid's effects work will help us better understand more complex titles.

SUGGESTED ASSIGNMENTS

1. Open the Title Tool and choose a font size.
2. Type a title.
3. Click on the Selector Tool and drag the right-hand selection handle to make the title fit on the line.
4. Move the title around inside the frame.
5. Add a drop shadow. Increase and decrease the depth and direction of the shadow.
6. Change to a depth shadow.
7. Save your title.
8. Close the Title Tool and cut the title into your Timeline. If you need to, create a V2 track.
9. Render your title.
10. Open the Title Tool. Create a light-colored title. Add a depth shadow. Now create a blend for that title.
11. Close the Title Tool and cut this title onto V2.
12. Render it.
13. Open the Title Tool. Create a title. Draw a rectangle. Place the title on top of the rectangle.
14. Close the Title Tool and cut this title onto V2.
15. Render it.

10

Effects

I learned to make films before I ever worked in video, and I guess that's why it took me a while to take advantage of Avid's extensive effects. Effects are so expensive in film that you use them only when nothing else will work. Put in a few freeze frames and a strobe effect, toss in a flop to change screen direction, and suddenly you're writing checks for thousands of dollars to an optical house in New York or Los Angeles. And then you wait weeks to see how those effects come out. When I started working in video, effects were certainly faster, but only marginally cheaper. Go into an online editing suite that has a sophisticated effects generator, and the bill you get when you're finished can grab your attention pretty fast.

It's different on an Avid. The effects are free, and you don't have to wait more than a few minutes—and usually much less—to see what they'll look like. It's true that if you're using the Avid as an offline machine—meaning you'll finish the project on film or at an online tape facility—you'll need to worry about your budget. But for all of the projects you can finish on the Avid, don't worry. Use as many effects as the show demands.

Keep in mind that not every project benefits from a lot of effects. Scenes involving strong performances by talented actors are usually hurt by visual effects because they steal the scene from the actors. Montage sequences that are music-driven or contain stunning cinematography are great candidates for effects because the right effect heightens the mood and visual impact of the sequence. Rock videos, which are designed to be viewed many times, benefit from complex visual effects. Otherwise, the video becomes stale after one or two viewings. Title sequences, show openings, and transitions between acts are usually polished with visual effects as a means of grabbing the audience's attention. The same can be said of television commercials, which are often packed with stunning visual effects.

Some editors think of effects as "crutches," used to mask serious problems in the material. Others think they needlessly junk up a show. I think this is another area where the Avid comes in handy. Try it with effects, and try it without. You can then make your decision based on what it looks like when you play the sequence. To evaluate the effectiveness of an effect, you must really watch. You must turn yourself into a critical viewer, which, as we've said before, is the editor's most important skill.

KINDS OF EFFECTS

There are two categories of effects: transition effects and segment effects. *Transition effects* are applied at the cut point or the transition point in the Timeline. These effects change the way Shot A transitions to Shot B. A dissolve is an example of a transition effect. Instead of a straight cut, Shot A fades out while Shot B fades in, creating a melting of the two shots.

Segment effects are applied to the entire clip or segment in the Timeline. You might have a shot in the sequence where your actor is facing screen left-to-right, and by applying a *flop*, the screen direction of the entire shot is changed so the actor is facing screen right-to-left. When you use a segment effect, you are affecting a segment in the Timeline.

Segment effects can work on one video track, like the flop, or on several video tracks. For instance, you might have an image on V2 interact with an image on V1. In a multilayered effect, V1 is always the background layer, and V2 (and V3, V4) is layered on top of the background.

Many effects work as both transition effects and segment effects. They can be applied to either a transition or a segment. Applying effects to a transition or segment is really simple. Getting them to do what you want is a bit more complicated.

EFFECT PALETTE

Let's take a look at the Effect Palette. Go to the Tools menu and select Effect Palette. Or simply go to the Project window and click on the little tab that looks like one of those naval flags that's used to signal by semaphore. Once the Effect Palette opens, you'll see a box with two columns.

The left-hand column lists the categories of effects. Once you click on a category, a list of the types of effects your system offers is displayed in the right-hand column. In Figure 10.1, I've clicked on the Box Wipe category, and my choices are listed in the right-hand column.

Click here to open the Effect Palette.

Figure 10.1   Effect Palette

Scroll through the category list, clicking on the different categories, and look at the many choices offered. For instance, under the Blend category, you see six different blend effects (Figure 10.2).

Figure 10.2   Blend effects

APPLYING AN EFFECT

It's easy to apply an effect. Just click on the icon for the effect you want, and drag it from the Effect Palette to the Timeline. Release it when you've reached the transition or segment of your choice.

Let's try a transition effect. Let's use a squeeze effect. Click on the Squeeze category to see the choices. There are quite a few squeeze effects to choose from. Let's try a Centered Zoom.

Here is Figure 10.3—the outgoing shot of people climbing into a van, and Figure 10.4—a dolly shot past a row of houses in Soweto, outside Johannesburg.

Figure 10.3

Figure 10.4

Now I'm going to click on the Centered Zoom icon in the Effect Palette, drag it onto the transition point in the Timeline, and release it. There. I've got a centered zoom squeeze between the two shots.

Drag the icon to the Timeline and release it.

Figure 10.5 gives you some idea of what the effect looks like. The house starts out small and then gets bigger and bigger as it squeezes out the shot of the people and the van.

Figure 10.5

Xpress DV RealTime Effects Button

As you may recall from the last chapter, Xpress DV users don't always have the same title and effects capabilities as Media Composer and Xpress users. You can't see your titles or your effects in the default mode. Examine your Timeline toolbar and see if the RealTime Effect toggle button is green (it looks like a ball). If it's blue, you won't be able to play your effects. Click on the blue ball so it's green. Now your effects will play.

RealTime Effect toggle button

You should also go to the Clip menu (Special menu for Media Composer) and make sure Render On-the-Fly is selected.

Applying More Effects

Let's try applying some different effects to other transitions. Click on the category called *Shape Wipe*. Click and drag the effect called *Horizontal Bands* to a transition in your Timeline.

Admittedly, some of the effects are fairly goofy—transitional effects that only George Lucas could love.

Now let's try a segment effect. Scroll down the Effect Palette until you see the category "Image" in the left-hand column. Click on it. Now click on the effect called Flop. This effect changes the screen direction of a shot. Here's a shot showing South Africa's second black president, Thabo Mbeki, talking to South Africa's last white president, F.W. De Klerk.

To change the clip's screen direction, I simply drag the Flop icon onto the clip itself, not onto the transition, and presto, the screen direction changes (Figures 10.6 and 10.7).

Figure 10.6

Figure 10.7

COLORED DOTS

When you look at an effect in the Effect Palette or at the effect icon in the Timeline, you'll see a colored dot. These dots tell you how complex the effect is and whether it will play in real time, or if it will need to be rendered. We discussed rendering in Chapter 9. As you recall, an effect, like a title, is a new image or creation. To see this new creation, the effect needs to be created by the computer so that new media sits on your media drive, the way a master clip does; however, the Avid has the ability to play most effects in a sort of preview mode. These effects, which can be played in the Timeline even though they have not been rendered, are called *real-time effects*.

The Xpress DV has a simple color scheme to tell you which effects are real-time effects. Effects with green dots are real-time effects—they will play in the Timeline if the RealTime Effect button is green. Effects with no dots are complex effects. When you place an effect that has no dot in the Effect Palette into the Timeline, a blue dot appears. The blue dot means it has to be rendered.

The Media Composer and Xpress use a more complex system. Some dots are orange, some are green, and some are blue. Which effects have which dots depends on the Avid model you're working on. Honestly, this whole dot business is fairly confusing and counterintuitive. Here's a quick guide that helps (I hope):

- The effects with *no dots* are the most complex effects and will take a long time to render. They turn blue when placed in the Timeline.
- The effects with *green dots* are less complex; sometimes you'll be able to play them in real time, and sometimes you'll have to render them to see them.
- The effects with *orange dots* are the least complex, and you should always be able to play them in real time.

THIRD-PARTY PLUG-IN EFFECTS

The latest Avid models come with effects created by Avid, as well as by other companies that specialize in visual effects. If you look at the Effect Palette in Figure 10.1, you'll see two categories that contain special plug-in effects: AVXSample and Illusion FX. All of the icons for plug-in effects look like electrical wall outlets. Normally, these are not real-time effects, they are complicated, and they take a long time to render. Let's skip them for now, until we have mastered the less complicated ones.

EFFECT EDITOR

So far we've looked at some fairly straightforward effects. As you can see, it's not all that difficult to apply an effect to either a transition or a segment in the Timeline. Now let's look at effects that can be changed in significant ways by using the *Effect Editor*.

Almost all effects have *parameters*, which are specific features that can be altered or adjusted. For instance, you might have one shot on the screen and then a second image appears inside a box. The image in the box may start out small and gradually fill the frame, covering up the first image. There are a lot of parameters you could manipulate to enhance this effect. You could, for instance, give the box a border. You could give the border a color. You could create a path for the box to follow as it moves around the screen. You could have the box get bigger as it moves around the screen. These are all parameters you can control with the Effect Editor (Figure 10.8).

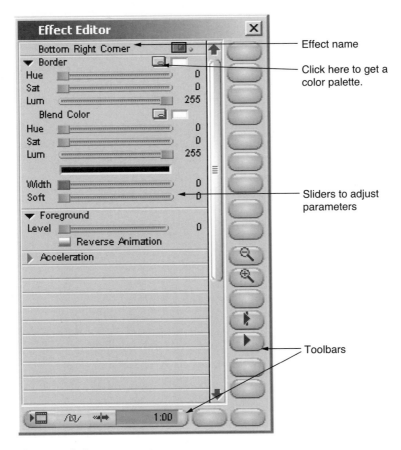

Figure 10.8 Effect Editor

You can also open the Effect Editor from the Tools menu, or, if you're going to be working with several effects that are already in the Timeline, you can get into Effects Editing Mode by selecting it from the Toolset menu.

Opening the Effect Editor

After you have applied an effect to the segment or transition in the Timeline:

1. Place the blue position indicator on the effect's icon in the Timeline.
2. Click the Effect Mode button on the Timeline toolbar or the Source/Record Fast menu. This opens the Effect Editor.

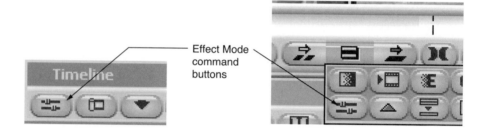

You'll see that the Record Monitor changes. It is now officially called the *Effect Preview Monitor* (Figure 10.9). Now you're looking at just the clip containing the effect, not the entire sequence. Notice that two key frames are already set in the position bar.

Figure 10.9   The Effect Editor and Effect Preview Monitor

Let's examine the Effect Editor. The one in Figure 10.8 is for a Peel effect called "Bottom Right Corner." At the top of the Effect Editor you'll see the name of the effect you are editing. In the middle area you'll see the parameters that can be changed. Triangle-shaped openers give you access to sliders, which control the amount or quantity of a particular parameter. Click on a triangle to show or hide the sliders.

Each effect will have different parameters because each effect behaves differently; however, the effects within a category usually have similar parameters. Figure 10.10 shows the Effect Editor at work. The Peel effect has been applied to a transition between a map of South Africa and a group of South Africans.

Figure 10.10

Using the Effect Editor, I created a border, which makes the peel look like a page that's turning, and then I gave the border a cream color.

Here are some of the different parameters you'll encounter:

Border. This changes the color of the border, or box, that surrounds an image. You can also change the border's width and transparency.

Foreground Level. On most transitional effects, this represents the proportion of incoming to outgoing frames. On blends and key effects, this represents the video's transparency.

Reverse. This reverses the parameter you have set. Instead of a box starting out small and getting bigger, it will start big and shrink.

Acceleration. This controls the start and end of a move, so the move isn't too abrupt.

Scaling. This changes the size of the box. You can manipulate the width and height of boxes.

Most boxes have handles that you can drag to change the shape of the box. You can also click in the center of the box and drag it to a new position.

Effect Editing Tools

Several important buttons can help you work with each effect and control its parameters. You'll notice that when you open the Effect Editor, the Record side of the Source/Record Monitor changes into the Effect Preview Monitor. The position bar offers a different set of command buttons, and it contains two key frames: one at the beginning and one at the end. You can add additional key frames with the Add Key Frame command.

Key frames enable you to change a parameter's look over time. For instance, you might place a box around an image and start that image on the far left of the screen. That's Key Frame Number One. Then you move the box a little toward the center of the frame and set the next key frame. Move the box some more and set another key frame. You could have the box go all over the place by setting multiple key frames. The number of key frames available on any given effect will depend on the version of Avid software you have. Some effects might have only four key frames, whereas others might have unlimited key frames.

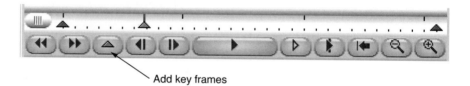

Add key frames

The Effect Editor also has toolbars containing helpful tools (Figure 10.11). One tool will render the effect, and another allows you to type in a new length for a transitional effect. Just type a new value and press Return or Enter.

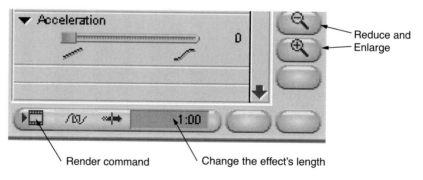

Render command   Change the effect's length

Figure 10.11

Another command lets you reduce the frame, so you can start an effect off-screen, and then enlarge the frame to return the screen to normal.

Let's work with a segment effect and use the Effect Editor and key frames to change the way a parameter works. We'll use the segment effect called *Superimpose* and work with the Level parameter. The Superimpose effect is available in the Blend category of effects.

For a superimposition to work, you need two images. First I add a second video track, V2. I simply go to the Clip menu and select New Video Track. Then I overwrite the second clip onto track V2. Figures 10.12 and 10.13 show the two clips. Next I drag the Superimpose icon from the Effect Palette onto the V2 image.

Figure 10.12   The image on V1

Figure 10.13   The image on V2

Now I open the Effect Editor by placing the position indicator on the effect icon and pressing the Effect Mode button on the Fast menu.

Effect Editor
Superimpose
Foreground
Level ———————————————— 50
   Reverse Animation
Acceleration

Right now the effect gives me a superimposition of the image on V2 over the image on V1. The level is set at 50, meaning that the two images are blended evenly together (half and half, or 50 percent). If I play the image by clicking on the Play Forward or Play Loop button, I'll see that the two images remain blended at this level throughout the length of the clip. That's not what I want. What I want to do is change the amount of superimposition over time. To do that, I will need to change the Level parameter (which affects the amount of V2's opacity) and set key frames in the effect's position bar, which will affect the Level changes over time.

First, I click on the first key frame in the position bar to make it turn pink and to put the position indicator on top of it. I always do this whenever I'm working with the Effect Editor, to make sure I'm starting at the beginning.

Now I go to Effect Editor and drag the Level slider to the left, resulting in 0 percent opacity. When I do that, the foreground image, V2, will not be seen at all. I want this to be the case at the beginning of the effect.

Effect Editor

Superimpose
▼ Foreground
Level ⬛━━━━━━━━━━━━━━ 0
☐ Reverse Animation
▶ Acceleration

Now I place a second key frame farther along the position bar, as shown in Figure 10.14. To place a key frame, just drag the position indicator to a spot farther along the position bar and click on the Key Frame button. Xpress users can also press the letter N on the keyboard, the same one you used to set audio key frames. Next click on the key frame to make sure it's pink. Now go to the Effect Editor and move the Level slider to 25.

Figure 10.14

Now I place a third key frame, farther along on the position bar, and click on it to select it, and change the opacity to 75.

Now the foreground image really starts to come through the background image.

Finally, I set the last key frame at the end and change the opacity to 100.

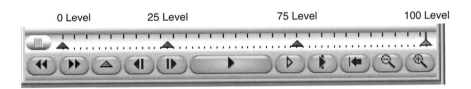

Now I've created my effect. The image begins with V1 totally filling the frame—Level is set at 0 (Figure 10.15). Over time, the image on V2 slowly takes over, as increasing amounts of opacity are set at those key frames (Figure 10.16), until finally the opacity is set to 100 and only the V2 image appears on the screen (Figure 10.17).

Figure 10.15   Begin with just V1.

Figure 10.16   V2 is supered over V1.

Figure 10.17   V2 takes over the screen.

Manipulating Key Frames

- After you have created a key frame, you can move it by holding the Option key (Mac) or Alt key (Windows) and dragging it to a new position.
- You can change the parameter for any given key frame by clicking on it (it turns pink) and changing the parameters in the Effect Editor.
- You can delete a key frame by selecting it and hitting the Delete key.

EFFECT QUICK REVIEW

Steps for adding effects:

1. Load a sequence into the Timeline.
2. Open Effect Palette from the Tools menu or from the Project window.
3. Choose the effect and drag it into the Timeline.
4. Adjust the effect's parameters with the Effect Editor (open it from the Tools menu, Timeline toolbar, or Fast menu).

DELETING EFFECTS

It's easy to delete an effect you don't want anymore. Here are two ways to get rid of both transitional and segment effects.

To delete a transitional effect:

- Put the position indicator on the transition. Press the Remove Effect button from the Fast menu.
- Go to the transition and enter the Trim Mode. Press the Delete key.

Remove Effect button

To delete a segment effect:

- Put the position indicator on the effect icon. Press the Remove Effect button from the Fast menu.
- Hit a Segment Mode button and select the segment in the Timeline. Press the Delete key.

ADDING DISSOLVES

Dissolves are so common that there's a Dissolve key on the keyboard (the "\" key), a Dissolve button on the Fast menu, and one on the Timeline toolbar. Just follow these steps to get the dissolve you want:

Add Dissolve button

1. Put the blue position indicator on the transition.
2. Hit the Add Dissolve button.
3. A dialog window appears, giving you choices to control how the dissolve will look.
4. Choose the duration. A 30-frame dissolve is the default length.
5. Choose whether the dissolve is centered on the cut, starting on the cut, ending on the cut, or custom-designed by you.
6. Choose the target disk.
7. Click Add to place the dissolve on the transition, or choose Add and Render to place it on the transition and have it rendered. I usually just click Add.

SAVING AN EFFECT AS A TEMPLATE

After doing all of the work involved in setting the many parameters for an effect, you can save those parameters so that you can use them again on another transition or segment in the Timeline. Simply drag the icon in the Effect Editor window to a bin. Rename it in the bin. You have just created a template. To place the template you created on a different transition or a segment, simply click on it in the bin and drag it to the Timeline.

Click and drag
the icon to a bin.

There are two important effects that aren't found on the Effects Palette: freeze frames and motion effects.

FREEZE FRAMES

Freeze frames are given special status and are found in the Clip menu. Just follow these steps to create your first freeze. After you've done it once, you'll be able to do it in your sleep.

1. In the Timeline, go to the tail of the shot you want to freeze and put the position indicator on the last frame. Remember, in the Timeline Option-Command-drag (Mac) or Ctrl-Alt-drag (Windows) the position indicator to jump to the clip's tail frame.
2. Select "Match Frame" (Fast menu item), and the clip will appear in the Source Monitor with that frame marked by an IN.
3. Go to the Clip menu and choose Freeze Frame.
4. Select the length. Click OK. A new clip is created, labeled "Clip name" FF. Open it in the Source Monitor.
5. Mark an IN and an OUT in the Source Monitor.
6. In the Timeline, go to the first frame of the next shot and mark IN.
7. Splice in the freeze.

Remember, there will be no sound.

MOTION EFFECTS

This special effect has its own button in the Source Monitor's toolbar on the Xpress or on the Fast menu on the Media Composer. With this tool you can create slow and fast motion, reverse the motion, or create a strobe effect. You'll be working in the Source Monitor. You place the shot you want to change in the Source Monitor, mark the part you want to change, and the Avid creates a new effect, which you cut into your Timeline. All of the motion effects share the same dialog box (Figure 10.18).

Motion Effect   ☒

- ☑ Variable Speed

	Current	New	
Duration	456	912	Frames
Rate	30	15.00	FPS
		50.00	% Speed

○ Fit To Fill

○ Strobe Motion

Update every [5] frames

Render 2-Field Motion Effect Using:

[Duplicated Field ▼]

Target Drive (⊏ Data1 (E:) ▼)

(Create) (Create and Render) (Cancel)

Figure 10.18

Motion Effect
command

Slow Motion/Fast Motion

1. Select a clip in a bin that you want to apply a motion effect to, and double-click to open it.
2. In the Source Monitor, mark an IN and an OUT to show the section of the clip you want to use for the effect.
3. Press the Motion Effect button. A Motion Effect dialog box appears (see Figure 10.18).
4. Fifteen frames per second (fps) and 50 percent are the default settings. The resulting shot is twice as long, which is another way of saying it appears to be twice as slow as normal.
5. Choose another setting, such as 8 fps, to make it even slower.
6. When you click on Create and Render, the motion effect appears as a new clip in the bin. Now you open that clip and splice or overwrite it into your sequence.

Reverse Motion

This is useful, for instance, if you have a zoom that goes in and you want to make the zoom go out.

1. Select a clip in a bin that you want to apply a motion effect to, and double-click.
2. In the Source Monitor, mark an IN and an OUT to show the section you want.
3. Press the Motion Effect button.
4. Put a minus sign (–) in front of the fps or percent rate. Choose 30 fps if you want it to play at normal speed.
5. After clicking on Create and Render, cut the new clip into your sequence.

Strobe

1. Select a clip in a bin that you want to apply a motion effect to, and double-click.
2. In the Source Monitor, mark an IN and an OUT to show the section you want.
3. Press the Motion Effect button on the Source Monitor toolbar.
4. Click on the Strobe Motion box and deselect the Variable Speed box.
5. "Update Every 5 Frames" is the default setting. This means every fifth frame is displayed, creating the strobe effect. Try 5 frames and then try another number.
6. After clicking on Create and Render, cut the new clip into your sequence.

The motion effects on many DV systems need to be rendered before they will play in the Timeline. That's why I suggest you choose Create and Render, rather than simply Create. Media Composer users can click on the Create button, however.

RENDERING

No matter how many real-time effects you use, at some point you'll need to render your effects to send your work out to tape. If you use third-party plug-in effects, they'll probably need to be rendered before they'll play in the Timeline. Rendering can take up a lot of time and some space on your hard drive, so render as late in the editing process as possible, and render only those effects you know are going in the final sequence. If you have several effects bunched together in the Timeline because you're creating a complex visual look, and they won't play because they are so complex, try selecting

Expert Render from the Clip menu. The Avid will figure out the least number of effects that will need to be rendered to get the effects to play together.

Xpress DV users will need to render all of their effects (and titles) before they can go out to tape.

Rendering Single Effects

1. Place the blue position indicator on the effect's icon in the Timeline.
2. Click the Render Effect button in the Fast menu, or choose Render from the Clip menu.
3. When the dialog box appears, choose a target disk.
4. Click OK.

Render Effect ——————   —— Remove Effect

Rendering Multiple Effects

First, click the Track Selector boxes to choose the track(s) holding the effects you want to render.

1. Mark an IN before the first effect and an OUT after the last effect.
2. Go to the Clip menu and select Render In/Out.
3. When the dialog box appears, choose a target disk.
4. Click OK.

Some of you may recall that in Chapter 5 we learned how to place menu items on the keyboard, and to practice this, we placed the Render In/Out on the keyboard. We placed it on the Shift-R key. So, whenever you have several effects to render, place IN and OUT points, and then, instead of going through the menus to find the command you want, simply hold the Shift key and then press the R key.

WAITING FOR EFFECTS TO RENDER

If you have complex effects to render, the process can take a long time. I've waited 5 minutes for a single effect to render. Five minutes might not seem like a long time, but if you're really in a flow and coming up with a lot of ideas, it can seem painfully slow.

One strategy is to wait until you've created several effects and then render them all at once, while you go do something else. Lunch is one possibility.

NESTING

Nesting is a fairly advanced technique. It lets you add an effect to an effect by permitting you to jump inside the first effect. You'll use either of the Segment keys to nest. You can nest any segment effect, but I most often use it with titles.

Let's create a title and put an image inside the letters. If the image has movement, we'll see that movement inside the letters. First, create a title with large letters. I used a point size of 96 to spell "South Africa." Next, I cut the title into the Timeline. But instead of placing it over another shot, I spliced it into V1, so I get white letters over a black background (Figure 10.19).

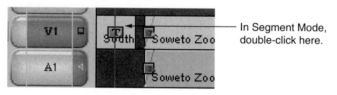

Figure 10.19

Now I click on either Segment Mode button and then click on the title segment in the Timeline—the segment is highlighted. Now I double-click on the title segment in the Timeline. It opens up to show nested tracks—1.1, 1.2, and 1.3. Get out of Segment Mode by clicking the segment button again.

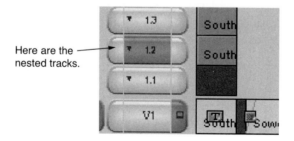

Next I select a clip that I want to "see" through the letters. I put it into the Source Monitor, mark an IN where I want it to start, and then overwrite it onto the nested track 1.2. To do this, patch the source track on V1 to 1.2. Then mark the clip in 1.2. You've got three marks. Now overwrite.

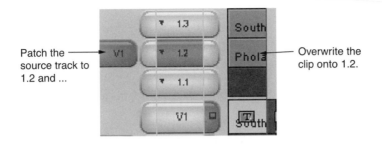

Patch the source track to 1.2 and ...   Overwrite the clip onto 1.2.

Now get back into Segment Mode and double-click the title segment in V1. The nest collapses and you're back to the regular Timeline. The result of our work shows the clip moving through the letters in the title (Figure 10.20).

Figure 10.20

Now that was pretty simple, wasn't it? Instead of having a shot travel through the letters over a black background, I could have placed the title on V2, so that it was superimposed over a shot on V1, and then done the same thing. Then I would have had a shot travel through letters over a visual. To do this, start with a shot on V1 and a title on V2, and nest a shot inside the title on V2.

Nesting works with any segment effect, letting you add an effect to an effect. For instance, you can have a segment on V1 and a segment on V2. Now place the Picture-in-Picture (Blend) effect onto V2, so that you have a picture (the shot on V2) inside the segment on V1. If you get into Segment Mode and double-click on the segment in V2, you can drag the Color Effect from the Image category onto V2's nest (onto 1.2). Now open the Effect Editor to change the color, and finally double-click on the segment on V2 to collapse the nest. Now you have a color effect just on the picture-in-picture, while the background image on V1 maintains its color.

COLOR CORRECTION

The only way you used to be able to change the color of a clip or segment in the Timeline was to drag the Color Effect icon (Image category) to the segment, open the Effect Editor, and manipulate a few parameters.

Now the latest versions of Avid come with a powerful Color Correction Tool, which you'll access via the Toolset menu. Color Correction acts like an effect, but it's in the Toolset menu because it changes the appearance of the Avid screen rather dramatically (Figure 10.21). The tool is designed for professional colorists and experienced Avid editors. It's quite complex, but hopefully I can help break its code so that even a beginner can tap its power.

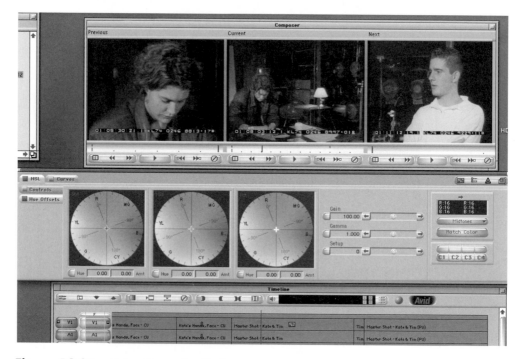

Figure 10.21   Color Correction Tool

You don't use the Effect Editor with Color Correction. Everything is done using the tool itself. As soon as you select the Color Correction Tool, you'll see three monitors showing you three segments (or clips) in the Timeline. Color correction is relative. Changing the color of one segment without seeing how it looks in comparison with the segment before (and after) would be a mistake because shots would not match the surrounding shots.

The middle monitor is the one showing you the clip or segment that the position indicator in the Timeline rests on. That's the segment whose colors you are changing. The left-hand monitor shows you the segment just before it, and the right-hand monitor shows you the segment just after it. Each monitor has a position indicator and commands so that you can navigate the segment. If you look at the three monitors, from left to right, you'll see the names Previous, Current, and Next. If you click and hold on the name, you'll see a pull-down menu that lets you change the segment that monitor is showing (Figure 10.22). The menu item Reference lets you lock a frame from a segment in one monitor. (I use the left-hand monitor whenever I want to do this.) With the left-hand monitor on Reference, I can hold a segment in that monitor and then move through the Timeline, looking at and fixing specific segments in the middle monitor, and I always have this frame as a reference. Maybe I want to use flesh tones or a shirt color as a reference.

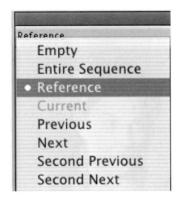

Figure 10.22

Using this pull-down menu, you can also turn these monitors into Waveforms and Vectorscopes. (There are several menu items not shown in Figure 10.22.) In Quad View, you can place your color reference tools in a single monitor, so you can examine them all at once.

The Color Correction Tools look dauntingly complex, but let me explain a few features, so you can try them out. There are two primary tools or groups: the HSL Group (*Hue, Saturation, Luminance*) and the Curves Group. You choose one or the other by clicking on the tab. The tiny box on each tab is called the *Enable button*. Click on that when you want that particular tool to be active, and the box turns pink.

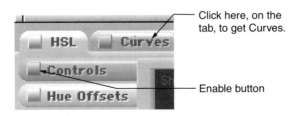

The HSL Group has two tabs: Controls and Hue Offsets. In the Controls Mode you adjust the hue, saturation, brightness, and contrast using sliders to enter specific values. In the Hue Offset tab you have three color wheels that allow you to change the color cast of your segments. I believe the HSL Group is best suited for experienced colorists. The Curves Group is easier to play with because there are fewer variables. If you've ever used Curves in Photoshop, you're already familiar with this tool.

The Curves Group gives you four graphs, representing Red, Green, Blue, and Master. Master lets you change the brightness of the segment. It's easy to adjust the color of a segment by dragging the 45-degree line in any of the three color graphs to create a curve that either increases or decreases the amount of that color in your image. Watch the middle monitor to see the segment's colors change as you drag on the 45-degree line.

If you don't like what you've done, it's easy to return to the default setting. Simply Alt-click (Windows) or Option-click (Mac) the Enable button. You can also click the Enable button to turn off (or on) any changes you've made.

After making changes to a clip, you can drag the Color Correction icon to a bin to use it as a template. You'll also notice that as you color correct a segment in the Timeline, the Color Correction Tool places a Color Correction icon in the Timeline. Just work through the Timeline until all of your shots are color corrected to your satisfaction. You can get rid of an effect using the Remove Effect command.

A WORLD OF EFFECT

We could devote several chapters to the Color Correction Tool and write a whole book on effects. We've just touched the surface in this chapter. There's the whole subject of third-party plug-in effects, which I barely mentioned, and the many three-dimensional effects, which come as a standard feature on many Avid models, which I didn't discuss at all. To give you an idea of how much information is available, consider that the effects manual Avid used to give out with its products is more than 300 pages long. The Avid Help menu has some information, as does the CD-ROM that comes with the Avid software. I hope you have enough information here to get you started. Through practice and experimentation, I think you'll do fine.

SUGGESTED ASSIGNMENTS

Take the information provided in this chapter and apply it to as many effects as you have time to play with. Just drag the effect you wish to examine onto the Timeline, open the Effect Editor, and manipulate the parameters. Use key frames to change the parameters over time.

11

Saving Your Work

IF IT'S A COMPUTER, IT WILL CRASH

Not too long ago there were articles in newspapers, weekly magazines, and online news sites about the convergence of television and computers, with companies arguing over whether we should be watching TV on a computer monitor or viewing our favorite Internet site on the old RCA or Sony Trinitron. One scribe who favored the television monitor said he didn't want to be watching the SuperBowl and have the system crash during a game-winning touchdown drive.

There is some truth to that observation. Computers do crash, they have bugs, and they are susceptible to viruses and other infestations. When you stop and think about it, those are problems we don't encounter on any of the other countless electronic products that surround us. My microwave doesn't crash, my television doesn't have bugs, and my CD player hasn't caught a virus, although I've loaded hundreds and hundreds of CDs into it.

That said, the various Avids that I've been using for 5 years have been quite dependable. (Yes, the sound you hear is my knuckles striking wood.) It has never quit on me. It has crashed only about 30 times, and I have never lost more than about 10 minutes of work. Given how much I've used it, and the service it has rendered, I figure it's one of the most dependable things in my life!

Another testimonial: The Avids I use to teach my digital editing classes have behaved beautifully. I've had only about three crashes in front of a roomful of students. That's an amazing record of performance. So, I'm a satisfied customer, and I don't hesitate to praise the machines whenever I'm asked. My point, however, is that although Avids are incredibly dependable, they will crash. And when they do, you'd better be ready.

BACKING UP

If there is a system crash, hard drive glitch, or any number of horrors just waiting to befall you, *all* of your work can be lost—unless you back up your work. By that I mean placing the information about your bins and sequences on a Zip disk, USB Flash drive, or CD. Here's how:

1. When you finish editing for the day, and after you save all of your work, close the project and quit the application. You are returned to the desktop, or Finder.
2. Double-click My Computer (Windows) or the Macintosh HD (Mac).
3. Windows users go to Program Files\Avid\Avid Xpress DV (or Media Composer). Look for the folder called "Avid Projects."
    Mac users, go to the Users folder, then to Shared, and there you'll find Avid Projects.
4. Double-click the Avid Projects folder (Figure 11.1).

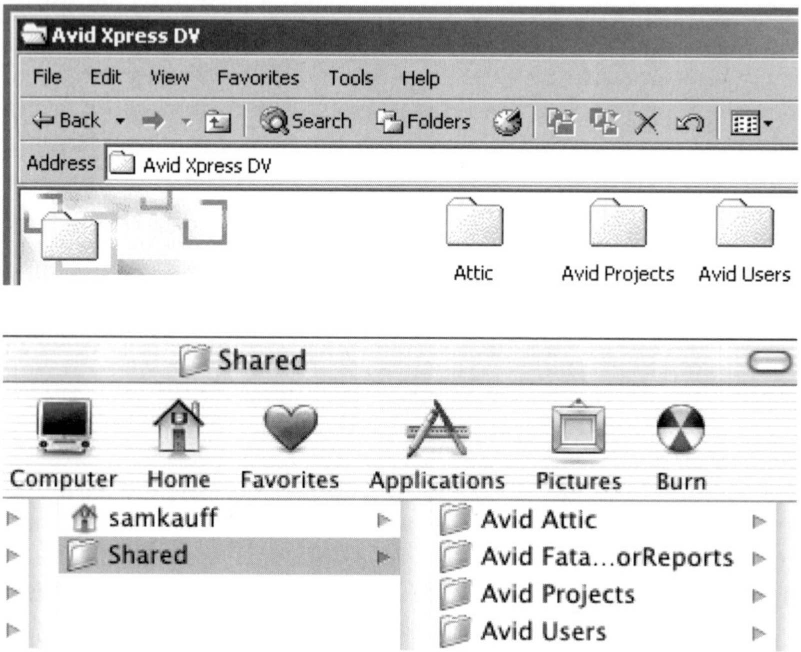

Figure 11.1   The Avid Projects folder on Windows and Mac

5. Scroll through it until you find your project—the one you named.
6. Insert either a CD-RW or a Zip disk into the computer's CPU slot for that type of disk. (Make sure your disk is not carrying a virus!) A USB Flash drive will work as well.

7. When the storage device appears on the desktop, drag the project folder containing your project's name onto the device's icon (Figure 11.2). The computer will automatically begin to copy to that disk.

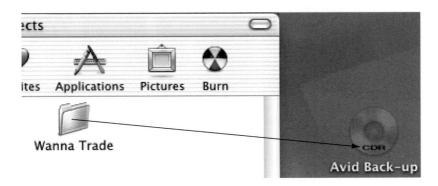

Figure 11.2   Backing up (Mac)

8. If you have placed your project folder on a CD, you'll need to burn it before ejecting.

That wasn't so hard. Remember to do it daily.

Examine the contents of the Zip disk named *Avid Back-Up* (Figure 11.3), which contains the "Wanna Trade" project folder. Notice that there is one for April 14 and another for April 15. As I said, you should do this at the end of every editing session, and then rename the latest version with the current date, so you can easily find the one with the most recent changes.

Avid Back-Up		
18 items	62.8 MB in disk	
Name	Size	Kind
▷ 📁 S. Kauffmann	—	folder
▷ 📁 Wanna Trade? April 14	—	folder
▷ 📁 Wanna Trade? April 15	—	folder

Figure 11.3

All of the project settings, sequences, and bins, including all of your titles, effects, clips, subclips, and audio clip information—everything—is copied to your backup disk. Open the most recent folder and you'll see that everything associated with the project has been backed up onto the backup disk, as in Figure 11.4.

Figure 11.4   Contents of the "Wanna Trade" folder

It's important to note that none of the media files—none of the digitized picture or sound—is copied to the Zip disk or CD. Only the information the Avid has created about the project is copied, but that's usually all you'll need.

AFTER THE CRASH

If there is a bad crash and your project is missing or badly corrupted, or if someone removes your project from the CPU, you can reload all of your files onto your Avid. All you have to do is insert your CD, Flash drive, or Zip disk into the CPU's disk drive and drag your project folder to the Avid Projects folder. Launch the Avid program, and your project and all of the clip information will be there. It will all be listed as "Media Offline," but you can easily re-record the clips. Once you re-record the clips, all of the sequences that you've edited using those clips will be just the way you left them, like magic. We'll learn to re-record your clips later in this chapter.

SAVING USER SETTINGS

You can back up your user settings the same way. All of the user settings you made in the Settings area—how Trim Mode works, how the keyboard is configured, how auto-save works, the color of your tracks in the Timeline—are saved under your name in the Avid Users folder.

COPY USER SETTINGS TO A CD OR ZIP DISK

When you are on the desktop or Finder (the application is closed and the CPU's hard drive is open), repeat the steps you used to get to the Avid Projects folder, and there you'll see the Avid Users folder (see Figure 11.1).

Double-click on the Avid Users folder and then drag your User Settings folder to a disk, as shown in Figure 11.5.

Figure 11.5   Locate your Avid Users folder and drag it to the backup disk.

THE ATTIC

If you recall the work we did with Settings, you'll remember that Bin Settings was one of the first settings we examined (Figure 11.6). There you told the Avid how often and when you wanted your work saved to the *attic*. The attic, you'll recall, is like an attic in a house, where old items get stored. In this case, the old items are previous versions of your work. If there is a crash, if you lose a sequence, or if something happens during an editing session, you can go to the attic and retrieve the last 30 versions, one of which is only 10 or 15 minutes old.

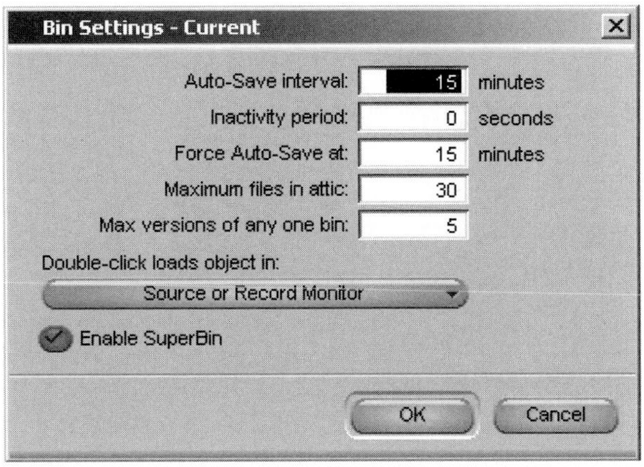

Figure 11.6

Whatever you're looking for, it's probably in the attic (Figure 11.7). You'll find the Attic folder on the hard drive, where the Avid Projects and Avid User folders are located.

Figure 11.7 The Attic folder

Double-click to open it, and you'll see all of the files that have been saved (Figure 11.8). The Avid doesn't just save sequences; instead, it saves the contents of an entire bin.

Figure 11.8 Bins that have been backed up

RETRIEVING A FILE FROM THE ATTIC

1. In the Project window, close all of your bins.
2. Minimize the Avid screen in Windows; on a Mac, hide the Avid screen by pressing Command-H.
3. Open the hard drive on the desktop.
4. Look for the Attic folder in the same place you found the Avid Projects and Avid User folders (see Figure 11.1).
5. Open it.
6. Scroll through it until you find your project—the one you named. Open it.
7. Look for the bin you want. The bin with the smallest number (binname.1) will be the oldest and the bin with the largest number will be the most recent version.
8. Select the bin file(s) you want.
9. Windows users, drag the bin to the desktop. Mac users, option-drag the bin to the desktop.

10. Now open the Avid program from the task bar or Dock.
11. When the Avid program opens, click on the Project window to make it active.
12. From the File menu, choose Open Bin. Navigate inside the directory until you find the bin you just created. It's on the desktop. Select it, then click Open.
13. Now create a new bin. Call it *Restore*.
14. Select the sequence you want from this attic bin, and then option-drag (Mac) or drag (Windows) the sequence to the Restore bin. Close this attic bin.
15. You'll see a folder labeled Other Bins. Open it and now delete the bin you got from the attic (see Deleting Bins).
16. When you quit for the day, you'll see that attic bin on your desktop. Drag it to the Trash.

DELETING BINS

Up to this point we really haven't needed to delete any bins. It's a piece of cake (unless you're in SuperBin Mode). Just click once on the bin icon in the Project window and press the Delete key. The bin will go into the Trash. The problem comes when you're in SuperBin Mode, because clicking once on the bin icon doesn't select the bin—it opens the bin and places it in the SuperBin. The solution is to first hold down the Shift key and then click on the bin icon. That will select it. Now press the Delete key. The bin will go into the Trash.

Once the bin is in the Trash, click and hold on the Project window's Fast menu and select Empty Trash.

BACKING UP MEDIA FILES

Your media files can be quite large, and to back them up you'd need a DVD burner. Because that feature is becoming standard on many systems, you should consider archiving your media files to DVD.

The Avid Unity MediaNet and Avid Unity LANshare are Avid's shared storage products. They allow multiple Avid machines to share the same media, but they also allow you to set them up to automatically back up any and all of your media files. For instance, if you had a system with 640-GB capacity, you could use 320 of those gigabytes for media and the other 320 GB as backup. That way your media files would be 100 percent backed up. Or, you might use 400 GB for storage and 240 GB for backing up only the most critical media files, such as files that are graphics and effects intensive and that can't be easily redigitized or re-recorded. LANshare EX has a more than respectable 1.9-terabyte capacity.

Batch Recording Offline Material

If your material goes offline (on purpose or by accident) or if you are going to record/digitize material that you logged, the process of batch recording/ digitizing is the same. Batch recording/digitizing works only with material that has timecode (e.g., DV, Betacam SP, or DAT tapes containing timecode).

Examine Figure 11.9, which shows a bin in Frame View. The clip on the left is offline. The clip information is there, but the media file either has been erased or was never digitized in the first place.

Figure 11.9

Before you record/digitize anything, you must have the source tapes in front of you. You also need to connect your equipment so that you can send your video and audio signals from the tape deck to the Avid. Take a look at Chapter 6 to review the steps you take to digitize. Once you're set up, follow these steps:

1. In the bin, select all of the video or audio clips that you wish to redigitize or re-record.
2. You can lasso the clips or shift-click the clips.
   - You can first sort the bin to find all of the offline material. Click on the offline column, and press Command-E (Mac) or Ctrl-E (Windows).
   - If all of the clips in the bin were offline, you could press Command-A (Mac) or Ctrl-A (Windows) to select all of the clips.
3. When all of the offline clips are highlighted, go to the Toolset menu and select Record/Digitize.
4. Choose:
   - Your target bin
   - Your resolution
   - Tracks (V1, A1, A2, TC)

5. Go to the Bin menu (Xpress) or Clip menu (Media Composer) and chose "Batch Record/Digitize."
6. A dialog box will open. Make sure "Offline media only" is selected. Then click OK.

The Avid will then ask you for the first tape. You should have all of the source tapes nearby and insert them as the Avid asks for them.

Once the Avid begins to digitize the offline clips, you can watch the process in action. Once a clip is digitized, it is no longer highlighted, so over time the list of highlighted clips gets smaller and smaller, until none are highlighted.

You can abort the batching process at any time. To abort, click on the Trash icon on the Record/Digitize Tool.

Back Up Daily

Now you know *why* you must back up your projects and *how* to do it. You also know how to restore lost or missing projects, how to retrieve files from the attic, and how to redigitize/re-record offline media. And you've been told that one of these days, your beloved Avid is going to crash. Don't say I didn't warn you.

SUGGESTED ASSIGNMENTS

1. Open the CPU's hard drive and examine the folders it contains.
2. Find the Avid Projects folder, the Avid Users folder, and the Attic folder.
3. Open the Avid Projects folder and back up your projects onto a CD or Zip disk.
4. Back up your user file to a CD or Zip disk.

12

Keeping in Sync

SYNC PROBLEMS

When I write about sync problems in this chapter, I have more in mind than just picture and audio tracks falling out of sync. To me, if a music cue is supposed to be heard as soon as a door opens, and instead it comes in 2 seconds late—it's out of sync. If you spend a lot of time getting narration, music, or effects to land perfectly with a visual, and suddenly they don't—you're out of sync. If you have a lower third title on V2 that says "Nelson Mandela," and when you play your sequence, the title comes up over a shot of a building, your title is out of sync. You have sync problems.

Getting out of sync can be an editor's worst nightmare, especially if a client or producer is in the room. One second you're splicing shots, trimming transitions, building tracks, and working at a nice clip, and the next second you're lost. The sound is out of sync with the picture, the music comes in at the wrong moment, the titles land on the wrong shots—you don't know what's happened. As you try to solve the problem, the client is behind you, pacing back and forth, looking at the clock, and sighing meaningfully. It's not helping. If you haven't had this experience, you will, and if you have, I don't need to go any further because you've been there.

Before the use of digital editing equipment, editors working in film experienced these sort of sync problems far more frequently than editors working on tape machines. Because film uses a "double system," meaning the sound is physically separated from the picture, it's easy for the sound and picture to become separated. With a tape-editing machine, the picture and sound occupy the same tape, so sync problems are less frequent. Of course, film editors *want* the separation between picture and sound because it means they possess far greater flexibility and creative control.

The Avid provides the same flexibility that a traditional film-editing machine provides, and with that flexibility comes sync problems. In fact, because you can easily add multiple video and audio tracks to your sequences, the Avid actually increases the potential for sync problems. When you're working with three video tracks and six audio tracks, a sync problem results in a confusing mess in the Timeline. Fortunately, some tools can help you get back into sync quickly, and there are things you can do to avoid going out of sync in the first place.

THE SOURCE OF YOUR PROBLEMS

Before we talk about solutions, let's review the ways you can get out of sync. Know what can go wrong, and you'll be able to avoid the problem. Know what can go wrong, and you're in a better position to identify and fix the problem.

How did you get out of sync? Here are the three actions most often responsible for sync problems. They are what the police would call "the usual suspects."

- Single-roller trimming—adding material to or subtracting it from one track, but not the other(s)
- Splicing material to one track but not to the other(s)
- Extracting material from one track but not from the other(s)

Now that you know who they are, keep an eye on them. Stay alert whenever you're performing one of these three actions.

SYNC BREAK INDICATORS

If your audio and video were digitized at the same time, the Avid will lock the two together. If you go out of sync, *sync break indicators* will appear in the Timeline to show you exactly how many frames out of sync you've fallen. Numbers appear in the Timeline on the video and its associated audio track, indicating precisely what went wrong and by how much.

| | | Master | | Kate's CU | −9 | Tim's CU | −9 |
| | | Master | | Kate's CU | 9 | Tim's CU | 9 |

In the example here, I made the mistake of entering Single-Roller Trim Mode on just one track. I inadvertently added nine frames to Kate's picture but not to her sound. The sync break indicator shows the sync break, as well as the number of frames by which the entire sequence has been thrown out of sync. It also tells me in which direction I need to go to get back in sync.

To get back in sync, use Single-Roller Trim and add or subtract the number of frames indicated. Here, I need to either subtract nine frames from Kate's picture (−9) or add nine frames to Kate's sound.

MANY TRACKS MEAN MANY SYNC PROBLEMS

If you lose sync when cutting a sequence containing just a few tracks, you'll be able to restore sync without much trouble. But once you start adding tracks containing additional material into your sequence (such as narration, sound effects, titles, and music), sync problems can become more frequent and more confusing.

Figures 12.1 and 12.2 show a sequence containing material on two video tracks and three audio tracks. The main visual material consists of a dolly shot past rows of houses, with a title superimposed over the shot. Audio track A1 holds narration; A2 and A3 hold the sync audio.

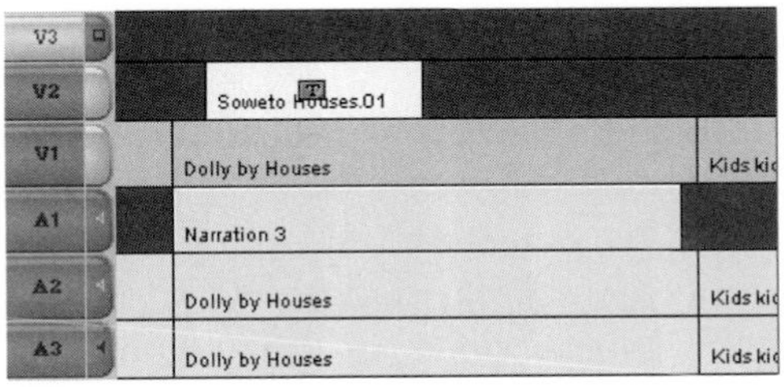

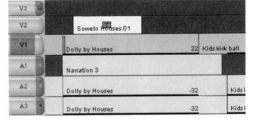

Figure 12.1   Before Single-Roller Trim

Figure 12.2   After trim, showing sync break

Let's see what happens if I get out of sync. To get out of sync I place the Single-Roller Trim just on V1 and not on any other tracks, and trim (shorten) it by 32 frames. Immediately, sync break indicators appear.

Notice that the sync break indicators show that the Dolly shot is out of sync by 32 frames. What you don't see is that the title on V2 and the narration on A1 are out of sync as well. If you are going to add or trim material from one track, you must add or trim material on *all* tracks; otherwise, you will get out of sync.

Why doesn't your Avid show that your title track (V2) and narration track (A1) are out of sync? Sync breaks work only with pictures and sounds that were digitized together. The video and audio tracks containing material that you added later—the titles, narration, sound effects, and music—won't show sync breaks because they are independent of any video.

There are several ways to solve this problem. I'll show you one of the quickest methods.

LOCATORS

Locators are handy "tabs" that you can place on any and all tracks in the Timeline to show you that you are in or out of sync. You can also use them to leave neat little messages in the Composer/Record Monitor.

If you click on the Add Locator command button, a locator will appear in the Timeline on whichever track is active. As you may recall, in Chapter 3 (pages 76-77) we opened the Command Palette and mapped the Add Locator button to the F5 key on the keyboard. Just select a track in the Timeline by clicking on its Track Selector button and pressing F5. It's also on the Source Monitor toolbar on the Xpress and on the Fast menu on the Media Composer.

For sync purposes, you want to place the locator on all of the tracks so that the locators line up in a straight vertical row. In Figure 12.3 you can see that I have placed locators on every track that contains a clip. You must place the locators on each track, one at a time. I deselected all of the tracks except V2, and then I hit the Add Locator button. Then, without moving the position indicator, I deselected V2 and selected V1 and pressed the Add Locator button again, and so on until all of the tracks have locators.

Look what happens if any of my tracks get thrown off (Figure 12.4). The sync break indicators tell me that the Dolly shot and its sync tracks are out of sync, but now because we added the locators, we can see that the title and narration are also out of sync.

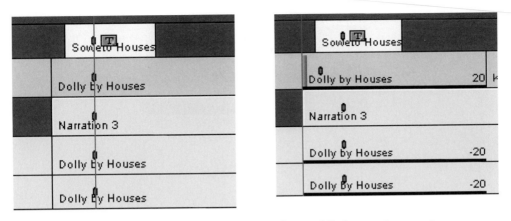

Figure 12.3 Tracks in sync **Figure 12.4** Tracks out of sync

You don't need to put locators everywhere in the Timeline, but I would suggest you place a vertical row of them every 5 minutes or so in your project. That way if you get out of sync, you don't have far to go before you have a checkpoint.

Locator Information

While we're discussing locators, let's look at the message function that's part of this handy tool. To write a message, click on the Track Selector box containing the locator. Then drag the position indicator until it lands on the locator. When the locator appears in the Record Monitor, click the mouse pointer on the red locator in the Record Monitor (not in the Timeline). A message box appears. Just type your message in the box.

In Figure 12.5, I typed the question, "Do we need this shot?" When I click OK, the message appears in the Record Monitor window whenever the position indicator stops on that frame in the Timeline (Figure 12.6). (Sometimes you have to use the one-frame step key to land precisely on it.)

Locators - Rough Cut 8-01

TC	Track	Comment
00;00;34;28	V1	
00;00;49;08	V1	
00;00;56;13	V1	
00;01;03;03	V1	
00;01;03;03	V2	
00;01;03;03	A1	

Do we need this shot?

Click on the locator, and a message box appears.

Figure 12.5

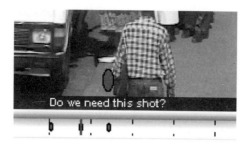

Figure 12.6

Deleting Locators

If you want to delete the locator (and its message), click on the locator in the position bar (the window under the monitor). If it doesn't appear in the monitor window, step-frame until it does, and then press the Delete key.

EDITING TRICKS TO STAY IN SYNC

In Chapter 8, we examined the topic, "Trimming in Two Directions." Because this is a vital skill, let's take a moment to review it.

Trimming in Two Directions: A Review

If you want to add material (or trim material) using Single-Roller Trim Mode, you must trim all of your tracks to keep their relationship the same. If you just trim V1 and A1 (picture and sync sound), all of the music and narration will fall out of sync.

- Go into Single-Roller Trim Mode.
- Add rollers on the "fill" or black side (shift-click on a transition to add a roller).
- Do this even if the rollers aren't all on the same side or going in the same direction.

As you trim, Avid will add or take away black fill to keep all of the tracks in sync.

In Figure 12.7, when we drag Tim's CU on track V1 and his overlapped audio on track A1 to the left, we are adding to it, or making the shot longer. That would normally throw the music out of sync. But if we place a Single-Roller Trim on the fill side of the music on track A2, then as we drag left, the Avid *adds* black fill, and sync is maintained. If we shortened Tim's shot

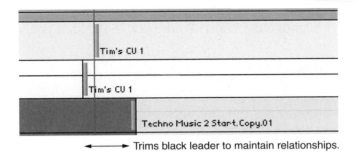

Trims black leader to maintain relationships.

Figure 12.7

by dragging right, the Avid would take away black fill to keep the music in sync. Remember, put the roller on the fill side of the music, not inside the music itself.

But what happens if you want to trim a shot in a sequence containing many tracks similar to the one in Figure 12.8? Let's say you're doing an hour-long show, and you have three video tracks and five or six tracks of audio. Let's say that the distance between where you want to trim and some of these other elements is too great to easily add rollers to them.

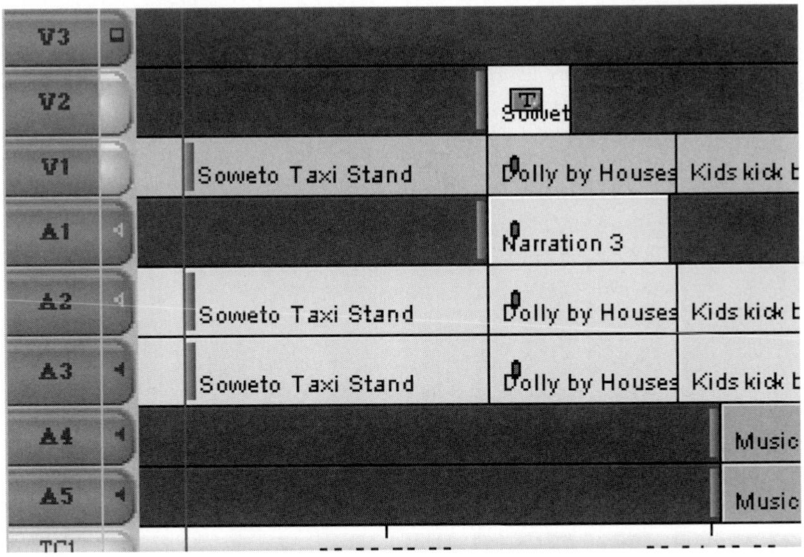

Figure 12.8

You can easily place single rollers on V2, V1, A1, A2, and A3. Tracks A4 and A5 are a slight pain to add rollers to, but not a huge deal. But you can't even see the material on track V3, and unless you expand the Timeline and add a roller to the clip on V3, it will go out of sync as soon as you trim. And don't forget, you have to move the Watch Point back to the shot you want to trim.

Add Edits in Black Fill

One solution is to lasso the transition that you want to trim, as I've done in Figure 12.9, and then hold the Option key (Mac) or the Alt key (Windows) while pressing the Add Edit key.

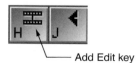

Add Edit key

When you press the Option key (Mac) or the Alt key (Windows) together with this key, the Add Edit is placed in the black fill. When you're in Trim Mode, rollers will automatically jump to all of the Add Edits, just like in Figure 12.10.

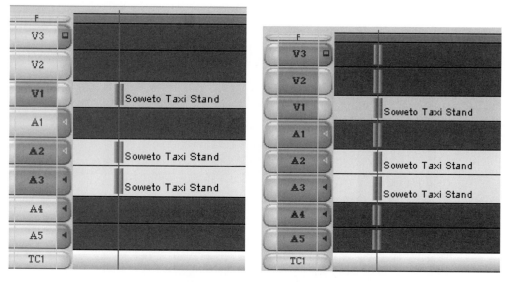

Figure 12.9   **Figure 12.10**

Now, if you want to use Single-Roller Trim, just click on the A-side or B-side of the Trim Mode Display, and the rollers will jump to that side.

Remember, the Option/Alt Add Edit only puts the Add Edits in black, but this is good. You don't want an Add Edit in the middle of a shot. Now trim to your heart's content and know that the Avid will trim the fill to keep your tracks in sync.

These Add Edit lines in the black fill can serve another function. During editing, they act as sync reference points, just as the locators do. If the lines don't line up, something has moved.

Deleting Add Edits

There's now a command for this task. Select the tracks containing the Add Edits you want to remove, then go to the Clip menu and select "Remove Match Frame Edits," which is another name for Add Edits. If you want to remove some, but not all, don't use that menu item. Instead, get into Dual-Roller Trim Mode (so you have dual-rollers on top of these edit lines in the Timeline), and hit the Delete key.

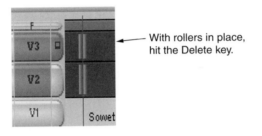

With rollers in place, hit the Delete key.

SYNC LOCKS

The Avid knows how important it is to maintain sync, especially when you're getting toward the end of editing and the tracks are filling up with titles, visual effects, sound effects, and music. So it gives you a tool in the Timeline that enables you to lock your tracks together; it's aptly named *sync locks*.

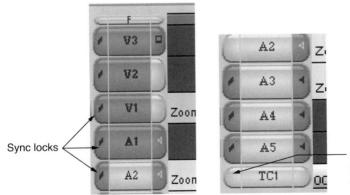

Sync locks

Click here to place sync locks on all tracks.

In the Track Selector area, there is a small box just to the left of the tracks. By clicking in the small box, you can place a sync lock on your track. You can lock two, three, or all of your tracks together. Click in the empty box in the TC1, or timecode track, and you'll place locks in all of the boxes.

Sync locks are supposed to work only in Trim Mode, but you'll find that they also work with Lift and Extract. Their main function, however, is to prevent you from going out of sync when in Single-Roller Trim. In Single-Roller Trim Mode, the Avid will maintain the proper relationship with all of your other tracks.

Figure 12.11 shows an example. I've placed single rollers on the A-side of this transition, on tracks V1, A2, and A3, but I forgot to place trim rollers on the narration on A1 and the music cue on A4 and A5. What happens if I trim this shot? I'll throw the narration and music cue off because I haven't trimmed in two directions. Right? Wrong. Because the sync locks are "on," the Avid will keep the A1, A4, and A5 tracks locked together with V1, A2, and A3. It will automatically adjust the fill to keep all of the tracks in sync.

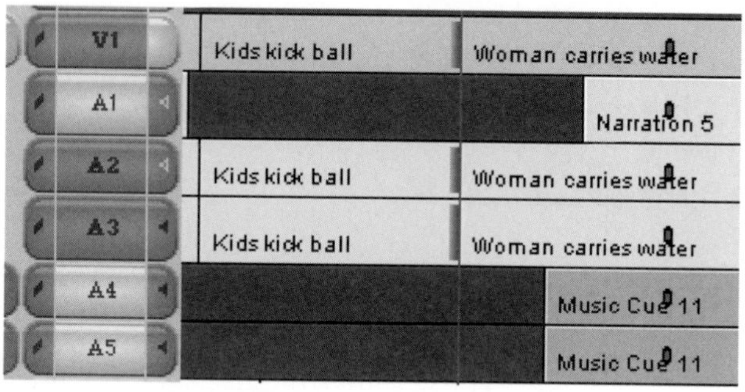

Figure 12.11

Don't believe me? Examine Figure 12.12. Although the "Kids kick ball" shot has been shortened, the music and narration are still in sync. The Avid shortened the black fill on A1, A4, and A5 to keep the narration and music cues where they belong. Even though I didn't trim in two directions, the Avid's sync locks did it for me.

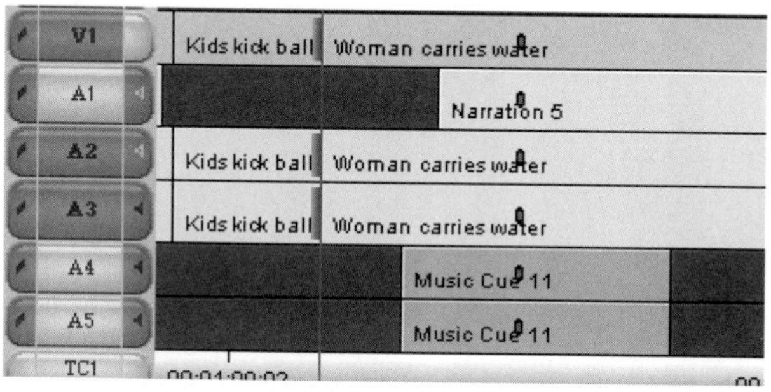

Figure 12.12   Even though there are no rollers on A1, A4, and A5, they will stay in sync because the sync locks are on.

"Hey," you might say, "if this works so well, why did you spend so much time teaching us about trimming in two directions, Watch Points, and placing add edits in fill?" My answer is twofold. First, you need to know about all of those other things to fully understand the value of sync locks, but mainly because sync locks don't always work. Another way to put it is that they work *too* well.

With sync locks, if the other tracks in line (vertically) with the tracks you are cutting are empty, the Avid adds or subtracts fill to keep your tracks in sync—and everyone is happy. But if the other tracks have material in line with the tracks you are cutting, the Avid cuts material from those tracks as well. This is a problem. Suddenly your narration and your music have disappeared. You're in sync, all right, but you've lost your narrator! Or a chunk of your music is missing!

Look at Figure 12.13. I have sync locks on all tracks, and I'm going to extend the tail of the shot—the A-side.

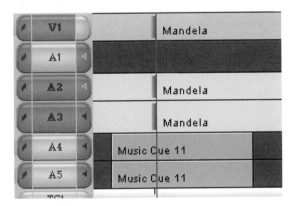

Figure 12.13

Watch what happens with the sync locks turned on. Examine Figure 12.14.

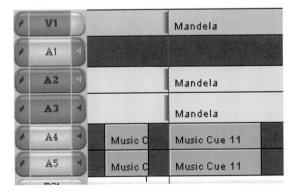

Figure 12.14

Whoa! My music cue has been cut in two and a chunk of black fill (silence) has been added. I certainly didn't want *that*. Why did it happen? Because even though A4 and A5 weren't selected for trimming, they're sync-locked to the other tracks. With the sync locks on, I used Trim Mode to extend the tail of my shot. The Avid did whatever it took to keep my tracks in sync, even if that meant adding fill in the middle of my music cue.

Figure 12.15 shows another example. I've got single rollers on the B-side video and sync audio tracks, but not on the narration. I want to extend the head of the "Girls watch bus" shot by 10 frames.

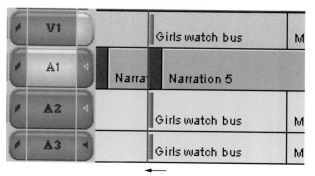

Figure 12.15

Look what happens in Figure 12.16 when I drag the rollers to the left to extend the shot. Yikes! The Avid has added black fill in the middle of the narration. That's not going to sound very good.

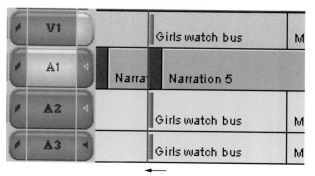

Drag rollers to the left to extend.

Figure 12.16

So, as you can see, sync locks work some of the time, but not all of the time. Remember, with sync locks on, the Avid will do whatever it takes to keep the tracks in sync. If the other tracks in line (vertically) with the tracks you are editing are empty, sync locks can be fast and foolproof. But, if the other tracks have material in line with the tracks you are cutting or trimming, the Avid will blindly remove important material in its quest to keep you in sync.

That's when all the work we've done before we were introduced to sync locks starts to pay off. Take the situation in Figure 12.17. To extend the "Girls watch bus" shot, we don't use sync locks. Instead, we'll trim in two directions by placing a roller in the fill side of A1—the narration. Now when we drag left to extend the shot and its sync tracks, the narration will stay in sync.

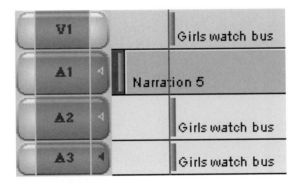

Figure 12.17

LOCKING TRACKS

Xpress and Xpress DV editors can now do what Media Composer editors have long been able to do: They can lock their tracks to prevent accidental changes. Locking is different from sync locking. When you lock a track, no further editing can take place on that track. You can lock picture and/or audio tracks. Say you have several sync dialog tracks and a narration track that are all in perfect sync with the video tracks, and you need to work on your music and sound effects tracks. You can lock the picture, narration, and dialog tracks. Now you don't have to worry about messing up those tracks while you work on your music and sound effects tracks.

To lock tracks:

1. Select the tracks you want to lock and deselect the others.
2. From the Clip menu, choose Lock Tracks. A padlock icon appears in the track lock indicator space.

Because you're beginning to take advantage of all the Avid has to offer, you're in danger of going out of sync. You're adding video tracks for titles and effects. You're adding tracks to hold music and narration. Once you go beyond cutting just a few tracks, sync problems can really cause you heartache. We've spent a lot of time on the subject of sync because losing it can be so painful.

My best advice is to keep it as simple as you can for as long as you can. Don't add titles, music, and sound effects until you've reached a fine cut. Tell the story first. Otherwise, you'll spend your time repairing sync, rather than editing.

SUGGESTED ASSIGNMENTS

1. Place a single-roller (Trim Mode) on one track and not the other. Drag left and look at the sync break. Leave Trim Mode. Now go back into Trim Mode and fix the sync break.
2. Place a row of locators on your tracks.
3. Leave yourself a message, using the locator message function.
4. Delete the locator.
5. Enter Trim Mode and Option/Alt-Add Edit.
6. Use Single-Roller Trim Mode to add or remove material on all of your tracks.
7. Delete the Add Edits.
8. Place sync locks on your tracks. Try extracting material. Try single-roller trimming.
9. Place locks on one or more tracks. Try editing the locked tracks.

13

Importing and Exporting

For those of you who have imported and exported various files before, this chapter may seem a bit simplistic. Accept my apologies. It's just that I'm not worried about you. You simply need to be shown how to use Avid's import and export tools, and off you'll go. This chapter is aimed at those of you who have never imported or exported files before and who think the whole business sounds incredibly difficult. I've streamlined and simplified the process as much as possible so you'll be able to master it, if you give it a try.

TYPES OF FILES

Because the Avid deals with digital information, just about any digital information can be brought in or sent out of the Avid. Here are several examples:

- You could import a music track from a CD.
- Using Adobe Photoshop, you could create an opening title that combines text with a special blurring effect. You could save that title as a graphic file, import it into one of your bins, and then cut it into your sequence.
- You could create an image or sequence of images in the Avid, export it as a file to a program such as After Effects, make changes to create a special look, and then reimport it into a bin and cut it into your sequence.
- You could take an audio clip that has sound problems and export it as an audio file. You could then bring it to a sound facility with Pro Tools for audio sweetening and reimport it back into the Avid.

You can import and export many kinds of graphic files, picture files, animation files, and audio files. Here is a partial list:

- *Graphic and Animation File Types*
  PICT
  Alias PIX animation
  QuickTime
  OMF Interchange
  Photo CD
- *Audio File Types*
  Audio Interchange File Format (AIFF)
  Sound Designer II
  OMF Interchange
- *Shot Log Files*
  FLEx File
  ATN File
  FTL file

IMPORTING

To import, there must first be a file to import. It can be located on the Avid hard drive or on a Zip disk, floppy, or CD that you've inserted into your CPU.

To import, simply select Import from the File menu. If Import is dimmed on the menu, it's because a bin has not been selected. Click anywhere in the bin to which you want to import the file. After you select Import, an Import dialog box opens. I've included the boxes for Windows and Macintosh Avids (Figures 13.1 and 13.2).

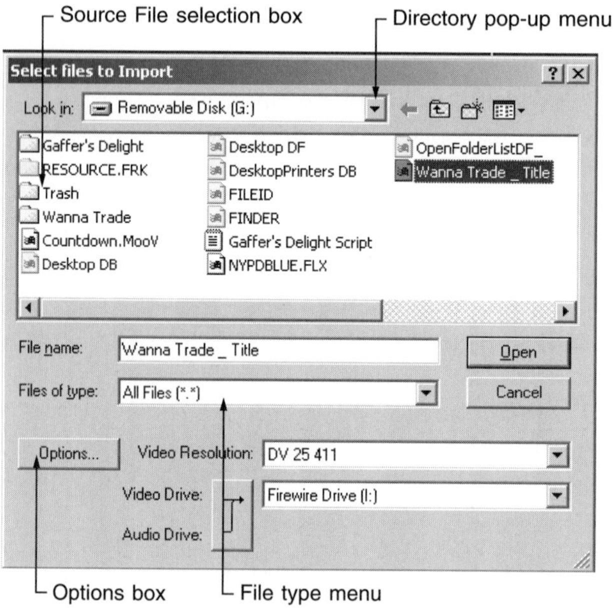

Figure 13.1   Windows Import dialog box

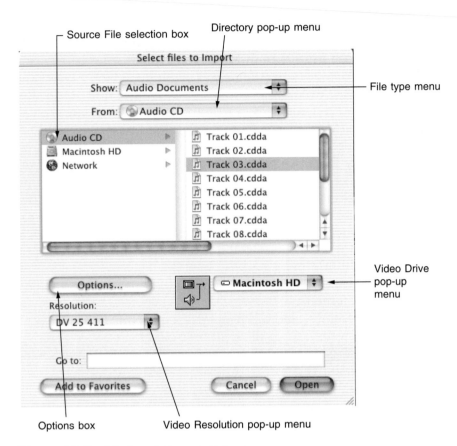

Figure 13.2   Macintosh Import dialog box

As you can see, although they appear quite different, the Mac and Windows Import windows offer the same choices.

IMPORTING A PICTURE FILE

Perhaps the most confusing aspect of importing is the various options you need to set for each kind of file. I'm going to walk you through the Import of a picture file created using Adobe Photoshop and saved as a PICT file. It's a title I designed for "Wanna Trade." I place the title on a Zip disk and carry it from my home computer to the Avid. I insert it into the Zip disk drive on my computer, and then, using the Import dialog box's Directory pop-up menu, I'll search the computer's hierarchical file system and find it.

Let's trace the steps I'll take to do this Import, and then we'll examine the choices I made and why. Examine Figure 13.1 (Windows) or 13.2 (Mac) as you follow my steps.

1. First I select a bin by clicking on it. In this case I've created a new bin called *Imported Files*.
2. Then I choose Import from the File menu.
3. From the Files of type (Windows) or Show (Mac), I select the sort of document I'm looking for: Graphic, Audio, and so on. Because my title is a PICT file, I choose Graphic Files (Windows) or Graphic Documents (Mac). If, for some reason, the Import box won't recognize your file type, or you're not sure what type of file it is, change back to Any Documents (Mac) or All Files (Windows), as I've done in Figure 13.1.
4. Using the Directory pop-up menu, I navigate through the desktop or hard drive. I double-click on disks and folders in the list to open them, and I scroll through them to locate the file I want. (Mac users, drag the horizontal slider all the way to the left to get to the desktop, where you'll find your Zip disk or CD.)
5. Once I find it in the Source File selection box, I simply click on it, so it's highlighted.
6. I click on Options, and a box opens. See Figure 13.3.

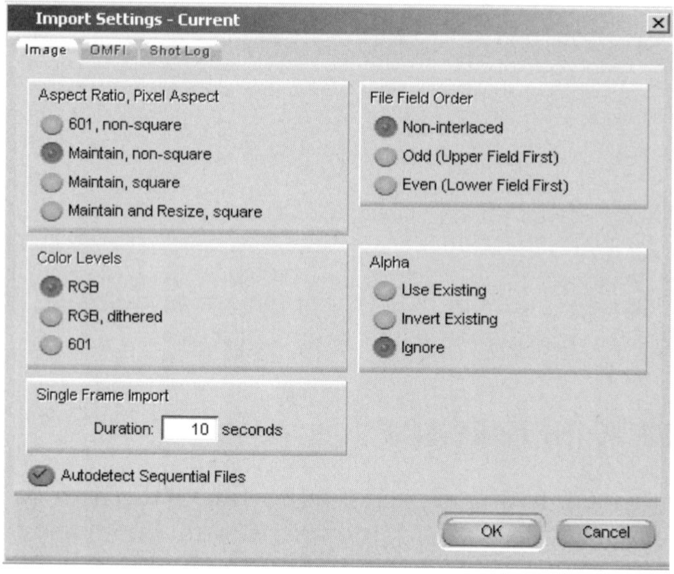

Figure 13.3 Graphic options dialog box

7. Media Composer and Xpress users, choose 601, non-square. Xpress DV users, choose Maintain, non-square.
8. I choose Non-interlaced in the File Field Order box.
9. In the Color Levels, I choose RGB.
10. In the Alpha, I select Ignore.

11. In the Single Frame Import box, I choose 10 seconds as my duration. If I want it to be longer or shorter, I change the number.
12. I click OK. The Options box closes.
13. Back in the Import Tool, I choose a Video Drive to store the media.
14. Because it's a graphic, I select a resolution in the Video Resolution box that matches the resolution of my sequence.
15. When I'm finished, I click Open.

I look in my bin. There it is, saved as a master clip that is 10 seconds long.

Now that I've walked you through an import, let's examine the rationale behind the choices and settings we made.

COMPUTER VERSUS TELEVISION

Most of the problems associated with importing files into the Avid stem from the fact that you are creating your files on a computer; although the Avid is a computer, it doesn't behave like one. It behaves like a digital television set. A computer and the Avid deal with images differently. The main differences involve aspect ratio, pixel shape, and color.

Aspect Ratio

Aspect ratio refers to the dimensions of a rectangle. In our case the rectangle is a picture image, film or video frame, or screen size. You determine a rectangle's aspect ratio by dividing its width by its height. (A square has an aspect ratio of 1:1 because the width is the same as the height.) Look at any standard television screen. It's not a square; it's a rectangle. The frame is wider than it is high. On a standard analog television set, the aspect ratio is 4:3. Filmmakers are more familiar with the number 1.33:1, which comes from dividing 4 by 3.

The new standard for high-definition television (HDTV) presents an even wider frame, with an aspect ratio of 16:9.

In the computer domain, the image is usually described in terms of pixels: the number and shape of the pixels that make up the image. Graphic artists often work on a computer creating images that have a frame of 648 (width) by 486 (height) *square* pixels. Divide 648 by 486 and you get an aspect ratio of 4:3, or 1.33:1.

The Avid's frame in pixel terms is slightly different because it comes from the Avid's video capture board. It is 720 (width) by 486 (height), *non-square* pixels. When you do the math, you see that instead of an aspect ratio of 1.33:1, you get an aspect ratio of 1.48:1 (720 divided by 486). This never made sense to me. Why would a video capture board give you an image that didn't match the 4:3 standard for all analog television screens? The answer lies in the pixel shape the Avid creates. It's not shaped like a square; it's tall and thin.

Square pixel   Avid's non-square pixel

If those non-square pixels were square, like the ones a computer generates, the aspect ratio would be wrong. But because the pixels are horizontally *squeezed*, 720 of them take up the same space as 648 square ones. So Avid's 720 × 486 non-square pixels provide the same aspect ratio as a computer's 648 × 486 square pixels, namely 4:3.

The number 601 I chose in the dialog box refers to the digital video standard known as *ITU-R 601*.

DV Aspect Ratio and Pixels

Although the DV frame has the same aspect ratio, 4:3, as standard NTSC video, it has six fewer horizontal lines. So instead of 486 vertical lines, it has 480. Inside the Avid, instead of 720 × 486, it's native size is 720 × 480.

Color

At this level you don't need to know that much about the different ways the Avid and a computer monitor handle color. Just remember that computer color is referred to as *RGB color*, whereas the Avid's color conforms to the ITU-R 601 digital video standard.

IMPORT OPTIONS

Now, armed with this information, let's look again at the Options choices for Importing a graphic file. You see that the Avid is asking for information about your file so that it can properly translate it into the Avid's format.

The first box you'll see is labeled "Aspect Ratio, Pixel Aspect." There are four choices: (1) 601 non-square, (2) Maintain, non-square, (3) Maintain, square, and (4) Maintain and Resize, square.

601, non-square takes graphics with the correct aspect ratio, no matter what the pixel shape, and makes them fit the Avid's 601, non-square standard. So if the title you created in Photoshop has the right aspect ratio for the Avid, but has square pixels, select this option and it will import nicely. This is the default setup.

Maintain, non-square is the correct choice for Xpress DV users who are bringing in files that are correct for digital television (720 × 486). It cuts off the top four lines and the bottom two lines to conform to the NTSC DV standard of 480 horizontal lines.

Maintain, square keeps the graphic just the way you designed it, with no change in size. For instance, you might not want a logo to fill the Avid's frame, but stay in the corner of the frame. This setting will do that. It will keep your image size and shape just the way it was created.

Maintain and Resize, square forces the graphic to fit the Avid's frame no matter what. The Avid often places a black border around your image to make it fit. Use if the file is the wrong size and shape, but you want it to fill the frame anyway.

File Field Order

The choices here are Non-interlaced, Odd (Upper Field First), and Even (Lower Field First).

The latest Xpress and Media Composer Avids all use a Meridien video capture board, whereas the older ones use an ABVB board. The Meridien board captures two-field video differently from an ABVB board, and this is part of the reason why there's a File Field Order selection. The ABVB Avid wants the odd field first, whereas the Meridien wants the even field first. Remember, a video signal is made up of two fields: one containing all of the odd lines and the other containing all of the even lines. The Meridien wants the even line first. When you're working with graphics involving the ordering of fields, you should set the field order to match the Avid you're going into—even for Meridien, odd for ABVB.

All PAL Avids are Odd (Upper Field First).

The Xpress DV acts just like the Meridien board. It wants the even field first for NTSC projects. Choose Even (Lower Field First).

File Field Order

◯ Non-interlaced

◯ Odd (Upper Field First)

◉ Even (Lower Field First)

If the file you are importing doesn't deal with fields (e.g., a PICT file), then Non-interlaced is the correct choice. I chose Non-interlaced when I imported the title I designed with Photoshop because it was a PICT file, not a video file.

Color Levels

Color Levels deals with the color issue. If the file you are importing was created on a computer, then it probably has RGB color levels. If it came from a videotape or video camera, select 601. The title I designed using Photoshop was created on a computer, and RGB is the correct setting.

If the picture image you created has fine gradient, and you see some ugly banding when you import it and then cut it into your sequence, try importing it again using RGB, dithered.

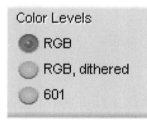

Alpha

If the image you are importing has some opaque areas and some transparent areas, known as the *alpha channel*, then you need to tell the Avid how the image was created. Most animation and graphic applications set up the alpha channel so that black is the transparent layer and white is the opaque layer. This is the opposite of what the Avid wants. So if that's how your application works, and you're bringing in a file to an Avid, you want to select "Invert Existing." If your files have the layers set up so that white represents the transparent layer, then select "Use Existing."

The title I created has white letters over a black background, so transparency isn't an issue. I chose "Ignore." But you can create titles using graphic programs such as Photoshop that will superimpose over a background shot. Keep the layers separate; don't "flatten" the image. If you have a transparent background, then select "Invert Existing."

Single Frame

I created a single-frame title using Photoshop. Once I import it, the Avid is going to turn that single frame into a master clip. In the Options box, I tell the Avid how long I want that master clip to last. The default is 10 seconds.

That's plenty for such a short title. If I had created a list of credits, I might choose a longer duration.

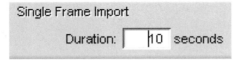

IMPORT PRACTICE

Let's create a title using Adobe Photoshop, import it, and cut it into a sequence. It's true that Avid has a Title Tool, but you might not be able to spend as much time on the Avid as you can on your home or office computer. Or perhaps Photoshop has an effect that your Avid doesn't have. Whatever the reason, it's handy to be able to import graphic files from programs such as Photoshop.

Creating a Photoshop File

Because of the difference between square pixels and non-square pixels, you often have to create titles and graphics that have the wrong aspect ratio so that when they are imported into the Avid, they come out looking correct. Let's create a simple title using Photoshop to illustrate this point.

When I open Photoshop, the first thing I do is set the aspect ratio in the New File dialog box. Remember that 648×486 pixels is correct for most graphic applications, but the Avid uses non-square pixels. Therefore we must slightly distort the image to get it to come out correctly once it's imported into the Avid. First, set the Photoshop image at 720×540 pixels, as in Figure 13.4. Xpress DV users, set to 720×534.

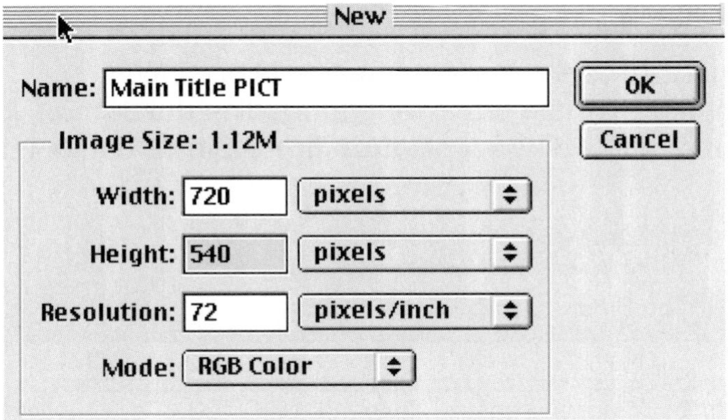

Figure 13.4   Adobe Photoshop's New File dialog box

After placing the text and a line beneath it, I created a weird shadow and applied some distortion and blur. Now I pull down the Image menu and select Image Size. In the dialog box, I remove the Constrain Proportion check and *change* the pixel size from 720 × 540 to 720 × 486, as in Figure 13.5. Xpress DV users, change to 720 × 480.

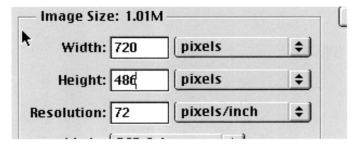

Figure 13.5   Adobe Photoshop's Image Size dialog box

This will squash the letters horizontally, making them appear shorter. This looks wrong, I know. But this is what I want, because when I import the graphic into the Avid, the letters will be squished vertically because of the non-square pixel issue. The result will be perfectly proportioned letters. I will save this title as a TIFF, PICT, or Photoshop file, and save it to a Zip disk. I repeat the steps for importing a picture file listed on pages 282-283.

Remember to make sure a bin is selected, otherwise the Import option in the File menu is dimmed. After navigating through the Directory pop-up menu, finding the file on my Zip disk, and selecting it, I open Options and choose:

1. 601 (or Maintain, non-square for DV projects)
2. Non-interlaced
3. RGB
4. Ignore Alpha
5. 10 seconds

I click OK and then in the Import window, I click Open.

Here's the title in the bin after Import. The duration of this clip is 10 seconds because that's how we set it up in the Single Frame Import option.

When I double-click on the clip icon, it opens in the Source Monitor. I mark an IN and an OUT. Then I mark an IN in the Timeline and splice the title into my sequence.

Here's my title, in the Source Monitor. Yeah, I know. Needs work.

Importing Audio from a CD

This is a great way to bring in sound effects from a sound effects library, temp music for editing, or music cues from your composer. The process goes much faster if you have already picked out the track(s) you want to import.

1. Place a CD into the computer's CD drive.
2. In the Avid application, select a bin and choose Import from the File menu.
3. Select Audio Documents in the Show menu (Mac) or Audio Files in the Files of type menu (Windows).

4. In the Directory pop-up window, navigate through the folders on your computer to locate the CD.
5. Choose the track you want.
6. Click Open.

Audio CDs are sampled at 44.1 kHz. If you're editing at 48 kHz, you'll get a message telling you that the sample rate of the track you're importing doesn't match your project and asking if you want the sample rate converted to 48 kHz. Click Yes. The file will be converted to 48 kHz. The import will take several minutes, and when the track comes into your bin as a clip, it will be too loud to use.

Double-click the clip's icon to put it into the Source Monitor. Go to the Tools menu, open the Audio Mix Tool, click on the Gang button for tracks 1 and 2, and then lower the volume to around –11 dB. Adjust from there.

This is a nice feature. In the past, getting a CD track into the Avid was a real pain.

Importing Color Bars

Let's import something else. Normally, when you send a sequence to video-tape (which we'll do in Chapter 16), you put SMPTE Bars at the head of the tape, so a video engineer can use them as a reference to properly set up the playback monitor and tape recorder. Let's import the SMPTE Bars that come bundled with the Avid software. This file is already loaded on your computer.

1. When you are in your project, click on a bin.
2. From the File menu, select Import. The Import window opens.
3. Select Graphic for the File Type.
4. Navigate the Source Files until you get to your computer's internal hard drive. You are looking for the Avid folder, then the Supporting Files folder, and inside that the Test Patterns folder (Figure 13.6).

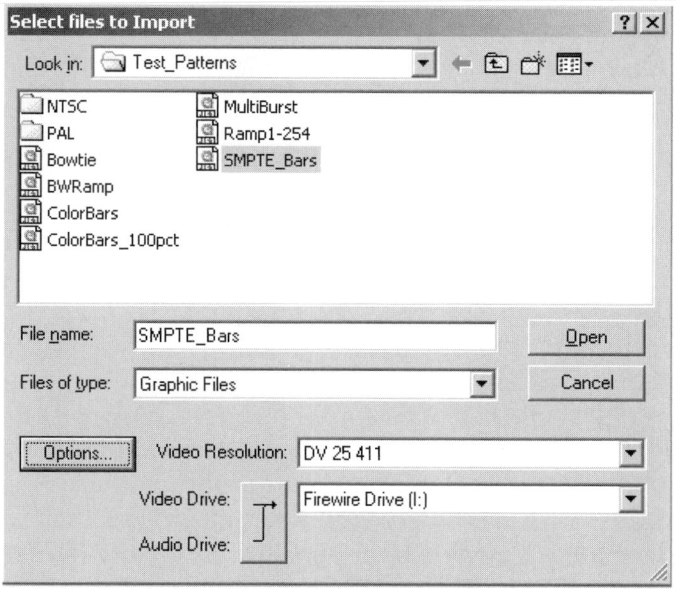

Figure 13.6

5. When you locate the folder, double-click on it and look for a file called SMPTE Color Bars, or SMPTE_Bars.pct.
6. Select it.
7. Select the Video Drive and Video Resolution.
8. Click on Option.
9. Choose 601, non-square. Xpress DV users select Maintain, non-square.
10. On a Meridien-based machine or Xpress DV, choose Even (Lower Field First).
11. In the Color Levels box, select 601. This choice is correct because the file was created on video, not on a computer.
12. Choose 60 seconds.
13. Click OK.
14. In your bin you will find a clip called SMPTE Bars. Double-click to open it, and cut it into the head of your sequence.

IMPORTING OTHER FILE TYPES

The figure on the next page contains a list of file types this Avid supports.

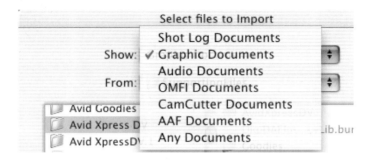

In Chapter 17, we'll learn about Shot Logs. The Avid can import several different audio files. OMFI stands for Open Media Format Interchange and is designed to help you import files that were created on different computer platforms and across many different applications.

You'll want to import many different files. Now that you know the parameters, you should be able to import just about any file successfully. As with anything else discussed in this book, you'll learn only through practice and experimentation. Try importing different types of files and playing with the many options. Keep a written record of what settings work. If you have a file you want to import, there's a way to do it. Just keep trying.

EXPORTING

There are hundreds of computer applications that can change, alter, sweeten, and enhance your Avid-generated picture, sound, or both. There are lots of outlets for the work you create on the Avid, including the Web and CD-ROMs. To take advantage of all of these applications and avenues for distribution, you need to understand the basics of exporting.

A quick aside: In the last few years, Avid has made the entire exporting process much easier. When I wrote the first edition of this book, this was by far the most difficult section to explain. It's not exactly a breeze now, but it's sure a lot simpler than it once was.

Here are four situations in which you might want to export frames or sequences from the Avid:

- Create a newsletter or flyer to advertise your project. You could export a still frame from a sequence, retouch the image in a program such as Photoshop, and place the retouched photo in the flyer or newsletter that you've designed using page layout software.
- Export audio tracks for sweetening in Pro Tools. You could then re-import the sweetened tracks back into the sequence.

- Export part of a sequence to Adobe After Effects, make changes, and reimport it into the Avid.
- Export a QuickTime Movie to be used as part of a Web page.

To really learn about exporting, you need to be familiar with the software application to which you are exporting. Often, you'll be exporting files for tweaking in applications such as Pro Tools, After Effects, Photoshop, 3D Studio Max, and countless others. If you don't have much experience with audio and graphic software, ask for guidance from the graphic artists, sound engineers, and animators living in your area, who work with the software application on a daily basis. Ask them to walk you through the settings and options required for a successful export for each specific application.

Preparing to Export

There are several things you should do to make sure your export goes smoothly:

- If you are exporting a sequence, or the audio tracks from a sequence, you should duplicate the sequence before initiating an export. Create a new bin for the duplicate and export it. If anything goes wrong, you have an original to return to.
- If you're exporting a frame, there's no need to duplicate anything.
- Make sure you render any and all effects that exist on the track(s) you are exporting.
- If you're exporting more than V1, make sure the Video Track Monitor is on the highest level.
- Make sure the material you want to export is selected.
  - If it's a frame, mark the frame by placing a Mark IN. If you have no marks, place the position indicator on the frame.
  - If it's one or more tracks, click on the Track Selector panel to select the ones you want and deselect the ones you don't want.
  - If you want to export a section of a sequence, place IN and OUT marks in the Timeline.

EXPORT DIALOG BOX

Let's start by exporting a frame from a sequence. Perhaps we want to include it in a flyer or other publicity material. This is pretty simple to do, and it'll give us a chance to learn about the various Export windows.

Put a sequence in the Timeline, and place a Mark IN on the frame you'd like to export. Now go to the File menu and choose Export. The Export Dialog box will appear as shown in Figure 13.7 or Figure 13.8 for Windows.

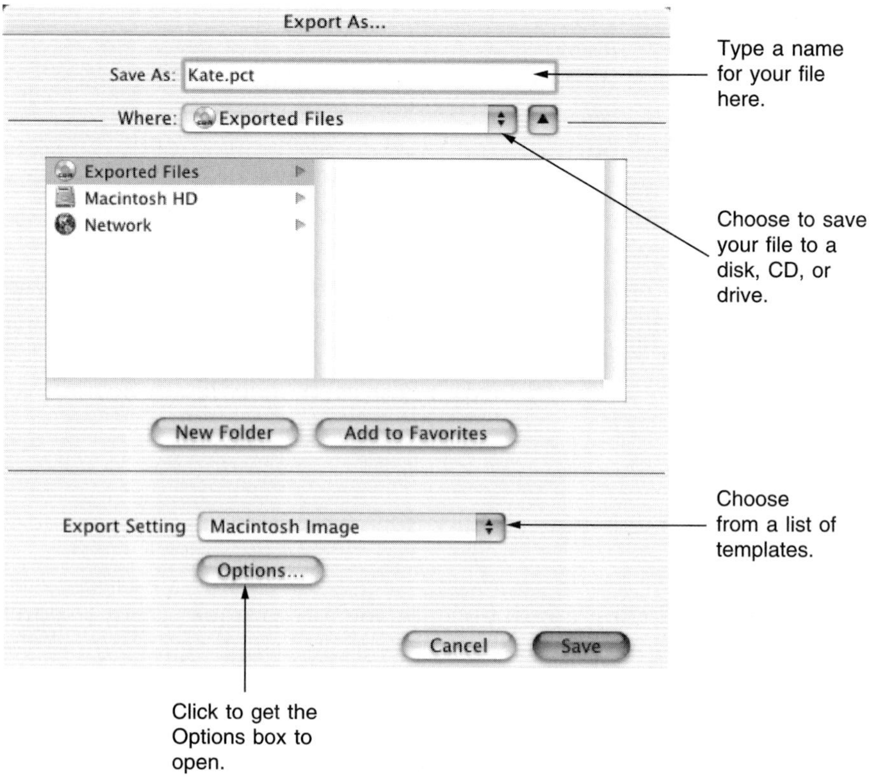

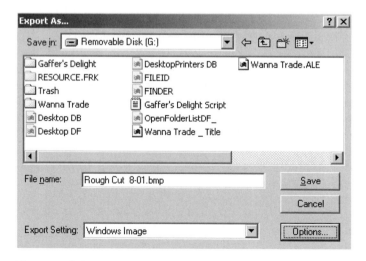

Type a name for your file here.

Choose to save your file to a disk, CD, or drive.

Choose from a list of templates.

Click to get the Options box to open.

Figure 13.7   Export Window (Mac)

Figure 13.8   Export Window (Windows)

Exporting a Graphic Image

The Avid knows that exporting a frame from a sequence is a common task, so there is actually a template for this task. Go to the Export Setting window (Figure 13.9) and select either Windows Image or Macintosh Image (depending on the machine you're on). Now press the Options button to open a box containing your Export settings.

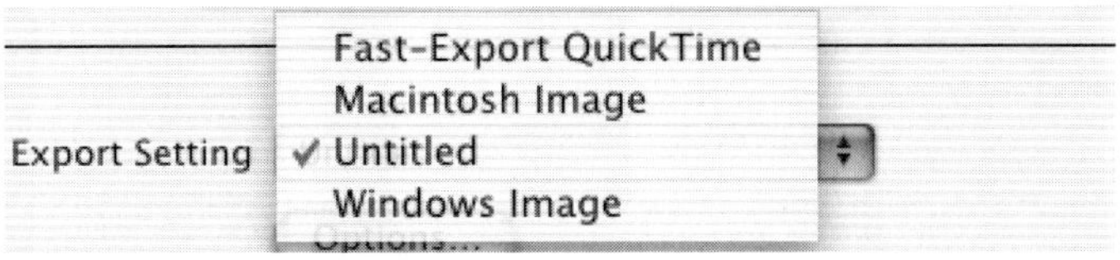

Figure 13.9

As you can see in Figure 13.10, there are several settings to select. Let's go through them.

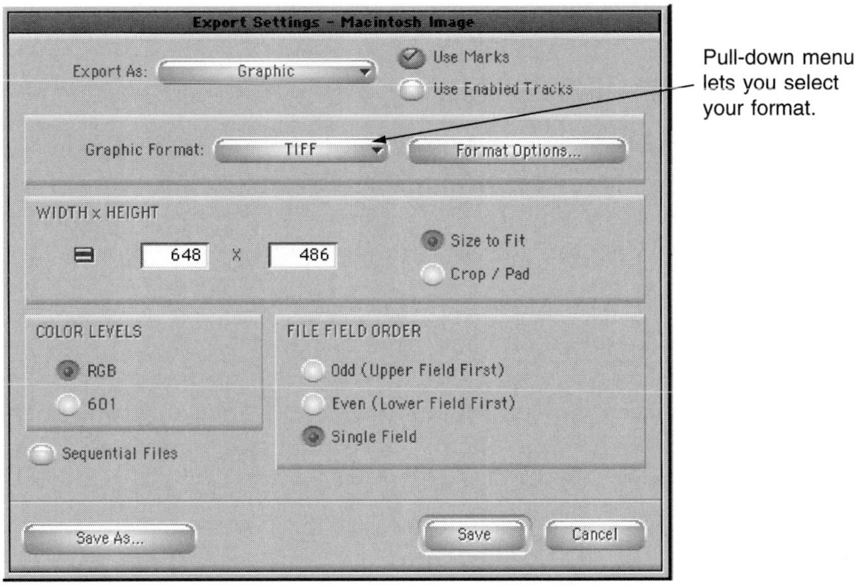

Figure 13.10 The Export Settings for a Graphic

1. In the Export As menu, Graphic will be chosen automatically because we asked for the Macintosh Image, and the Avid knows it's a graphic file.

2. Because I want to export a specific frame, I choose Use Marks. Remember, we placed a Mark IN in the Timeline on the frame we wanted to export.
3. In the Graphic Format window, select TIFF.
4. In the Width × Height Fast menu, select 648 × 486 (4 × 3 square pixel). This works best for printing.

5. Choose Size to Fit. Select Crop/Pad only when exporting a frame for use in a DVD project.
6. Choose RGB. As with importing, graphic files are usually RGB, whereas video files are usually 601. This is a graphics file.
7. Choose Single Field. When exporting a still image (an individual frame of a sequence), this option works best. We'll use Even (or Odd) for exporting a file as video.
8. Make sure Sequential files is not selected.

If you are going to be doing this a lot, then select Save As. A dialog box will open; give it a name (Macintosh Image TIFF), and you'll find all of your settings saved as a template under that name in the Export Settings window. If you don't expect to export graphics much, just hit Save. You'll return to the Export window.

1. Type a name for your file, such as Kate.pct.
2. Choose where you would like to save the file, such as on a CD, Zip disk, or your hard drive. In Figure 13.7, I have inserted a CD-RW, entitled "Export Files," in the computer and navigated to it, so it appears in the "Where" window.
3. Press Save.

EXPORTING A QUICKTIME MOVIE

Let's export a QuickTime Movie. This is another common type of export, so the Avid has a template for that as well.

First, however, we need to select the sequence we'd like to export. The easiest thing to do is to go to the bin that contains the sequence and click on it so that it's highlighted in the bin. If you don't want the entire sequence, put it in the Timeline and place a Mark IN and OUT. Make sure all of your tracks are selected. Now click on the Record Monitor to make it active.

Here are the steps we will take to export a sequence:

1. Choose Export from the File menu.
2. Choose Fast-Export QuickTime from the Export Setting window.

> **Fast-Export QuickTime**
> **Macintosh Image**
> Export Setting ✓ Untitled

3. Press the Options button. The Export Settings window opens (Figure 13.11).

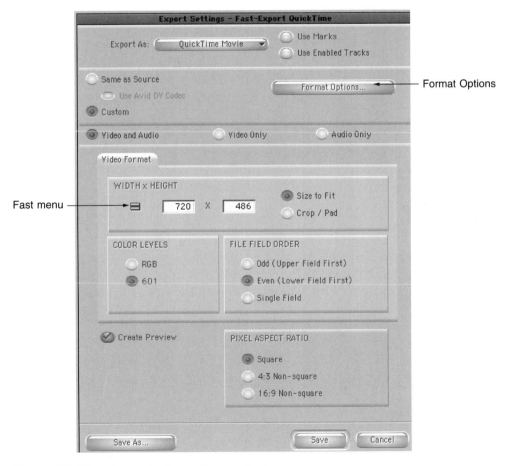

Figure 13.11 Export Settings—Custom Settings

4. In the Export Settings window, Export As: QuickTime Movie should be selected.
5. Now:
    *   Choose Use Marks if you have IN and OUT marks in the Timeline.
    *   Deselect *both* Use Marks and Use Enabled Tracks if you want the entire sequence.

5. Choose Same as Source to use the same compression as your footage. If you're working in 2:1, that will be the compression.
6. If you're working on an Xpress DV system, and you'll be exporting to your hard drive or to another Xpress DV system, chose Same as Source and check Use Avid DV Codec.
7. If you're going to a system that doesn't have the Avid DV Codec, deselect Use Avid Codec.
8. Select Video and Audio.
9. Select Create Preview (all this does is put a picture frame on the file's icon).
10. Select 4:3 Non-square.
11. Click Save (or Save As and name).
12. When you are returned to the Export window, name the file (the name of the sequence will be the default name).
13. Choose where (e.g., CD, hard drive) you want to save the file.
14. Click Save.

This creates a QuickTime Movie that is of the same quality as your recorded video. That's perfect for exporting several clips or an opening sequence to After Effects, where you'll add an effect and then reimport it back into your Avid. It's also great for showing a short scene or two to a friend on his or her computer. But remember that if your project is DV, 3:1, or 2:1, and your sequence is longer than a couple of minutes, this can be a very large file. If you want to post it on a Website or send it as an e-mail attachment, you'll need to compress it quite a bit. For that you'll need to customize your settings.

Custom Settings

If you deselect the Same as Source button, and select Custom, many familiar choices open up (see Figure 13.11). We've already discussed many of these variables earlier in this chapter.

You know, for instance, that you'll want 601 and not RGB for all Quick-Time movie exports. If your video system is NTSC and not PAL, you'll want Even (Lower Field First).

Use Figure 13.11 as a guide. These settings should work for all NTSC QuickTime exports. The only setting that isn't obvious is the WIDTH × HEIGHT Fast menu (Figure 13.12). Here are a couple of hints:

- Use 720 × 486 when exporting to After Effects or a similar program, or when you plan to reimport back into your Avid.
- Use 648 × 486 for the Web.

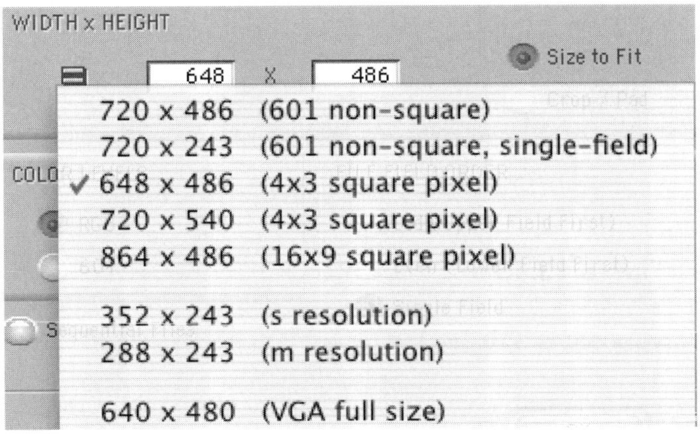

Figure 13.12 Width × Height choices

Now there's one more set of choices we need to examine. Click on the Format Options button (see Figure 13.11). Here you'll find boxes that contain settings for Video, Sound, and Internet Streaming. Inside the Video box, for instance, you can click on Settings and scroll through to find many standard video compression settings. In Figure 13.13, I have selected Sorenson 3, which provides a great deal of compression, appropriate for delivery to the Web.

You can also choose the frames-per-second rate, the frame size, and the audio compression. There's also a section specifically for Internet Streaming. Knowing which program, application, or delivery medium you're exporting to will help you select the right settings from the many choices. Obviously, if you find the settings that work well for you, you should click Save As and save them as a template.

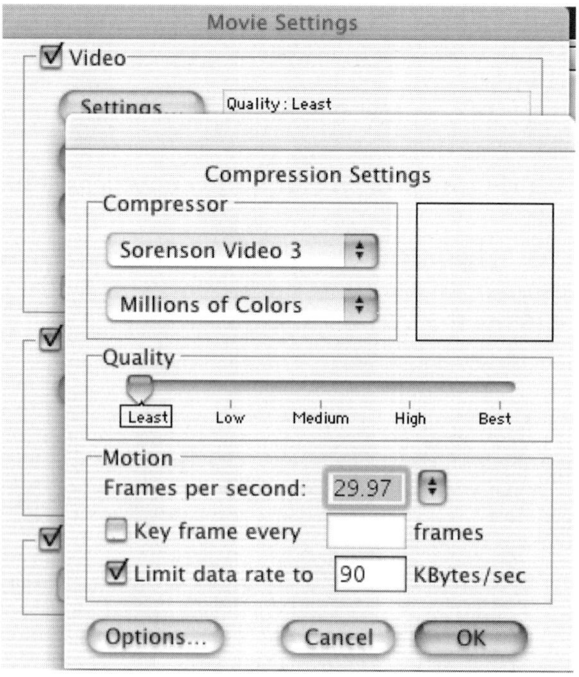

Figure 13.13

Exporting Audio to a Digital Audio Work Station

Although the Avid is capable of fairly sophisticated audio manipulation, it's not as sophisticated as Pro Tools or other dedicated digital audio workstations (DAWs). Although you may be a great editor, sound mixing is probably not your specialty. Sometimes it's worth going to a professional sound mixer—someone who does this sort of work every day. Not only can these professionals solve your sound problems, but they can also set perfect levels for any number of distribution formats, including videotape, DVD, and film magnetic and optical tracks.

Because Pro Tools is one of the most common audio workstations, we'll review the steps you should take to export your audio to Pro Tools. If you think you'll be going to a Pro Tools workstation, or some other DAW, talk to the sound engineer before following these steps, in case he or she would like something a little different. This outline will give you a great place to start the conversation. Then you can make whatever changes the sound engineer suggests to this list of steps before you export your files.

The basic idea is that you will be sending the audio's master clips and the media files to a CD-R or to a media drive, such as your FireWire drive, which you will disconnect from your Avid and carry to the DAW station. Because audio takes up far less space than video, a CD or Jaz disk can probably hold all of your master clips and media files.

1. Make a duplicate of your final sequence. Create a new bin, labeled Pro Tools Sequence, and place the duplicate in the bin.
2. Place the sequence in the Record Monitor and, in the Timeline, delete the video track(s) by selecting them and deselecting all audio tracks. Hit the Delete key.
3. Make sure all of your audio effects are rendered and all of your tracks are enabled (selected).
4. Select the sequence in the bin, and choose Export from the File menu.
5. Click Options in the Export window and, when the Export Settings window opens, drag down the Export As window and choose OMF 1.0.

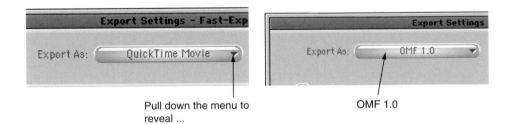

Pull down the menu to reveal ...

OMF 1.0

- You should ask the sound engineer if he or she would prefer OMF 2.0.
6. Select: Include All Audio Tracks In Sequence.
7. Deselect: Include All Video Tracks In Sequence.
8. In Audio Details, choose Consolidate and Link to Consolidated Media (Figure 13.14).

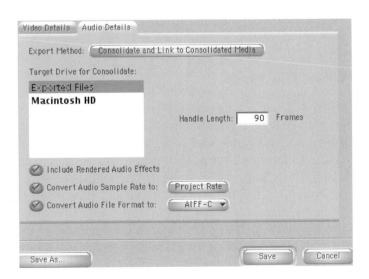

Figure 13.14

9. Select a Drive for Consolidation. In Figure 13.14, I have selected a CD-R called "Exported Files," which I have already inserted into the computer's CD burner.
10. Type 90 in the Handle Length box.
11. Check:
    - Include Rendered Audio Effects.
    - Convert Audio Sample Rate to Project Rate.
    - Convert Audio File Format to AIFF-C.
12. Click Save As. Name it Pro Tools (or DAW). Then click OK.

When you return to the Export window, you'll now see Pro Tools as a template that you created.

13. Now click Save.

The Avid will send the audio master clips in your final sequence, and all of the media files linked to those clips, to your CD. Burn the CD and bring it to your mixer; the sequence and all of the audio files will be on the CD. Most mixers will want a video copy of the final sequence to play in sync with the audio as they sweeten and mix your tracks.

Exporting Other File Types

If you look at the Export As menu (Figure 13.15), you'll see that there are several file types to choose from. In the chapter on film (Chapter 17), we'll learn about Avid Log Exchange and Tab Delimited.

A QuickTime Reference Movie isn't a real movie file, but rather a shell that connects to the media on your Avid. If you want to work with another application that uses QuickTime Movies, and that application is on the same computer as your Avid software, this is the best method because it's fast and takes up no media drive space. But it won't work on any other computers because then it's an empty shell without access to the media on your Avid's media drive.

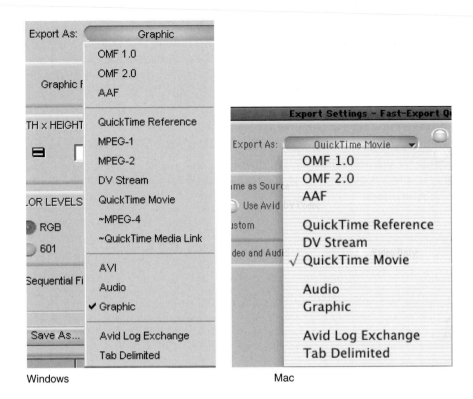

Windows   Mac

Figure 13.15 File types

MPEG-2 is used by some DVD authoring software. AVI was Microsoft's first attempt at competing with Apple's QuickTime.

We've discussed only two kinds of graphic files: TIFF and PICT. There are scores of other supported file types. It all depends on the application to which you're exporting the material.

Exporting is more complicated than importing because you could be exporting to hundreds of applications, but you're importing to only one application—your Avid. Just as I did with importing, I've tried to make exporting as simple as possible. Needless to say, I haven't covered all of the hundreds of choices or options.

To become an expert at exporting, you need to learn about the applications you're exporting to, such as After Effects, Photoshop, and Pro Tools. The more applications you master, the more valuable you are to your client or employer. If you're editing your own projects, the fewer outside vendors or freelance people you'll need to hire (all the better for your budget).

SUGGESTED ASSIGNMENTS

1. Import Color Bars from the Avid Test Patterns folder.
2. Import a file created in Photoshop. If you don't have a file, borrow one from a friend. Ask him or her to save it as a TIFF or PICT file.
3. Cut it into a sequence.
4. Export a frame from a sequence.
5. Open the file in Photoshop. If you don't have Photoshop, ask a friend who does to open it for you.
6. Export a sequence as a QuickTime Movie and play it on another computer.

14

16:9 Widescreen Television

Although widescreen cinema has been with us for many decades, television has remained wedded to its boxlike shape. The tide is slowly turning, and the day will soon come when we'll all replace our box-shaped televisions with sleek, widescreen versions. Although many uncertainties remain in terms of the type of video signal our new televisions will display, one thing we do know is the aspect ratio will be 16:9.

In Chapter 13, we discussed the topic of aspect ratios. To recap, a square's aspect ratio is 1:1 because its height is identical to its width. Most feature films shown in today's multiplex theaters are projected with an aspect ratio of either 1.85:1 or 2.35:1. These formats are much wider than they are high, especially when compared with the aspect ratio of a standard television screen—1.33:1 (or 4:3).

Let's compare the frame size of standard television with the widescreen, 16:9 version. As you can see in Figure 14.1, I've placed a 4:3 standard television frame inside a 16:9 television.

WHERE THE NUMBERS COME FROM

The 16:9 aspect ratio is becoming the standard for all high-definition televisions (HDTVs). This aspect ratio comes from one of the earliest proposed HDTV formats. In this one there are 1920 pixels (wide) × 1080 pixels (high). Divide 1920 by 1080 and you get a ratio of 1.7777778:1. That's rather cumbersome to bring up in daily conversation, so 16:9 is used instead. Divide 16 by 9 and you get 1.7777778.

STANDARD NTSC VIDEO—NOT BIG ENOUGH

If you play your standard NTSC video on a 16:9 monitor, it will not fill the screen. It will sit in the middle of the screen, looking sheepishly undersized,

4:3 inside a 16:9 screen

Figure 14.1

with black bands on the left- and right-hand sides. If you have letterbox video, it's even worse. Not only do you have black bands on the left and right, but on the top and bottom as well.

This chapter explains how you can produce true widescreen video, using the Avid to do much of the work. Before explaining that process to you, a little background information on the whole high definition (HD) mess is perhaps in order.

THE ROOT OF THE FORMAT PROBLEM

A few years back, when the U.S. Federal Communications Commission (FCC) ruled that all television entities in the United States must move to digital television, it left it up to the networks and cable companies to determine their own distribution format. Perhaps that was a mistake. The problem with not mandating a digital format is that each company has come up with competing and incompatible formats. There are four variables that determine these competing formats:

- The number of horizontal lines
- The aspect ratio of the frame
- The frames-per-second rate
- The way in which the lines are scanned

The standard NTSC television of today has 525 horizontal lines, with an aspect ratio of 4:3, running at 29.97 frames per second, using interlaced scanning. As things stand, the four U.S. networks have chosen four different digital formats. Most people call these new formats HDTV, although some have more definition than others.

Although the story may change, as of now it looks like CBS and NBC have chosen an HDTV signal that has 1080i (lines interlaced); ABC has chosen a format of 720P (lines progressive); and Fox will accept three formats: 420P,

480i, and 720P. Europe has proposed several other HDTV formats. Most people who have done the math and examined the various choices say there are a total of 18 different HDTV formats under consideration. What a mess! The problem for those of us who are trying to produce material for the networks and cable companies is this: How do we provide shows that are compatible with all of these competing formats? As editors, what do we say to our clients when they ask for 18 different versions of an hour-long show?

If I weren't an optimist, I'd be discouraged. Let's face it: If all of these billion-dollar television entities can't get it together, what chance do we have of coming up with solutions? Where does it leave the rest of us? Well, one answer is that although we are creators of content, we are also consumers of that content, and what are we consumers doing? We're pricing and buying widescreen, HD-ready televisions.

Only a small portion of the viewing public is watching HDTV, but most of our friends and neighbors are buying widescreen, HD-ready televisions. We can't wait for the dust to settle on the various competing HD formats. We need to start producing products for widescreen television—not tomorrow, but today. As I see it, here are the paths we can take. They range from the extremely expensive to the relatively cheap.

YOUR WIDESCREEN CHOICES

Expensive

If you can afford it, shoot your project on 35mm film. I know, I know, it's hugely expensive, but I'd be remiss if I didn't propose it. You can transfer it to any existing or future format. It offers the best resolution, and it is the archival medium of choice everywhere on the planet. (That's why so many television shows are shot on film rather than video.) I'm not going to go into much detail because it's probably not an option for you, but if you have the money, it's the simplest and the safest choice.

The video format of choice is HD video running at 24 frames per second and using a progressive, not an interlaced, scan. This format is often simply referred to as *24P*. Many bright people have determined that this HDTV format is compatible with nearly all of the other competing HDTV formats, as well as film. George Lucas used this format to shoot his latest Star Wars trilogy. Brad Anderson (*Next Stop Wonderland*) was one of the first filmmakers to shoot a feature film using an HDTV camera, when he shot *Session 9*. Both Lucas and Anderson have used Sony's HDW-F900 video camera. The key to this format is that, like film, it runs at 24 frames per second, and also like film, each frame is unique, courtesy of progressive scanning. Costs associated with shooting in 24P HD are comparable with 35mm film.

Less Expensive

The Super-16mm film format has a lot of appeal for mid- to low-end producers and students. Super-16's aspect ratio is almost identical to HDTV's aspect ratio. Film is 24P. Film cameras run at 24 frames per second, and each frame is unique and stands by itself. It's a progressive rather than interlaced medium. The resolution of Super-16mm film rivals HDTV.

Super-16mm equipment rents for hundreds less per day than comparable professional video packages, and to get comparable image quality in video, you'd have to move up to HDTV, which is a far more expensive option. Many film schools have 16mm cameras that can be converted to Super-16.

To fill a widescreen television, you need to use an anamorphic process. I'll explain this process in detail later in the chapter.

Newer video cameras are coming out with true 16:9 chips that capture the image onto a 16:9 digital target. These are not HDTV cameras, but they share the same aspect ratio. Because there are more pixels available per frame, there's more information on each frame of video.

Least Expensive

Digital video, whether DV, DVCAM, or DVCPRO, has become wildly popular because it offers good image quality for comparatively little money. The most popular camera models are now offering a 16:9 setting among their extensive menu options. I don't recommend this as a viable choice for acquiring 16:9 images. These cameras use a 4:3 digital capture area, and they manipulate the pixels to fill a 16:9 frame. Unfortunately, there just aren't enough pixels or picture information to do this successfully.

There is a way to use DV cameras to get 16:9 images. You place an *anamorphic converter* on the front of your DV camera and then use an NLE editor, such as the Avid, to give you 16:9 widescreen video (Figure 14.2).

Figure 14.2   16 × 9 Anamorphic attachment. (Courtesy Century Optics.)

The two options I want to discuss in detail are Super-16mm and digital video because I believe they offer the rest of us a chance to produce widescreen material. Both choices use an anamorphic process to provide a 16:9 image that will fill a widescreen television.

ANAMORPHIC PHOTOGRAPHY

We've all been to an amusement park and stood in front of those funny mirrors. One makes you look tall and thin and the other one makes you look short and wide. These mirrors use the same principle that gave rise to CinemaScope movies in the 1950s. Scope pictures, with their 2.35:1 aspect ratio, are still in vogue today. Early on, cinematographers placed anamorphic converters in front of their lenses to achieve the widescreen effect, but today companies such as Panavision manufacture a wide range of anamorphic lenses for use on 35mm and 70mm cameras and theater projectors.

The anamorphic converter, or lens, compresses the image in one plane and not the other. The converter compresses or squeezes the image horizontally, while keeping the vertical image fixed. Look at a film shot with an anamorphic lens. The people and objects look as if they have been placed in a vise and squeezed together (Figure 14.3). Now project that same film with a projector outfitted with an anamorphic lens, and the image is stretched horizontally. The people and objects are restored to their normal proportions, but you also have a much wider screen image—the amusement park mirror without the distortion (Figure 14.4).

Figure 14.3 Image anamorphically squeezed

Figure 14.4 Image stretched during projection

Anamorphic DV

If you place an anamorphic converter on a DV camera, such as the one shown in Figure 14.2, you get the same squeezing of the horizontal plane—just like a widescreen Hollywood movie. Play that tape on a standard NTSC monitor and everything looks squeezed; however, when you display your videotape on one of today's 16:9 monitors, electronics in the monitor stretch the image to fill the 16:9 widescreen, as you can see in Figure 14.5.

Figure 14.5 A widescreen television monitor

Super-16

Super-16mm film is really just 16mm film. Instead of manufacturing it with perforations (or sprocket holes) on both sides of the film, the manufacturer makes a single-perforated version. With a row of perforations removed, there is more usable negative because the area taken up by the perforations is replaced by more exposable film. The frame isn't any higher, but it is much wider. If you use a 16mm camera converted for shooting this wider image area, you can take advantage of the additional negative space to create high-quality widescreen projects. (Super-16 was originally used for blow-ups to 35mm for theatrical release.)

Double-perforated 16mm film has an aspect ratio of 4:3. If you remove one row of perforations, you have a wider usable area with an aspect ratio of 1.66:1. You could use standard 16mm film and crop the top and the bottom of the frame to get a widescreen look, but using Super-16 gives you 47 percent more image area! The aspect ratio of 1.66:1 is very close to 16:9.

Anamorphic Film-to-Tape Transfer

Instead of using an anamorphic converter on the lens of a 16mm camera, you can get a superior picture by anamorphically squeezing the image during the film-to-tape transfer.

When the Super-16 film is scanned during telecine, the image can be squeezed and stored that way on any standard NTSC tape (e.g., Beta SP, DVCAM, D-1). When you display this tape on a standard 4:3 monitor, the actors will look squeezed—tall and thin. If you use one of the new widescreen televisions, however, electronics in the monitor can stretch the image to fill the 16:9 frame. This is often called *anamorphic video*. Look at the television monitor in Figure 14.5. This image was shot on Super-16mm film and then transferred anamorphically to video. When played on this widescreen monitor, the squeezed image is stretched to fill the entire 16:9 frame.

Obviously, not all film-to-tape transfer machines have anamorphic capability. You need a flying-spot scanner, or its equivalent. I recently did a transfer using a Cintel Ursa Diamond at a post house in Boston, Massachusetts, called *Finish Edit* (Figure 14.6).

Figure 14.6   A colorist adjusts levels during a film-to-tape transfer

Using Super-16 film, with its wide image area, and then doing a transfer anamorphically, gives spectacular results. When played on a widescreen television, the picture quality rivals 35mm.

Super-16mm to HDTV

There's another reason why I'm pushing Super-16 as the format of choice for many projects. Right now, I'm not recommending that you transfer your film to HD tape because there's so little demand for it. But unlike all of the NTSC video formats currently available, Super-16 film can be transferred to HD tape beautifully. When demand for HDTV warrants the conversion, you can transfer your Super-16mm film to just about any HDTV format and end up with a true HDTV project.

PRACTICE FOOTAGE

As part of the DVD that comes with this book, I have included a project entitled "Gaffer's Delight." The project was shot using a Super-16mm camera, and then, after the film was processed, the negative was anamorphically squeezed during the telecine. If you follow the mounting instructions at the end of the book, you will have 16:9 clips to work with. We'll also use these clips in Chapter 15, when we learn about Script Integration.

16:9 AVID EDITING

You may shoot your own footage using a video camera with a true 16:9 chip or a DV camera using an anamorphic converter on the lens. Or you may shoot with a film camera using Super-16mm film and then transfer it anamorphically; the end result is NTSC video with squeezed people and objects.

The latest Avid software, including Xpress DV, can easily change the shape of the Source and Record Monitors so that you can edit in the 16:9 aspect ratio. To the Avid it's all just pixels to be manipulated.

To get the Avid to change the aspect ratio of the monitors, Media Composer users go to Settings and double-click on the Composer Settings. Select the 16:9 Monitors button.

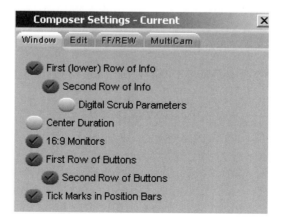

Xpress and Xpress DV users simply go to the Source/Record Monitor and click on it to make it active. Then go to the Clip menu and select 16:9 Monitors. It's that simple.

As you can see in Figure 14.7, the Avid changes the shape of the Source and Record Monitors to accommodate the 16:9 images. You may have to resize the Timeline and various bins to get everything to fit nicely on your computer screen.

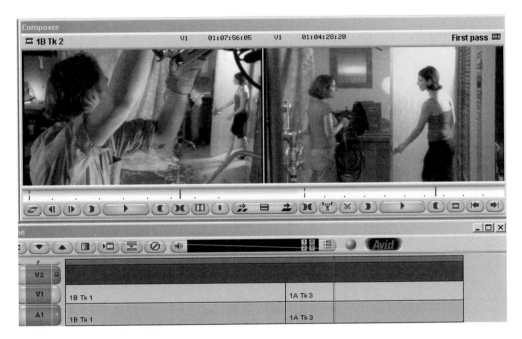

Figure 14.7

16:9 Titles

When you create titles using the Title Tool, the Avid will know to create them as widescreen 16:9 titles. Just open the Title Tool and create your titles as you would in a 4:3 project.

Your Finished Project

Once you're through editing the 16:9 project, you can output it to any tape format. The tape will contain the squeezed material, but a widescreen TV or video projector will easily stretch the footage. In fact, today's video projectors can make this video material look as if it were shot in 35mm by displaying it in a widescreen format. With DVD a popular choice for distribution, you can also burn your project to DVD, select 16:9 as your aspect ratio, and maintain the widescreen look. We examine how to do this in Chapter 16.

MULTIPLE FORMATS

Although having a widescreen version is great, you will also want the option of playing your project on any standard television, not just the widescreen ones. The Avid has tools to create a 4:3 version and a 4:3 letterbox version as well. You can record those out to tape or DVD and therefore have several options for showing your work.

Creating a letterbox version is amazingly simple and, depending on your software, can be done in a matter of minutes. With letterboxing, you get to keep the widescreen composition, but to do so, you have to put black bands above and below the picture information.

Creating a 4:3 Letterbox Version (Media Composer Only)

1. Go to Settings, Composer Settings, and deselect 16:9 Monitors.
2. Create a V2 track. Make sure nothing else is on it. (If there is, create a V3 track.)
3. Click the Monitor track box so the icon moves up to V2.
4. Go to the Effect Palette, click on the Reformat category of effects, and drag the 16:9 Letterbox icon to the V2 track (see Figure 14.12).

You will now see your sequence with normal 4:3 proportions, but with the widescreen composition maintained, thanks to the letterboxing. Look at Figure 14.8.

Figure 14.8

Creating a 4:3 Letterbox Version (Xpress and Xpress DV)

The Xpress doesn't have the Reformat category of effects. Even if it did, I've encountered a problem with the way Xpress DV handles certain effects. The Xpress DV won't allow you to place an effect, such as Mask or Resize, onto an empty video track. You can't place an effect on V2, so the effect is a layer above your clips in the Timeline. (Xpress users don't have this problem and can skip step number 3.)

I've discovered a work-around, however. Examine Figure 14.9. If you place anything at the head of V2 (or V3), such as a title, you can then drag an effect, such as Resize, onto V2. Once you've done that, the effect can work on all of the clips in the Timeline. Without this ability, you have to drag the Resize icon onto each and every clip. In Figure 14.9, you can see that by placing a title in V2, I was able to drag the Resize Effect onto the entire V2 track.

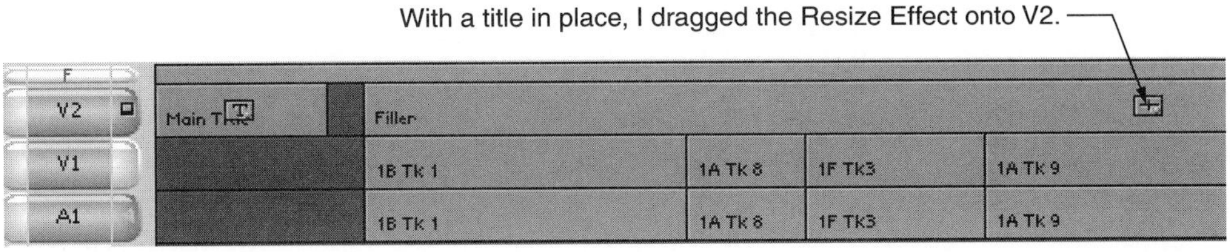

With a title in place, I dragged the Resize Effect onto V2.

Figure 14.9

Follow these steps to create a letterbox version on your Xpress and Xpress DV:

1. Click anywhere on the Source/Record Monitor to make it active.
2. In the Clip menu, deselect 16:9 Monitors so that you're back in 4:3 mode. Everything will appear squeezed.
3. Create a title and splice it so that it's on V2, before the clips in your sequence, as shown in Figure 14.9.
4. Go to the Effect Palette > Image and drag the Resize icon to the V2 track. You will have one solid effect covering the whole track.
5. Placing the blue position indicator on the Resize Effect icon in the Timeline, open the Effect Editor (Figure 14.10).
6. Under Scaling, select:
   Width 100 (normal)
   Height 75

That's all there is to it. You now have reformatted your entire sequence to 4:3.

Figure 14.10

Creating a 4:3 Pan & Scan Version for a Standard TV

Most video distributors of feature films believe that viewers won't accept letterboxing of any stripe, so they crop all feature films, cutting off the edges and showing you what occurs in the center of the frame or panning to the left or right if the composition warrants it. Networks and cable companies do the same whenever they show feature films on television. But for true film lovers, this seems like a bad compromise. You're not seeing the film's original composition—you're not seeing the sets, or the art direction, or some of the action because large sections of the frame are being cropped out. Fortunately, more and more DVDs are offering a widescreen version that, when played on a widescreen television, shows you the entire widescreen picture.

For now, you will still need a 4:3 version of your project, and like Hollywood, you will need to crop your project to conform to the 4:3 aspect ratio of standard television. We'll first capture the center of the widescreen composition, dropping off the sides of each shot in the sequence. Then we'll recompose the image, panning left or right, to make each shot compositionally more effective.

The simplest method uses a feature available on Avid's newer models called Pan & Scan, which I'll explain in a bit. But first, let's look at a workaround for those systems, such as Xpress DV, that don't have Pan & Scan. We're going to use the Resize Effect, just as we did with the letterbox version.

Using the Resize Effect

1. Click anywhere on the Source/Record Monitor to make it active.
2. In the Clip menu, deselect 16:9 Monitors so that you're back in 4:3 mode. Everything will appear squeezed.

3. Go to the Effect Palette > Image and drag the Resize icon to the first clip.
4. Placing the blue position indicator on the Resize Effect icon in the Timeline, open the Effect Editor (Figure 14.11).

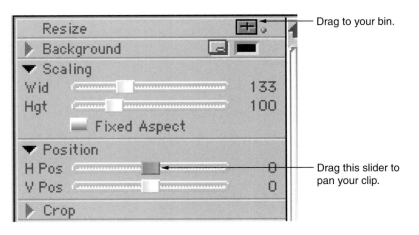

Drag to your bin.

Drag this slider to pan your clip.

Figure 14.11

5. Set the Scaling to:
   Width 133
   Height 100
   You'll see that your first clip now has a perfectly proportioned 4:3 image. That part was easy.
6. Now, create a template for this effect by dragging the effect icon from the Effect Editor to a bin. Name it "Resize 4:3."
7. Place this template on all of the shots in your sequence.
   Now you have resized all of your shots, and all of your composition has the middle of each shot, with the sides dropped out. But it might look better if some shots were panned left or right.
8. Re-open the Effects Editor.
9. Open the Position Triangle (see Figure 14.11).
10. Set the opening key frame by clicking on the opening key frame and then moving the H Pos slide to pan either left or right.
11. Copy that H Pos setting and paste it onto the end key frame.

This will maintain the same composition—the pan—throughout the shot. You can use multiple key frames to pan during the shot. Set an opening composition on the first key frame and then add key frames and change the H Pos slider at every key frame. You can even make several templates and use them for a variety of similar clips requiring the same composition. Using the Pan & Scan Effect is a much better choice, if you have it.

Pan & Scan Effect

The newer Media Composers have a Reformat category of effects that allows you to reformat to different aspect ratios, as well as Pan & Scan. Currently, Avid doesn't ship the Xpress DV or Xpress with Pan & Scan. Pan & Scan makes the process of panning a bit easier than the method I just described, but not much.

When you are through editing, leave your Source/Record Monitor in the 16:9 mode. Now follow these steps:

1. Create a video track that is above your titles and clips, either V2, V3, or higher.
2. Go to the Effect Palette and click on Reformat (Figure 14.12).

Figure 14.12

3. Drag the Pan & Scan Effect icon to the top-most video track—the one that is empty.
4. Placing the blue position indicator on the effect icon in the Timeline, open the Effect Editor.

5. Click on the Aspect Ratio triangle so that it opens. In the Source pop-up menu, select 16:9 Anamorphic. In the Target pop-up menu, select 1.33 (4:3).

Now you'll see a wire frame inside the Effect Preview Monitor. Usually the Pan & Scan chooses the middle of the widescreen frame as its default selection. If that works as a starting point for all of your shots, go to the Actions triangle and click on Establish Origin. If that doesn't work as a starting point for most of your shots, move the wire frame with your cursor to select a more appropriate composition and then click on Establish Origin.

Under the Actions triangle, you'll see Subdivide Effect. If all of your shots in your sequence needed the same amount of panning, then you could leave the Pan & Scan Effect just as it is, but of course just about every shot will have different panning requirements. That's where Subdivide Effect comes in. It breaks the Pan & Scan Effect into sections that match the length of each clip in your Timeline.

Now you need to go to each clip that needs recomposing, open the Effect Editor, and using key frames, either drag the wire frame or use the H Pos slider in the Position triangle to set the panning. If at any time you want to get back to your starting point, click on Reset Origin in the Action section and you'll return to your original, or base, composition.

GO WIDE

The anamorphic process seems strange at first, but it's a great way to produce projects for the widescreen monitors that are starting to appear in our neighbors' apartments and homes. The Avid handles the material effortlessly. There's no going back, so we might as well embrace this format and make all of our projects HD-ready. With a little bit of help from the Effect Palette, you can simultaneously create a letterbox and standard 4:3 version as well.

SUGGESTED ASSIGNMENTS

1. Open the "Gaffer's Delight" project and place several clips in the Source Monitor.
2. Media Composer users, go to Settings and double-click on the Composer Settings. Select the 16:9 button.
3. Xpress users, go to the Clip menu and select 16:9 Monitors.
4. Edit several clips together and then letterbox the sequence.
5. Use Pan & Scan to get a 4:3 version or use the Resize effect if you don't have Pan & Scan.

15

Script Integration

Script Integration is found on Media Composers and the latest Xpress models. I believe it is the most dynamic and exciting tool found on any NLE system in the world. Yet despite its strong points, Script Integration is perhaps the least used of all of Avid's features.

Why? First, you have to have a script. For many films and videos, from experimental to cinema verité, there's no script, so there's no script to integrate. Yet even those filmmakers who work from a script often think Script Integration is just too much work. You can't just open a bin and start editing. You must import the script, drag all of your clips to it, and mark individual lines of dialog or action. At first glance, it seems like a waste of good editing time; however, the time spent on the front end is more than made up on the back end. Once you get the hang of it, you'll wonder how you ever got along without it.

Xpress DV users, you must have PowerPack to access Script Integration.

HOLLYWOOD-STYLE EDITING

Script Integration is based on the style of editing commonly used on feature films. During production, information about the way each scene was shot gets written on the script by the script supervisor. The script supervisor draws lines through the script, indicating the amount of the scene each camera angle covers. At the end of production, the editor receives a copy of this "lined script." With the lined script in hand, the editor knows what footage is available for each line of action and dialog. The script supervisor also makes detailed notes about how many times each camera setup was repeated and which are the preferred takes.

An Avid with Script Integration follows this lined script system but adds its own powerful digital editing tools. You import the script right into the Avid. You then select the portion of the script that is covered by a particular clip and drag the clip to that section of the script. Each camera setup is represented by a *slate*, showing a frame from that clip (Figure 15.1). Different takes are indicated by tabs at the bottom of the slates. Once all of the clips are linked to the appropriate sections of the script, you can click on a line of dialog and have the takes play automatically, so you can compare them. When you're ready to start editing a scene, you can quickly go through the script, double-click on the preferred takes, and create a rough cut in a matter of minutes.

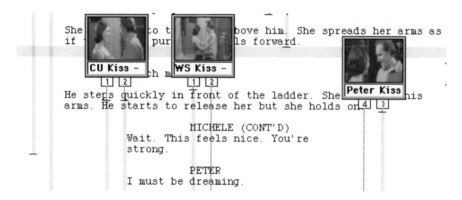

Figure 15.1   A script with attached clips and slates

The Avid can handle documentary scripts as easily as narrative scripts, and the setup and procedures are the same.

AN EXAMPLE

The screen captures in this chapter are from a scene entitled "Gaffer's Delight," which I made with the help of students and staff members at Boston University. A copy of the project files, media files, and the script can be found on the DVD that comes with the book. A copy of the lined script is at the end of this chapter.

The scene was covered with a master shot, showing both actors, and then shot again from many different angles to cover the actors as they moved around the set. Each camera setup was repeated several times, as take 1, take 2, and so on. Follow the DVD instructions at the end of this book to mount the project and media files onto your Avid. I'll explain how to bring in the script shortly.

USING TWO MONITORS

This is one editing mode where having two monitors can be helpful. One monitor holds all of the bins, including the script, and a second monitor holds the Source/Record Monitors and the Timeline. You can do it with one monitor, because the script can be resized and moved around the screen, but it's a lot easier with two. For Xpress DV users, setting up a second monitor is pretty easy. Read your computer guide to find out how to hook up a second monitor and how to set the second monitor's screen resolution. You want *dual display* rather than *mirroring*. In dual-display mode, the second monitor extends the real estate of the Avid, so you can drag the Script window to the second monitor. Video mirroring simply shows the same Avid screen on both monitors. You might have to go to your local computer store to get the right cable to run from your computer to a second monitor. I did.

NAMING CLIPS

Before you even digitize your material, you should give some thought to how you name your clips. Long clip names, such as "Over-the-Shoulder on Peter" or "Close-up on Hands," are easy to read in your bin when you're in Text Mode, but they don't work as well with the slates, which are the heart of Script Integration. Try using clip names such as "1D Tk 1" to indicate the scene, camera setup, and take because they will fit more easily on the script page. If your clip names are too long, the Avid will shorten them, but in doing so the Avid might hide important information.

For the purposes of this book, I have used clip names that describe the action to make it easier for the reader to follow. On the DVD, for those of you who will actually edit the scene, I have used the shorter scene and take numbers, such as "1D Tk 1."

GETTING THE SCRIPT

I use Final Draft, the popular scriptwriting software, as do many of my students. Because Avid and Final Draft have collaborated on Script Integration, you can bring a Final Draft script into the Avid.

1. Open your script in Final Draft, then choose Save As from the File menu.
2. In the dialog box, go to the Format box and choose "Avid Script Based Editing," and click on Save (Figure 15.2).

Place a copy of this script onto a Zip disk, CD, or DVD and bring it to your Avid system. If you're on a network, you can leave the file on your computer and get it once you're on your Avid. In case your version of Final Draft isn't compatible with the latest application software, go to the Format box and save your script as ASCII Text with Layout.

Once you're on the Avid, place the Zip disk, CD, or DVD in your drive (or get it from the network). Those of you who have loaded the "Gaffer's

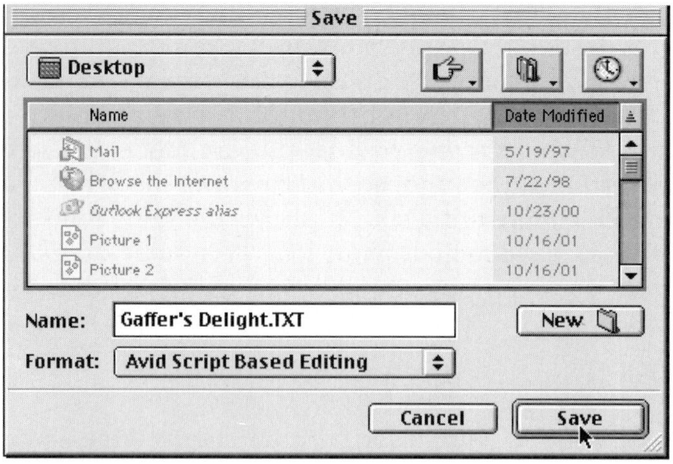

Save

Desktop

Name	Date Modified
Mail	5/19/97
Browse the Internet	7/22/98
Outlook Express alias	10/23/00
Picture 1	10/16/01
Picture 2	10/16/01

Name: **Gaffer's Delight.TXT**   New

Format: **Avid Script Based Editing**

Cancel   Save

Figure 15.2

Delight" files can get the script from the DVD that comes with this book. Then launch your Avid software, open the project, and follow these simple steps:

1. Click on the Project window to make it the active window.
2. Select New Script from the File menu.
3. Search through the directory dialog box that appears, and find the script file (Gaffer's Delight script).
4. Select the file and click the Open button.

Your script will appear in the Bin monitor, looking much like this (Figure 15.3):

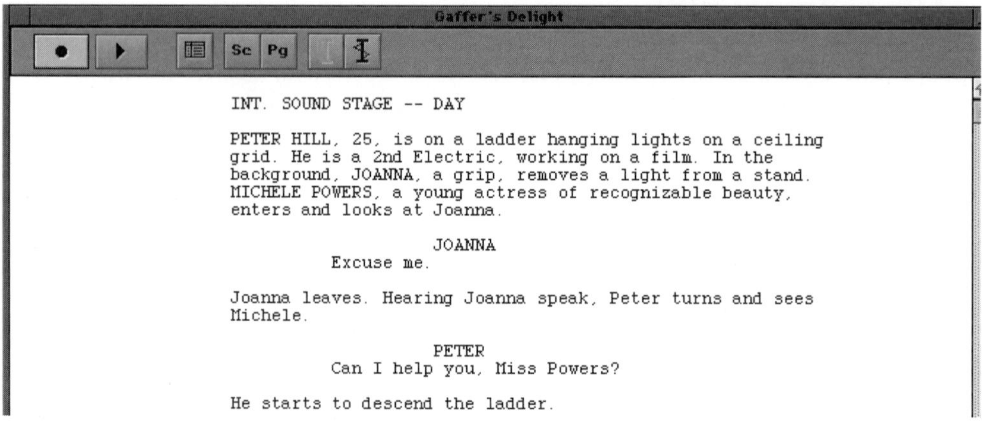

Gaffer's Delight

● ▶   ▦   Sc   Pg   ⌐

```
INT. SOUND STAGE -- DAY

PETER HILL, 25, is on a ladder hanging lights on a ceiling
grid. He is a 2nd Electric, working on a film. In the
background, JOANNA, a grip, removes a light from a stand.
MICHELE POWERS, a young actress of recognizable beauty,
enters and looks at Joanna.

                    JOANNA
          Excuse me.

Joanna leaves. Hearing Joanna speak, Peter turns and sees
Michele.

                    PETER
          Can I help you, Miss Powers?

He starts to descend the ladder.
```

Figure 15.3   The script, as it appears in the Avid

The Avid will also create a special script bin, bearing the same name as the script file you're bringing in. When you close the script, it will go inside the script bin as shown in Figure 15.4.

Figure 15.4

GETTING STARTED

Your script should look like it did in your screenplay software. You can make changes to the script once it's in the Avid. You can delete lines of dialog or action (the Delete key won't work—use the Cut command to remove text instead), and you can move segments or scenes around, but you can't change individual words. In fact, you can't even select a word. The smallest segment of the script you can work with is an individual line. You'll see that this makes sense, once you start working with it. It's editing software, not script-writing software.

The way you select lines or sections of your script is pretty standard. You either lasso the line(s), using the mouse, or click on one line and keep pressing the Shift key to include more lines. You'll find lassoing text the best way to go.

LINKING CLIPS TO THE SCRIPT

Bringing clips from your bin to the script and linking them to specific lines is actually quite simple:

1. Open the script by double-clicking on it in the script bin.
2. Open the bin containing your clips (Figure 15.5).
3. Select the part of the script you want the first clip to cover by lassoing the script lines with the mouse. That portion of the script becomes highlighted.
4. Go to your clips bin, select the first clip, and drag its icon from the bin to the script.

A *slate*, or frame from that clip, will appear above the text (see Figure 15.5). The slate will show a frame from that shot, include the name of the clip, and have a box (or boxes) at the bottom to show different takes.

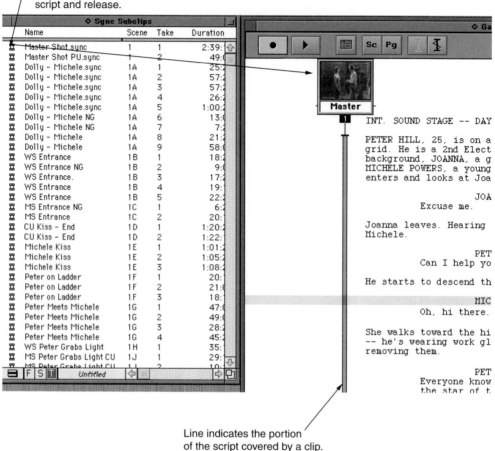

Figure 15.5

Once you've placed the first clip onto the script, you'll want to drag additional takes to that slate.

ADDING TAKES

The process of adding takes to a slate is similar to placing the first clip onto the script. Whichever take you brought over first establishes the slate. The next take goes on top of that slate and adds a second little box at the bottom. There's no difference, really, between the first take—the one you dragged onto the script first—and the second take. But first, you must create a column for the takes in your bin, so take numbers appear in the little boxes below the slate.

Takes don't show up in Brief View, so you need to switch to Text View.

1. Go to the Headings column in the Bin menu and select it.
2. In the list of headings, find the Take heading and click on it to select it.
3. Click OK.
4. In the bin, scroll to the right and find the Take column heading, click on the word Take so that the whole column is highlighted, and then drag the column all the way to the left, just next to the Name column.

Now, enter the take information by clicking in the column (Figure 15.6).

Name	Take	Start	End
1 Master Shot	1	01:00:01:26	01:02
1 Master Shot – P. U.	2	01:02:40:08	01:03
1A Tk 2	2	01:03:29:04	01:04
1A Tk 3	3	01:04:25:20	01:05
1A Tk 5		01:05:27:05	01:06
1A Tk 8		01:06:20:12	01:06
1A Tk 9		01:06:40:22	01:07

SuperBin: Dailies — Brief Text Frame Script

Figure 15.6

To add takes to a slate:

1. Lasso the portion of the script that the second take covers.
2. In your shots bin, click and drag the clip that represents the second take and drag it onto the slate already in the script.

Now you see that the slate has two boxes hanging from it, one for each take (Figure 15.7). Let's call them *take tabs*. Clicking on either take tab will

Figure 15.7 Take tabs

select that take. The frame in the slate will change depending on which take is selected.

There's a faster way to create slates and add takes to that slate. Say you have a shot with five takes. Simply lasso the portion of the script the shot covers, lasso or shift-click all five takes in the bin, and drag them all to the script at once. In Figure 15.8, you can see that I've dragged several clips, some with multiple takes, onto the script.

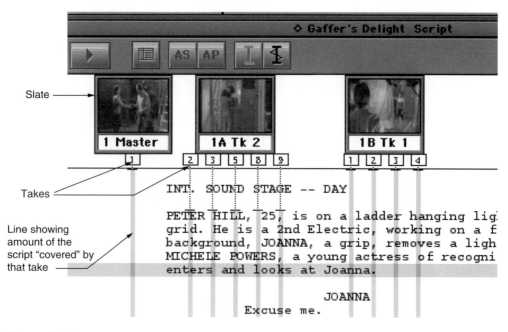

Figure 15.8

Remember that the key to this process is lassoing portions of the script that are covered by that particular clip. Once the portion is highlighted, when you drag the clip, the Avid will place the vertical lines appropriately. The end result will look like a professionally lined shooting script.

CHANGING THE SLATE

You can make the same changes to a slate as you would to a frame in Frame View in the bin. To change the size of the slate, choose Enlarge or Reduce from the Edit menu.

To change the representative frame that appears in the slate:

1. Select the take you want to change. Click on the take tab or take line.
2. Press the Step-one-frame or Step-10-frames key, stepping either forward or backward.

Don't use the J, K, and L keys, because that won't work. Click on the take tab and then press and hold the Step-one-frame forward key (the number 2 on the keyboard) to go forward. Press the Step-one-frame back key (the number 1 on the keyboard) to step backward.

REVIEW

In "Gaffer's Delight" I have a complicated Dolly shot (1A). Because there is a lot of actor and camera movement, we shot it nine times, resulting in nine takes (only five of the nine were worth digitizing). First I highlight the portion of the script that the first good take covers. Then I click on that take and drag it to the script. A slate appears with a box and a line running through the script all the way to the last line covered by that Dolly shot. If all of the other six takes ended at about the same place, I would shift-click on them in the bin and drag all of them onto the slate that's there.

Individual takes often end at a different point in the script. Takes 2 and 3 might get cut early because there's a bump in the Dolly shot or an actor flubs a line. Only the completed takes end at the same point. If I have shorter takes that are worth looking at, I'll treat each take individually. I lasso the portion of the script that Take 2 covers and drag it to the slate. Then I lasso the area Take 3 covers and drag it to the slate. Another way to handle this is to adjust the take lines.

ADJUSTING TAKE LINES

The vertical lines showing how much of the script a single take covers are called *take lines*. Where the line begins and ends is denoted by a short horizontal dash. Let's say that you highlighted too much of the script, and the vertical line the Avid draws goes beyond where the shot actually ends, or the take starts later than indicated. It's easy to correct where these lines start and end (Figure 15.9).

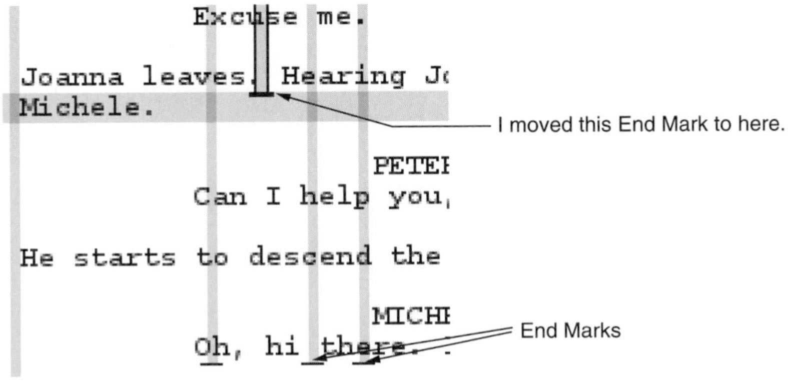

Figure 15.9

1. Go to the End Mark (or Start Mark) and hold down the Command key (Mac) or the Control key (Windows). The icon changes shape.
2. Drag the mark to the correct line in the script and release it.

SELECTING MULTIPLE TAKES

It's helpful to be able to select more than one slate or take at a time. To select a single slate or take, just click on the take tab. Shift-click to add additional slates or takes. Another way to select multiple takes and slates is to lasso the portion of the script covered by the takes you wish to select.

MOVING SLATES

You might find that a slate ends up obscuring a line of dialog from view and you want to move it to another place on the script page. Just click on the slate with your mouse and drag it to the left or right, or up and down. If you want to move the slate vertically, however, and at the same time change the position of the take lines, hold down the Command (Ctrl) key as you move the slate.

DELETING TAKES AND SLATES

You may make a mistake and put the wrong take on a slate or put the wrong clip in the script. To delete a slate or take, click on it and press the Delete key. The resulting dialog box looks intimidating (Figure 15.10). Just press OK. The takes in the bin will still be there, but the slate (here made up of two takes) will be removed from the script.

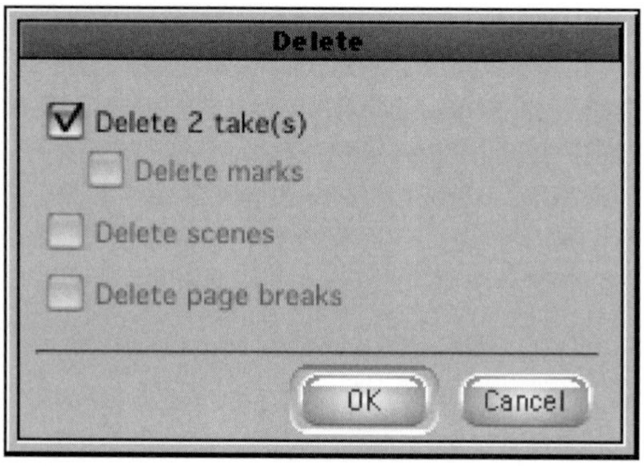

Figure 15.10

LOADING AND PLAYING TAKES

We still have more work to do before the script is truly integrated and we can take advantage of all that Script Integration has to offer. But before we take the next step, let's play around a little to get some satisfaction for our work. If you double-click on a take tab, the clip will load in the Source Monitor. If you want to select all of the takes for a shot, just lasso the take lines and they will all be selected, then double-click on any take and they'll all move to the Source Monitor.

You can play takes in two different ways. You can use the Play keys or J, K, and L keys once the clips are loaded into the Source Monitor, just as you would with any other clips. A better way is to lasso the take lines, or shift-click the take tabs, and then press the Play key at the top of the Script window (Figure 15.11). Those of you with Xpress DV 3.5 or higher can use the spacebar.

Figure 15.11

Either method will play the clips you selected one after another in a continuous loop. Now you can get a sense of the power of Script Integration. You don't have to waste time messing with the Source Monitor menu or using Play keys. One button will load the takes in the Source Monitor *and* play them. If you want to stop at any point, hit the spacebar.

THE TAB KEY

This special Play key works great, but it's especially useful when used with the Tab key on the keyboard. After selecting the takes you want to look at, press this special Play key, and they will load in the Source Monitor and begin to play in order. If you want to see the next take, without waiting for the current one to finish, press the Tab key. The Tab key gives you control over what you watch. Often, you don't want to see the rest of the take. You want to jump ahead to the next one, and the Tab key gives you that ability.

This works with slates as well as takes. If you lasso a section of your script, including one or more slates, all of the takes for every shot will load and play. Let's practice.

1. Select one or more takes by:
   - Lassoing a portion of the script covered by several takes, *or*
   - Clicking on a take tab (or shift-clicking on several take tabs).

   You will see that the tabs are dark (selected).

2. Press the Play key at the top of the Script window.
3. Press the Tab key to jump to the next take.

On most systems, the next take will start playing as soon as you press the Tab key. On my Xpress DV, pressing the Tab key moves you to the next take, but you have to press either the special Play key or the Spacebar to get that next take to play.

Now you're probably saying to yourself, "That was interesting." You like being able to sit back and watch as the takes play in a continuous loop, one after another. But watching every take from start to finish, one after another, isn't what you had in mind. You want to look at a specific portion of the take—the portion you will be editing first. If that's what you think, then good. That's exactly what Script Integration is all about.

To harness the power of Script Integration, we need to take one more step. We need to place *Script Marks*. These marks, when placed in the script, will allow you to look at all of the material covering any portion of the script you want—and only that portion (Figure 15.12). It's time-consuming at first to place all of these marks, but once you get the hang of it, it's not so bad.

Three Script Marks—one on each take.

Figure 15.12

When you place a Script Mark, a double-sided arrow appears on a take line. When you double-click on this arrow, the take loads in the Source Monitor on that precise line. You don't have to look at what comes before it.

PLACING SCRIPT MARKS

To place Script Marks, you'll need the command that places Script Marks in the script. Go to the Tools menu and open the Command Palette.

Go to the "Other" tab and you'll see the Add Script Mark (Figure 15.13) button. With the "Button to Button" Reassignment box selected, click and drag the Add Script Mark button to any one of your Source Monitor buttons, as I have in Figure 15.14.

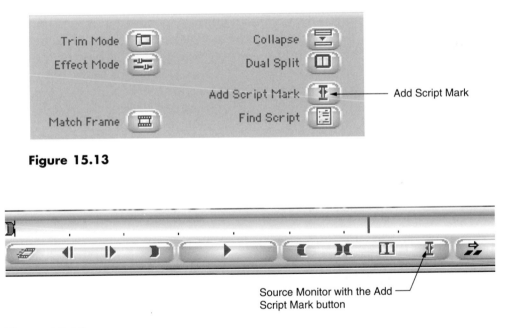

Figure 15.13

Figure 15.14

Now go to the script and find the take you want to mark first. Let's say you want to place a Script Mark on Take 3, where Peter says, "Everyone knows who you are." Double-click on the spot where the take line intersects with that line of dialog, as shown in Figure 15.15. Take 3 will be selected, it will load in the Source Monitor, and that line will be highlighted.

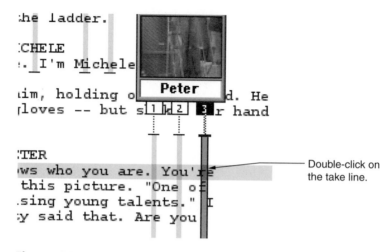

Double-click on
the take line.

Figure 15.15

Right now, the entire take will load from the beginning of the clip. You must play the clip in the Source Monitor as you normally would, using the J, K, and L keys or the Play button. When you get to the part of the clip where Peter is about to say the line, press the Add Script Mark button. A double-sided arrow will appear at that spot in the script. Now that point in the script is linked to that point in the clip (Figure 15.16).

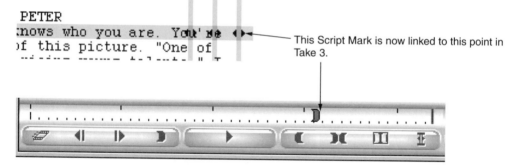

This Script Mark is now linked to this point in
Take 3.

Figure 15.16

I prefer to click on the Add Script Mark button just before the actor speaks the line. That way, when it plays, I get a chance to hear the whole line, not a clipped version.

Let's add script marks to the other takes of this line of dialog:

1. Double-click on the spot where the take line for Take 2 intersects with the line of dialog. Take 2 will load in the Source Monitor.

2. Play through the clip until the actor reaches the line, and then shuttle back until just before he speaks.
3. Press the Add Script Mark button or key. A Script Mark appears in the script.

Repeat these steps until all the takes of this line of dialog have Script Marks, as in Figure 15.17.

All the takes have Script Marks.

Figure 15.17

PLAYING MARKED TAKES

Let's see how this works. With your mouse, lasso Peter's line of dialog so that you are lassoing all of the take lines and script marks.

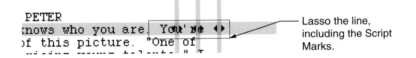

Lasso the line, including the Script Marks.

Now press the Play button on top of the Script window. All four takes will load into the Source Monitor and start playing, not from the beginning of the clip, but starting just before the line. They will keep playing in a continuous loop—first Take 1, then Take 2, and so on. Use the Tab key to jump to the next take.

You'll notice that if the takes are long and have a lot of material after the line you've marked, you'll want to keep placing marks at other points on these takes. I like to place a Script Mark whenever an actor starts a new segment of dialog.

In Figure 15.18, I have placed additional marks on Peter's next line of dialog in the script, right before he says, "Me?" When I lasso the first row of script marks and press the Play button above the Script window, Take 1 loads and starts where I want it to and loads the next take as soon as the line is spoken, rather than playing the rest of the material on that take.

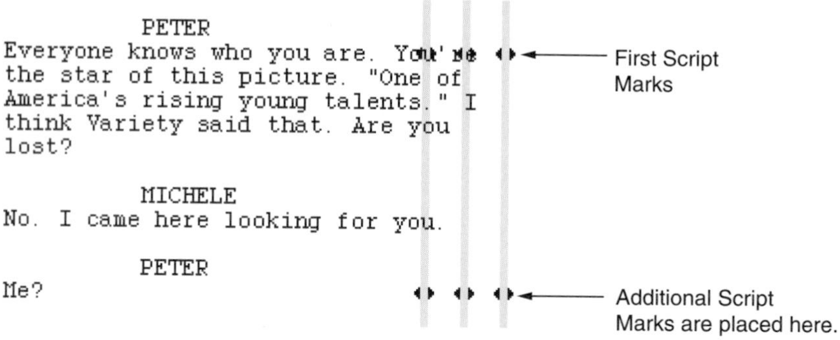

```
        PETER
Everyone knows who you are. You're
the star of this picture. "One of
America's rising young talents." I
think Variety said that. Are you
lost?


        MICHELE
No. I came here looking for you.

        PETER
Me?
```

First Script
Marks

Additional Script
Marks are placed here.

Figure 15.18

Now I'm able to concentrate on just one section of dialog and have all of the takes of that line play in a loop. I can see and hear the differences and decide which one works best.

A FASTER WAY TO PLACE SCRIPT MARKS

In the previous section I described how to manually place Script Marks. There's a faster way, although it's trickier to master. This involves playing the take and clicking on the take line at the point where you want to insert a Script Mark.

1. Select the first take you would like to mark by clicking on the take tab.
2. Go to the top of the Script window and press the Record Marks button (pink) (Figure 15.19).

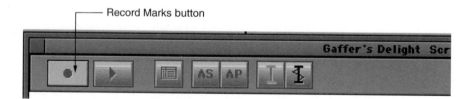

Record Marks button

Figure 15.19

The first take's vertical line will turn green, and the clip will load into the Source Monitor. It will start to play.

3. As soon as the dialog or action appears in the Source Monitor, position the mouse and click on the take line in the Script window (not the Source Monitor) where you want the Script Mark placed. A Script Mark will appear.

4. Move down the take line with your mouse, and as the take plays in the Source Monitor, keep clicking on the take line to place additional script marks.
5. Click on the keyboard's spacebar to stop the process.
6. Now select the next take tab and repeat the process.

This method is obviously faster, but it's tricky because the marks don't always link to the clip where you want them to link. In my experience, they link a few beats after the line of dialog you want marked. That's a problem because the whole point of marking the script is to take you to the lines you want to review, not halfway into the next line.

Fortunately, there are several remedies for this problem. You can click the Record Marks button again, then click on a line that already has a Script Mark. You'll replace that mark with a new one and "correct" the sync point in the clip. If the Script Mark is way off, you can delete it. Just click on it and press the Delete key. A dialog box appears. Click OK.

THE FASTEST WAY

Perhaps the fastest way of all is to have an assistant editor do all of this work for you. Really, in some ways, Script Integration was designed for feature-length projects, particularly the ones employing several assistants. On the other hand, because most people have never taken the time to learn Script Integration, this might be a good way for you to get your foot in the door and land that first job on a feature. You master this technique and you'll have skills few others possess.

MOVING SCRIPT MARKS

You may find that the Script Mark is in the wrong place on the script. That's an easy fix. Just press the Command (Ctrl) key. The cursor changes. Click on the script mark, and drag it up or down on the take line.

LOOKING AT YOUR COVERAGE

Not only does this system work for takes involving a specific slate (or camera setup), but it is also designed to show you all of the choices for a specific portion of your script. Take the time to place script marks on all of the takes for all of the slates covering a section of your script. Now, lasso *all* of the script marks for a specific line of dialog, including all of the coverage. As you can see in Figure 15.20, I have lassoed the Wide Shot and the Medium Shot of Peter. Now, when I press the Play button at the top of the Script window, I'll see Peter saying his line in the wide shot, and as soon as that is finished, I'll see in quick succession Take 1, Take 2, and Take 3 from the Medium Shot.

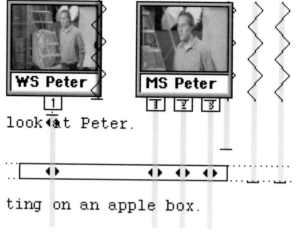

lookat Peter.

ting on an apple box.

Figure 15.20

PAGE AND SCENE NUMBERS

Although your script has scene and page numbers, they aren't really recognized by the Avid. You'll need to add new ones. The steps for adding scene and page numbers are the same:

1. Go to the first line of the new page and/or new scene and click it.
2. Click either the Add Scene or Add Page button on the Script Window (Figure 15.21).

Add Scene and Add Page number

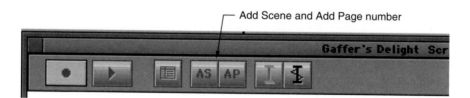

Figure 15.21

A dialog box appears.

3. Type the page/scene number and click OK.

The nice thing about adding page and scene numbers is that you can now use the Go to Scene or Go to Page commands in the Script menu (see Figure 15.23, page 341) to jump to the scene or page you want. Without page and scene numbers, a 120-page script would be difficult to work with. To change the number, repeat the process. The dialog box will now say Change Scene or Page number.

To delete page and scene numbers, select the line containing the number and press Delete.

FIND SCRIPT

The Find Script button is another handy command button that helps you stay in control of your script. Place this command key on one of your rows of buttons in your Source Monitor or a Fast menu. You need to go to the Command Palette to find it. It's in the Other tab (see Figure 15.13).

Say you have a clip loaded in the Source Monitor and you're not sure which part of the script it comes from. Just click on the Find Script button, and the Avid will scroll to the place in the script where the clip is linked and will highlight that section.

OFF-SCREEN DIALOG

When shooting a scene involving two actors, more often than not the director will shoot it several times from different camera angles. In the simplest form of coverage, there is a master shot of both actors and individual close-ups of the two actors. When the close-ups are shot, one actor is on-camera (onscreen) and the other actor is standing off-screen, but saying his or her dialog so that the onscreen actor has someone to act with. When the script supervisor "lines the script" during shooting, jagged lines are drawn on the script to indicate off-screen dialog. You can easily add these jagged lines to the script in the Avid:

1. Lasso the portion of the script where you want to place off-screen marks. Make sure you lasso only those take lines that represent off-screen dialog (Figure 15.22).

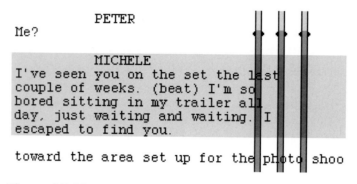

Figure 15.22

2. Click on the Off-Screen button.

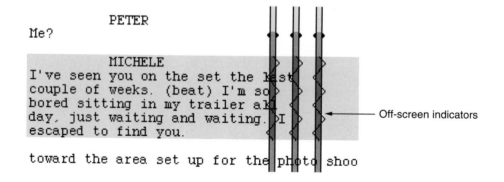

Your script will now have a series of jagged lines indicating that these takes, covering this dialog, take place off-screen.

ONE TAKE LINE ONLY

Sometimes, when you have a lot of takes for a particular shot, all of those take lines can overwhelm the script and make it hard to look at. To show only one take line, go to the Script menu and deselect Show All Takes. Only one take line will appear on the page, and all of the rest will disappear; however, if you then select a slate by clicking on it, all of that slate's take lines will appear. That makes sense. You want to see all of the take lines for the slate you're working with and get all of the others out of your way.

If you select Show All Takes from the Script menu, you'll reverse the action, and all of the take lines will appear once more.

COLOR LINES

Last but not least, you can place one of six colors on your take lines to indicate a preferred take, a problem, or whatever you want to highlight. Just go to the Script menu (Figure 15.23) and select Color; a choice of six colors will appear. Select one.

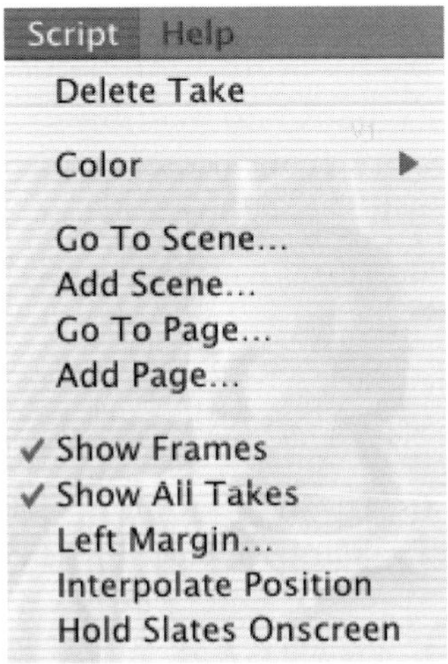

Script	Help
Delete Take	
Color	▶
Go To Scene...	
Add Scene...	
Go To Page...	
Add Page...	
✓ Show Frames	
✓ Show All Takes	
Left Margin...	
Interpolate Position	
Hold Slates Onscreen	

Figure 15.23   The Script menu

Now follow these steps:

1. Lasso the portion of the take line (or the entire take) that you want to color.
2. Click on the Color button on top of the Script window.

Lassoing the colored section and clicking the Color button again will remove the color.

Identifying the Preferred Take

The ability to mark the preferred take with a color is all part of the organizing process that takes place before the editor even walks in the door. On a feature film, the director will often indicate which take is the preferred one during the screening of the dailies. Using the notes supplied to the editorial department, an assistant links all of the takes to the script and highlights the preferred takes in red. With all that done, the editor can sit down and put together a rough cut of the scene in a matter of minutes.

With the preferred takes color-coded, the editor needs only to go through the script and click on the Script Mark for the take marked in red. The preferred take will load into the Source Monitor, with a Mark IN already in place. The editor then plays to the spot where she wants to end the shot and places an OUT and then hits Splice or Overwrite. She clicks on the next color-coded take and splices that into the Timeline, repeating the process until each color-coded take has been placed in the Timeline.

It'll be a bit rough, but using Single-Roller Trim, she cleans up each transition and in a matter of minutes, the entire scene has been put together.

Now the real editing can begin. Maybe a preferred take doesn't work as well as hoped once it's been cut into the sequence. It's easy to replace it. Try another take. Often, it's better to whittle away all of the choices, put together a rough cut, and work from there, rather than going over all of the choices a hundred times, until everything looks like a blur and you're lost in the land of indecision.

OTHER MENU ITEMS

There are a few Script menu items we haven't discussed that you may find useful. Examine Figure 15.23. These menu items let you fine-tune the appearance of the script or make it easier for you to navigate through it.

Left Margin

You can drag the box located in the lower right-hand corner of the script to resize the right-hand margin, but not the left-hand margin. Left Margin lets you make this adjustment.

Interpolate Position

With this command, you can click in a take line within a script, and the image in the Source Monitor updates to the approximate position in the take where you have clicked. If you deselect this option, the Source Monitor does not interpolate when you click in a take line.

Hold Slates Onscreen

With this command selected, when you scroll through the script, the slate will stay in view until you scroll past the point covered by that slate, at which point it will disappear. This lets you see the slate for as long as possible as you scroll through the script.

A SELECT FEW

You are now one of only a handful of people who know how to use Script Integration. I think we can all agree that Script Integration doesn't make sense for every project, but for those script-based projects involving lots of camera coverage with multiple takes, it's worth the effort. If you have an assistant to do the grunt work, think how quickly you can really get to the heart of the scene. If you're the person hired to do the grunt work, maybe Script Integration doesn't seem so special. But, hey, at least you've got a job.

Script for "Gaffer's Delight"

The three-page lined script for the scene "Gaffer's Delight" can be found on pages 344–346.

1   INT. SOUND STAGE -- DAY
               1A   1B

PETER HILL, 25, is on a ladder hanging lights on a ceiling
grid. He is a 2nd Electric working on a film. In the
background, JOANNA removes a light from a stand. MICHELE
POWERS, a young actress of recognizable beauty, enters and
looks at Joanna.

                   JOANNA
         Excuse me.
                                1F

Joanna leaves. Hearing Joanna speak, Peter turns and sees
Michele.

        1   PETER
         Can I help you, Miss Powers?

He starts to descend the ladder.

                  MICHELE
         Oh, hi there. I'm Michele Powers.
                                1G

She walks toward the him, holding out her hand. He hesitates
-- he's wearing work gloves -- but shakes her hand after
removing them.

                   PETER
         Everyone knows who you are. You're
         the star of this picture. "One of
         America's rising young talents." I
         think Variety said that. Are you
         lost?

                  MICHELE
         No. I came here looking for you.

                   PETER
         Me?

                  MICHELE
         I've seen you on the set the last
         couple of weeks. (beat) I get so
         bored sitting in my trailer all
         day, just waiting and waiting. So I
         escaped to find you.

She walks toward the area set up for the photo shoot.

                   PETER
         I've worked on ten pictures and,
         well, this is a first.
                               1M

                  MICHELE
         What are you doing?

2.

1   1M

Peter walks up and stands near her.

                PETER
          Talking to a movie star.

Michele smiles.

                PETER (CONT'D)
          I'm pre-rigging lights for
          tomorrow. The fashion model scene.

                MICHELE
          Right.   1K

She walks to the ladder and starts to climb up.

                PETER
          Whoa! Not so fast.

He chases after her and reaches the foot of the ladder.
               1E
                MICHELE
          It's fun up here.

                PETER
          You fall and get hurt, I'm
          unemployed.

She descends to two steps above him. She spreads her arms as
if to fly and purposely falls forward.

                MICHELE
          Catch me!   1L
          1D

He steps quickly in front of the ladder. She lands in his
arms. He starts to release her but she holds on.

                MICHELE (CONT'D)
          Wait. This feels nice. You're
          strong.

                PETER
          I must be dreaming.

                MICHELE
          Will you kiss me?

Peter looks into her eyes and is encouraged by the warmth he
sees. He kisses her gently, softly. Finally, she breaks off.

                MICHELE
          Oh my God! Can you kiss!

3.

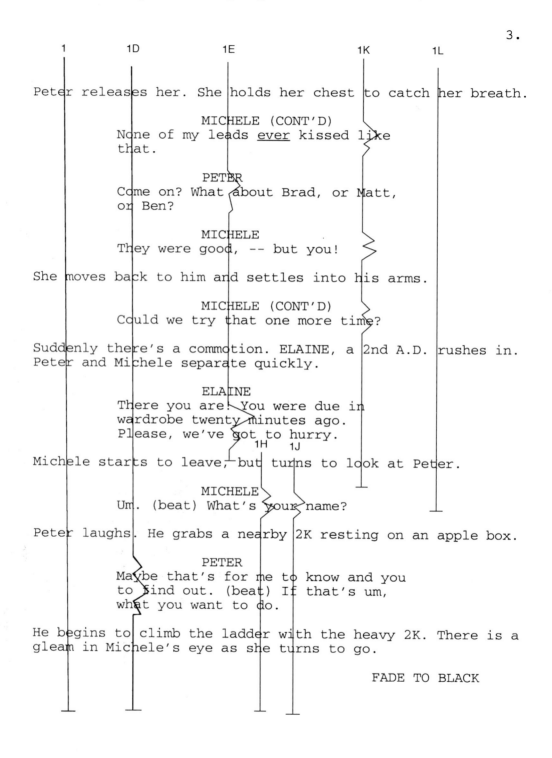

    1   1D   1E   1K   1L

Peter releases her. She holds her chest to catch her breath.

                     MICHELE (CONT'D)
          None of my leads _ever_ kissed like
          that.

                     PETER
          Come on? What about Brad, or Matt,
          or Ben?

                     MICHELE
          They were good, -- but you!

She moves back to him and settles into his arms.

                     MICHELE (CONT'D)
          Could we try that one more time?

Suddenly there's a commotion. ELAINE, a 2nd A.D. rushes in.
Peter and Michele separate quickly.

                     ELAINE
          There you are! You were due in
          wardrobe twenty minutes ago.
          Please, we've got to hurry.
                 1H   1J
Michele starts to leave, but turns to look at Peter.

                     MICHELE
          Um. (beat) What's your name?

Peter laughs. He grabs a nearby 2K resting on an apple box.

                     PETER
          Maybe that's for me to know and you
          to find out. (beat) If that's um,
          what you want to do.

He begins to climb the ladder with the heavy 2K. There is a
gleam in Michele's eye as she turns to go.

                            FADE TO BLACK

16

Finishing

I think successful videomakers and filmmakers are product oriented. Let's face it, a lot of people start films and videos, but only the truly dedicated finish them. It's easy to give up, to run out of steam, to take a never-ending break from a project. Making a film or video is a lot of hard work, and often you do it for little reward. I think the reason some people finish their projects, whereas others abandon theirs, is that they love having a product. They can't stop until they hold something in their hands, whether it's a videotape, film, or DVD.

"Here," they say, "is my project. Come look at it."

They're the ones I admire, no matter how many problems appear on the screen. They did it. They finished. It's an accomplishment worthy of our praise. Let's be like them. Let's learn how to finish a project on the Avid.

PATHS TO THE FINISH LINE

Here are four paths that lead to a finished project:

1. You can output your sequence to videotape.
2. You can create an Edit Decision List (EDL) and take your tapes to a tape facility for an online editing session.
3. If your project originated on film, you can create a Cut List so that a negative cutter can conform your camera negative to the Avid sequence, and from that you make a 16mm or 35mm print.
4. You can create a DVD.

Chapter 17 is devoted to path number 3. It takes you through all of the steps involved in getting a print of your film. In this chapter, we're going to concentrate on outputting your sequence to tape, creating an EDL, and sending your project to a DVD.

ROOM ON THE MEDIA DRIVES

Most Xpress and Media Composer users digitize their footage at a low resolution, such as 20:1. Once they finish editing and want to output to tape, they redigitize their footage at a finishing resolution, such as 2:1 or even 1:1. This process is called *up-rezing*.

As we'll see shortly, this isn't all that difficult a task because the Avid handles most of the work automatically. The difficulty comes in finding space on your media drives to accommodate the high-resolution material.

Xpress DV users don't encounter this up-rezing process because they record their tapes at DV's native resolution, but knowing how to find more space on your media drives is an important skill. This is especially true if you need to bring in additional footage late in the editing process and you don't have enough room on your media drives to do it.

Usually, by the time you're ready to output your project, all of your drives are full. If you can rent, borrow, or purchase additional drives, then by all means do so. But if you can't, and you must use the drives you've got, then you need to make space. Something has to be tossed out or at least taken offline if you're going to clear enough space on the drives. Sometimes you have to make difficult decisions about what to keep and what to erase. You'd probably like to keep the low-resolution sequence online, in case you need to cut another version later on, but you might not be able to. Some of the decisions are easy. Getting rid of unreferenced precomputes is a no-brainer, once you know what they are. Unreferenced precomputes are the mohair sweaters of the digital editing world—they take up space and you never use them.

Deleting Unreferenced Precomputes

A *precompute* is the new media the computer creates when you render an effect or a title. If, while editing your sequence, you change or delete some of your titles or effects, those old precomputes don't get deleted. They remain on the media drive, taking up valuable space. These hidden media drive hogs are called *unreferenced precomputes*. It's frightening how many of them you'll find and amazing how satisfying it is to blow them away.

Why are they still there? Why, when you delete unwanted effects, does the Avid hold on to the precomputes? One reason, I'm told, is so that you can use Undo to change your mind. The Avid knows you pressed the Remove Effect key, but it worries that you might change your mind 30 minutes later and press Undo. If it didn't hang onto the precompute, it couldn't perform the Undo. You also may want to remove the effects from sequence 5 but keep them for sequences 1 through 4. Because the Avid doesn't know what you want, it holds onto the unreferenced precomputes. Fine, I understand all that; however, I do think Avid should rewrite the software so that you can determine a length of time, in days or weeks, by which unreferenced pre-computes are automatically removed from your system. You shouldn't have to keep tracking them down, like some Arnold Schwarzenegger wannabe.

You'll use the Media Tool for this mission (Figure 16.1). Go to the bin that holds all of your sequences and shift-click on all of the ones you still use.

Figure 16.1 Media Tool

1. In the Tools menu, open the Media Tool.
2. In the Media Tool Display, click on All Drives and Current Project.
3. Select Precompute Clips. Deselect the other choices.
4. Now go back to the bin that contains your sequences. Make sure the sequences you care about are highlighted. If not, shift-click to select them. Go to the Bin Fast menu and choose Select Media Relatives.

The precomputes that are connected to your sequences are selected in the bin and in the Media Tool.

5. Go to the Media Tool window and click on the title bar to activate the window. All of the precomputes associated with the selected sequences are highlighted. They're the ones you want to keep.
6. Go to the Media Tool's Fast menu and choose Reverse Selection. Now all of the unreferenced precomputes are revealed.
7. Press the Delete key. In the Delete Media dialog box that appears, make sure that only the precomputes are selected (Figure 16.2).

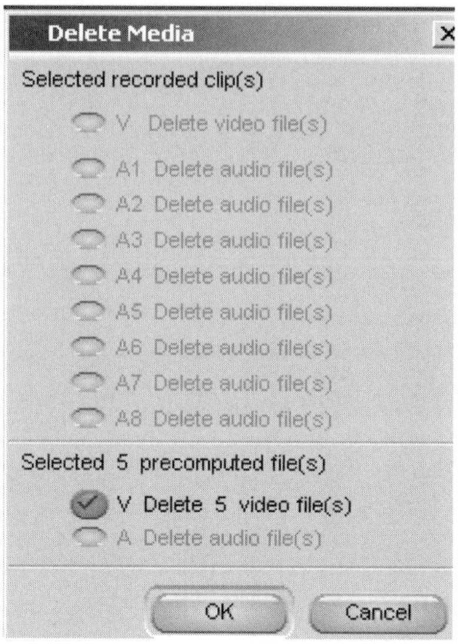

Figure 16.2

There are only five unreferenced precomputes in this project. Often there are lots more of the pests lurking about. I once found 200. Press OK and they're gone.

Media Composer and Xpress users, as satisfying as it is to delete all of your unreferenced precomputes, your drives are probably still full with all of the low-resolution footage you digitized when you began the project.

Checking for Space

You can check to see if you have enough room on your media drives. Put your sequence in the Timeline, choose the Digitize/Record Tool, and set it to your finishing resolution—2:1, 1:1, or DV-25. Next to the name of the drive you'll see a time display, showing you how many minutes are available at the selected resolution. Check the other drives connected to your system for space. Add up the total minutes and see if you have enough.

You can also check drive space by choosing the Hardware Tool in the Tools menu (Figure 16.3).

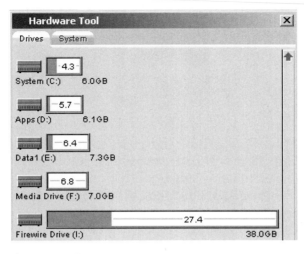

Figure 16.3

XPRESS DV USERS CAN SKIP AHEAD

The next few steps are for Xpress and Media Composer users who are going to redigitize their clips to a higher resolution. If you like, you can follow along in case your next project is on Media Composer or Xpress. Otherwise, jump ahead to the section called "Rendering Your Effects." Filmmakers using Xpress DV machines, who plan to use FilmScribe to make 16mm or 35mm prints, should follow along closely.

BLOWING IT ALL AWAY

Media Composer and Xpress users, you may find that there's not enough space on your drives to redigitize your project at the highest resolution. If that is the case, you'll need to take all of your video offline. Once done, when you play your sequence, the Record Monitor will display the dreaded words "Media Offline." Don't worry. Soon you'll be redigitizing it to 2:1 or 1:1, and your sequence will look so beautiful that you'll never miss the old low-resolution version.

DELETING YOUR LOW-RESOLUTION MEDIA

1. Go to the Tools menu and select the Media Tool.
2. In the dialog box, select All drive(s). Select Current Project. Check Master Clips and Precompute Clips, and deselect the last one—Individual Media Files.

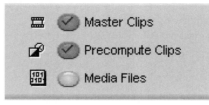

3. Click on the Media Tool and press Command-A (Mac) or Ctrl-A (Windows). This will select every clip in your project.
4. Press the Delete key.
5. In the Delete Media Files dialog box, check the box "V"—Delete video file(s) (Figure 16.4).

Figure 16.4

6. Make sure you deselect all of the "Delete audio file(s)" choices. Do not delete your audio!
7. Hit OK.

Now your drives will be practically empty, giving you plenty of room to redigitize the clips in your sequence at the finishing resolution of your choice.

PREPARING TO REDIGITIZE YOUR SEQUENCE

There are several steps you need to take before you start to redigitize:

1. Make sure you have all of your source videotapes with you.
2. Go to the Project window and click on the Settings button. In the scroll list, double-click on "Digitize." Click on the box that instructs the Avid to go to the next drive as the selected drive becomes full.
3. Create a new bin and call it "Online."
4. Duplicate your final sequence (select it and hit Command-D or Ctrl-D) in its original bin and drag the duplicate copy to the new Online bin.
5. Change the name of this sequence by adding "Online" to it. For example, change "Fine Cut 9-15" to "Fine Cut 9-15 Online."
6. Delete all of the audio tracks in the duplicate. To do this, place the online sequence in the Record Monitor so that the tracks appear in the Timeline. Select the audio tracks and deselect the video tracks. Hit the Delete key.
7. Close all of your bins except the newly created Online bin.

REDIGITIZING YOUR SEQUENCE

To redigitize your sequence at a higher resolution, you'll need to hook up your videotape deck. See Chapter 6 for suggestions on how to do this. Remember to open the Video Tool and set it to component, composite, S-video, or Serial digital. Once you're connected:

1. Select the sequence in the Online bin (it should be the only one there).
2. Get the Digitize Tool from the Tools menu.
3. Choose the target drive (the darkest one on the drive menu).
4. Select the finishing resolution—2:1, 1:1, AVR 77.
5. Select Batch Digitize from the Bin menu (Xpress) or Clip menu (Media Composer). If it is grayed out, click on the sequence in your Online bin.
6. In the Batch Digitize dialog box, deselect the option "Digitize only those items for which media currently is unavailable."
7. Choose a handle length of 30 or 60.
8. Click OK.

The Avid will ask you for the first tape by name. Feed it the tapes as it asks for them. The process takes a while, but it's exciting to see the footage looking so sharp after all the time you've spent at a lower resolution.

TIMECODE BREAKS

When the Avid is searching for the next clip to batch digitize, you will sometimes suddenly get an error message saying the Avid can't execute the preroll. Don't panic. The Avid is trying to get to the timecode for the next clip, but it bumps up against a break in the timecode. Put your tape deck in Local Mode and fast-forward until you find the timecode it is searching for. You are crossing over the timecode break. Now return the deck to Remote Mode and click "Try again" in the Batch dialog box. Now the Avid will find the timecode and continue batch digitizing.

DECOMPOSE

One of the nicest features on the Media Composer is one with perhaps the most gruesome name—Decompose. When you decompose your sequence right before redigitizing, it breaks the sequence into all of the many clips that are part of that sequence. Once the sequence is broken down this way, you can organize the clips in any way you wish. Without Decompose, the Avid controls the redigitize process, and there's no way to change or stop it. With Decompose, you can organize the clips by tape, by clips that need color correction, by clip length—whatever you wish. You can redigitize some clips today, then quit, shut down, and do the rest tomorrow.

In the "Redigitizing Your Sequence" section, substitute these commands:

1. Select the sequence in the Online bin (it should be the only one there).
2. Choose Decompose from the Clip menu.
3. Deselect the choice, "Decompose only those items for which media is currently unavailable."
4. Select a handle length of 30 or 60.
5. Click OK.
6. Organize the "new" clips that appear in the Online bin in any manner you choose. Now select the ones you would like to up-rez first.
7. Get the Digitize Tool from the Tools menu.
8. Choose the target drive (the darkest one on the drive menu).
9. Select the finishing resolution—2:1, 1:1, AVR 77.
10. Select Batch Digitize from the Bin menu (Xpress) or Clip menu (Media Composer). If it is grayed out, click on the sequence in your Online bin.

The Avid will ask for the tape(s) corresponding to the order you selected. Remember, you don't have to batch all of the clips today. Do the ones you choose. Do the rest tomorrow.

REPLACING YOUR AUDIO TRACKS

When the redigitizing process is complete, you'll see that you need to restore the audio tracks that you deleted earlier.

1. To get your sound tracks, open the bin that contains the final sequence—the one at the low resolution.
2. Drag the sequence icon to the Source Monitor.
3. In the Source Monitor, go to the first frame of the low-rez sequence. Mark IN. Go to the last frame and mark OUT.
4. Now make your Timeline active and go to the first frame of the online sequence. Mark IN.
5. Now you're ready to splice the sound tracks into the Timeline of your online sequence. To do this you will need to create new audio tracks—as many as there are source tracks (Command-U or Ctrl-U).
6. In the Timeline, select the audio tracks and deselect your video tracks. Now hit the Splice button. All of your audio should splice into the Timeline.

RECREATING TITLE MEDIA

Your sequence probably will not play because you may still have all of those titles that you created at a lower resolution, whereas everything else is at a higher resolution.

1. Select all of your titles by selecting the video tracks and marking an IN and an OUT in the online sequence Timeline.
2. Go to the Clip menu and choose Recreate Title Media. Your titles will be recreated at your new resolution.

You will need to render those recreated titles, as well as all of your audio and visual effects.

RENDERING YOUR EFFECTS

Xpress DV users, as well as Media Composer and Xpress users, will need to go through their tracks to make sure all of their titles and effects are rendered. Xpress DV users should press the green RealTime Effects toggle button so that it turns blue. Select each track and mark an IN and an OUT. From the Clip menu, choose Render In/Out. All of your titles and effects will be rerendered.

If I have a lot of effects to render, I usually don't do all of them at once. I usually either mark an IN and OUT on one track at a time or mark just a section of the Timeline.

CHECKING AUDIO LEVELS

Before you output the final sequence to tape, check your sound levels one last time. Get a pair of isolating headphones that prevents you from hearing anything other than what's coming through the earpieces. Open the Audio Tool and set the Input/Output toggle to O, so you're monitoring the levels you are sending out.

CHECKING FOR OFFLINE MEDIA

If you are editing a long project or if you're in a real hurry to put your sequence out to tape, you might not have the time to play the entire sequence to make sure all of your clips are now online. Believe me when I say that I've made the mistake of putting an hour-long show to tape, only to discover that several clips were still offline. There's now a handy way to check:

1. Click on the Timeline to make it active.
2. In the Timeline Fast menu, select Clip Color and hold the cursor until the arrow opens up the submenu (Figure 16.5).
3. Select Offline.

Now scroll through the Timeline; any offline clips will be bright red. Those clips still need to be digitized.

Figure 16.5

OUTPUTTING TO TAPE

Now your sequence is just as you wished. It looks and sounds perfect. You're itching to get it onto tape, but you need to do a few things first to get ready.

You should import SMPTE Color Bars and cut them into the beginning of your sequence. Chapter 13 walks you through the process. Make sure you import the file at the correct resolution and that you bring in 60 seconds. Cut the SMPTE Color Bars into your sequence. If you sync-lock all of your tracks before you splice in the bars, everything will stay in sync.

Now cut in a reference head tone at 1000 Hz to go with the SMPTE Bars. To create this tone:

1. Get the Audio Tool from the Tools menu.
2. Click and hold on the Peak Hold box in the Audio Tool. A menu will open. Select the last option in the menu, "Create Tone Media" (Figure 16.6).

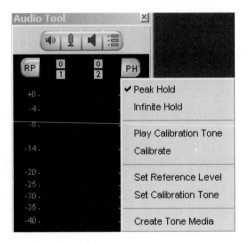

Figure 16.6

3. In the dialog box, set the reference tone to a desired decibel and choose the length of tone in seconds. A tone of –14 dB is the default setting, which works nicely. You need a length to match your SMPTE Bars—60 seconds.
4. Click OK.
5. The 1000-Hz tone appears in your bin as a clip. Overwrite it into your sequence so that it lines up with the bars. Now you have "Bars and Tone."
6. Put in 15 seconds of black (fill) on all of your tracks between the bars and tone and the first frame of your show.

7. If you want to start from black, rather than from the SMPTE Bars, go to the Clip menu and select Add Filler at Start. The Avid will place 1 second of fill at the start of your sequence.

CONNECTING THE AVID CABLES TO THE TAPE DECK

Xpress DV users have only one cable to deal with, and it's probably already connected. If not, run the DV cable from the computer's FireWire port to the deck or camera's DV In/Out—the FireWire port. Recording from the camera/deck to the Avid uses the same cable, connected to the same ports, as recording from the Avid to the camera/deck.

Media Composer and Xpress editors, if you've just finished redigitizing your sequence to the highest resolution from your source tapes, you're going to have to switch the video cables around. You were sending video signals out from the tape deck to the Avid, and now you need to connect the cables so that they run from the Avid to the deck. Connect your video cables from the Avid's Video Out to the tape deck's Video In. You also need to connect the audio cables so that they go from the Avid's Audio Out to the videotape deck's Audio In.

If your Avid facility has some sort of patching panel, you may not need to touch any cables at all. Just select the right buttons.

MANUAL RECORDING OR CRASH RECORDING TO TAPE

The simplest method of recording to tape is called *manual recording*. You don't need to be a video engineer to get it to work. You simply set your video deck or camera to record and play your sequence.

The only problem you may encounter with this method occurs at the end of your sequence, especially with Xpress DV projects. (But we can fix the problem.) When you manually record to tape, the last shot sometimes holds onscreen or doesn't completely fade out. Part of the reason for this is that it's so difficult to add filler at the end of your sequence. There's a menu command to add filler at the start but not at the end. There's a trick to fix this problem.

Go to the end of your sequence and add two clips. The first one should be 15 seconds long and the last one should be 1 second long. Now you've got two shots that you don't want at the end of your sequence. Mark the first of the two clips with IN and OUT marks and then lift it out of the sequence. Now you have 15 seconds of black between the last shot of your sequence and that 1 second clip at the end. Now place a Fade Out on your last real clip (Figure 16.7).

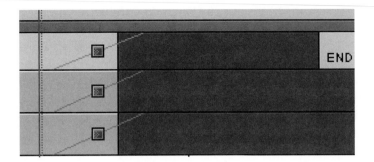

Figure 16.7

Your fade will be perfect, and you'll have 15 seconds to press the Stop button on your camera or record deck when manual record is over. Try it.

Now, with your online sequence in the Timeline, and the cables hooked up and patching connected, you're ready to complete one of the following series of steps for manual recording.

Manual Record to a DV Deck or DV Camera

1. Put a new tape in the deck.
2. Pack the tape. To do this, fast-forward the tape and then fast-rewind it.
3. Place the position indicator at the start of your sequence.
4. On the DV deck, set the Remote-Local switch on the video deck to Local.
5. On the DV camera, place the Camera-VTR switch to VTR.
6. On the DV deck, press the Record button (or Play/Record), count 10 seconds, and play your sequence on the Avid.
7. On the DV camera, on the VTR controls panel, press the Record (or DV Record) button and the blank button to its right, count 10 seconds, and play your sequence on the Avid.
8. When the sequence is over, press Stop. (If you have added a shot at the end to create 15 seconds of black, make sure you stop the deck before you reach this extraneous shot.)

Manual Record to an Analog Deck
(Beta SP or VHS) or Digital Deck

These instructions work for Media Composer, Xpress, and Xpress DV users:

1. Put a new tape in the deck.

2. Pack the tape. To do this, fast-forward the tape and then fast-rewind it.
3. Set the Remote-Local switch on the video deck to Local.
4. On the video deck, press either Pause/Play/Record or Stop/Record, so you can monitor your audio levels without recording.
5. Play the sequence and monitor the audio levels on the video deck's audio meters, adjusting the input pots on the tape deck.
6. Check the picture on a monitor attached to the tape deck.
7. Once you are satisfied with the levels, park the blue position indicator at the head of your sequence in the Timeline.
8. When everything is set, press Play and Record together, count 10 seconds, and play your sequence on the Avid.
9. When the sequence is over, press Stop. (If you have added a shot at the end to create 15 seconds of black, make sure you stop the deck before you reach this extraneous shot.)

There. You're finished. Congratulations.

DIGITAL CUT

Using the Digital Cut Tool, you can get a frame-accurate recording using timecode. The Avid acts as the edit controller for the video deck. This is the preferred method for projects that will be aired by a television station. It can be a lot more complicated and, if you're using a DV deck, it's not always frame accurate.

To use the Digital Cut Tool, you must use a master videotape that has been striped and blackened. A *striped and blackened tape* is one that has had a "black" video signal and timecode striped onto the entire tape. With time-code already on the master tape, the Avid can control the tape deck. The advantage to this method, compared with a manual recording, is that you can make changes to the master tape without re-recording the entire sequence. You can go back later and perform an insert edit.

For instance, I once recorded a sequence to a master tape and then later, while playing back the master, noticed a bad sound level halfway through an hour-long show. Instead of having to redo the entire tape, I went to the Timeline and adjusted the audio. Then, using the Digital Cut Tool, I inserted the "corrected" audio onto the master tape.

You can purchase a blackened tape from a tape facility. Obviously, it costs more than a blank tape. Or you can set your deck's timecode and blacken a tape yourself. Ask the owner of the deck how to set up the deck to do this because each deck is configured differently. It's not that difficult.

Starting Sequence Timecode

The Avid sets each sequence you create to start at 1:00:00:00. Most television stations want the show's first frame to start at this timecode, but if you add 60 seconds of bars and tone before the beginning of your show and 15 seconds of black fill before the first frame, as you should, then the show's first frame will be 1:01:15:00. You need to change the sequence's starting timecode. Go to the Settings window and select General. You can set the starting timecode to whatever you want, and the next sequence you create will start with that timecode. Type 58:45:00 in the box. Type colons if your show's timecode is non–drop-frame and semicolons if it's drop-frame. (Look at your sequence, or see Chapter 17, for the section "Types of Timecode.") Return to your online sequence, select all of your tracks, mark an IN at the first frame and an OUT at the last frame, and copy it to the clipboard. Go to the Clip menu and create a new sequence. Now open the Clipboard Monitor, mark an IN at the first frame and an OUT at the last frame, and splice your show onto the Timeline of this new sequence. Your new sequence will have a starting timecode of 58:45:00. Name this new sequence "Online."

When you order your blackened tape, instruct the tape facility to stripe the tape so that the timecode they lay down starts at 58:30:00. Then the timecode on the tape will lock up with the timecode on your sequence, and you can perform a digital cut using "Sequence Time." If the need arises, you can insert material onto the master tape later. Make sure to tell the tape facility whether your sequence contains semicolons for drop-frame timecode or colons for non–drop-frame timecode.

To perform a digital cut:

1. After connecting the cables from the Avid to your timecode deck, place the deck's Remote/Local switch on Remote.
2. Load your online sequence into the Record Monitor.
3. Choose Digital Cut from the Clip menu (Xpress and Xpress DV) or Output menu (Media Composer). The Digital Cut Tool opens (Figure 16.8).
4. Make sure all of the tracks you wish to record are selected.
5. Check the box Entire Sequence.
6. Select Add Black at Tail and then type a number, such as 00;00;10;00, for 10 seconds of black.
7. Select Sequence Time in the menu window.
8. Choose a deck from the Deck Selection pop-up menu.
9. Press the Preview button on the Digital Cut Tool (see Figure 16.8). The Avid will play the sequence, and you can make sure everything plays correctly. When you're satisfied:
10. Press the Record button.

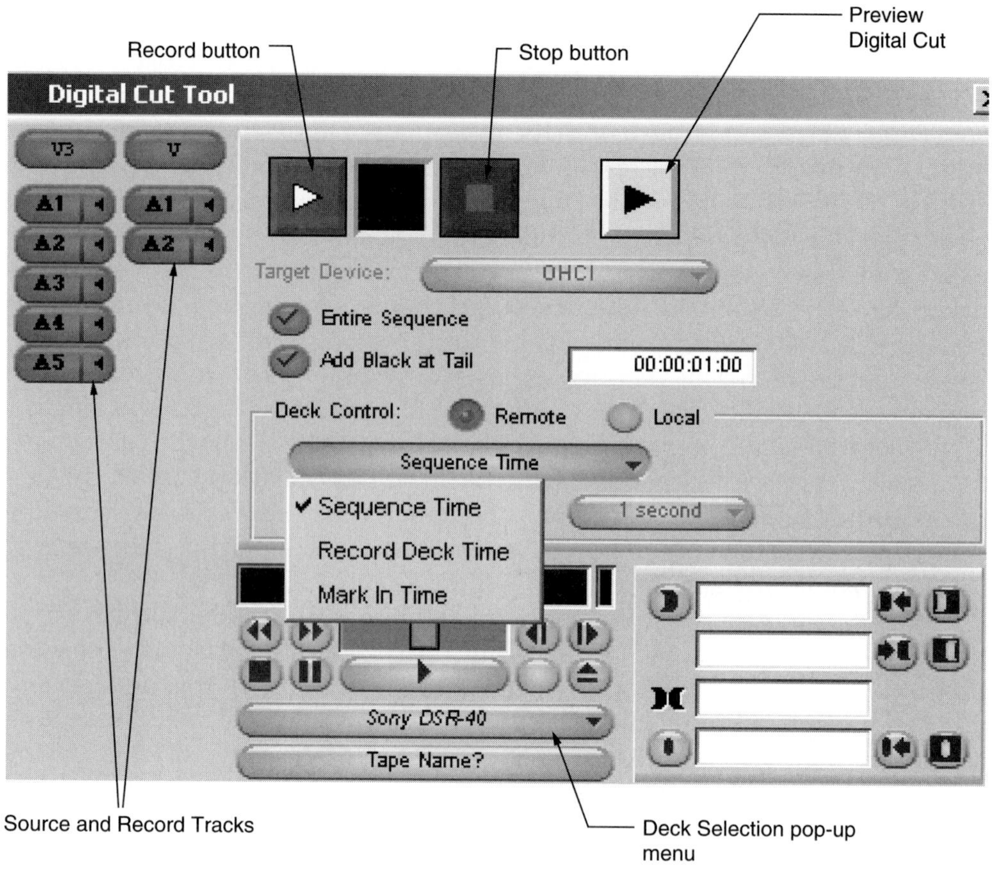

Figure 16.8 Digital Cut Tool

The Avid cues up the tape and begins recording your sequence to tape. If you need to stop at any time, press the Stop button.

INSERT EDITING

If you want to insert material later, for instance to replace a shot or raise the volume of one clip in the Timeline, you must set up the Digital Cut Tool a little differently. Let's pretend we want to do just that. Imagine that there's a clip with inaudible audio on A1 and A2, and we don't discover it until after we have recorded the entire sequence to tape.

First we'll fix the clip's audio level in the Timeline, and then we'll place IN and OUT marks in the Timeline to mark the clip that needs to be inserted over the inaudible clip on the tape.

1. Go to the Settings window and open the Deck Preferences setting.
2. Click on the button for "Allow Assemble Edit for digital cut."
3. Click OK.
4. In the Digital Cut Tool you'll see a new pop-up menu (Figure 16.9).
5. Select "Insert Edit."
6. Deselect the box Entire Sequence. Select Sequence Time.
7. Make sure A1 and A2 on both the Source and Record side are selected and everything else is deselected.
8. Go to the Digital Cut Tool's Mark IN and Mark OUT windows and type the sequence timecode for the section of audio you wish to replace—corresponding to the IN and OUT marks in the Timeline.

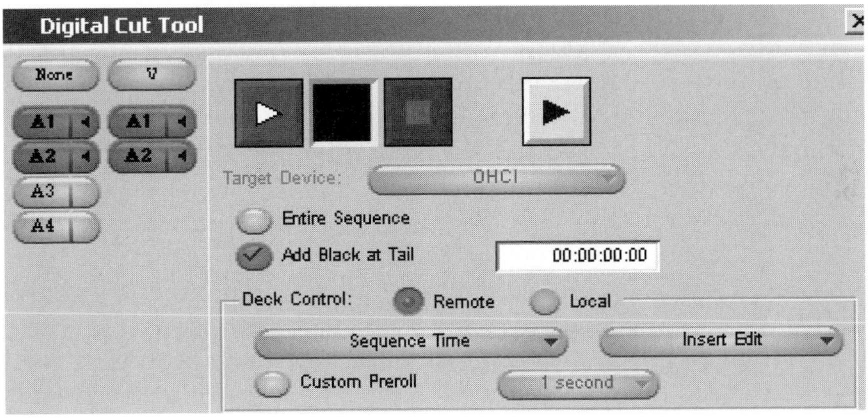

Figure 16.9   Insert Mode

When you press the Record button, the Avid will cue up to the insert points and perform an overwrite, replacing the old audio with the new.

EDIT DECISION LIST (EDL)

For a while, it looked as though companies such as Avid were going to make obsolete the process of generating an EDL for conforming your project back to videotape. With the advent of 1:1 resolutions on the Avid, there appeared to be no need to ever go back to tape. Just finish on an Avid and all of the effects you've generated can be re-created perfectly. The finished show can be totally uncompressed, conforming to every cable and broadcast company's specifications. You could up-rez your show without the hassles or the expense of an online tape-to-tape session.

Well, the coming of high definition (HD) has brought the online tape session back in vogue. Many projects will either shoot on HD tape or shoot on film and transfer to HD tape. Because HD tape requires such massive amounts of storage, many users will "downconvert" their tapes to standard-definition tape, edit on an Avid or other NLE, and go into an online session to create high-definition and standard-definition tapes for NTSC and PAL.

Xpress DV users should pay particular attention to the EDL process. In many ways the Xpress DV is the perfect offline machine, set up to deliver an EDL. In fact, this is what I find so incredible about the Xpress DV. For less than $2000, you can edit any NTSC video project, shot on any tape format. You could edit PBS documentaries, television commercials, rock videos, made-for-TV movies—the list is incredible. High-end projects that were shot on film (35mm or 16mm) and then transferred to Digital Betacam or that were originally recorded on Digital Betacam are perfect candidates for Xpress DV offline editing. Just have the producer make a DVCAM copy that has the same timecode as the Digi-Beta and you're good to go. Edit your project, and then have the Avid spit out a list of all of your editing decisions, listed according to the timecode numbers.

In theory, generating an EDL and handing it to a tape facility is simple. With your EDL and the source tapes, the online facility can finish your program using a sophisticated videotape system and edit controller, such as those manufactured by CMX, Grass Valley Group, Ampex, and Sony. They will deliver your show to you on the tape format of your choice, whether it's Digital Betacam, D1, D2, or some other high-end tape format.

What Exactly Is an EDL?

Basically, an EDL is just what the name implies—a list of all of your editing decisions. It lists all of your shots and figures out where on a master tape or record tape those shots will be recorded. The EDL doesn't use clips in a sequence. It replaces your clips in the Timeline with source tape timecode numbers and record tape timecode numbers.

The EDL is made up of lines, showing all of your editing decisions. Every line is made up of at least four sets of timecode numbers. The first pair of timecode numbers usually gives the IN and OUT timecode for the first shot you used in your edited sequence. The second pair of numbers shows where that clip will be placed on the master, or record tape.

Examine the EDL in Figure 16.10. The first shot in the sequence is 10 seconds long. In the EDL, it is event 001, and we see that its starting timecode is 01:06:45:01 and its ending timecode is 01:06:55:01, for a total of

10 seconds. That's the source tape. On the record tape (the master tape), this clip would be recorded at 01:00:00:00 and run until 01:00:10:00, for a total of 10 seconds. The second shot is 2 seconds and six frames long. You can tell by the timecode of the source tape where that shot would end in the master tape.

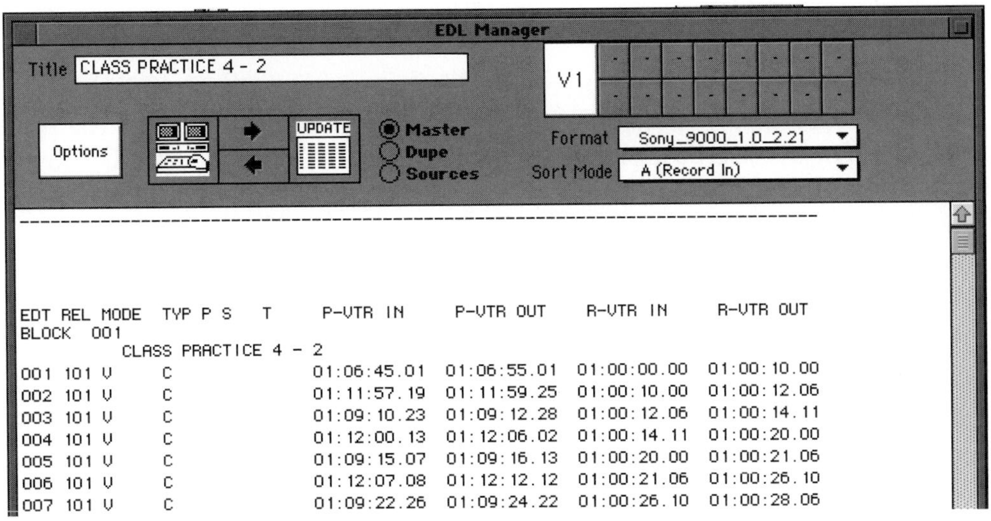

Figure 16.10 EDL Manager window

Talk to Your Online Facility

This is the first step, after getting prices from a variety of suppliers. Once you've selected a postproduction facility to do your work, you need to have a long, detailed conversation about your job and their requirements.

For instance, your Avid will print out and put onto a disk all of your editing decisions in a form that can be read by many different edit controllers. Your first step is to ask the online facility what tape edit controller they'll be using. The Avid will support many different edit controller formats, but because so many of them are incompatible, you must provide the right one. An EDL formatted for a Sony 9500 won't do your tape house much good if they have a CMX machine.

All of the steps listed here should be used as a guide to make your conversation with the online editor at your tape house more productive. There's no way for me to know what settings are correct for their equipment, but I want you to be able to find the options and select the settings asked for by your tape facility.

Getting Started

First, make a new bin, call it "EDL Sequence," and duplicate your final sequence and place the duplicate inside this EDL Sequence bin. Now place this sequence in the Record Monitor. Now minimize the Avid (Windows) or hide the Avid with Command-H (Mac).

Finding the EDL Manager

The EDL Manager is a separate piece of software that comes with the Avid software; hopefully you installed it when you installed the rest of the Avid software. On the Media Composer there is actually a menu item. Go to the Output menu, select EDL, and the Avid launches the EDL Manager. Xpress users have to find it.

- In the Windows world, go to the Start menu, go to Programs, then to Avid, and then to the EDL Manager. Select it.
- In the Mac world, open the Macintosh Hard Drive, click on Applications, click on the EDL Manager folder, and double-click the EDL Manager icon (Figure 16.11). If the EDL Manager does not open, go to the Windows menu (in the menu bar at the top of your computer screen) and select EDL Mgr.

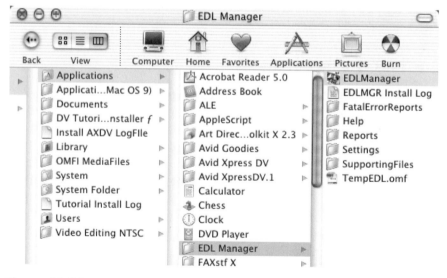

Figure 16.11

Once you've launched the program, you will need to get the sequence and have the Avid place it inside the EDL. Leave the EDL Manager open and visible on the desktop.

To get an EDL:

1. Click on the EDL Manager window so that it's active.
2. Click on the arrow between the drawing of a computer editing system and the UPDATE box (the arrow points to the right). Your sequence should appear in the EDL Manager window. The default setup might not be correct for your online facility.

3. To make changes to the default setup, go to the Windows menu (in the menu bar at the top of your computer screen) and choose Options.

The Options window opens (Figure 16.12).
4. Select the options asked for by your online facility.
5. In the Format window, select your format, such as Sony 9000 or GVG_7.0_7.0.
6. In the Sort Mode menu, select the Sort Mode.
7. Click on the Apply button, which flashes if you have made changes, to apply your changes.
8. Most likely you will be asked to deselect the audio tracks or the video tracks. Click on the EDL window and click on the tracks (see page 368). A menu will allow you to change the tracks or deselect them (as indicated by a horizontal line). Press the flashing UPDATE box to apply any changes.

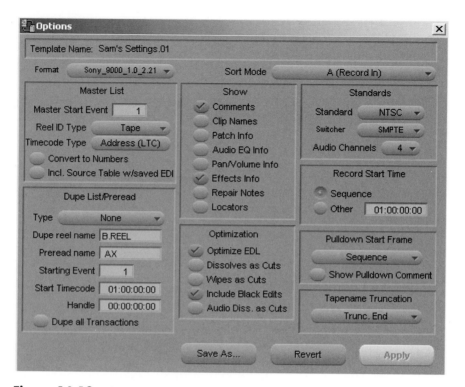

Figure 16.12 Options window

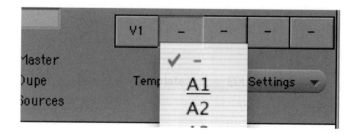

9. From the File menu, choose Save As. . . and save it to your disk.

I'll admit, the Options window looks complicated. These choices determine the order in which your source tapes will be used, the way visual effects will be handled, and the kind of information that will be included on the EDL. Don't worry, just select the items your online facility asks for.

Saving the EDL to a Disk

The steps involved in saving your EDL can be the most complicated part of the EDL process. The problem most people face when bringing a project to an online editing facility is that most of these online editing controllers are quite old. Many were built at the dawn of PCs (circa 1985) and won't accept a standard floppy or Zip disk. Some require a diskette you probably have never even seen before, such as an RT11 diskette, or can barely remember, such as a double-density disk. Your Avid might not even recognize them if you were to insert one into your floppy drive (if you have a floppy drive). You really must work closely with the online facility you've chosen. Often, they will send you a couple of disks already properly formatted for use in your Avid. The File menu has RT11 commands you may be asked to use. They may ask you to send the EDL by modem or a high-speed connection. The File menu also has commands for sending and receiving EDLs over the telephone or cable.

EDL and Audio

The EDL is often for your video tracks only. Your audio will already have been mixed by a professional mixer on a DAW. You'll then bring the mixed audio to the online session and have the online editor lay the final mixed tracks to the online tape.

Sometimes the EDL is all about the audio. In Hollywood, the sound editor often asks the film editor to provide an EDL of the audio tracks, so she or he can go back to various reels and tapes that were used to digitize the sound into the Avid.

Visual Effects

If there aren't too many visual effects, it's not that difficult for the online tape facility to reproduce your sequence based on an EDL. But if your sequence consists of many multilayered effects that took a lot of time to render, chances are the online facility will be hard-pressed to recreate them accurately. You might find that the whole process costs a lot of money. Most offline editors work closely with the online facility during the editing stage so that there aren't any expensive surprises when they go into the online session. If you have clips and effects on V2 (V3, V4), you will need to create a separate EDL for each video layer.

OUTPUT TO DVD

If you have a DVD burner attached to your Avid and DVD authoring software, you can burn your sequence onto a DVD. Not surprisingly, the Windows and Macintosh applications handle this task differently.

Whichever system you're on, remember that the process can be exceedingly slow, taking many, many hours. It can also be exceedingly frustrating. I suggest you start by burning a very short sequence—no longer than a minute maximum—to work the kinks out.

DVD on Windows

Select your sequence in its bin and place it in the Record Monitor. Make sure all of the tracks are selected and the highest level video track is monitored.

1. Go to the Export window, open the Options window, and in the Export As menu, choose MPEG-2.
2. Deselect both Use Marks and Use Enabled Tracks (so you'll send out the entire sequence).
3. Choose Slow, High Quality.
4. Choose 4:3 (most likely) or 16:9 (if your footage was shot in this aspect ratio).
5. Select Save As, and call it "MPEG-2". Close the Export window.
6. Go to the File menu and select Create DVD.
7. A Create DVD window opens. In the Function menu, select Create DVD Volume and Write to DVD.
8. Click on the Browse button to select a destination on your hard drive to store the files before they get burned onto the DVD.
9. Make sure the Export Setting is MPEG-2. Click Modify to check your export settings.
10. Click OK.

DVD on MAC

You need to have a DVD-authoring application on the computer, such as iDVD or the more complicated DVD Studio Pro.

Select your sequence in its bin and place it in the Record Monitor. Make sure all of the tracks are selected and the highest level video track is monitored.

1. From the File menu, choose Send To DVD.
2. In the Send To DVD dialog box, click on the Send To menu.
3. Choose iDVD or DVD Studio Pro.
4. Select the Auto Launch Application button.
5. In the Destination for Export Files, click on the Browse button to select a destination on your hard drive to store the files before they get burned onto the DVD.
6. Choose 4:3 (most likely) or 16:9 (if your footage was shot in this aspect ratio).
7. Deselect both Use Marks and Use Enabled Tracks (so you'll send the entire sequence to DVD).
8. DVD Studio Pro—select Use QuickTime for MPEG Encoding.
9. Click OK.

SUGGESTED ASSIGNMENTS

If you are in a classroom setting, sharing media files with other students, it's difficult to practice the space-saving steps explained in this chapter because you may wipe out someone else's media. If that is the situation:

1. Go through each of the space-saving steps, examining the dialog boxes and windows, but stop short of actually pressing the final OK or Delete button.
2. Output your sequence to tape.
3. Using the EDL Manager, get an EDL of your sequence.

If you are working alone, on your own Media Composer or Xpress system, and have finished editing a sequence:

1. Select the final sequence and then delete your unreferenced precomputes.
2. Select the final sequence, duplicate it, create an online bin, and strip out the audio tracks.
3. If you have space, redigitize this sequence to a "finishing" resolution.
4. Splice in your audio tracks.
5. Re-create your titles and render all effects.
6. Output your sequence to tape.
7. Using the EDL Manager, get an EDL of your final sequence.

If you are working alone on an Xpress DV system:

1. Select the final sequence and then delete your unreferenced precomputes.
2. Output your sequence to tape.
3. Using the EDL Manager, get an EDL of your final sequence.

Finishing on Film

This chapter is designed to help those of you who want to cut a film project on your Avid that will result in either a 16mm or 35mm projection print. Media Composer and Xpress users will need Avid's FilmScribe software. Xpress DV users will get FilmScribe if they purchase the FilmMaker's Toolkit. The information provided in this chapter will be particularly useful to editors who don't have access to an Avid Film Composer or to a Media Composer with 24 frames-per-second (fps) capabilities.

WHY FILM?

The main problem with video as a medium of distribution is that there are just so many video formats and standards in use around the world. There are three "standards" to deal with: SECAM, PAL, and NTSC. Each of these standards has at least 10 different tape formats. None of them plays on any other format's tape machines. And now we must deal with the confusion over which of the competing digital television formats will be adopted. Will it be 1920 × 480 interlaced at 29.97, 1280 × 720 progressive at 59.94, or 1920 × 1080 progressive at 23.976? What a mess.

The great thing about a film print is that there is only one standard and only a couple of formats. A 16mm or 35mm print can be shown at festivals and theaters anywhere in the world, from Afghanistan to Zimbabwe, from Sydney to Cannes. And it can be transferred to any analog or digital tape format—now or in the future. Making that film print can be a challenge, however.

FILM AND THE AVID

There is now a way to transfer film directly onto a disk for the Avid, but unless you have a lot of money and one of the most expensive Avids, you'll first transfer the film to videotape. Once your film is on tape, you can digitize it, using the Record/Digitize Tool, just as you would any other videotape.

THE FILM-TO-TAPE TRANSFER

After you have shot your footage, you take the exposed film to a laboratory for processing. Once the film has been processed, it has an image, either negative or positive. You then take your processed film to a telecine facility (many labs have them) for a film-to-tape transfer. The film's individual frames are projected or scanned onto videotape. A variety of telecine systems are in use today, ranging from film projectors beaming the film's image onto a video camera to highly sophisticated machines using a flying-spot scanner, capable of incredible image manipulations. Many flying-spot systems cost more than $500,000. The film is transported on rollers that never touch the image surface, so your film won't get scratched or damaged. A flying-spot scanner can also transpose a negative image to a positive one. So if you shoot negative film, as most people do, you don't have to make a positive print of your film to get it transferred.

FINISHING ON FILM OR FINISHING ON TAPE

Television commercials, rock videos, and many episodic television dramas are shot on film, but the finished product is a videotape. If the end result of your film project is a videotape, then once the film is transferred, you no longer need the film. To be honest, you also don't need to know much about the film-to-tape process.

If you plan to make a projection print of your film, however, which is currently the case for all feature films and many student film projects, then you need to pay *a lot* of attention to the film-to-tape transfer. Why? Because after cutting your project on the Avid, you will then ask a negative cutter to go back to the original film and conform that film to match your Avid sequence. Think about it. The negative cutter must be able to locate hundreds of strips of film and splice those strips together in the right order and at the right length, based on an edited sequence that was digitized, not from that film, but from a video copy of that film! Needless to say, the process is far from straightforward. You can help the negative cutter do the job correctly, and save yourself a lot of money, if you know how the process works.

HIRE A NEGATIVE CUTTER FIRST

Usually, filmmakers finish editing their films and then they go in search of a negative cutter. That's not a good idea when cutting your film on an Avid. The negative cutter can help you even before you send your exposed film to the lab. By the end of this chapter, you and your negative cutter will speak the same language. In fact, you'll probably know more about the overall process than most negative cutters. Still, I urge you to contact a negative cutter even before you send your film for processing.

THE $64,000 QUESTION

The key question when editing a film project on the Avid is this: Which frame of film was placed on which frame of video during the film-to-tape transfer? Everything depends on that. The Avid can tell you which frame of video you edited. That's easy. The difficult part is figuring out which film frame that video frame represents. What's the big deal, you ask? Film runs at 24 fps, and video doesn't. That, as they say, is a problem.

THE 2-3 PULL-DOWN

Film intended for projection in a theater is shot at 24 fps. Videotape travels at different speeds, depending on the country you live in and the tape standard that country has adopted. In the United States we use the NTSC standard, and NTSC tapes travel at approximately 30 fps. Transferring film onto tape in an NTSC country is a bit tricky, as you can imagine. How do you transfer 24 frames of film onto 30 frames of video? And how do you do it in a way that will allow a negative cutter to go back to the film and cut the correct frame?

Fortunately, it's not that difficult to get 24 frames to fit nicely onto 30 frames. Each frame of videotape consists of two fields. (Each field contains half the frame's total lines, which are scanned horizontally. Odd lines are scanned first, then even lines to give the total image.) During the transfer process, the telecine machine places four frames of film onto five frames of video, using the two fields to make the math work. Examine Figure 17.1.

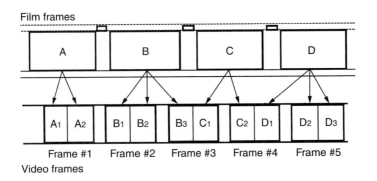

Figure 17.1

The first film frame, called the *A-frame*, goes onto the first two fields of the videotape. The second frame of film, called the *B-frame*, goes onto three fields. The third film frame, the *C-frame*, goes onto two fields, and the fourth film frame, the *D-frame*, goes onto three fields. Two fields then three fields, two fields then three fields, and on and on like that. Hence the name "2-3."

As you can see in Figure 17.1, four film frames are transferred onto five video frames. If you do this six times (6×4 film frames = 24, or 1 second, and 6×5 video frames = 30, or 1 second), you have a second of film and a second of video.

Look closely at this diagram. Notice that each frame of film (A, B, C, D) is transferred differently. The A-frame is the only one that is transferred onto a single frame of video, all by itself. The C film frame is like the A film frame, in that it covers just two fields, but the C film frame is transferred onto two different video frames. B and D are transferred onto three fields, but the way each goes onto those three fields is different. If you transfer 10,000 frames, each frame is either A, B, C, or D.

The way the four film frames are placed on the video is called the *frame pullin* and is critical to the process of identifying which video frame holds which film frame.

IT'S REALLY 29.97

Another complication arises from the fact that NTSC video doesn't actually run at 30 fps. It used to, but with the development of color television many decades ago, the frame rate of NTSC videotape changed to 29.97 fps.

It turns out that the difference between 30 and 29.97 is 0.1 percent. So what film-to-tape transfer facilities do is actually slow the film down by 0.1 percent when doing the film-to-tape transfer. The film is slowed down from 24 fps to 23.976 fps. The difference between 23.976 and 24 fps is 0.1 percent. I know I'm repeating myself, but yes, the film's running speed is "slowed down" by 0.1 percent during transfer.

KEYCODE AND TIMECODE

Knowing that we can accurately transfer from film to tape doesn't entirely solve the problem of identifying which frame of videotape contains which frame of film. In the beginning of this textbook we discussed the timecode system that video uses to identify every frame. Using a system based on clock time, every video frame has its own unique number. Film has a corresponding system using *key numbers*, which look something like this: KL74 0246 8805, where the two letters indicate the film's manufacturer and the film type, the first six digits identify the film roll, and the last four digits provide the footage count on that roll.

Strictly speaking, *keycode* is a machine-readable bar code version of the key numbers, but most people just say keycode when referring to the numbers as well as the bar code version. Keycode isn't placed on every frame of film. In 16mm, for instance, the key numbers are placed every 20 frames. (There are 40 frames in 1 foot of 16mm film, so every half-foot.) But even though there isn't keycode on every frame, it's easy to identify each frame by counting the frames between the keycode. Computers are good at this sort of counting, and during the transfer from film to tape, not only is the keycode read by a *keycode reader*, but the frames between the keycode are counted and given numbers. Those numbers are called the *frame offset*.

Pretend you're the negative cutter. Examine the strip of film and try to find the frame that is six frames past the frame containing the key number KL74 0246 9612.

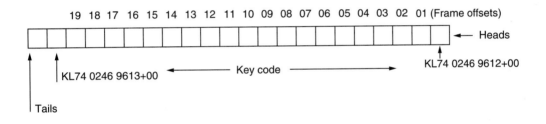

Because the film has keycode and the videotape has timecode, during the film-to-tape transfer, you place the keycode information onto the videotape, together with the tape's timecode information. But there's one more crucial piece of information needed—the frame pullin. Remember that the 2-3 pull-down process places four frames of film (A, B, C, or D) onto five frames of video. Each frame of video must contain this pullin information. Each video frame must say, "I've got an A-frame," or "I've got part of a B-frame," or "I've got the other part of the B-frame," for the negative cutter to know which frame of film that videotape frame holds.

During the film-to-tape transfer, a machine locks together each frame's keycode information, timecode information, and frame pullin information. Because this information is critical, it is "burned" onto the videotape so that all of the information is visible whenever the tape is played. As you can see in Figure 17.2, the timecode information is displayed on the left and the keycode, with frame offset (count) and pullin, is displayed on the right. This frame of video contains the film frame that is six frames past the frame containing the key number KL74 0246 9612. It is a C pullin.

Figure 17.2 A video frame displaying the timecode, keycode, frame offset, and pullin

PROBLEMS WITH THE TRANSFER

It's easy to accurately burn the timecode onto the tape, but as Figure 17.3 illustrates, the device that reads the keycode is some distance from the telecine's film gate, and problems do crop up. If the film is not threaded properly into the telecine machine, the keycode can be off. This should not happen, but it does.

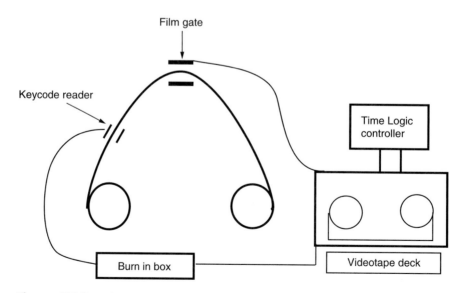

Figure 17.3 The telecine process

IDENTIFYING THE FIRST FRAME WITH A PUNCH

As I said before, it's critical for the negative cutter to know which video frame holds which film frame. The pullin (A, B, C, D) helps us know which film frame landed on which video frame. But for this to work, we need a place to start, so that everyone knows which is the first frame.

After processing the film, your lab should punch a hole in the frame containing the first visible key number at the head of each camera roll—the "dot frame" or 00 frame. The telecine facility then lines up that punched frame so that it is an A-frame pullin. All of the timecode and keycode numbers, all of the frame offsets, and all of the pullin letters have that punch as a common reference point. Many labs punch only the first 00 frame in a lab flat, which may contain three camera rolls, which can be a big problem. Be explicit in your work order, and then don't accept this sort of shoddy work.

As the film is transferred, the keycode numbers are sent to a box that burns them onto the videotape. Part of the process involves a controller, such as a Time Logic controller, which keeps the timecode locked together with the keycode coming from the keycode reader.

CHECKING THE NUMBERS

Errors do occur, so it is a good idea to check the accuracy of the transfer. Do the key numbers on your tape match the key numbers on the negative? One way to find out is to ask your negative cutter to go through the negative rolls and create a keycode log. Have the negative cutter fax the log to you, and then check to see if the numbers on the negative match those displayed on the Avid. On big-budget features, a workprint is often made, so the editor or assistant can check the numbers without having to pull the negative out of the vault.

TYPES OF TIMECODE

Speaking of timecode, there are actually two kinds of timecode: non–drop-frame and drop-frame. As previously mentioned, videotape used to run at 30 fps, but when color was introduced, the rate was changed to 29.97 fps. Because of that slight difference, whenever non–drop-frame timecode is used, a show's running time and its timecode time can be off by several seconds during an hour-long show. To solve this problem, drop-frame timecode was introduced. No frames are actually dropped, but some frame numbers are dropped to make up for the difference between 30 and 29.97. Video engineers prefer drop-frame because an hour-long show equals 1 hour of timecode, but the film industry uses non–drop-frame, and you should always specify non–drop-frame when given a choice.

How do you tell the difference? The Avid can tell, almost as soon as you feed a tape into the deck during digitizing. Non–drop-frame will display colons: 01:23:54:21, whereas drop-frame will appear with semicolons: 01;23;54;21.

WORK ORDER TO YOUR LAB

As mentioned earlier, you should speak with your negative cutter before taking any film to the lab to be processed and transferred to tape. The negative cutter can offer suggestions about how he or she wants the camera rolls prepared. The main points you would stress in your work order to the lab and transfer facility are as follows:

Lab

- Develop all rolls Normal.
- Prep negative for video transfer.
- Punch the head of *each* camera roll at the first visible key number/dot frame (the "00" frame).
- Please send prepped negative to your transfer facility for a film-to-tape transfer.

Transfer Facility

- Perform a 2-3 pull-down starting with the A-frame at head punch of each camera roll and at the starting hour of timecode.
- Use non–drop-frame timecode.
- Transfer the camera negative to the enclosed Beta SP (or DVCAM) tapes with timecode and keycode burn-in on one tape and simultaneously transfer to the second tape so that both tapes have identical timecode, but the second tape is clean, with no burn-in.
- On the first tape, place the burn-in at the bottom of the frame, within the safe title area.
- The telecine must be controlled by a Time Logic controller or other sync-lock device.
- Provide a log file on a disk (floppy disk/CD).

My students save money by purchasing the tape stock themselves and sending it to the transfer facility, rather than having the transfer house gouge them for the tape stock.

CLEAN VIDEO COPY

Because many Avids are capable of outputting the final edited sequence at high resolution (2:1 or even 1:1 resolution) or the native DV resolution, you can ask the transfer facility to make an additional Beta SP/DVCAM copy of the film-to-tape transfer—one with no burn-in information. This copy is made at the same time the film is transferred to the master tape, and it contains the same timecode as the master tape. Because it is "clean" (contains no burn-in information), you can up-rez your final sequence to tape, using these clean tapes, rather than the ones with the burn-in. You'll do this after making a video copy of the final sequence containing all of the burn-in numbers. (Xpress DV users, follow the steps in Chapter 16, the section entitled "Blowing It All Away," to replace the burn-in footage with clean video.)

With this method, you can have beautiful tapes to give to festivals, actors, agents, and so on. It's fairly simple to take this extra step. Let's say you shot eight 400-foot rolls and need two 60-minute tapes. Instead of sending two tapes, send four, and include instructions asking that a copy be made containing the same timecode but without the burn-in.

THE CUT LIST

Any number of negative cutters in New York City could take a video copy made from your sequence on the Avid and, using the numbers on the screen, look at each cut point and then go to the negative film and conform it perfectly. Using just the video copy, they could "match back" the film to the video copy of your sequence.

But most negative cutters outside of New York use the videotape and an Avid-generated *Cut List*. A Cut List is like an Edit Decision List but with key numbers instead of timecode numbers. Avids with matchback software can generate a list of all of the edit points, showing the key number and pullin for each transition point. Avid calls its matchback software *FilmScribe*.

Unfortunately, neither the Avid nor FilmScribe can read the keycode, offset, and pullin information when you digitize the videotape. You must input that information yourself. Only then can the matchback software produce a Cut List.

There are two ways that you can feed the keycode information into the Avid: typing each number by hand or importing the numbers into your bins from a disk provided by the transfer facility. Guess which one is easier. Good. Now guess which one is cheaper.

TELECINE LOG FILE

If the price is right, you should ask the transfer facility to make a Telecine Log File. This is a file containing all of the timecode, keycode, and pullin information pertaining to your film-to-tape transfer. It contains all of the information you, the Avid, and your negative cutter will need to conform the film to the Avid version. It eliminates the need for logging each take on each camera roll. A FLEx file is perhaps the most common type, and it is created whenever the transfer facility has used a Time Logic machine during the transfer. If an Aaton system was used, the file will be an ATN file, and if an Evertz was used, the file will be an FTL. Some transfer facilities charge a lot of money for the Telecine Log File. One New York transfer facility was asking more than $100 for each one, and there's one for each tape. Others charge you no more than the price of the floppy disk. Shop around. Bargain.

You need to convert these log types to Avid log format. Fortunately, the Avid gives you a utility, already installed in your computer, to do this. Usually the files come from the telecine facility on a PC disk, but don't worry if you are using a Mac because they can read PC disks these days. I've imported only FLEx files, so they're the files most often discussed in this chapter. You don't even have to know what kind of file you have. Just set the Avid Log Exchange (ALE) utility to Automatic (Figure 17.4), and it will figure it out for you.

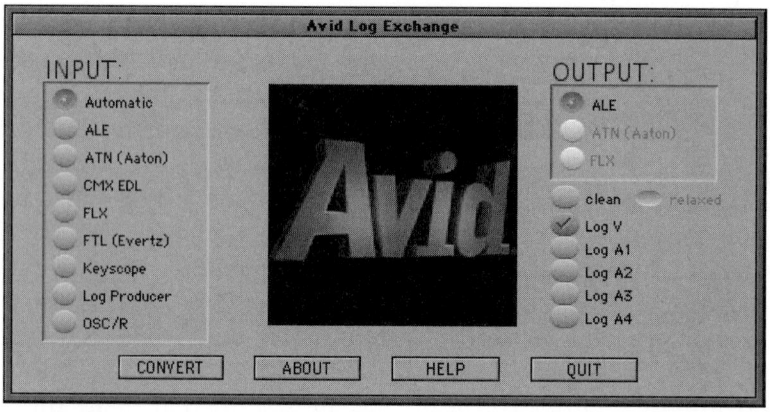

Figure 17.4

Steps for importing a FLEx file:

1. Insert the disk containing the FLEx file into the CPU's drive.
2. Open the disk and drag the file onto the desktop.
3. Look for the ALE folder on the CPU's hard drive, either in the Applications folder or the Avid Utilities folder.

4. Open (double-click) the ALE utility. There are two columns—one for input and one for output.
5. Select: Input—Automatic; Output—ALE.
6. Unless you had the transfer facility sync up your audio and lay it onto your video, deselect the Log Audio Tracks, keeping only Log V for Video.
7. Click Convert.
8. The Select File to Convert dialog box appears. Navigate until you find your Log file on the desktop of your computer. Click on it.
9. Click on Open. Your file will be converted to ALE.
10. Quit the Avid Log utility.

SETTING UP YOUR AVID

Now launch the Avid software and create a new project. After naming the project, make sure you select Matchback. Once you do, several choices become available. Select either 16mm or 35mm in the Film Type pull-down menu (Figure 17.5).

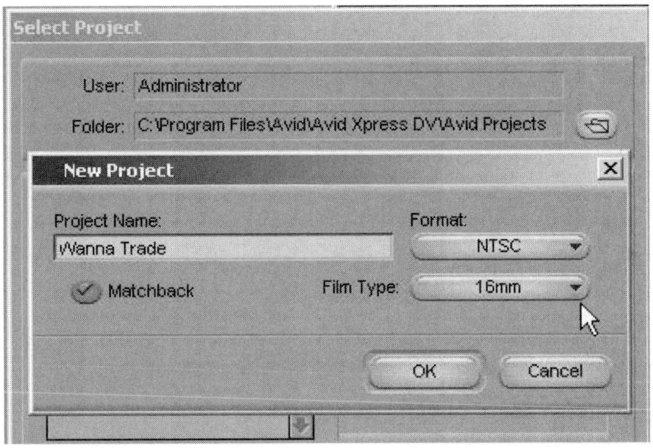

Figure 17.5

Once you're in the project, go to the Settings window and double-click on Film. In the window, choose the options that are right for your project. Normally, a 16mm project would be set up as shown in Figure 17.6. The Ink Number Format is every 20 frames because the key numbers are found every 20 frames. Don't worry about the Auxiliary Ink Format, unless you're working on a project in which the negative was workprinted, ink numbers were applied, and the workprint was transferred to tape. Usually that process is used only on large-budget features.

Figure 17.6

Now create a new bin and name it "Dailies Day 1" or "Camera Roll 1." To import the file:

1. Click on the bin to make it active.
2. Choose Import from the File menu.
3. In the Import window, select Files of type (Windows) or Show (Mac) and choose Shot Log Documents.
4. Scroll through the directory until you find your file "Name-ALE." It's on the desktop.
5. Click Open.

Depending on the transfer facility, in the bin you will either see just a single master clip of the entire camera roll (if you have a really lazy facility) or all of the scenes and takes (a good facility), with the start and end timecodes.

To see the key numbers, you'll need to get into Text View. Then go to the Bin menu, choose Headings, and select Camroll, KN Start, KN End, KN Duration, Pullin, Scene, and Take. A faster way to select these headings is to go to the window next to the bin's Fast menu and click on "Untitled." A menu appears. Select Film.

Now record/digitize the takes. Just select all of the clips in the bin and batch record/digitize (Clip menu—Media Composer; Bin menu—Xpress and Xpress DV).

I suggest you create a new bin for each camera roll and import the log file for that camera roll into that bin.

LOGGING KEYCODE BY HAND

If you don't have a log file, you can enter the information by hand. It's not as fast, nor as much fun.

1. In the New Project window, name the project by its title. Then select Matchback and choose the 16mm or 35mm option.
2. Click OK.
3. Create a new bin and give it a name: "Dailies—Day 1."
4. Go to Text View.
5. In the Bin menu or the Bin Fast menu, select Headings.
6. Select: Camroll, KN Start, KN End, KN Duration, Pullin, Scene, Take.
7. Open the Record/Digitize Tool. When it asks for a tape, insert the videotape and click New Tape. Then name the first tape "Tape 001."
8. Place the Record/Digitize Tool into the Log Mode and enter start and end keycodes for each take of the first camera roll. To do this you find a point before the clapstick and Mark IN on an A-frame. Make sure it's an A-frame. Then go to the end of the take and Mark OUT, hit Log, and enter the keycode information in the bin by typing in the heading "Keycode Start."
9. The keycode should look like this: KL 236892 0512 +00A.
10. Type the letters and all of the numbers, without spaces, and the Avid will set spaces and add the "+" sign.
11. Hit the Tab key and enter the pullin frame in that column. (A will probably be there already. If it's not an A-frame, type the right letter.)
12. The Avid will supply the Keycode End.
13. Enter the scene, take, and camera roll information.

To avoid having to enter key numbers for *each* take, you can create what's known as the *Phantom Master Clip*. It sounds like a low-budget horror film, but it can save you a lot of time and money. Most transfer facilities badly overcharge you for Telecine Log Files. If the lab won't give you a reasonable rate for the log files, do it yourself by using the Phantom Master Clip method.

PHANTOM MASTER CLIP

1. On the videotape, go to the hole punch at the head of the first camera roll, and in Log Mode, mark an IN. Write down on a piece of paper the keycode number at this punch frame. You should see the camera roll's first keycode number, plus 00 frame, and an A-pullin. Go all the way to the end of the camera roll, where there is still keycode, and Mark OUT. Hit the Log button. Now you've set the timecode information.

2. Now type the keycode information, which you wrote down on the paper, in the bin heading "Keycode Start."
3. Type the letters and numbers without spaces, and the Avid will set spaces.
4. Hit the Tab key and enter the pullin frame in that column. (A will probably be there already.)
5. The Avid will supply the Keycode End.
6. Enter the scene, take, and camera roll information.

Now you can play the tape and log your individual clips or takes, choosing IN and OUT points with the Record/Digitize Tool. The Avid will provide the keycode numbers, which it gets from the Phantom Master Clip, automatically. After logging all of the takes, batch record/digitize all of the takes you logged. Be careful not to record/digitize the Phantom Master Clip! Just record/digitize the clips inside of it.

Sometimes the keycode numbers in the bin will be correct but the pullin may be listed as an X-pullin. I asked Tom Ohanian, one of the people who created the Avid, about this X-pullin, and he said, "You don't need to futz with the pullin. As long as the master clips have the correct key number that they obtained from the Phantom Master, you're all set."

Keep in mind that every camera roll has different keycode, so you have to enter keycode information, not by the videotape, but by the camera roll. A videotape might contain three or more camera rolls.

SOUND AND THE AVID

When you record your field tapes on either a Nagra or a DAT recorder, you set those machines to work with a film camera running at 24 fps. To do this you use a Nagra set at 60Hz or a DAT set to record at 30 fps, non–drop-frame.

Remember that your film was slowed down in the telecine from 24 to 23.976 fps. It was slowed down by 0.1 percent. For your field tapes to sync up with the film, they will need to be slowed down as well. During postproduction, they need to be played back at a speed that is 0.1 percent slower than normal to be in sync with the picture that's already inside the Avid.

For a hefty fee, your transfer facility will do this for you. They will play the field audio tapes from the Nagra or DAT, slow them down, and then lay your audio in sync with the picture on your videotape. That way, when the videotapes are delivered to you, you can digitize picture and sound together. You no longer have to deal with all of the issues of slowing down the sound or syncing up the rushes. They've done it all for you. Needless to say, it's quite expensive.

NAGRA 4.2

You can save a lot of money by syncing the field tapes yourself. Many students and low-budget filmmakers use analog Nagras to record sound for their films because they're reliable, inexpensive (relatively speaking), and provide great sound. Always have your Nagra set to run at 60Hz (NTSC). It will be set up that way, so you don't need to do anything, but don't let anyone talk you into a different setup.

Once the sound has been recorded in the field, you can slow your Nagra down and transfer the sound into the Avid by using a device that slows the Nagra down from 60Hz to 59.94Hz (0.1 percent). I bought one of these devices from Equipment Emporium in Mission Hills, California (www.equipment-emporium.com). They call it a TX-8 59.94 Crystal. It's a snap to use. Just plug it into the Pilot Socket where the "crystal cap" goes.

For those of you using the Xpress DV to edit your film projects, this is a fairly inexpensive solution. You need a deck capable of acting as a transcoder—one that can convert an analog signal to DV. Most of the medium-priced models can do this. Now plug your Nagra into this DV deck, with this attachment hooked up to the Nagra. Use the deck as a transcoder to convert the analog signal to a DV signal. You slow the Nagra down with this 59.94 Crystal device as you record your tapes into the Xpress DV.

Media Composer and Xpress users could transfer their Nagra field tapes right into the Avid using the 59.94 Crystal device to slow the field tapes down.

FIELD RECORDING WITH A TIMECODE DAT

If you recorded your field tapes on a sophisticated DAT machine, such as an HHB or Fostex, you can record your sound in the field using a sampling rate of 48.048K. Then when you re-record it at a sample rate of 48K, you will automatically slow the audio by 0.1 percent.

If your DAT can't record at this faster sample rate, you'll need to slow the DAT when you record/digitize it. No matter what your sample rate, you want the DAT set up to run at 30-frame, non–drop-frame. That's important—always 30 NDF.

SLOWING DOWN THE DAT DURING DIGITIZING

If you haven't slowed down your audio, using one of the methods described previously, then you must slow them down as you play them into the Avid. One method is to use the pitch adjustment on the DAT recorder and set the pitch to –0.1 percent when digitizing into the Avid. A better method is to send a video signal (at 29.97) to the DAT recorder and have the DAT recorder use this video reference to determine its clock or speed. Because the DAT was recorded at 30 fps, this slows the tape by the requisite 0.1 percent. Because it's a timecode machine, the Avid can control the DAT deck, just as it would a videotape deck.

ONE BIN PER AUDIO TAPE

I usually set up a separate bin for each audio tape and record/digitize the clips into that bin. I usually don't digitize the audio as individual takes, but as larger master clips, containing six to eight takes each. Once the audio is in the bin, I'm ready to sync up the sound takes to the picture takes.

SYNCING RUSHES

Syncing picture and sound is a time-consuming endeavor. Usually you have a lot of takes on a camera roll, and each one has to be synced by hand. Of course, the process is the same if you are on a KEM or Steenbeck. Film projects usually hire assistant editors to do the syncing. If you have 50 rolls of film and you've had your fill of syncing after just three rolls, you might think about finding an assistant editor.

There are probably three different ways to sync your sound to your picture clips. The one outlined here seems as straightforward as any and takes advantage of the Avid's AutoSync feature:

1. Create a new bin and call it "Synced Takes." Now create a second new bin and call it "Sync Subclips."
2. Open the bin with the picture clips: "Dailies—Day 1."
3. Open the first clip to be synced: Scene 1 Take 1.
4. In the Source Monitor, find the first frame where the clapstick closes. If there was sound, it would "crunch" here. Mark this frame with an IN. Go to the end of the take and mark an OUT.
5. Make a subclip of this by holding the Option key (Mac) or Alt key (Windows), clicking on the picture in the monitor, and dragging the picture to the "Sync Subclips" bin. (You should see the subclip symbol.)
6. Press the Caps Lock key so that you can use "digital scrub" to hear the sound.
7. Locate the audio clip for the first scene: Scene 1 Take 1. Open it.
8. In the Source window, find the first full frame of "CRUNCH." Use the Step-one-frame button to locate it precisely. Mark an IN.
9. Go to the end of the take and mark an OUT.
10. Make a subclip of this audio by holding the Option key (Mac) or Alt key (Windows) and dragging the audio to the "Sync Subclips" bin. (You should see the subclip symbol.)

11. Now you have two subclips in the bin, each with an IN point referenced to the clapsticks. Shift-click so that both subclips are selected. Go to the Bin menu and choose AutoSync.
12. A dialog window appears. Select the "Inpoints" box and click OK.
13. A third subclip is formed, combining sound and picture locked in sync. Drag that to the "Synced Takes" bin.
14. Hit Command/Ctrl-S to save what you have done.
15. Play it in the Source Monitor to check sync.
16. If there is a problem with the sync, delete it, and the subclips you used to make it, and try it again.
17. Now sync up the next take in the same way.
18. It's slow going at first, but after you do it for a while, it'll get a lot faster.

DUPE DETECTION

When you are editing your sequence, you may inadvertently use the same shot or part of a shot twice. That second use of the same material is called a *dupe*. It's done all the time with video projects, but film is different. There is only one negative, and the negative cutter can't use the negative twice. So if you use even one frame more than once, you'll have to pay big bucks to duplicate that single frame. Avids with FilmScribe have a feature, found in the Timeline Fast menu, that when turned on will warn you if you use any material more than once.

Don't forget also that the negative cutter needs at least half of a frame to make a cement splice, so you have to make sure you leave that "extra" frame.

First, go to the Settings window and double-click on the Timeline setting. Click the Edit tab and in the Dupe Detection Handles pull-down menu, select 0.5 frames. To turn on Dupe Detection, go to the Timeline Fast menu and select it.

If you use a frame more than once, you'll now see a colored bar in the Timeline on the video segments that are dupes. The first color you'll see is red. It there are more instances of dupes, other colors will appear.

EFFECTS

Fades and dissolves are the only effects that I recommend you add to your sequence. You can do wonderful things with the Effect Palette, but each effect you add to your sequence will cost you hundreds, if not thousands, of dollars to recreate on film. Fades and dissolves can be created when you make a 16mm or 35mm print. A single fade or dissolve adds only about five dollars to your laboratory bill, but all the other effects available on the Avid will cost you serious, eyepopping, wallet-breaking money.

When placing fades and dissolves in your Timeline, choose them by seconds and parts of seconds, and then translate that into video frames. For example, choose a 30-frame fade-in if you want a one-second fade to go into your film. Choose a 45-frame fade if you want the fade to last a second and a half.

ADD EDITS

Once you've finished cutting your film on the Avid, go through and delete any add edits that might appear on your video track. You don't want them to throw off your Cut List.

SMPTE LEADER AND BEEP

You need an SMPTE leader at the head of your film, so the negative cutter wants to see one at the head of your Avid sequence. The easiest way to accomplish this is to digitize an SMPTE leader (ask your lab to splice one onto the negative before the transfer, so it's on your videotape) and cut it into your Timeline. Take out any bars and tone you might have added to your sequence. The Picture Start frame on the SMPTE leader must be the first frame in your sequence. The 8, 7, 6, 5, 4, 3 will follow until the single frame of 2 appears. After the 2-frame, there is a precise amount of black: 47 film frames on the leader or 59 video frames in the Avid. The next frame is the first frame of your picture—whether it is a shot, a title, or a fade-in of a shot. Once the SMPTE leader has been cut into your Timeline, splice in a single frame of 1000-Hz tone (the beep) into your audio tracks in sync with the number 2 on the SMPTE leader.

The Picture Start frame becomes the 0 point of your footage on the Avid, and if you have cut the SMPTE leader in correctly, the first frame of your show (48 frames after the 2) would be listed in the Cut List as starting at 4 feet and 32 frames (4 + 32). Look at the Cut List on page 393. When you preview the Cut List, check this number. If your first shot doesn't start at 4 + 32, recut the SMPTE leader until it does. In the list shown on page 393, my first shot is an optical effect.

OPENING THE CUT LIST TOOL

Once you have a final sequence, it's not that difficult to get a Cut List. After loading your sequence into the Record Monitor, open the Cut List Tool. Media Composer users will find the tool in the Output menu.

Xpress DV users need to open the FilmScribe utility. Windows users go to Start > Programs > Avid > FilmScribe. Mac users will find it in the Applications folder. Generally, you will find the FilmScribe utility in the same place you found the EDL Manager and Avid Log Exchange utility.

The FilmScribe utility is a complex piece of software. It has all the capabilities you'd find on an $80,000 Film Composer. I've tried to make it easier for you by providing suggested settings for the many different options.

Media Composer users:

1. Load your sequence into the Record Monitor.
2. In the Output menu, select Cut List.
3. Click on Get Sequence from the Cut List Tool or Open from the File menu.
4. Navigate through the directory window until you get to Avid Projects > your project > and finally the bin containing your sequence.

Xpress DV users:

1. Launch the FilmScribe utility.
2. Go to the File menu at the top your screen and select Open.
3. Navigate through the directory window until you get to Avid Projects > your project > and finally the bin containing your sequence.
4. Click on the name of the bin containing the sequence you want. Then click Open. If you can't select the bin for some reason, change the Files of type or Show window to All Files or Any Documents.
5. In the dialog box that appears, double-click on the sequence you want.

The Cut List Tool will open, similar to the one in Figure 17.7.

Select the video tracks you want to include, so that they are highlighted. Usually select just V1, unless you have multilayered effects and the money to pay for them.

The right-hand side of the Cut List Tool shows the Global Options. This is where you tell the Avid what kind of project you've been editing and how you want the lists to appear. I've set this one up for a standard 16mm project. Follow my settings and you'll be fine. If you shot 35mm film, you'll want to indicate that in the Running Footage menu and find out from your negative cutter whether she will be conforming using Single Strand or Double Strand.

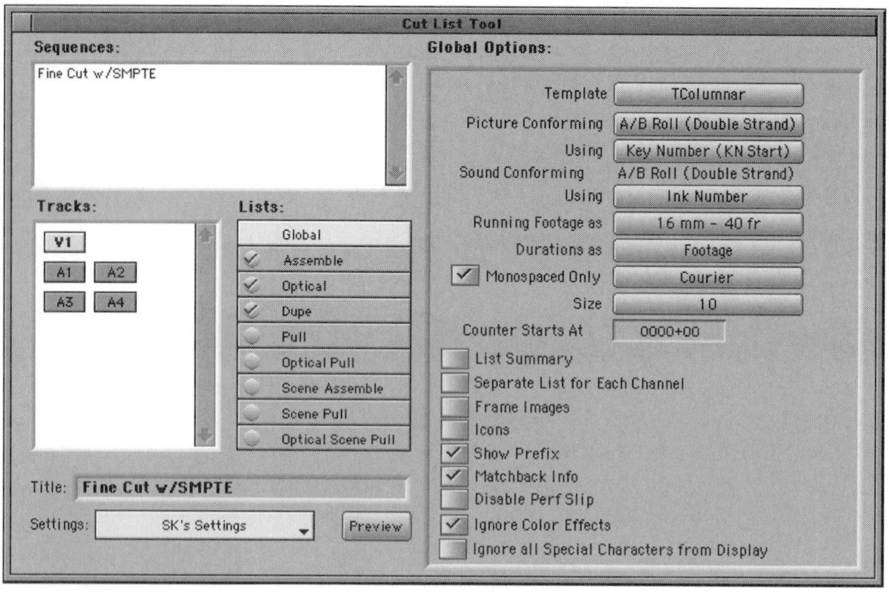

Figure 17.7 Cut List Tool with Global Options

The Avid generates eight different lists. The most important list is the Assemble list. Click on the button to select it, and then click on the Assemble box, so that the Assemble List Options window opens (Figure 17.8).

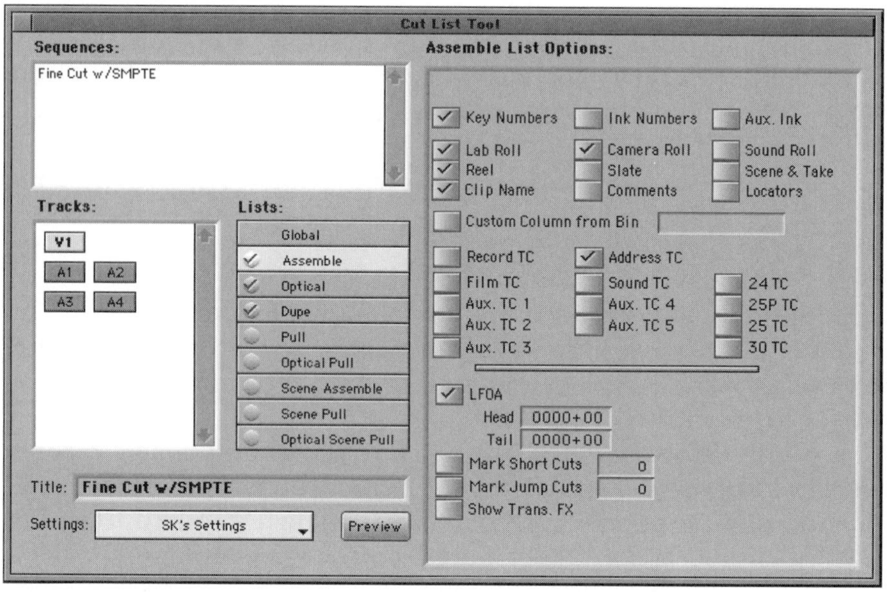

Figure 17.8 Assemble List Options

Again, I have made choices that will work well for almost all of your projects. The other lists you may need to check are the Optical list and Dupe list. A true optical effect, such as a freeze frame, would require that the negative cutter pull the shot from the negative camera roll and have it sent to an optical house. If you have a true optical, then the negative cutter would need this list as well as the Pull list. If you have any opticals, understand that they will take time to prepare and cost serious money.

The Dupe list shows you where you have used any footage or frames more than once. If you have used Avid's Dupe Detection feature, you shouldn't have any dupes, but just in case, check this one off. Get the Dupe list and make sure there are no dupes. If you have dupes, find out where they are and use some other footage or be prepared to pay for optical printing.

All of the lists have a List Options window in which you can determine how you want the list to look. Fortunately, the Avid takes the options you used when setting up the Assemble list as the default setup for all of the other lists. So you don't have to check off any more boxes, unless your negative cutter asks you to make changes. I have saved all of these settings under my initials in the Settings window.

Now click the box that says Preview. Several dialog boxes may appear, saying that the sequence has no edgecode track or the SMPTE leader has no key numbers. Just click OK until your list appears, like the one in Figure 17.9. Now go to the File menu and choose Save As. Save your lists to a floppy, Zip disk, or CD.

Cut List

Footage	Duration	First/Last Key	Address TC	Cam Roll	Sc/Tk	Clip Name
1. 0+00 4+31	4+32	NO EDGE NUMBERS				ACADEMY LEADER
2. 04+32 20+06	16+15	Opt 1-0000+00 Opt 1-0050+06				OPTICAL #1
3. 20+07 25+23	5+17	KL 74 0246-8770&19 KL 74 0246-8781&15	01:04:54:29 01:05:03:29	1		2B/1CU HANDS
4. 25+24 28+38	3+15	KL 74 0246-8795&18 KL 74 0246-8802&12	01:05:15:23 01:05:21:11	1		2B/1CU HANDS

Matchback shortened the tail of the clip by 1 frame.

Figure 17.9

Back at your office/apartment, insert your disk or CD into your computer and open the lists with any popular word-processing program. The resulting columns of numbers and text are easier to read when you set your page orientation to horizontal, rather than the standard vertical page setup. You may have to fiddle with the columns, using the Tab key to line things up. Once they look good, print them.

The negative cutter will also need a video copy of your finished project, showing the timecode and keycode burn-in clearly visible. Some negative cutters want a VHS copy, but others want Beta SP. You can also export the sequence as a QuickTime Movie, but make sure your negative cutter would prefer this format. Armed with Cut Lists, the video copy of your film, and the negative camera rolls, the negative cutter can now conform and A&B Roll your film.

"MATCHBACK SHORTENED THE TAIL OF THE CLIP BY 1 FRAME"

Look at the Cut List in Figure 17.9 and you'll see a message saying, "Matchback shortened the tail of the clip by 1 frame." Because the Xpress and some Media Composers aren't true 24 frames-per-second (fps) machines, when you make a cut to your sequence, that cut point corresponds to a video frame, and that video won't always conform to a film frame. (Look at a C-frame for an example of this situation.) Because you can't split a film frame in half, the Avid will adjust the length of a clip by shortening or lengthening it by one film frame to get things to work out. You can be out of sync by a frame, but that will be made up, or corrected, at the next cut point.

MIX AND OPTICAL SOUND TRACK

After you've locked your picture and done your sound work, you can do a sound mix on the Avid. Check your levels by playing your tracks with the Audio Tool open, set to Output. Use isolating headphones as you watch your levels. Once you're happy with everything, you can send your final mixed tracks to DAT. The DAT becomes your Mixed Master. Now you're ready to make the optical sound track, either a 16mm mono track or a 35mm stereo track.

Xpress DV users can record their final sound tracks to DVCAM at the 48K sample rate and either dub that to DAT or see if the sound facility that will make the optical track can handle the DVCAM format.

Most people suggest that you not speed up the sound yourself; let the sound facility do it when they make your optical track. Remember, you slowed the sound down by 0.1 percent to match the telecine process, which slowed the film down. Rather than speeding it up yourself to match the 24-fps film print, let the sound facility do that for you. If you're using a DAT deck, transfer your sound to DAT set at 30 NDF with the pitch shift off.

Send the DAT (or DVCAM tape) to the sound facility with instructions that say "The DAT tape is referenced to video," or that it is "recorded at 59.94." They will speed it up 0.1 percent so that it will sync up with your film print. Remember to ask for a B-wind optical track.

CHECKING SYNC

If you are nervous about sync—and who wouldn't be—try the following: Have the lab make a silent answer print from the A&B Rolls. Then have the sound facility make a magnetic film track (mixed mag) from your DAT before you have an optical track made. Make sure they have correctly "sped up" the audio that's on the magnetic track.

Once you have the "sped-up" magnetic track and the silent answer print, get on a Steenbeck and check out the sync by lining up the number 2 to the beep. Obviously, it should all be in sync. If it isn't, you can at least figure out why before you have an optical track and a married print made.

IT WORKS

For the past few years, I've taught a class called *Film Production III*. Undergraduate students in the class use Avids with matchback software to cut their senior thesis films. Many of the films produced in that class have been made into 16mm prints, and quite a few have won recognition at film festivals. The steps I've outlined here are the same steps my students used. In fact, we worked together, often by trial and error, to come up with them.

One recent student didn't plan to make a 16mm print of his project, but he went through all of these steps just in case. Then, when his film was nominated for a Student Academy Award, he needed a print fast. Needless to say, he was quite happy that he'd gone through all of this trouble because he was able to get a 16mm print ready in time for the judging.

NEXT STOP, CANNES

Is it simple? Not exactly. But then, what in life that's worth doing ever is? Don't be afraid to ask for guidance from your negative cutter, film lab, transfer facility, and sound studio. Remember, you're paying them, not the other way around. Keep at it, and soon you'll have a print that you can show anywhere in the world.

Bon chance.

Present and Future

WHERE DO YOU GO FROM HERE?

If you want to make videos and films, then go make videos and films. You now know enough about the Avid to edit your own projects, and what you don't know, you can figure out. If you want to be an Avid editor, however, this book is a beginning, not an end. I'll be the first to admit that this book doesn't cover every Avid command or examine all of Avid's capabilities—far from it. I've tried to give you all of the information you need to efficiently edit your projects, but there is certainly more to learn. There are several excellent books on the market that I urge you to read. *The Avid Handbook* by Steve Bayes covers, in great detail, many areas that I have treated lightly. It's for advanced users, but you're fast becoming one.

The Avid Digital Editing Room Handbook by Tony Solomons is particularly helpful for those of you hoping to edit feature films on an Avid. *Digital Film-making* by Thomas A. Ohanian and Michael E. Phillips provides a vast amount of information about nonlinear digital editing and digital production techniques. The chapters on 24P and HDTV are particularly relevant. Although it's not a book on nonlinear editing, I also recommend *The Filmmaker's Handbook* by Steven Ascher and Edward Pincus. This book covers nearly every aspect of video and film production and will answer just about any question you might have about moviemaking. Jon Fauer's *DVCAM* is another production-oriented book, which has information about DV cameras and decks.

There are three books about the art of editing that are worth reading: *The Techniques of Film Editing*, by Karel Reisz and Gavin Millar; *On Film Editing*, by Edward Dmytryk; and *In the Blink of an Eye*, by Walter Murch. The first two were published decades ago but are valuable for their insights and the historical perspective they provide. Walter Murch's book is the most recent and contains some interesting observations about the pitfalls of digital editing. I highly recommend it.

Last but not least, I recommend the various user manuals that Avid supplies when it sells a system. Much of my understanding of Avid's products comes from these manuals, which are often clearly written. The problem with all manuals is that everything is treated as if it is of equal importance to you, when clearly some things deserve more attention than others. You also need to buy an Avid system to get the Avid manuals, which is one reason why I wrote this book. This book might seem expensive, but you didn't have to shell out thousands of dollars to get it.

INFORMATION ON THE INTERNET

Like all modern companies, Avid has a well-maintained Website. To visit it, go to www.avid.com. You'll find lots of hype, as well as information about new products and upgrades. There are several user groups on the Internet that discuss digital products such as the Avid. One of the most helpful ones I've encountered is called the *Avid-L*. The vast majority of Avid-L subscribers are professional Avid editors, living and working all over the world. Most of the postings are by editors seeking specific help for problems they're having on real projects. The answers come from experienced editors who've encountered similar problems and are offering suggestions, work-arounds, and quick-fixes. You can learn a lot just by following the postings over time. Although Avid is now the host site for the group, these editors owe no allegiance to Avid and are just as likely to blast the company for its missteps as to praise it for its achievements.

To subscribe to the Avid-L, go to Avid's Website and click on Community or go to www.avid.com/community and scroll down until you find the Avid-L. You'll find other user groups listed there as well. Creative Cow has an Avid forum that many people new to Xpress DV have found helpful. Go to www.creativecow.net. Also try www.wwug.com.

DV magazine has many articles that relate to the Avid and digital editing in general. It has a useful Website as well. Visit www.dv.com. Another Website devoted to digital video editing is www.digitalvideoediting.com, which often has interesting columns and product reviews.

There's a wealth of information about HD and 24P issues at www.24P.com, hosted by Avid guru Michael Phillips. Another of Avid's most knowledgeable employees, Alan Stewart, has a Website containing lots of in-depth tips and links to Avid-related sites. His page is at www.zerocut.com.

GETTING A JOB AS AN AVID EDITOR

If you want to be an Avid editor, I suggest that you find an entry-level position or internship at an editing facility that uses Avids and work on the sorts of projects you're interested in. I know it's wrong to generalize about people, but it's been my experience that editors are the most down-to-earth and helpful people in the film and television industry, and many of them enjoy sharing their knowledge. Once you get a foot in the door, seek out a mentor and ask her or him to teach you what she or he knows in exchange for loyal and dependable assistance. Ask if you can get on a machine after-hours and try your hand at cutting the day's work. Employee turnover at some post houses can be amazingly fast, and you may find yourself moving up the ladder quickly. You need to demonstrate four things: your reliability, your proficiency with the equipment, your ability to please clients, and your creativity; you'll find the order of importance varies from company to company.

OTHER AVID PRODUCTS

Avid now offers a full range of products on both Macintosh and Windows platforms. Avid divides its products into three basic groups: Post, Broadcasting, and Storage. The Broadcast group products are aimed at the television news editor, working under tight deadlines. The broadcast journalist's script is at the heart of the NewsCutter interface.

In the Post group you'll find the Media Composer and Symphony line (and I'll toss the Xpress into this group). These products are designed for mainstream picture and sound editing. If you're cutting a documentary or narrative film, a Media Composer or Xpress is for you. The Avid Symphony is for "finishing" projects. Symphony looks and behaves like a Media Composer but offers more visually sophisticated tools to make the finished show look even slicker.

The Avid | DS product line is for graphics- and effects-centric programs. Television commercials, station promos, bumpers, and music videos would benefit from the tools that make up the Avid | DS. This is the software Avid got when it purchased a Montreal-based company called *SOFTIMAGE*. Over time, Avid has been trying to make the interface more like the Media Composer so that all of those Avid editors can move more easily to the Avid | DS. This is also the product line that has Avid's high-definition system, the Avid | DS HD.

The Avid Storage group offers a variety of storage devices, many of which work with its shared storage software. Avid Unity LANShare works well with 10 or more Xpress DV stations, whereas the Avid Unity MediaNetwork lets groups of Media Composer and Symphony stations share storage.

When it comes to storage, formats such as HD require many times more space than the analog television shows of the 20th century. The standard 4:3 aspect ratio signal with its 720×486 pixel matrix uses about 22 megabytes per second. HDTV, with its 16:9 aspect ratio, is made up of 1920×1080 pixels and uses about 120 megabytes per second, or about 7 gigabytes per minute! An hour-long show would need at least 420 gigabytes.

AVID'S FUTURE

When I wrote about Avid's future in the first edition of this book, I wrote primarily about Avid's inability to listen to its customers. At that time Avid had needlessly alienated most of them.

A case in point: In 1999, when Avid announced with great fanfare its extensive plans for Avids on Windows at the National Association of Broadcasters (NAB) annual convention, a lot of Avid customers got terribly upset. Based on what Avid said about its big plans for Windows systems and its meager plans for Macintosh systems, they thought Avid was going to abandon the Mac platform. These customers felt they were being forced to move to a Windows system if they wanted to get the latest software and the top-of-the-line machines. To add insult to injury, the prices Avid offered to those who wanted to make the move from their Macs to Windows machines were exorbitant. It seemed as if Avid was punishing people who had bought Macintosh Avids.

This was strange behavior, indeed, especially when you consider that, at the time, Avid hardly had any customers who didn't have Macintosh Avids. For years the critics were right. Avid did favor the Windows operating system.

There are plenty of PC users out there, and Avid was smart to make its product line available on Windows, but Avid made a big mistake when it treated the Mac as a second-class system. Many talented people saw a cheaper and more comfortable path and moved to Apple's Final Cut Pro, and the bleeding became harder and harder to ignore. Avid finally realized that if students and independent filmmakers first learn to cut on Final Cut Pro, that's the system they'll fight for when their careers take off.

But now, Avid is starting to get it. No longer is Avid sitting by and letting an entire generation of filmmakers move to another system. Avid has finally responded with the latest version of Xpress DV—one that works flawlessly on both the Mac and the PC. It's a great product, at a price we can afford. And it enables editors to move easily from one Avid system to another.

Avid is back in the game, and it will win or lose based on two things: the merits of its software and the strength of its customer support. I have complete faith in the former, but am less certain about the latter.

Avid has long enjoyed a reputation as a company with a big brain, but it has often appeared to possess small ears and tunnel vision. To continue to be successful, Avid must learn to listen to you, the Avid editor. I hope they do—you are Avid's future. Don't be afraid to tell them what you think. If you do and they pay attention, they'll be around a long time, and your investment in time and money will pay off.

Index

DVD-ROM Instructions

This DVD-ROM contains all the video and audio clips for two projects. The first one is a short scene entitled "Wanna Trade." You will want to load this onto your Avid before starting Chapter 1. The second scene, "Gaffer's Delight," is more challenging. The action is covered by many different camera angles and each angle has multiple takes. In all there are 36 clips. The clips are in the 16:9 widescreen format. Wait until you reach Chapter 14 to load this project. The DVD-ROM also contains the three-page script for "Gaffer's Delight." Following instructions in Chapter 15, you will learn to import the script and edit the scene using Avid's Script Integration features.

The DVD-ROM will mount on Macintosh and PC platforms, and should work with Media Composer version 9.0 and higher, Xpress 3.0 and higher, and Xpress DV 3.0 and higher. All the audio is sampled at 48K. There are instructions provided here, explaining how to mount the projects onto your Avid. Depending on your platform and software version, find the correct mounting instructions and follow them carefully.

Instructions for Mounting "Wanna Trade" onto Your Media Composer or Xpress on a Macintosh Computer (These instructions are not for Xpress DV users.)

Insert the DVD-ROM in the DVD-ROM drawer. If your DVD Player starts, quit the DVD Player. Double-click on the DVD-ROM's icon. Once the DVD-ROM opens, you'll see four folders and a script. One folder is called *Wanna Trade* and another is called *Wanna Trade Media*.

1. Open your computer's Macintosh (internal) hard drive. Find the folder called Avid Projects. Now, drag the Wanna Trade folder from the DVD-ROM to the Avid Projects folder and release it. It should copy in seconds. Close the folder.
2. All your external hard drives should be visible on the desktop. Double-click on one of the external hard drives to open it. Once opened, you'll see an OMFI MediaFiles folder on the hard drive.
3. Go to the DVD-ROM's folder and double-click on the Wanna Trade Media folder. There you'll find an OMFI MediaFiles folder.

Double-click to open it. You'll see audio and video media files. Select all the media files by pressing Command-A. They will all be highlighted. Now drag them to the drive's OMFI MediaFiles folder and release. It will take several minutes for these files to copy onto the hard drive.

4. Now, close the Hard Drive folder, then close the DVD-ROM folder. Eject the DVD-ROM.

Instructions for Mounting "Wanna Trade" onto Your Media Composer or Xpress on a PC Computer (These instructions are not for Xpress DV users.)

Insert the DVD-ROM in the DVD-ROM drawer. If your DVD Player starts, exit the DVD Player. Double-click on the DVD-ROM's icon. Once the DVD-ROM opens, you'll see four folders and a script. One folder is called *Wanna Trade* and another is called *Wanna Trade Media*.

1. Double-click on My Computer.
2. Double-click on the external media drive. Locate the OMFI Media-Files folder. Double-click on My Computer again.
3. Click on the purple (or top) bar and drag it so you can see both screens.
4. Double-click on the DVD-ROM's Wanna Trade Media folder to open it. There you'll find a folder labeled OMFI MediaFiles. Open it. Select all the media files (Ctrl-A) in the folder and drag them to the OMFI MediaFiles folder on the external media drive. It will take several minutes for the media files to copy onto the external media drive.
5. Now, click on your computer's internal drive—the C: drive. Now, double-click on the Program Files.
6. Double-click on the Avid folder to open it. Then double-click on the Avid Xpress or Avid Media Composer folder. Now, double-click on the Avid Projects folder.
7. Go to the DVD-ROM folder and drag the Wanna Trade folder from the DVD-ROM to the Avid Projects folder and release. It should copy in seconds.
8. Looking at the Avid Projects folder you will see the Wanna Trade folder. Right-click on the folder and the Properties menu will open.
9. Click on the Read Only radio button so that the check mark is removed (empty). Click Apply. Another dialog box appears. There are two radio buttons. Make sure the Apply Changes to this Folder, Subfolders and Files radio button is checked. If it isn't, click on it. Now click OK. Click OK again.
10. Close all the folders including the DVD-ROM folders, external drive folders, and C: drive folders. Now eject the DVD-ROM.

Instructions for Mounting "Wanna Trade" onto Xpress DV

Unfortunately, the Xpress DV handles media differently than either the Media Composer or Xpress. You cannot compress Xpress DV files the way you can compress Media Composer files. So, in order to get both "Wanna Trade" and "Gaffer's Delight" to fit onto one DVD-ROM, I've used a Media Composer to compress them. They are not native DV files. What this means is that you are going to have to work a little harder to get these files into your Xpress DV. You are going to import them (pages 280–281). The process takes longer, and the images aren't quite as beautiful as native DV files, but certainly useable.

Instructions for Mounting "Wanna Trade" onto Your Xpress DV on a Macintosh Computer

Insert the DVD-ROM in the DVD-ROM drawer. If your DVD Player opens, quit the DVD Player (Command-Q). Double-click on the DVD-ROM's icon. Once the DVD-ROM opens, you'll see four folders and a script. One folder is called *Wanna Trade* and another is called *Wanna Trade Media*.

1. Open your computer's Macintosh HD (internal) hard drive. Find the folder called Avid Projects (Users>Shared>Avid Projects). Now, drag the Wanna Trade folder from the DVD-ROM to the Avid Projects folder and release it. It should copy in seconds. Close the folder.

2. Go to the DVD-ROM folder and find the Wanna Trade Media folder. Drag the folder to your computer's Desktop and release it. It will take several minutes for these files to copy onto the drive.

3. Launch the Avid Xpress DV software. Click on Shared, and then click on the Wanna Trade project. Click OK. You will get a warning, saying, "The Temporary Directory is no longer valid...." Don't worry. Simply click, "Use this Directory Always." Nothing bad will happen.

4. When the Avid Xpress software opens, you'll see the Project window, which contains four small tabs. The Bins tab is selected. Click on the Settings tab. A list of settings appears. Double-click on Audio Projects setting. In the window that opens, choose 48K in the Sample Rate pulldown menu. Choose OMF (AIFF-C) in the Audio File Format pulldown menu. Click the close button.

5. Now scroll down the list of Settings and double-click on the Media Creation setting. Deselect Filter Out System Drive. Deselect Filter Out Launch Drive. Click OK.

6. Click on the Bins tab in the Project window. You now see two bins: Assembly and Dailies Day One. If the Dailies Day One bin is open, click on it so the bar is purple. If it isn't opened, double-click on the Dailies Day One bin icon so the bin opens and all the clips are visible.

7. Go to the File menu at the top of the computer screen and pull down the File menu. Select Import. (If the Import is grayed out, click on the Dailies Day One bin.)

8. The Import dialog box opens. In the "Show" window at the top of this dialog box, click and hold on the pulldown menu and select Any Documents. In the "From" window just below that, click and hold on the pulldown menu and select Desktop (not Macintosh HD or the DVD).

9. In the directory box that lists all the files available to you, click on the Wanna Trade Media folder. It opens to reveal the OMFI Media-Files folder. Click on that and you'll see all the media you need to bring into the Avid. There are 18 audio files, which end with the letters .aif, and 9 video files, which end with the letters .omf. Click on the first file and then scroll down to the bottom and Shift-click on the last so that all the files are selected. Now click the Open button at the bottom of this dialog box.

10. A dialog box will open saying "Master Clip Conflict Found." Among the choices given is "Yes To All." That's the one you want to click.

11. The files will begin to load into the Avid. Be patient. This can take as long as an hour. Once all the clips appear in the bin, don't worry if they don't look great. Quit your Avid software and eject the DVD. Now re-launch your software. Select Wanna Trade. When the project opens the images will now look good. Begin Chapter 1.

12. If at any point during the import process, you get an error message, click the button that directs the Avid to skip that file. See the "Troubleshooting" section on p. 412.

13. Once all the files have been successfully imported, you can drag the Wanna Trade Media folder on your Desktop to the trash and empty it.

Instructions for Mounting "Wanna Trade" onto Your Avid Xpress DV on a PC Computer

Insert the DVD-ROM in the DVD-ROM drawer. If your DVD Player starts, exit the DVD Player. Double-click on the DVD-ROM's icon. Once the DVD-ROM opens, you'll see four folders and a script. One folder is called *Wanna Trade* and another is called *Wanna Trade Media*.

1. Click on your computer's internal drive—the C: drive.
2. Double-click on the Program Files.
3. Double-click on the Avid folder to open it. Then double-click on the Avid Xpress DV folder.
4. Double-click on the Avid Projects folder.

5. Now go to the DVD-ROM folder and drag the Wanna Trade folder from the DVD-ROM to the Avid Projects folder and release. It should copy in seconds.

6. Looking at the Avid Projects folder you will see the Wanna Trade folder. Right-click on the folder and the Properties Menu will open.

7. Click on the Read Only radio button so that the check mark is removed (empty). Click Apply. Another dialog box appears. There are two radio buttons. Make sure the Apply Changes to this Folder, Subfolders and Files radio button is checked. If it isn't, click on it. Now click OK. Click OK again.

8. Go to the DVD-ROM folder and copy the Wanna Trade Media folder to your local hard drive. It will take several minutes for these files to copy onto the drive.

9. Launch the Avid Xpress DV software. Click on Shared, and then click on the Wanna Trade project. Click OK. You will get a warning, saying, "The Temporary Directory is no longer valid...." The options are Persist and Use Once. Click Persist. Don't worry. Nothing bad will happen.

10. When the Avid Xpress software opens, you'll see the Project window, which contains four small tabs. The Bins tab is selected. Click on the Settings tab. A list of settings appears. Double-click on Audio Projects settings. Choose 48K in the Sample Rate pulldown menu. Choose OMF (AIFF-C) in the Audio File Format pulldown window. Click the close button.

11. Now scroll down the list of Settings and double-click on the Media Creation setting. Deselect Filter Out System Drive. Deselect Filter Out Launch Drive. Click OK.

12. Click on the Bins tab in the Project window. You now see two bins: Assembly and Dailies Day One. If the Dailies Day One bin is open, click on it so the bar is purple. If it isn't opened, double-click on the Dailies Day One bin icon so the bin opens and all the clips are visible.

13. Go to the File menu at the top of the computer screen and pull down the File Menu. Select Import. (If the Import is grayed out, click on the Dailies Day One bin.)

14. The Import dialog box opens. In the "Look in" window, browse to the Wanna Trade Media folder you just copied to your local hard drive in step #8. In the "Files of Type" window at the bottom of this dialog box, select All Files.

15. In the directory box that lists the files available to you, you'll see the OMFI MediaFiles folder. Click on that and you'll see all the media you need to bring into the Avid. There are 18 audio files, which end with the letters .aif, and 9 video files, which end with the letters .omf.

Press Ctrl-A so that all the files are selected (or shift-click on the files until all are selected). Now click the Open button.

16. A new dialog box will open saying "Master Clip Conflict Found." Among the choices given is "Yes To All." That's the one you want to click.

17. The files will begin to load into the Avid. Be patient. This can take as long as an hour. Once all the clips appear in the bin, don't worry if they don't look great. Exit your Avid software and eject the DVD. Now re-launch your software. Select Wanna Trade. When the project opens the images will now look good. Begin Chapter 1.

18. If at any point during the import process, you get an error message telling you that the Avid is having trouble importing a particular file, click the button that directs the Avid to skip that file. See the "Troubleshooting" section.

19. Once all the files have been successfully imported, you can send the Wanna Trade Media folder on your Desktop to the trash and empty it.

Instructions for Mounting "Gaffer's Delight"

Follow the instructions provided above for mounting "Wanna Trade" onto your Avid. Wherever the instructions mention the Wanna Trade folder or the Wanna Trade Media folder, substitute the corresponding Gaffer's Delight folder, which you'll find on the DVD-ROM that comes with your book.

Media Composer and Xpress users will find the process takes just a few minutes. Xpress DV users will find that it takes several hours to move all the media onto their Xpress DV computers.

After bringing in all the files, you will find that there are two clips, 1 Master Shot and 1A Tk3, that seem to have no audio. For some reason the Source track sound monitor for these two clips is off. To hear the sound, place either one of the clips in the Source Monitor. Now look at the Timeline. The tiny speaker icon to the left of the Source track is missing. Click in the empty space and the speaker icon will appear (see page 164–165). Now you'll hear the audio. Do the same for the other clip. I believe you'll find that the audio is on A2 rather than A1. Simply patch the Source track A2 to the Record track A1 before splicing or overwriting (see page 166–168).

Troubleshooting

Chances are good that you'll never need this list, but if you find that any of the files don't import properly, or if you get an error message and have to skip a file when importing, you can try re-importing the file that is missing. Here is a list of all "Wanna Trade" and "Gaffer's Delight" files. In the left-hand column, you'll see the names of the clips as listed in the bin, and on the right-hand columns, you'll see the specific media files associated with those clips. Notice in the example, Kate's Entrance—WS, that the media file name is extremely long. Instead of listing the entire file name, I've listed the last six numbers that come just before the .omf or .aif designation.

Let's say that when you imported all the files, everything came in smoothly, except there's no image for Kate's Entrance—WS. The audio is there, but there's no video. To get the missing video, you follow the importing instructions for your PC or Mac. Instead of importing all the files found inside the Wanna Trade Media folder, you find the file CF7390.omf and import just that file. It imports in a few minutes and now you've got the picture. If you have the picture but no audio, shift-click CF7380.aif and CF7370.aif—the audio files for that clip—and import them.

Wanna Trade Project Files

What the files look like inside the Wanna Trade Media folder:
Kate's Entrance—WS: video   WannaTraV01.3DB01BF6.CF7390.omf
                      audio 1   WannaTraA01.3DB01BF6.CF7380.aif
                      audio 2   WannaTraA02.3DB01BF6.CF7370.aif

The shortened version:

Clip Name	The Last Six #s .omf # (video)	.aif # (audio)	.aif #
Kate's Entrance—WS	CF7390	CF7380	CF7370
Kate's Hands, Face—CU	E3CB90	E3CB80	E3CB70
Master Shot Kate & Tim	F21AB0	F21AA0	F21A90
Master Shot Kate & Tim (PU)	0DA280	0DA270	0DA260
Tim's CU Tk1	19C6F0	19C6E0	19C6D0
Tim's CU Tk2	317760	317750	317740
Tim's CU Tk3	494DF0	494DE0	494DD0
Kate's CU	62BDA0	62BD90	62BD80
Kate's MS	7A5990	7A5980	7A5970

Gaffer's Delight Project Files

What the files look like inside the Gaffer's Delight Media folder:
1 Master Shot   video: 001A919AV01.3DB02843.D042F0.omf
                     audio: 001A919AA02.3DB02843.D042E0.aif

The shortened version:

Clip Name	The Last Six #s .omf # (video)	.aif # (audio)
1 Master Shot	D042F0	D042E0
1 Master Shot (PU)	F87EC0	F87EB0
1A Tk 2	060D70	060D60
1A Tk 3	15D480	15D470
1A Tk 5	25E7C0	25E7B0
1A Tk 8	35ADD0	35ADC0
1A Tk 9	3CBF70	3CBF60
1B Tk 1	4C9900	4C98F0
1B Tk 2	521B30	521B20
1B Tk 4	561C90	561C80
1B Tk 5	5C8C10	5C8C00
1D Tk 1	62EEDO	62EEC0
1D Tk 2	798310	798300
1E Tk 1	8F30E0	8F30D0
1E Tk 2	9FE350	9FE340
1E Tk 3	B19A70	B19A60
1F Tk 1	C40260	C40250
1F Tk 2	CA6420	CA6410
1F Tk 3	D0DF50	D0DF40
1G Tk 1	D6BF40	D6BF30
1G Tk 2	E387B0	E387A0
1G Tk 4	F0CE20	F0CE10
1H Tk 1	FD0420	FD0410
1J Tk 1	070E70	070E60
1J Tk 2	0F6920	0F6910
1J Tk 3	13DCC0	13DCB0
1K Tk 1	1CCAE0	1CCAD0
1K Tk 3	23F9C0	23F9B0
1K Tk 4 PU	37E850	37E840
1L Tk 1	B94C50	B94C40
1L Tk 2	454910	454900
1M Tk 1	52E770	52E760
1M Tk 2	5B24D0	5B24C0
1M Tk 3	63C4D0	63C4C0
1M Tk 4	6C4490	6C4480
1M Tk 7	73C670	73C660

LIMITED WARRANTY AND DISCLAIMER OF LIABILITY

FOCAL PRESS AND ANYONE ELSE WHO HAS BEEN INVOLVED IN THE CREATION OR PRODUCTION OF THE ACCOMPANYING CODE ("THE PRODUCT") CANNOT AND DO NOT WARRANT THE PERFORMANCE OR RESULTS THAT MAY BE OBTAINED BY USING THE PRODUCT. THE PRODUCT IS SOLD "AS IS" WITHOUT WARRANTY OF ANY KIND (EXCEPT AS HEREAFTER DESCRIBED), EITHER EXPRESSED OR IMPLIED, INCLUDING, BUT NOT LIMITED TO, ANY WARRANTY OF PERFORMANCE OR ANY IMPLIED WARRANTY OF MERCHANTABILITY OR FITNESS FOR ANY PARTICULAR PURPOSE. FOCAL PRESS WARRANTS ONLY THAT THE MAGNETIC DVD-ROM(S) ON WHICH THE CODE IS RECORDED IS FREE FROM DEFECTS IN MATERIAL AND FAULTY WORKMANSHIP UNDER THE NORMAL USE AND SERVICE FOR A PERIOD OF NINETY (90) DAYS FROM THE DATE THE PRODUCT IS DELIVERED. THE PURCHASER'S SOLE AND EXCLUSIVE REMEDY IN THE EVENT OF A DEFECT IS EXPRESSLY LIMITED TO EITHER REPLACEMENT OF THE DVD-ROM(S) OR REFUND OF THE PURCHASE PRICE, AT FOCAL PRESS'S SOLE DISCRETION.

IN NO EVENT, WHETHER AS A RESULT OF BREACH OF CONTRACT, WARRANTY OR TORT (INCLUDING NEGLIGENCE), WILL FOCAL PRESS OR ANYONE WHO HAS BEEN INVOLVED IN THE CREATION OR PRODUCTION OF THE PRODUCT BE LIABLE TO PURCHASER FOR ANY DAMAGES, INCLUDING ANY LOST PROFITS, LOST SAVINGS OR OTHER INCIDENTAL OR CONSEQUENTIAL DAMAGES ARISING OUT OF THE USE OR INABILITY TO USE THE PRODUCT OR ANY MODIFICATIONS THEREOF, OR DUE TO THE CONTENTS OF THE CODE, EVEN IF FOCAL PRESS HAS BEEN ADVISED OF THE POSSIBILITY OF SUCH DAMAGES, OR FOR ANY CLAIM BY ANY OTHER PARTY.

ANY REQUEST FOR REPLACEMENT OF A DEFECTIVE DVD-ROM MUST BE POSTAGE PREPAID AND MUST BE ACCOMPANIED BY THE ORIGINAL DEFECTIVE DVD-ROM, YOUR MAILING ADDRESS AND TELEPHONE NUMBER, AND PROOF OF DATE OF PURCHASE AND PURCHASE PRICE. SEND SUCH REQUESTS, STATING THE NATURE OF THE PROBLEM, TO ELSEVIER SCIENCE CUSTOMER SERVICE, 6277 SEA HARBOR DRIVE, ORLANDO, FL 32887, 1-800-321-5068. FOCAL PRESS SHALL HAVE NO OBLIGATION TO REFUND THE PURCHASE PRICE OR TO REPLACE A DVD-ROM BASED ON CLAIMS OF DEFECTS IN THE NATURE OR OPERATION OF THE PRODUCT.

SOME STATES DO NOT ALLOW LIMITATION ON HOW LONG AN IMPLIED WARRANTY LASTS, NOR EXCLUSIONS OR LIMITATIONS OF INCIDENTAL OR CONSEQUENTIAL DAMAGE, SO THE ABOVE LIMITATIONS AND EXCLUSIONS MAY NOT APPLY TO YOU. THIS WARRANTY GIVES YOU SPECIFIC LEGAL RIGHTS, AND YOU MAY ALSO HAVE OTHER RIGHTS THAT VARY FROM JURISDICTION TO JURISDICTION.

THE RE-EXPORT OF UNITED STATES ORIGIN SOFTWARE IS SUBJECT TO THE UNITED STATES LAWS UNDER THE EXPORT ADMINISTRATION ACT OF 1969 AS AMENDED. ANY FURTHER SALE OF THE PRODUCT SHALL BE IN COMPLIANCE WITH THE UNITED STATES DEPARTMENT OF COMMERCE ADMINISTRATION REGULATIONS. COMPLIANCE WITH SUCH REGULATIONS IS YOUR RESPONSIBILITY AND NOT THE RESPONSIBILITY OF FOCAL PRESS.